Marketing in Travel and Tourism

Second edition

Victor T. C. Middleton

BUTTERWORTH
HEINEMANN

Butterworth-Heinemann
Linacre House, Jordan Hill, Oxford OX2 8DP
225 Wildwood Avenue, Woburn, MA 01801-2041
A division of Reed Educational and Professional Publishing Ltd

A member of the Reed Elsevier plc group

OXFORD   BOSTON   JOHANNESBURG
MELBOURNE   NEW DELHI   SINGAPORE

First published 1998
Reprinted 1988, 1989, 1990, 1992, 1993
Second edition 1994
Reprinted 1995 (twice), 1996, 1997, 1998

© Victor T. C. Middleton 1994

British Library Cataloguing in Publication Data
A catalogue record for this book is available from the British Library

ISBN 0 7506 0973 7

Printed and bound in Great Britain by The Bath Press, Bath

FOR EVERY TITLE THAT WE PUBLISH, BUTTERWORTH-HEINEMANN
WILL PAY FOR BTCV TO PLANT AND CARE FOR A TREE.

Contents

Foreword

In the foreword to the first edition of this book, published in 1988, I stressed that marketing was 'an integrated approach to the whole conduct of profitable business, within an overall corporate culture, focused on long-run customer orientation'.

The most important thing about marketing is that, practised correctly, it forces an organization to recognize and respond to the preferences of the customer in a way which builds consistent loyalty and, thereby, profitability.

Travel and tourism is now recognized as the world's largest industry. Continuing growth, coupled with increasing deregulation, is set to produce highly-intense levels of competition within each of its various sectors. The services and facilities we offer will, therefore, need to be geared sharply to the needs of the consumer, rather than to those of the producer. Consequently, the closer integration of marketing and production becomes not just a desirable objective, but a powerful imperative.

I have been pleased to learn of the international success of the first edition of *Marketing in Travel and Tourism*; and commend this second edition to marketing practitioners and students, alike. Systematic marketing will reward those who are willing to make the necessary effort to study, evaluate and innovate. This book plays a valuable role in communicating how to achieve those benefits in travel and tourism.

Sir Colin Marshall
Chairman
British Airways Plc

Preface

For the second edition, encouraged by reviews and comments on the first edition by many people in several countries, I have aimed to give the book a more broadly based international relevance. First, the information in each chapter has been updated for the 1990s. Second, the opportunity has been taken to revise the content of every chapter. Although the structure of the book remains as before, new material has been added to all chapters, diagrams have been modified, and recent illustrations from practice included. Third, the epilogue, which offers views on the future for travel and tourism marketing, has been completely rewritten and extended. It is designed to have broad relevance to worldwide travel and tourism, it contains views on the environmental issues surrounding the industry, and is written in the expectation of maturing markets and significantly slower growth in developed countries than is currently predicted by the World Tourism Organization and most other forecasters. The epilogue is also written in a rather different style than the main text, being intended to stimulate debate.

Also new in this edition are seven case studies, which appear as Part Six. These cases replace most of the shorter synoptic examples included in Part Five of the first edition. Reflecting marketing experience in North America, the Pacific area and the UK, each of these cases has been written by a leading contributor, using a broadly standardized format. It is hoped to extend and develop this approach in future editions of the book.

The structure of the book

The book is presented in six parts. The structure is designed to follow a logical development of the subject but, as every manager knows, marketing is a circular rather than a linear process. As far as possible, the parts are designed to be reasonably self-explanatory, with the intention that lecturers and students can fit the chapters into whatever pattern the logic of their courses suggests.

Briefly, Part One defines travel and tourism and the sectors within the industry, which are referred to throughout the book. The subject of marketing is introduced, especially for those who are coming new to the subject, and the characteristics of travel and tourism to which marketing responds, are set out. This part of the book also explains the factors in the external business environment that influence demand and customers' purchasing behaviour.

Part Two explains the *four Ps* of the marketing mix in travel and tourism and notes their significance for all marketing managers engaged in strategic and tactical decision-making. Part Three focuses on planning for marketing, and deals with marketing research, marketing strategy and tactics, and with the procedures for constructing and budgeting for marketing campaigns. Issues of organization and the role of marketing managers are also included in this part of the book. Part Four deals with each of the main tools or functions used in marketing practice, and emphasizes the role of print, distribution, and direct response marketing, which are especially important in travel and tourism.

Using a broadly common format, Parts Five and Six analyse the meaning and application in practice of marketing in five of the main sectors of travel and tourism. The Epilogue draws together the principal trends emerging in the book, and makes a series of ten predictions expected to influence the future for marketing in travel and tourism over the coming decade.

Victor T. C. Middleton

Preface to the first edition

This book is written in the belief that the marketing of travel and tourism is still in the early stages of a development that will influence travel and tourism to an increasing extent for the remaining years of the twentieth century. Marketing is a dominant management philosophy or culture, a systematic thought process, and an integrated set of techniques focused on customer needs and aspirations. Combined, the application of the thought process and techniques may be used in marketing-orientated organizations to guide the way they understand, respond to and influence their target markets, in a continuously changing business environment.

Marketing is an integrated approach to business in commercial and non-commercial sectors of travel and tourism. It is presented as a proactive management response, especially to industry conditions of excess capacity of production and volatile market demand, which are commonly found in international travel and tourism. Marketing perishable products in such conditions inevitably produces highly aggressive competition for market share and growth, and it is easy to predict that competition will intensify rather than diminish over the next decade. The rapid growth of tourism demand around the world from the 1950s to the 1970s served to cushion many producer organizations in travel and tourism from the full effects of competition and delayed the full application of marketing in many organizations. As travel markets approach maturity in many countries, and as the rate of growth slows, competition will be further stimulated by the growing marketing professionalism of the many large-scale producer organizations that developed so strongly in all sectors of the travel and tourism industry over the last decade.

Marketing is not viewed, however, as the only focus of business management. Throughout the book the requirement of meeting customers' needs is balanced against the essential need of organizations to make the most profitable use of existing assets, and to achieve integration of management functions around customer-oriented objectives. Nor does marketing necessarily determine the nature of an organization's long-run goal or mission. But its approach and techniques are always essential inputs to specifying revenue-earning objectives that are precise, realistic and achievable in the markets in which an organization operates. In this sense the adoption of a marketing approach can be as relevant to museums responsible to non-profit-making trusts and to local government tourist offices, as it is to airlines, hotels, or tour operators in the commercial sector.

The rigorous application of the modern marketing concept can also provide the route to achieving the marginal extra business volume and revenue on which the difference between profit and loss so often depends in the travel and tourism industry. Systematically applied, marketing can also secure marginal increases in the cost effectiveness of promotional and related budgets. This is a most important aspect of marketing, which this author terms *marketing the margin*. The concept is relevant both to strategy and tactics, and it is reflected throughout the book.

Marketing as a body of knowledge is international; like travel and tourism it observes no geographical boundaries. While many of the principles and techniques were developed originally in North America and Europe for selling manufactured consumer goods, they are now being practised and developed all around the world in service industries, too. For reasons that are set out in Chapter 3, this author believes that it is possible to construct an overall understanding of travel and tourism marketing based on three essential points. First, that the fundamental principles of consumer marketing are common to all its forms. Second, that service industries display particular generic character-istics, which do not alter the principles but must be understood before marketing can successfully be applied in practice. Third, that there are important common characteristics of travel and tourism, which require particular forms of marketing response.

It is certainly too much to claim that a theory of travel and tourism marketing exists. Yet the increasing consistencies of approach in marketing, adopted in the different sectors of travel and tourism to the opportunities and threats they perceive, do point to a coherent, systematic body of knowledge within the framework of marketing that is capable of being developed.

The aim of the book and its intended market

The book has three aims, which are to provide:

● A basic but comprehensive text about what marketing means in the travel and tourism industry.
● A balance of concepts and principles drawn from the study of marketing, with illustrations of recent practice.
● A necessary companion volume for all concerned with travel and tourism marketing, but not a substitute for the many excellent texts that explain marketing principles in their overall context.

On both sides of the Atlantic the better of the standard texts on marketing are now substantial volumes, many of them having developed over several editions. This book makes no attempt to replace them. It is intended instead to fit fully within a framework of internationally accepted marketing principles that have stood the test of time, and develop these concepts in travel and tourism. Suggested readings, indicating chapters in books that are typically recommended to students in the USA and Britain, are noted at the end of each chapter where relevant. Such books have the added advantage of dealing with the important principles in the wider industrial context in which marketing developed. Students in particular will profit from the breadth of understanding this conveys.

The book is written to meet the needs of students of travel and tourism and hospitality courses, and related leisure industry programmes. For all of them, marketing is likely to be a very important influence in their careers, whether or not they are directly engaged in marketing practice. The contents are developed from lecture material originally prepared for students, and judged to be suitable for all preparing for examinations in further and higher education courses with a travel and tourism component. They provide much material relevant to those on other courses, in which service industries are an important element.

But marketing is also a very practical subject, and the book is equally aimed at the great majority of managers in travel and tourism in the 1990s who have some responsibility for aspects of marketing but who have not studied the subject formally. Much of the contents have also been exposed to the critical reaction of managers in the industry, and modified in the light of their responses. The book is not an attempt to tell the practitioner how to make instant improvements to his marketing efforts, increase sales revenue, and reduce marketing expenditure overnight. It does not contain any 'golden rules'. But if people in the industry read the book with care, and relate its principles to the particular circumstances their own organizations face, most should perceive useful insights and ways to improve the effectiveness of their marketing decisions. If they do not, the author will have failed in his purpose.

Victor T. C. Middleton

Author's note

Repeated use of 'he or she' or of 's/he' can be cumbersome in continuous text. For simplicity, therefore, only the male pronoun is used throughout the book. No bias is intended and wherever 'he' or 'his' appears it applies equally to 'she' or 'hers'.

Acknowledgements

The second edition of this book is launched in the knowledge that the first edition sold well in the UK and internationally, with four reprints. No doubt many read it also in university and other libraries. It is a comfort for an author of a marketing book that the targeted audience appeared to find satisfaction with the product. My first debt of gratitude is to those readers.

It is impossible to list all who influenced this book with their insights, encouragement and sometimes much needed prods to get on with it. The most important group are undoubtedly the students on undergraduate and postgraduate courses at the Universities of Surrey and Oxford Brookes, to whom the contents were first exposed. Their reactions to the material and the ideas discussed improved my thought processes and communication skills more than they knew, and I am grateful to them. I appreciate, too, the views and reactions of many managers on short post-experience courses around the world, to which I have contributed in the last decade; they sharpened my appreciation of international marketing for travel and tourism. For stimulating my marketing thoughts in the 1970s and 1980s I am pleased to acknowledge my former colleague John Burkart of the University of Surrey.

For particular contributions to chapters in this book I wish to acknowledge Peter Allport, Marketing and Sales Director for HavenWarner; Emma Bannister, Environment Co-ordinator, British Airways; Nigel Embry, Chief Executive, Best Western Hotels (UK); Dr Rebecca Hawkins, my colleague at Oxford; Roger Heape, Managing Director of British Airways Holidays; Ken Robinson, Managing Director of Ventures Consultancy; Grahame Senior, Managing Director of Senior King; and Graham Wason, Partner of Touche Ross Management Consultants. The authors of the case studies in the appendix are Rosemary Astles, Marketing Director of Thomson Tour Operations; Nick Cust, Joint Managing Director of Superbreak Mini-Holidays; Robyn Griffith-Jones, Head of Marketing and PR for the Victoria and Albert Museum; Crawford Lincoln, President of Old Sturbridge Village in Massachusetts; Gordon D. Taylor, former Manager, Research and Analysis, for Tourism Canada; and John Yacoumis, Project Manager for the Tourism Council of the South Pacific. British Airways gave permission for use of material from one of their recent major campaigns.

For her much appreciated cheerful support with the seemingly endless task of typing for the second edition, I am very grateful to Sue Kitching. For her faith in the book and patience while I missed my deadlines I thank Kathryn Grant, Director of Business Publishing for Butterworth-Heinemann. Last and most, I acknowledge the support of Professor Rik Medlik, who persuaded me to write the first edition and prompted the second. Both the structure and the contents of the book owe much to his constructive criticism. All errors and omissions are the author's sole responsibility.

Figures

Tables

Part One

The Meaning of Marketing in Travel and Tourism

1

Introducing travel and tourism

This chapter introduces and defines the subject matter of this book. The intention is to identify the essential nature of travel and tourism, and the industry it supports, for practical purposes in marketing.

In essence, travel and tourism is a total market reflecting the demand of consumers for a very wide range of travel-related products. Depending on definitions used, this total market is now serviced by the world's 'largest industry' (WTTC: 1992). The market is of interest in most countries because of its recent growth and current size; its potential for further growth; its economic contribution measured in terms of investment, employment and balance of payments; its effects on host communities; and its impact on the physical environment of visited destinations.

In the last 5 years increasing interest has been shown in the potential of global travel and tourism as an important contributor to economic development. There is also increasing concern about the effects of tourism on the global environment, in terms of use of energy and water supplies; impact on global warming; and damage to marine environments and the ecosystems of destinations developed as major tourism resorts. Some of the influences on host communities and on the built and natural environment are positive and beneficial (WTTERC: 1992); others are undoubtedly negative and damaging. Marketing is a subject of vital concern in travel and tourism because it is the principal management influence which can be brought to bear on the size and behaviour of this major, global market.

Within the total market there are many submarkets, or segments, and many products designed and provided by a wide range of organizations, which are categorized in Figure 1.1. Because travel and tourism is defined as a market, it is best understood in terms of demand and supply. Marketing is introduced in Chapter 3 as a vital part of the linking mechanism between supply and demand focused on *exchange transactions*, in which consumers exercise preferences and choices, and exchange money in return for the supply of particular travel experiences or products. For reasons discussed subsequently, the practice of marketing is also highly relevant to tourism resources for which no market price is charged, such as national parks and historic towns. It is a vital role for national tourist offices and other area organizations, most of which are not directly engaged in the sale of products.

The chapter begins with an overview of travel and tourism demand, its international dimensions, and main components. A working definition of the subject is provided, with comments on the distinction between *tourism*, and *travel and tourism*, often a source of confusion to students. The components of demand and supply and the linking role of marketing are put together in diagrammatic form (Figure 1.2), which serves also to identify the main categories of supply within the travel and tourism industry. Suggestions for further reading will be found at the end of the chapter.

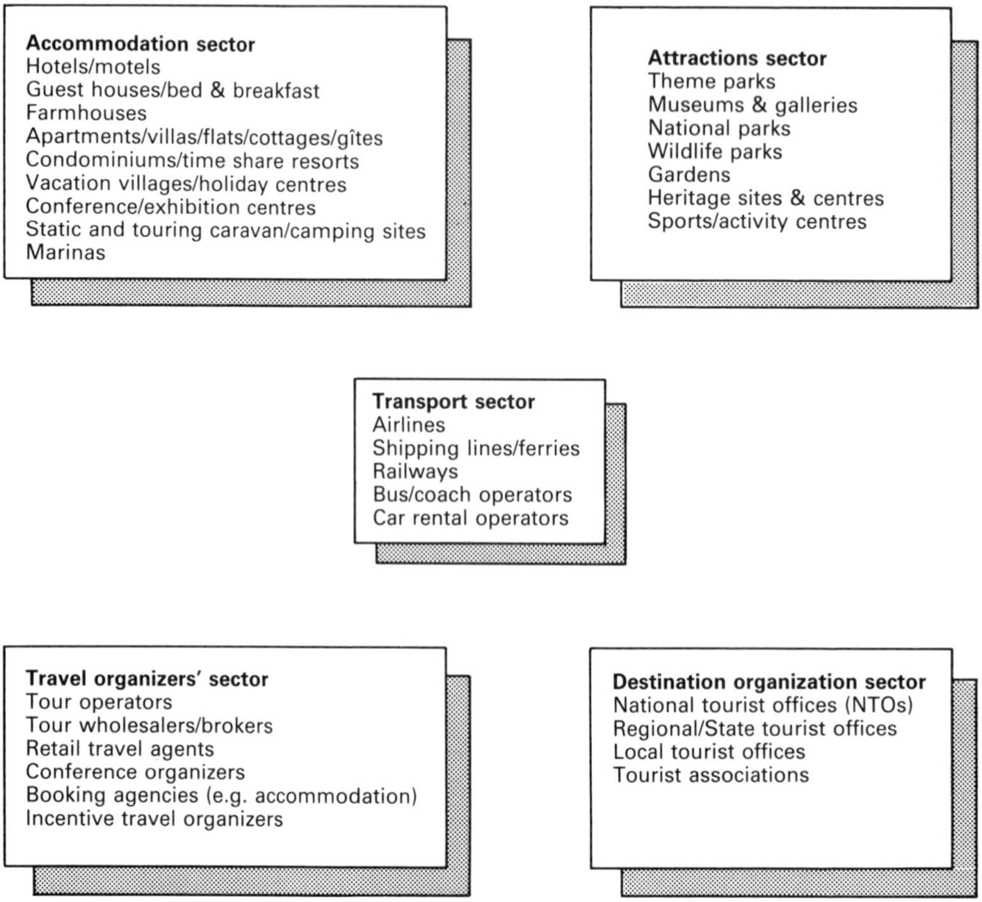

Accommodation sector
Hotels/motels
Guest houses/bed & breakfast
Farmhouses
Apartments/villas/flats/cottages/gîtes
Condominiums/time share resorts
Vacation villages/holiday centres
Conference/exhibition centres
Static and touring caravan/camping sites
Marinas

Attractions sector
Theme parks
Museums & galleries
National parks
Wildlife parks
Gardens
Heritage sites & centres
Sports/activity centres

Transport sector
Airlines
Shipping lines/ferries
Railways
Bus/coach operators
Car rental operators

Travel organizers' sector
Tour operators
Tour wholesalers/brokers
Retail travel agents
Conference organizers
Booking agencies (e.g. accommodation)
Incentive travel organizers

Destination organization sector
National tourist offices (NTOs)
Regional/State tourist offices
Local tourist offices
Tourist associations

Figure 1.1   *The five main sectors of the travel and tourism industry*

An overview of travel and tourism demand

In defining travel and tourism for the purposes of this book it is useful to follow the basic classification system, which is used in nearly all countries where measurement exists. This system is discussed in detail in most intro-ductory texts; see, for example, Burkart and Medlik (1981/41). It is based on three categories of visitor demand with which any country is concerned; each is a different sector of the total market:

1   International visitors, travelling to a country, who are residents of other countries (inbound tourism).

2 Residents of a country, travelling as visitors to other countries (outbound tourism).

3 Residents visiting destinations within their own country's boundaries (domestic tourism).

Defining travel and tourism is a primary responsibility for the World Tourism Organization (WTO), which undertook a major review of its definitions at an international conference on travel and tourism statistics in Ottawa in 1991. In 1993 revised definitions were put to the UN Statistical Commission. The following are the principal terms:

● *Visitors* to describe all travellers who fall within agreed definitions of tourism.
● *Tourists or staying visitors* to describe visitors who stay overnight at a destination.
● *Same-day visitors, or excursionists,* to describe visitors who arrive and depart on the same day. Same-day visitors are mostly people who leave home and return there on the same day, but may be tourists who make day visits to other destinations away from the places where they are staying overnight.

As outlined above, these three categories are easy to understand. In practice the technicalities of achieving statistical precision in measuring visitors are extremely complex and, despite various international guidelines, no uniformity yet exists in the measurement methods used around the world. For example, should visitors who are remunerated from within the countries they visit be counted as tourists? Should nationals of a country who are resident abroad be treated as foreign visitors for statistical purposes? At what point, measured in distance covered away from home, or time travelled, or activity followed, should a resident of a city be counted as a same-day visitor, as distinguished from a resident pursuing his or her normal daily activities? In cities, for example, some shopping trips are evidently tourist or recreational excursions, but other trips, to make routine purchases, are not.

While the definition of travel and tourism outlined in this chapter will be adequate for the working purposes of those involved in marketing, this book does not set out to be a detailed study of the nature of tourism. Readers seeking further elaboration of concepts and measurement issues are referred to the reading suggestions noted at the end of the chapter. Marketing managers will, of course, require their own definitions of the market segments with which they are involved, and these will be far more precise than the broadly indicative international categories referred to here (see Chapter 7).

International tourism

People who travel to and stay in countries other than their country of residence for less than 1 year are normally described as international tourists. They are usually treated as the most important market sector of tourism because, compared with domestic tourists, they spend more, stay longer at the destination, use more expensive transport and accommodation, and bring in foreign currency, which contributes to a destination country's international balance of payments.

Around the world, measured as *arrivals* or *trips*, the numbers of international tourists and their expenditure have grown strongly since the 1950s, notwithstanding temporary fluctuations caused by the international energy and economic crises of the 1970s and 1980s. The overall growth pattern is revealed in Tables 1.1 and 1.2, and the reasons for it are discussed later in some detail in Chapters 4 and 5. For the purposes of this introduction it is sufficient to note the recent growth and current size of the international market, and to be aware of consistently confident projections in the early 1990s that international tourism will continue to grow for the rest of the twentieth century. Although annual fluctuations in volume, reflecting economic and political events, are virtually certain, current expectations are for annual growth of the order of some 4 per cent per annum over the period 1992–2005 as a whole (see for example Edwards: 1992).

Table 1.1 *Growth in worldwide international tourist arrivals, 1950–2000*

Year	International arrivals (millions)	Index of growth for each decade
1950	25.3	–
1960	69.3	274
1970	159.7	230
1980	284.8	178
1990	443.0	155
2000	650.0[e]	147[e]

Note: e = forecast at 1992
Source: World Tourism Organization

At present, in Northern Europe, it is common for over half of the adult population to have made one or more international tourist visits during the previous 5 years, mostly on vacation. Experience of international travel is very much less for Americans, reflecting the size of the USA and the distances most of them would have to travel in making international trips. US interstate tourism, e.g. between the North East and Florida, should perhaps be viewed as similar in principle to tourism between European countries over similar distances.

Although not included in Tables 1.1 and 1.2, international same-day visits are an important market sector in countries with common land frontiers, such as the USA and Canada, the Netherlands and Germany, and Malaysia and

Table 1.2 *Forecasts of percentage shares of worldwide international tourism arrivals and expenditure, by world regions of origin, 1989–2005*

Year	Europe/ Mediterranean	North America	Far East/ Pacific & South East Asia	Central/ South America	Others	
In terms of visits abroad[a]	%	%	%	%	%	%
1989	70.4	15.5	5.7	4.4	4.0	100
1995	71.2	12.3	6.5	5.8	4.2	100
2005	71.8	10.2	7.8	6.0	4.2	100
In terms of tourist spending[bc]						
1989	49.5	22.7	17.5	3.5	6.8	100
1995	51.5	18.3	17.9	4.5	7.8	100
2005	54.6	14.6	18.4	4.6	7.8	100
In terms of nights abroad[b]						
1989	69.0	18.2	4.1	4.0	4.7	100
1995	68.8	15.6	5.0	5.2	5.4	100
2005	68.2	14.1	6.2	5.6	5.9	100

Notes: a = excludes day trips   b = main origin countries only   c = at constant prices and exchange rates, excluding fares.
Source: Edwards, A., *International Tourism Forecasts to 2005* (EIU Special Report No. 2454), with permission from the Economist Intelligence Unit, London, 1992.

Singapore. Because of the speed and efficiency of cross-Channel ferries and the Channel Tunnel, same-day visits between Britain and France, and Britain and Belgium, are also important.

Domestic tourism

People who travel and stay overnight within the boundaries of their own country are classified as domestic tourists. Estimates of the size of this sector of the market vary because in many countries domestic tourism is not adequately measured at present. In the USA, where good measurement does exist, Americans take only one trip abroad for every 100 domestic trips defined as travel to places more than 100 miles distance from home. Even for longer visits of over 10 nights' duration, international trips were no more than 3 per cent of the total. For the British, where the statistics are also good, and reflecting the shorter distances to travel abroad, there were some four domestic tourism trips (including overnight stays) for every visit abroad in the early 1990s. The comparative growth figures over the last 20 years are shown in Table 1.3.

Table 1.3 *Growth in domestic tourist arrivals and expenditure in the USA and UK, 1972–1990*

	USA*		UK†	
Year	Visits (millions)	Expenditure ($ millions)	Visits (millions)	Expenditure (£ millions)
1972	458ᵉ	na	132	1,375
1980	1,046	162,000	130	4,550
1985	1,078	245,000	126	6,325
1990	1,275	307,000	96	10,460

Note: na = not available, e = estimate.
* USA data include visits of 100 miles or more away from home, for any purpose, with or without overnight stays.
† UK data include visits, for any purpose, including at least one night away from home. Definitions changed between 1985 and 1990.
Sources:
* *Economic Review of Travel in America,* US Travel Data Center
† UK Tourism Survey, UK Tourist Boards

Evidence from surveys of the vacation market in Europe and North America in the early 1990s indicates that, in most countries, between a half and three-quarters of the adult population took holidays away from home in any 12-month period. This includes international and domestic holidays, although the latter are the largest category. Increasing numbers of people take more than one vacation trip a year, a factor of great importance to marketing managers, for reasons to be discussed later.

Market research data analysing the complete tourism experience of the same individuals over periods of more than 1 year are rarely available. But excluding the very old, the sick, the severely disabled, and those facing particular financial hardship, recent and frequent experience of some form of staying and same-day tourism now extends to over nine out of ten people in most economically developed countries.

Within the total, domestic same-day visits taking place within a country's frontiers are the most difficult to quantify. In most developed countries the frequency of day visits is already so great that it is not easily measured by traditional survey techniques, because people find it hard or impossible to remember the number of trips they have taken over a period of months or even weeks. In the early 1990s there is, however, a rough but useful estimate for developed countries, that there are at least as many domestic day visits for leisure purposes within a country as there are tourist days or nights spent away from home for all purposes. Thus, for example in the UK in 1989 an estimated 110 million domestic tourism visits for all purposes generated 443 million nights away from home. An additional 630 million same-day visits for leisure purposes were made by the British in the same year with a duration of at least 3 hours from home and a minimum distance of 20 miles. With a population of some 55 million in Britain, this is equivalent to over ten visitor days per person for leisure purposes over a year. UK estimates of day visits for business and social purposes do not exist, although such visits are obviously a very large market, for transport operators in particular.

To summarize, the total market for travel and tourism comprises three main elements: international visits inbound to a country, visits made to foreign destinations by a country's residents; and domestic visits including day trips. The total market has grown rapidly in recent years and it is very large indeed, comprising the great majority of the population of economically developed countries. Frequent, repeat purchases of travel and tourism products in any period of 12 months are already a normal experience for many people. Although the statistics are inevitably open to dispute, travel and tourism is already the largest sector of international trade and in developed countries usually contributes 5–10 per cent of Gross Domestic Product. One may safely predict that marketing in travel and tourism will be a subject of growing significance and interest.

A working definition of travel and tourism

Before drawing the discussion of the main markets in travel and tourism into a working definition, we need to clarify one important potential source of confusion. What, if any, are the differences between *tourism*, and *travel*, used on their own as single terms, and *travel and tourism* used as a combined term? What can a definition of tourism mean if it does not include travel? This book proceeds in the belief that an acceptable definition of tourism necessarily covers all relevant aspects of travel. In normal usage *tourism*, and *travel and tourism*, are terms that relate to exactly the same market and they are used interchangeably.

Travel and tourism tends to be the term used most often by managers, especially in North America, because it is convenient, practical, and widely understood. Accordingly, this usage is

adopted generally throughout the book. As the US Travel Data Center puts it, 'Tourism is synonymous with travel' (USTDC: 1987, Appendix B). Where, for the sake of convenience, *tourism* is used alone, it also means travel and tourism; students should be aware that no conceptual difference is implied between the two expressions in this book.

Although academics have debated conceptual definitions of tourism for several decades, and there are international agreements on statistical definitions, it was not until 1991–2 that the WTO endorsed the following statement 'Tourism comprises the activities of persons travelling to and staying in places outside their usual environment for not more than one consecutive year for leisure, business and other purposes', (WTO: 1992 – subject to ratification by the UN).

In the UK the Tourism Society adopted a definition in 1979 based on the work of Burkart and Medlik (1974), which in turn draws on earlier definitions and is widely accepted. 'Tourism is deemed to include any activity concerned with the temporary short-term movement of people to destinations outside the places where they normally live and work, and their activities during the stay at these destinations' (Tourism Society: 1979, p. 70).

There is nothing particular to the UK about this definition. It is comprehensive, it holds good for all countries and it encompasses all the elements of visitor categories noted earlier in the chapter. The new WTO definition is similar to it and it serves as the working definition of the total market that is relevant throughout this book.

The definition pulls together the three main elements of travel and tourism:

1 Visitor activity is concerned only with aspects of life outside normal routines of work and social commitments, and outside the location of those routines.
2 The activity necessitates travel and, in nearly every case, some form of transport to the destination.

3 The destination is the focus for a range of activities, and a range of facilities required to support those activities.

Five important points should be noted in relation to the definition.

● There is nothing in it that restricts the total market to overnight stays; it includes same-day visits.
● There is nothing in it that restricts the total market to travel for leisure or pleasure, and it includes travel for business, social, religious, educational, sports and most other purposes, provided that the destination of travel is outside the usual routines and place of residence or work.
● All tourism includes an element of travel but all travel is not tourism. The definition excludes all routine commuter travel and purely local travel, such as to neighbourhood shops, schools or hospitals.
● Travel and tourism includes large elements of individual leisure time and also many recreational activities, but it is not synonymous with them because the bulk of all leisure and recreation takes place in or around the home.
● All travel and tourism trips are temporary movements; the bulk of the total market comprises trips of no more than a few hours' or nights' duration.

One of the greatest difficulties in understanding and dealing with travel and tourism as a total market or industry is the extent to which so many of the supplying organizations see tourism as only a part of their total business operations. For example, airlines, trains, buses, restaurants and hotels, all deal with a wide variety of market segments, many of which do not fall within the definition of travel and tourism. Hotels have local trade for bars and meals, transport operators carry commuters. Many visitor attractions, such as museums, and most visitor information bureaux, also provide services to local residents.

This mixture of products designed to serve both tourism and other markets has great significance for marketing decisions; it is discussed in some detail in Part Five of the book which considers marketing applications in the component sectors of the industry.

The component sectors of the travel and tourism industry

Travel and tourism was discussed at the beginning of this chapter from the demand side and identified as a total market comprising three main sectors of international tourism, domestic tourism, and same-day visits or excursionism. It is appropriate to complete the introduction by discussing briefly the sectors on the supply side, which are loosely known as the *travel and tourism industry*.

From Figure 1.1 it is obvious that the 'industry' comprises the products or outputs not of one but of several different industry sectors, as these are conventionally defined and measured in most countries' economic statistics. In practice, convenient though the concept is for all working within it, travel and tourism is not an industry that is recognized as such by economists. In assessing the performance of industry sectors it is normal for economists and statisticians to measure the outputs of transport, accommodation, and catering separately. But they cannot easily distinguish what proportion of each output is generated by visitor spending. While this is a topic of almost infinite debate for statisticians and economists, and for complicated visitor survey techniques, it is fortunately not a matter of prime concern for marketing managers. Accordingly, the term travel and tourism industry is used throughout this book in the broad sense that it is recognized without difficulty in practice.

The five main component sectors of the industry noted in Figure 1.1 are reflected in the chapter headings and case studies included in

Parts Five and Six of the book. Each of them comprises several sub-sectors, all of which are increasingly concerned with marketing activities, both in the design of their products and the management of demand. This author considers that the classification in Figure 1.1 is justified by the existence within the sectors of certain common, integrating principles that underlie the modern practice of marketing. Such principles greatly facilitate the understanding of the subject and help to explain the common interests in marketing that practitioners recognize. Students may find it a useful exercise to extend the list in Figure 1.1, using the same five sector headings and aiming to produce up to fifty sub-sectors involved altogether in the *travel and tourism industry.*

It can be seen that some of the sub-sectors are fully commercial, operated for profit; some are operated commercially for objects other than profit; and some are in the public sector and operated mainly on a non-commercial basis. To illustrate, in the first category come most hotels; in the second category many attractions, such as safari parks and heritage sites; and in the third category many state-owned national museums, national parks, and most of the operations undertaken by tourist offices. Internationally, growing recognition of the value of marketing in non-commercial operations in the second and third categories has been a remarkable feature of the 1980s.

The systematic links between demand and supply and the role of marketing

Figure 1.2 is provided to show vital linkages between demand and supply in travel and tourism that are fundamental to an understanding of the role of marketing. The figure shows the relationship between market demand, generated in the places in which visitors normally live (areas of origin), and

product supply in areas of destination. In particular, it shows how the five main sectors of the industry set out in Figure 1.1 combine to manage visitors' demand through marketing influences. Noted as the *marketing mix,* in the centre of the diagram, this important term is fully explained in Chapter 6.

Readers should note that the linkages in Figure 1.2 focus on visitors in the left-hand box. A detailed knowledge of their customers' characteristics and buying behaviour is central to the activities of marketing managers in all sectors of the industry. Knowledge of the customer, and all that it implies for management decisions, is generally known as *consumer orientation;* a concept developed in the next chapter.

It should be noted also, in the lower half of the diagram, that not all visits to a destination are influenced by marketing activity. For example, domestic visitors travelling by private car to stay with their friends and relatives may not be influenced by marketing in any way. On the other hand, first-time buyers of package tours to exotic destinations in the Pacific area may find almost every aspect of their trip is influenced by the marketing decisions of the tour operator they choose. The operator selects the destinations to put into a brochure, the accommodation, the range of excursions, the routes, choice of airline, and prices. In between these two examples a traveller on business selects his own destinations according to business requirements but may be influenced as to which hotel he selects. The range of influences, noted as 'marketing mix', is obviously very wide, and it is varied according to visitors' interests and circumstances.

There are, of course, many other linkages between the five sectors of the travel and tourism industry, e.g. between national tourist organizations and suppliers at the destination. These additional linkages are not drawn into Figure 1.2, to avoid unnecessary confusion in this introduction. The linkages are identified subsequently in all parts of the book.

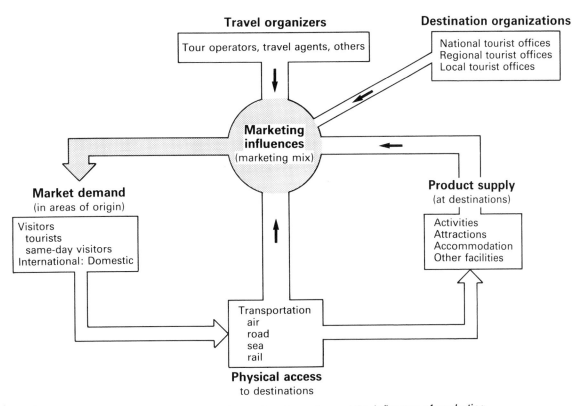

Figure 1.2 *The systematic links between demand and supply, and the influence of marketing*

Chapter summary

This chapter introduces travel and tourism as a nationally and internationally important market, in which the natural focus of management activity is on exchange transactions between visitors (demand) and producers (supply). The dimensions of the market are set out and key definitions provided in a form suitable for marketing purposes. The travel and tourism industry is outlined as five main sectors, the marketing practices of which subsequently form the subject matter of Part Five of the book. The chapter emphasizes that there are no conceptual differences intended between the use of the terms *tourism,* and *travel and tourism,* which are used interchangeably throughout the book. All the definitions are based on principles that are valid for all countries, whether they are economically developed or not, and whether their tourism industry is mature or just emerging.

The five sectors of the industry are brought together in the important diagram in Figure 1.2, which traces the main linkages between supply and demand and, in particular, indicates the area of marketing influence. This is analysed in depth in later chapters.

Students should be aware of a tendency among some authors of travel and tourism books and articles to state *or assume* that tourism is a sub-set of leisure and recreation. Such texts frequently identify tourism as essentially concerned with one or more forms of holiday. In fact as clearly endorsed by WTO in 1992, tourism encompasses travel for business, social and many other non-holiday purposes. For many hotels, airlines and for most travel agents, business travel is the most important sector for marketing purposes. For many visitor attractions, educational markets and same-day visits from home are more important segments than holiday visitors. It is important for marketing managers to keep firmly in mind this broad and internationally endorsed concept of travel and tourism.

For those who wish to consider the definitions of travel and tourism in greater depth, although this is not necessary for marketing purposes, further readings are given.

Further reading

Burkart, A. J., and Medlik, S., *Tourism: Past, Present, and Future,* 2nd edit., Heinemann, 1981, Chapters 4 and 7.

Holloway, J. C., *The Business of Tourism,* 3rd edit., Pitman, 1989, Chapter 1.

Murphy, P. E., *Tourism: A Community Approach,* Methuen, 1985, Chapter 1.

McIntosh, R. W., and Goeldner, C. R., *Tourism : Principles, Practices, Philosophies,* 6th edit., John Wiley Sons, 1990, Chapters 1 and 3.

2

Introducing modern marketing: the systematic thought process

This chapter explains the meaning of modern marketing as it is applied internationally to goods and services of all types. The intention here is to define the essential characteristics common to all forms of marketing, while Chapter 3 considers the special characteristics of travel and tourism marketing.

To explain marketing, it is necessary to distinguish between the familiar word in everyday use and the term as it is used professionally by marketing managers. Popular notions of marketing are probably more of a hindrance than a help to those studying the subject for the first time, because, before reading any marketing texts, readers will be aware already of the continuous and competitive process of persuasion and inducements of every kind to which we are all routinely exposed in the conduct of our lives. All of us are daily the targets of massive and sustained marketing activity in a variety of forms, which range from advertising on television and radio, in the press, on posters, on drink mats and on milk bottles, through promotional literature of all types, and through special offers and price reductions in retail stores. If we pause to think about it, the evidence of marketing activity surrounds us on every hand like the air we breathe and take for granted. We are continuously exposed to persuasion and inducements, not only from

national and international commercial organizations, but also from governments and their agencies.

However imprecise their initial understanding of the subject, most people approach marketing with the view that it is important both commercially and socially; many are suspicious about its potential influence on their lives, and some have serious ethical worries about its effects upon society. What consumers see of promotion and persuasion is of course only the visible tip of an extensive iceberg of marketing management activities, of which most people are completely unaware. Marketing, as an approach to the conduct of business, developed most strongly in countries in the Western world with highly developed economies, but the concepts are also found increasingly in less developed countries.

In the early 1990s, following the remarkable collapse of old-style communist economies in Eastern Europe and the former USSR, there has been a deliberate stimulation of market based organizations and marketing methods. If this succeeds, it will promote as powerful a socio-economic revolution as any we have seen this century. For many decades competition, profit, and promotional activity were seen in the communist world as wasteful and against the public interest. Now, even in countries such as

China, the speed of response to change and prospects for greater operational efficiency inherent (but not guaranteed) in marketing principles, are requiring radical rethinking of the traditional practices of centrally planned economies.

This chapter begins by explaining the essential idea of voluntary exchange between two parties, which underlies all marketing theories of the conduct of business. It proceeds to discuss what *marketing orientation* means in terms of management attitudes. This leads into formal definitions of marketing, from which five propositions are derived. The most important of these is that marketing is *a system* comprising a series of stages, which are represented in an important diagram shown in Figure 2.1. The final part of the chapter discusses the combined effect of the five propositions and explains the growing significance of marketing in the late twentieth century. While every aspect of this chapter is relevant to travel and tourism marketing, the intention is to introduce the subject as it applies to transactions generally for all types of goods and services.

Marketing means exchanges

Chapter 1 explains that travel and tourism is best understood in terms of demand and supply within a total market. At its simplest, marketing can be explained as a process of achieving voluntary exchanges between two individual parties:

- Customers who buy or use products.
- Producer organizations which supply and sell the products.

In terms of buyers, marketing is concerned with:

- Understanding their needs and desires (why they buy).
- Which products they choose, when, how much, at what price, how often.
- Where they buy them from.

- How they feel after their purchase and consumption of products.

In terms of producers, marketing focuses on:

- Which products to produce and why.
- How many.
- At what price.
- When and where to make them available.

Not all products are exchanged for money. For example, some visitor attractions are made available to visitors free of admission charges. But provided such visitors have choices as to how to spend their time, the central notion of exchange remains valid.

From this simple introduction it follows that marketing involves a *management decision process* for producers, focused on a *customer decision process*, with the two sets of decisions coming together in an *exchange transaction* – money for products in the case of commercial operators. Assuming that customers have choices between different products, which is nearly always the case in travel and tourism markets, it is easy to see that producers have a strong motivation to *influence* prospective customers to choose their products rather than a competitor's.

Throughout this book, especially in dealing with exchange transactions based on services rather than goods, it is convenient to refer to 'the conduct of business', or 'business operations', or 'the management of operations'. In every case exchange transactions are the focus of activity.

Management attitudes and the business environment

To get below the surface of promotional activity, which is all the typical customer ever sees of marketing, it is helpful to focus first on the attitudes of managers in producer organizations. The spirit of marketing, its driving force, and the reason that its professionals find the subject enormously stimulating, exciting, and satisfying, lies in the way in which it is carried out in practice. Important though they are, marketing skills and techniques do not explain what marketing is. Attitudes do. In a few lines it is impossible to communicate the excitement and energy surrounding successful marketing operations. Most managers will recognize the enthusiasm the subject inspires; students will have to take it on trust, though they should be aware that the subject has to be experienced 'live' before it can be fully understood.

Above all, marketing reflects a particular set of strongly held attitudes, and a sense of commitment on the part of directors and senior managers – not just marketing managers – which are common to all marketing-led organizations. Combined, the guiding principles that affect the whole of an organization are known as a 'management orientation' or 'corporate culture'. In the particular case of a *marketing orientation*, there are four key elements, as follows:

● A positive, outward looking, innovative and highly competitive attitude toward the conduct of exchange transactions (in commercial and non-commercial organizations).
● A continuous recognition that the conduct of business operations must revolve around the long-run interests of customers.
● An outward looking, responsive attitude to events in the external business environment within which an organization operates, especially the actions of competitors.
● An understanding of the balance to be achieved between the need to earn profits from existing assets and the equally important need to adapt an organization to achieve future profits, recognizing social and environmental constraints.

With these proactive attitudes integrated as the driving force in a management team, marketing techniques may be implemented with success and vigour, although it is never easy. Without the driving force, the most professional

skills are unlikely to succeed because their practitioners will usually lose heart and seek more productive working environments. Management attitudes are partly learned and partly a response to external circumstances, especially the current balance between the capacity of supply and the volume of demand in the markets which an organization serves. The next section considers some important effects of this changing balance or relation between supply and demand. The Epilogue (p. 359) discusses social and environmental constraints in tourism marketing.

A *marketing orientation* as described above is not the only choice for managers. At the risk of over-simplifying it is possible to comment on two other orientations, which at different times and in different market circumstances serve managers as the guiding set of principles for the conduct of their businesses.

Production orientation

This term is often used to summarize the attitudes and responses of businesses whose products are typically in strong and rising demand, and profitable. Because demand does not present problems, there is a natural tendency for managers to focus their main attention on more pressing decisions, such as those concerning production capacity, quality and cost controls, finance for increasing production, and maintaining the efficiency and profitability of operations generally. In the short run, where demand is buoyant and growing, an emphasis on production processes and financial controls appears both logical and sensible.

Consider the example of a small town with two hotels and one car rental operator. If the town's business community is prosperous and growing, it is likely that the hotels and the car rental operation will be profitable businesses and they are very likely to be production orientated. Such demand conditions are quite commonly found in travel and tourism, even in the late twentieth century. Readers should note that the focus of production orientation is *inward looking* toward operational needs.

Sales orientation

This term is often used to summarize the attitudes and responses of businesses whose products are no longer enjoying growth in demand, or for which demand may be declining to levels that reduce profitability. Production is not now the main problem; surplus capacity is. The natural management reaction in these conditions is to shift the focus of attention to securing sales. Increased expenditure on advertising and on sales promotion or price discounts is a logical response in an attempt to secure a higher level of demand for available production capacity.

In the small-town example noted above, suppose a third hotel of similar size and quality were built. The occupancy of the existing two would probably suffer an initial fall, and a sales response from their managers would appear to be logical and sensible. Such changes in demand conditions are also frequently met in travel and tourism in the late twentieth century. Readers should note that the focus of sales orientation is still essentially *inward looking* toward the needs of operations and their surplus capacity.

Marketing orientation

This term can now be defined as summarizing the attitudes and responses of businesses that adopt the four key principles noted earlier in this chapter. Readers should note that the focus of marketing orientation is essentially *outward* looking toward the needs of customers and the effects of a changing business environment on their operations. A marketing orientation is typically a response to business conditions in which there is strong competition and surplus capacity for the available level of demand. In the notional small-town example, suppose there were now five hotels of a similar standard for a current demand that will fill only three of them at profitable levels of room occupancy. In these conditions an inward looking concern with production and operational efficiency will not make much impact on demand, especially if competitors' products are of a similar standard and price. Similarly, a strong sales drive with its emphasis on increased promotional expenditure will not increase demand significantly if competitors quickly follow suit with matching expenditure, and the increased expenditure will erode profitability. Reducing prices to increase demand will not succeed if competitors are able to match the reductions, and profit will again be eroded.

In the strongly competitive business conditions noted above, which in fact are typical of those faced by most operators in the travel and tourism industry, survival and future success lies in rethinking the whole business from the customer's standpoint – in order to secure and sustain an adequate *share* of the available demand. This means, in other words, assessing the different groups of customers in the available market, identifying their particular interests and preferences, and then adapting the organization as smoothly as possible to meet those needs better and/or faster than competitors. Since customers' needs and market conditions are nearly always in a state of constant change, the involvement of managers with marketing also has to be continuous. Identifying, responding, and adapting to market changes ahead of competitors, is the essence of a successful marketing approach and the focus of this book.

Defining marketing

For a student approaching the subject for the first time, it would be highly convenient if there were one standard definition of marketing with which all authors agree. But, although the subject has been studied and taught in academic courses for over seventy years (Bartels: 1976), it is still evolving and most consider it as much an art as a science. There are literally dozens of definitions. Crosier, for example, reviewed over fifty (see Baker: 1979, p. 5). Fortunately, most of these definitions are individual variations within a broad consensus that the marketing concept is consumer- and profit-orientated. Consumer orientation does not always mean giving customers what they want, but understanding consumers' needs and wants in order to respond more efficiently in ways that make business sense for organizations - both in the short term of 6 months to a year, and in the long term of several years.

Kotler, the author familiar to most marketing students on both sides of the Atlantic, defines the marketing concept as follows: 'The marketing concept holds that the key to achieving organizational goals consists in determining the needs and wants of target markets and delivering the desired satisfactions more effectively and efficiently than competitors' (Kotler: 1991, p. 16). See also 'societal marketing' concept, discussed in the Epilogue.

The British Chartered Institute of Marketing defines marketing as: 'The management process responsible for identifying, anticipating and satisfying customer requirements profitably'.

Both these definitions hold good for any form of consumer or industrial product marketing, whether of goods, such as soap powders or pianos, or services, such as hotel rooms, theme parks or airline travel. The Kotler definition is equally relevant to the marketing of people, ideas and places, and to any exchange process where target markets and organizational goals exist. It also covers the products of non-profit organizations, such as trusts responsible for museums, or charities established to provide particular products on a subsidized basis, such as holidays for the disabled or elderly.

While this book is about marketing in travel and tourism, readers must appreciate that tourism marketing is not a separate discipline but an adaptation of basic principles that have been developed and practised across a wide spectrum of consumer products for more than four decades.

Both definitions noted above provide a basis for making five important propositions, which are entirely relevant to travel and tourism marketing but not derived from it.

Five marketing propositions

- Marketing is a management orientation or philosophy.
- Marketing comprises three main elements linked within a system of exchange transactions.
- Marketing is concerned with long-term (strategy) and short-term (tactics).
- Marketing is especially relevant to late twentieth-century market conditions.
- Marketing facilitates the efficient conduct of business.

The first proposition (management orientation) was discussed earlier. Each of the other four is developed below.

Three main elements linked within a marketing system

It is implicit in Kotler's view above and all other definitions, that marketing comprises the following elements:

- The attitudes and decisions of customers (target markets) concerning the perceived utility and value of available goods and services, according to their needs, wants and interests, and ability to pay.
- The attitudes and decisions of producers concerning their production of goods and services for sale, in the context of their business environment and long-term objectives.
- The ways in which producers communicate with consumers, before, during, and after the point of sale, and distribute or provide access to their products.

In other words, the key elements in any marketing system are the attitudes and thought processes of the two parties – buyers and sellers – in any exchange process or market transaction.

It should be noted that there is no natural or automatic harmony between what consumers want and will pay for and what producers are able or willing to provide. In practice there is usually continuing tension between a producer's need for profit and the efficient use of assets, and the customer's search for value and satisfaction. Marketing managers have to use judgement in balancing between the conflicting needs of the parties in the exchange process, and to do so with imprecise knowledge about their customers and about the decisions of other producers marketing competitive products. Their judgement is expressed in the third element of the system, distribution and communication, on which the bulk of marketing expenditure is spent.

The better the balance between the interests of the two parties in the exchange process, the smaller the marketing expenditure will need to be as a proportion of sales revenue, and vice versa. For example, if a tour operator has accurately designed, priced, and judged the capacity of his programme, sales will be achieved at a relatively low promotional cost. If, for whatever reason, the price is too high or the capacity excessive for the available demand, only massive promotional expenditure and discounting will bring supply and demand back into balance. (Chapter 24 develops this point in more detail.)

The marketing system for service products

The three elements in the marketing system are shown in more detail in Figure 2.1. This is an important diagram, which in addition to introducing all the main processes or stages involved in any form of marketing, also serves as a framework for the contents of this book.

In Figure 2.1 the logical flow and linkages between the main processes are shown as an integrated system; it is relevant to all forms of service products. The process begins with a detailed analysis of the external business environment, and works through marketing and campaign planning to produce business strategies and operational plans that identify the marketing activities to be undertaken. The research and planning stages of the process incorporate all that an organization knows about its customers and potential customers, their attitudes and buying behaviour. Business strategies express an organization's attitudes and decisions over a specified time period. As the stages proceed, plans are turned into costed action programmes, which express how an organization will communicate with and provide access for its potential customers. The marketing process ends with further research into customers' feelings about the satisfaction and value for money they received from the purchases they made.

To simplify the explanation, the marketing system is shown in Figure 2.1 as a series of logical steps with an obvious beginning and an end. In practice, as explained in subsequent chapters, the steps do not proceed in a straight line; they comprise a continuous cycle, or rolling programme of decisions, actions and research, which incorporate many feedback loops under constant management review.

Because this book is concerned with services rather than goods, production capacity is shown as being held within an inventory/reservation system. For an airline this would be a computerized reservations system for seats on flights; for a hotel, a reservation system for beds, and so on. For manufacturers of physical goods all the main stages in the marketing system are essentially the same, but transport, warehousing, and related physical distribution systems would be the relevant considerations for inventory.

The summary of the marketing system below is intended to be read with Figure 2.1, and it

Table 2.1 *Summary of the marketing system*

Process	Description	Main chapter reference
Marketing research and analysis	Continuous, detailed appreciation of the historic and projected trends in the external business environment; includes consumer research and evaluation of previous marketing expenditure and results.	4, 5 and 11
Business strategy and marketing planning	Developing research and analysis into overall business and marketing strategies and operational plans; includes product and capacity plans.	12 and 13
Campaign planning and budgeting	Producing costed operational programmes to integrate the four main marketing mix elements of products, prices, promotion and distribution.	6 and 14
Action programmes/implementation	Detailed programmes of weekly and monthly activity for all forms of promotion and distribution.	15 to 19
Evaluation, monitoring and control	Monitoring and evaluating the results of completed marketing activity; includes customer research. Feeds data into the next cycle of the marketing process. May involve adjustment of current action programmes.	11 and 14

notes (in Table 2.1) the main chapters in which each of the stages is explained and discussed in detail.

Concerned with long term and short term (strategy and tactics)

The meaning of strategy and tactics is discussed in Chapters 12 and 13, but in understanding marketing orientation it is always important to distinguish the time scale within which marketing decisions are taken. The short term (or short run) may be defined as the period of time in which an organization is able to make only marginal alterations to its product specifications and published prices. In other words, in the short run an organization has no choice but to offer its goods or services for sale within the limits of a set of constraints that were established in part by its own earlier decision process. In the long run, according to its view of future markets and customers' requirements, an organization may decide to alter product specifications, introduce new products or phase out old ones, alter its pricing strategy, or change its position within a market. Mergers and business acquisitions or disposals provide other long run options.

In the short run, organizations frequently find themselves unable to adapt their products quickly enough to changes in customers' needs or market circumstances. In order to survive, they have to stimulate the available demand

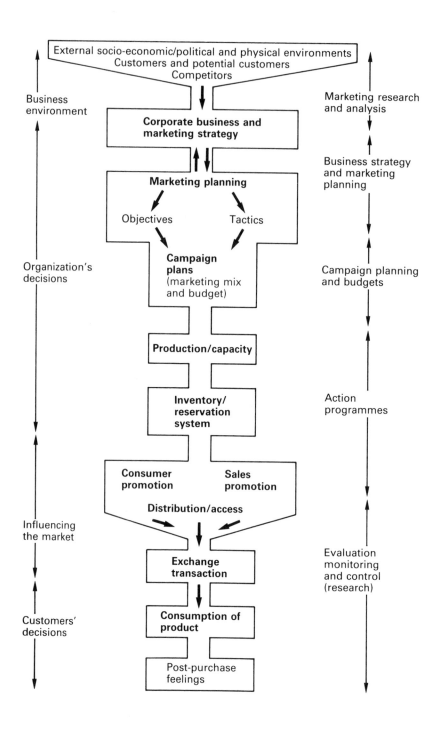

Figure 2.1   *The marketing system for service products*

through all the techniques of sales promotion, merchandising and advertising they can command. For example, if a rival airline gains permission to operate a scheduled route and reduces its competitors' seat occupancy (load factor) from, say, 64 to 54 per cent in the first 6 months of a new service, the immediate task for the competitor's marketing is to regain share and volume through aggressive sales tactics. What always distinguishes the marketing-led organization is not the objectives of its short-term tactics, but the speed and the way in which it uses and exploits its deep knowledge of customers to achieve its objects, while at the same time developing strategies aimed at long-run consumer orientation and satisfaction. Readers should note that most marketing definitions (including the Kotler version quoted in this chapter) are relevant primarily to the long run. In practice most marketing decisions are made in the tactical context of the short run. The constraints imposed by marketing highly 'perishable' service products with a fixed capacity on any one day, make short-run marketing decisions especially important in travel and tourism, a point which is explained in the next chapter.

It is not possible to set a precise time scale for either short or long run, because it varies from product to product. Suffice it to say that the short run typically means 6 months to a year ahead, and the focus of decisions is on this year's and next year's operations and marketing campaign. The long run typically means not less than 3 years ahead, and the focus of decisions is strategic.

In the ideal world of textbooks, products are mostly designed to meet customers' needs and they generate satisfaction and profit. In the real world of travel and tourism marketing, products are mostly less than ideal in one or more respects, and marketing managers have to live with the results of decisions that looked right when they were made some months or years previously but which have since been overtaken by unpredicted (and often unpredictable)

events. In 1991 the unpredicted and massive impact on international travel and tourism markets of the Gulf War was a classic if extreme illustration of circumstances that face marketing managers. Sometimes, as for Pan Am in USA or the International Leisure Group in the UK, such circumstances are overwhelming and business failures occur. Skilful marketing performs a vital compensating function for the gaps and mismatches between demand and supply, which occur inevitably when markets do not move in the ways predicted by managers.

Especially relevant to late twentieth-century conditions and large-scale operations

There is really nothing new in a marketing concept based simply on recognizing the need to satisfy customers, understand market trends, and exploit demand efficiently. As they are defined in many marketing textbooks, the essential characteristics of marketing have been practised by small businesses throughout history. No one survives long, especially in small service businesses, unless they understand their customers' needs, and provide satisfactory service at competitive prices. What distinguishes markets in the late twentieth century from those in any previous era, is a combination of powerful trends towards:

- Large, growing, highly competitive businesses with standardized products and relatively large shares of the markets they serve, operating on a national, international and increasingly on a global scale.
- Capacity of supply considerably in excess of what markets can absorb naturally (without stimulation).
- Large numbers of consumers in developed countries with sufficient disposable income and leisure time to indulge in non-essential purchases, many of them choosing to engage in frequent travel for leisure purposes.

These trends are obviously not unique to travel and tourism, but they are highly relevant to what is happening in marketing in the industry in the last part of the twentieth century. Large transnational corporations in travel and tourism around the world are increasingly able, through their marketing decisions, to influence customers' expectations of products and prices on the one hand, and lead the way in the development of marketing skills on the other. In this they are aided by modern information technology, which has greatly facilitated the speed and efficiency with which it is possible to manage and control large, multi-site operations. Among hotels, fast food restaurants, airlines, other transport operators, retail travel agencies, and tour operators, the conduct of operations in many different locations spread over a wide geographical area is already common. In each of these sectors a greater share of operations is becoming concentrated into fewer large-scale organizations.

This process has already produced giant organizations, such as Holiday Inns, Accor, Forte, Hyatt, Quality Inns, or Sheraton in the hotel sector; American Airlines, Delta, Japan Air Lines or British Airways in the airline sector; Hertz, Avis and Budget in car rental; American Express and Thomas Cook in travel organizations; and McDonald's, Burger King, Wimpy and Little Chef in fast food catering. These of course are only a few of the better-known major corporations competing for shares of travel and tourism markets, and students may find it a worthwhile exercise to expand this list around the industry sectors shown in Figure 1.1.

The emergence of large organizations in manufacturing industries has been well quantified in recent years in the USA, Britain and Continental Europe. The economic arguments of economies of scale, and the search for lower unit costs of production through the operation of larger capacity machines and equipment, are also well covered (see, for example, Pickering: 1974). Though less well analysed for the travel and tourism industry, the trends to larger scale have been in the same direction, for the same main reasons.

Without in any way denying the importance and future role in innovative marketing of the many thousand small businesses that still account for the largest part of travel and tourism supply in most countries, the recent emergence and growth of large international organizations justify the view that their marketing practices will be increasingly influential. They will tend to dominate customer expectations, product design, prices, and marketing techniques in all sectors of travel and tourism markets. The emergence of these corporations and their plans for expansion have greatly added to the surplus production capacity available, and therefore to the pressures of competition. As Baker puts it for industry as a whole, 'in the modern advanced industrial economy we have arrived at the point where the basic capacity to produce exceeds the basic propensity to consume' (Baker: 1979, p. 379). The same point, based on the capacity implications of technological innovation and slower growth in more mature markets, is highly relevant to travel and tourism in many countries now, and will be more so by the end of the century.

This author believes, and the view is reflected throughout this book, that the nature of modern international competition, and the continuous need to fill thousands of under-utilized beds, seats and other supply components, provide the most powerful motivating force now forcing the pace of modern marketing in the travel and tourism industry. There is no equivalent phenomenon on this scale in any previous period of history; it is the driving force that explains the current and future importance of marketing orientation and the need for improved marketing techniques. This view is further developed in the next chapter.

A quarter of a century ago large-scale operations were invariably associated with mass-produced products for mass-consumption markets. This is no longer true, however, and in manufacturing as well as in service operations global corporations increasingly have the technology not only to segment and respond to individual customers but also to customize products for them.

The commercial sector survivors of the 1990-3 international political upheavals and economic recession will not require reminding that large organizations are in some ways even more vulnerable than small ones when projected earnings fail to match actual costs as a result of falling demand. In such cases a combination of aggressive marketing and cost-cutting provides the only route to survival. The marketing route is positive, customer-orientated and proactive in the long run. Cost controls, however necessary, are essentially negative and reactive in the short run.

Facilitates the efficient conduct of business through monitoring and control

A marketing orientation is effectively forced upon businesses in competitive markets as a necessary method of survival. It is less clear from the definitions of marketing exactly how this orientation leads to the more efficient conduct of business. In practice efficiency emerges from the systematic way that managers undertake the processes set out in Figure 2.1. But it is not the processes themselves that are characteristic of marketing orientation; these processes are common to all larger organizations. What matters is the way that marketing procedures are integrated and co-ordinated with other core business functions, especially the production or operational processes, human resource management, and financial controls - backed up by management commitment to quality and long-run customer satisfaction.

All commercial organizations plan, promote and distribute products. Marketing-orientated businesses are characterized by the systematic organization of their planning processes, the precision with which they state their targets, the speed at which they act in relation to competitors, and their knowledge of the effects of their actions on their customers.

Throughout the book it is stressed that efficiency or cost-effectiveness in marketing is always based upon systematic planning and the specification of precise objectives and action programmes that can be closely monitored and evaluated. Precise marketing objectives also serve in practice as an integrating mechanism for all the operational departments in a business, and as a control system for measuring actual performance against targets. Tactical objectives may be evaluated against strategic marketing objectives and, if the organization is large enough, subsidiary objectives may be set for the profit performance of particular products or sub-divisions of a business, providing further ways to check on operational and marketing efficiency.

Chapter summary

This chapter defines the meaning of modern marketing, first as a management orientation, sometimes referred to as a management philosophy, and, second, as a systematic process comprising the techniques used by marketing managers to influence demand. To be effective in practice the orientation and the techniques must be integrated and co-ordinated within the management team. While the practice of marketing is most easily understood in commercial operations, the orientation and the techniques are increasingly applied in non-profit-making sectors also.

A marketing orientation is defined in contrast to other orientations based on production or sales. The latter tend to be inward looking and responsive to the needs of an organization and its operational requirements; marketing is outward looking and proactive to the changing business environment, and the needs, expectations and behaviour of customers. In distinguishing conceptually between production, sales, and marketing orientations, the differences appear quite clear. In practice no such clarity exists, and evidence of all three types of management orientation may be encountered within parts of the same organization at the same time.

Students of travel and tourism are reminded that a marketing approach is a response to business conditions, especially competition, and that such conditions are increasingly common to all producers of consumer goods and services in the latter part of the twentieth century. The particular conditions of fierce competition between large-scale, multi-site organizations, often with a considerable surplus of capacity of highly perishable products and seeking to influence available demand, are those which are now found frequently in travel and tourism markets in many parts of the world. The chapter stresses the role of these larger transnational organizations because of their influence over modern markets, but the importance of small businesses is not ignored. Competition between large organizations seems certain to leave many gaps and niches, too small to be profitable for big firms with their necessarily standardized operations, but highly profitable for smaller ones practising the same marketing orientation and techniques without competing head-on in large volume markets.

Figure 2.1 provides a step by step diagram of the modern marketing process, which also serves as a framework for the contents of the book. The diagram is one of the most important in the book and should repay careful consideration. It is applicable to all types of organization in the travel and tourism industry.

Above all, this chapter stresses that marketing is a proactive approach to business, conducted at best in a marvellously stimulating and positive spirit of competitive enthusiasm that no textbook can convey. There are three elements within it: the attitudes and decisions of managers, the attitudes and decisions of customers, and the ways in which the two parties communicate. Marketing focuses on exchange transactions and product sales, which yield satisfaction and value for money to one party, and a profitable long-run return on assets employed to the other.

Further reading

Because Baker in Britain, and Kotler in the USA and Britain, are commonly used marketing textbooks, these two authors are recommended for the chapters in this book that deal with basic marketing principles. Chapter 2 recommended reading is:

Baker, M. J., *Marketing: An Introductory Text*, 4th edit., Macmillan, 1985, Chapters 1 and 2.
Davidson, J. H., *Offensive Marketing*, 2nd edit., Penguin Books, 1987, Part 1.
Kotler, P., *Marketing Management: Analysis, Planning, Implementation and Control*, 7th edit., Prentice-Hall International, 1991, Chapter 1.

3

Special characteristics of travel and tourism requiring a marketing response: managing demand

Drawing on the contributions of widely recognized authors, Chapters 1 and 2 introduced the essential concepts of travel and tourism as a market, and of marketing as an approach to the conduct of modern business. This chapter focuses on the special characteristics of the supply side in travel and tourism, in response to which modern marketing is increasingly being adopted throughout the industry. Organizations in travel and tourism are a part of the *service sector* of an economy, as distinguished by economists internationally from the manufacturing, construction, and primary sectors. Understanding the special characteristics of travel and tourism services, which are common to all the 'industry' sub-sectors noted in Chapter 1, helps to explain the way in which marketing decisions are made and they merit very careful consideration. Travel and tourism operations are by no means unique in marketing terms but they do reflect common structural patterns which determine marketing responses.

This chapter begins by drawing some vital distinctions between the marketing of goods, on which much of the theory of marketing has been traditionally based, and the marketing of services. It notes the growth and importance of large-scale service organizations and identifies the characteristics common to most forms of service marketing before proceeding to identify the particular characteristics distinguishing travel and tourism services. The response of marketing managers to these characteristics, and the implications for demand management, are noted. The chapter ends by summarizing the basic differences between marketing as a set of principles relevant to all forms of exchange transactions, marketing for services generally, and marketing for travel and tourism in particular.

Marketing goods and services

The origins of marketing theory are generally attributed to the USA in the first part of the twentieth century (Bartels: 1976). The early contributions to the study recognized the growing importance of sales and distribution functions for manufacturers of consumer goods. They reflected opportunities provided by rapid improvements in transport and communication systems, and the consequent growth in the size of markets that businesses could reach with their products. For over 50 years the emerging theories focused almost exclusively on the marketing of physical goods, especially on the marketing of items manufactured on a mass production basis for consumption by the general public.

Until the 1970s the significance of service industries and service marketing generally were largely ignored on both sides of the Atlantic. Or they were discussed in crude simplifications, which lumped together as one broad category personal services such as domestic cleaning and hairdressing; commercial services such as banking, transportation, restaurants and tour operation; professional services such as medical and legal services; and public services such as education and health care. Yet in countries with highly developed economies the proportion of the working population employed in all forms of services has been rising rapidly in the last half of the twentieth century, to current levels of two thirds or more of all employment in many areas.

Between 1960 and 1990 the share of employment in service occupations in the USA rose from 56 per cent to around 70 per cent. In the UK, share of employment in manufacturing operations fell from 36 per cent in 1971 to 23 per cent in 1990, and services are also approaching the 70 per cent level (*Economist*: November 1991).

It was the rapid growth in the 1960s and 1970s of large-scale commercial service operations such as banking, insurance, and retail distribution, as well as transport, accommodation and catering, which prompted the shift of emphasis in marketing studies towards services. The first American Marketing Association Conference devoted specifically to service industries took place as recently as 1981, and there has been a massive output of articles and books on service marketing since the late 1970s. While it is beyond the scope of this book to trace and analyse the growth of service industries, the causes are related to increasing levels of consumers' disposable income, the development of rapid communications within and between countries, the growth of telecommunications and the emergence of computerized systems for management information and control purposes. Most importantly, associated with improved communications and control processes, the recognition of *economies of scale* in service operations has triggered much of the recent growth. Such economies are especially important in marketing. Developments in franchising and management contracts for services have also facilitated the speed of growth in large commercial organizations in service industries, both nationally and internationally. The 1980s were a decade in which major transnational service corporations helped to shrink the globe with their international brands.

Large-scale service operations

It is not easy to define the point at which a service producer becomes a large-scale operator; it tends to vary in different sectors of industry according to the nature of their operations. Large-scale operations in all parts of the world, however, usually display the following common characteristics, all of which have important implications for marketing:

1 Production and sale of purpose-designed, repeatable, quality controlled products.
2 Typically branded with the producer's name and bearing standard prices (with variations by place and time).
3 Products available at many places (multiple outlets).
4 Continuous production and availability, mostly on a daily basis, throughout the year.

5 Most marketing undertaken by head offices, which control and direct the activities at individual outlets.

These characteristics are common to most supermarket chains, fast food chains, post offices, banks, car rental and hotel corporations. They are not restricted to travel and tourism services.

Given the characteristics noted above, it should be appreciated that there are some strong similarities between the operating needs of large-scale service organizations and manufacturers of goods produced on a continuous mass-production basis. Levitt, for example, pushed this similarity to its logical conclusion in discussing the need to 'industrialize service production systems'. He suggested that this could be achieved by reducing the level of discretion available to service staff through the use of standardized procedures, and the use of what he calls 'hard', 'soft' and 'intermediate technologies' (Levitt: 1981, p. 37). Levitt cites McDonald's Corporation as an excellent illustration of the successful blending of industrial processes in food production and distribution, with quality control over every aspect of standardized operations, including the performance of the staff who provide service in the restaurants. The whole thrust of McDonald's international operations are firmly market-orientated as described in the previous chapter. Most airlines, hotel groups, tour operators, retail travel agency chains, and the larger tourist attractions, are striving currently to organize, control and deliver their continuous production capacity in equivalent ways, for the same reasons. It is a worldwide issue.

During the last 5 years considerable interest has been shown by service industries in recently developed systematic procedures for defining, regularly monitoring and providing certification for the quality of service products. Using a standards procedure based on the production of manuals, including regular assessments by external auditors, the process is known internationally as International Standard (ISO 9000), in Europe (EN 2900), and in the UK as British Standard (BS 5750). Not yet widely used in travel and tourism, these standards were being operated in some hotels and tour operations in 1993 and under active consideration in many others. Quality monitoring is not without considerable operational problems in multi-site services, but it is an interesting development for marketing managers whose product promises have to be based on expectations of satisfactory delivery. It draws marketing managers and operation managers closer together.

The recent developments in modern service industries noted above explain why the concept of services marketing set out in this book is primarily orientated around the marketing of large-scale, widely distributed, quality-controlled products. It has to be stressed that production on a large scale does not imply the mass production of undifferentiated products for all markets. All the complexities of market segmentation and product differentiation are as relevant to service producers as they are to manufacturers of physical goods; there is also ample room for market niches to be filled by the many small entrepreneurial businesses, which are important in travel and tourism in all countries.

From a cost-efficiency standpoint, the essential requirement of continuous production on a large scale lies in effective product design and quality control of operations. But once the technical problems of production have been solved, the ability to sustain production at efficient levels of utilization of premises and equipment, forces management attention on the systematic promotion of continuous consumption: in other words, ensuring that there is balance between the volume of demand and the volume of supply. If sufficient demand cannot be generated, massive financial losses are inevitable. Recent examples are the losses sustained internationally by airlines in the years 1979–82 and again in 1990–2, and by American and European car manufacturers over the same period. The larger the operator, the more important it is to secure and sustain a regular flow of customers to purchase the available capacity. This explains much of the modern focus on the role of marketing by these larger organizations.

It is interesting to speculate that the *size* of business operations is in fact more important in determining marketing responses than the nature of goods or services. As this author put it some years ago:

> It is the reality of large-scale continuous production of many service products, which provides the essential 'like with like' comparison with manufactured products. Of course, this characteristic has little if anything to do with lawyers, undertakers, cobblers or beauticians. But then neither has it any relevance to basket weavers, jobbing potters, saddle makers or gunsmiths. A dentist and a street corner shoe shiner have more in common (in marketing terms) with each other and with bakers and candlestick makers, than any of them have in common with large scale producers of goods or services (Middleton: 1983).

Services and their characteristics

The essential difference between goods and services, as noted by Rathmell in one of the earlier contributions to the subject, is that 'Goods are produced. Services are performed' (Rathmell: 1974). Goods are products purchased through an exchange transaction conferring ownership of a physical item that may be used or consumed at the owner's choice of time and place. Services are products purchased through an exchange transaction that does not confer ownership but permits access to and use of a service, usually at a specified time in a specified place. Thus, for example, the buyer of a ready-to-wear suit takes it from the store and wears it

when and where he pleases. The producer need have no further involvement unless the article is faulty. The buyer of a hotel room agrees to arrive alone or with a specified group, on a particular night or nights, and may forfeit a deposit if he fails to appear. Throughout his stay the traveller is closely involved with the hotel and its staff, and may participate directly in aspects of the service product by carrying his own bags, serving himself from a restaurant buffet, making his own tea, and in other ways.

The manufacturer or retailer of suits can put his products into warehouses and shops, and it may not be a vital concern if 6 months or more elapse between the completion of production and sale to the customer. But a hotel can perform its services once only on, say, 31 January; if customers are not available on that day, products are lost and cannot be resold the following day.

From this short introduction the principal characteristics of service products may be summarized as *inseparability* and *perishability*. From these two flow most of the distinguishing differences between goods and services that influence marketing.

Inseparability

This means that the act of production and consumption is simultaneous. The performance of the service requires the active participation of the producer and the consumer *together*. In the context of this book it also means that production and consumption takes place on the premises, or in the equipment (such as aircraft or hire cars) of the producer, and not in the consumer's home environment.

It means too that most of the staff of service companies have some consumer contact and are seen by the customer to be an inseparable aspect of the service product. Factory workers, managers and distributors do not usually meet customers; their attitudes, and the way they look and behave in the factory, are not necessarily relevant to product performance and customer satisfaction. Physical items can be tested and guaranteed, and precise product performance can be enforced by consumer protection laws. For services a wide range of product performance is determined by employees' attitudes and behaviour, for which there can be none of the normal guarantees and no prospect of legal enforcement. Staff cannot be forced to smile at customers, for example.

Inseparability of production and consumption is thus a vital concept in marketing services, but it does not mean that consumption and purchase cannot be separated. A primary aim of service marketing is to create ways to distance the act of purchase from the act of consumption. A hotel, for example, which has only 20 per cent of its capacity booked 12 hours before the scheduled performance of its particular service becomes highly dependent upon passing traffic for last-minute purchases. Customers at the check-in desk may well negotiate prices that are half or less of published tariffs. The same hotel, if it is 85 per cent pre-booked 3 months before the specified date of service production, is clearly in a much stronger position.

Perishability

It is convenient to treat perishability as a separate characteristic of services, although it follows from the fact of inseparability that service production is typically *fixed in time and space*. This means that if service capacity or products are not sold on a particular day, the potential revenue they represent is lost and cannot be recovered. Service production therefore is better understood as a *capacity to produce*; not a quantity of products. Capacity can be utilized only when customers are present on the producers' premises.

To illustrate the point, let us consider the example of a museum that has an effective visitor capacity (assessed as space in which to move in comfort around the exhibits) of, say, 500

visits per hour. This could mean 2,000 visits on a typical busy day, when open from 10 am to 6 pm, making allowance for peak and slack times of the day. If the museum closes 1 day per week it has a nominal 'production' capacity of 313 (days) × 2,000 visitors = 626,000 visits over 12 months. In practice such a museum is unlikely to exceed around 150,000 visits per annum and on, say 10 days it may be overcrowded with 3,000 visits per day, whereas on 100 days in the winter it may never exceed 200 per day. If 10,000 visitors want to visit the museum on a particular day, they cannot do so, because the display space cannot be expanded, and the inevitable queues would simply cause most prospective visitors to go elsewhere. A would-be Sunday visitor is unlikely to be impressed by the fact that he could visit on Monday if he is going to be back at work on that day.

Hotels with a fixed number of rooms, and transport operators with a fixed number of seats, face identical problems of matching available demand to perishable supply, although they can calculate their available capacity and probable demand with much more precision than museums or other visitor attractions. Perishability is linked in the case of travel and tourism services with seasonality, which is discussed later in this chapter.

No possibility of creating and holding stocks

It follows from the characteristics of inseparability and perishability that it is not possible for a service producer to create a stock of products to be used to satisfy daily fluctuations in demand. By contrast, manufacturers of Christmas goods, for example, are able to manufacture their products around the year and create stocks, most of which are sold to customers in December. The process of stock creation and physical distribution between factories, warehouses and retailers is expensive, but it does create a relative stability and continuity in the production process that is not available to service producers.

Perishability and the impossibility of stockholding does not mean, however, that inventory systems for services cannot be created, or that distribution processes are not a vital concern for service producers. On the contrary, one of the most interesting developments of the 1980s in service marketing was the refinement of systems making it possible to retain details of each year's production capacity in a computerized inventory, and then to treat the inventory in exactly the same ways that physical stocks are treated by producers of physical goods. Thus a hotel may keep an inventory of its production capacity for conferences for 2 or more years ahead of the actual performance of services, and market that capacity through contracts to deliver products at specified times.

Two other characteristics are sometimes said to distinguish products based on services from those based on physical goods: one is *heterogeneity* and the other is *intangibility* (see, for example, Stanton: 1981). Taken literally, heterogeneity means that every service performance is unique to each customer. Strictly, because human beings are not machines, this is true. But in practice it is a totally academic concept and it is absurd to apply it to frequently used service products such as those marketed by banks, transport operators, fast-food chains, and other large-scale service operators, all of which are committed to the specification and quality control of service performance.

Intangibility is an important characteristic of service products in the sense that most services cannot easily be measured, touched or evaluated at the point of sale before performance; it means, in other words, that many service products are 'ideas' in the minds of prospective buyers. But many physical goods, such as motor cars, perfumes or expensive leisure wear, are also 'ideas' in customers' minds at the point of sale, even though they can be inspected and guaranteed. On the other hand, bus services, fast-food restaurants, and even hotels, are hardly less tangible to those who use them regularly than Marks & Spencer's underwear or

a washing powder. Accordingly, although the intangibility of travel and tourism products requires careful understanding by marketing managers, and a particular response in the promotion and distribution of products, it is not a generic difference between goods and services of the same order as inseparability and perishability.

Table 3.1 summarizes the main generic characteristics that distinguish most goods from most services.

Particular characteristics of travel and tourism services

Associated with the basic or generic characteristics common to all services, there are at least three further features that are particularly relevant to travel and tourism services. These are seasonality, the interdependence of tourism products, and the high fixed costs of operations.

Seasonality and demand fluctuations

It is a characteristic of most leisure tourism markets that demand fluctuates greatly between seasons of the year. Residents of northern Europe and the northern states of the USA tend mostly to take their main holidays of the year in the summer months of June to September, because the winter months of December to March are generally cold and wet and hours of daylight are short. While such climatic variations are not so relevant to many Mediterranean, Middle Eastern, Pacific or Caribbean tourism destinations, their main markets are still accustomed to think of summer and winter months, while schools and many business year cycles reinforce such traditions. As a result, many tourism businesses dealing with holiday markets fluctuate from peaks of 90 to 100 per cent capacity utilization for 16 weeks in a year, to troughs of 30 per cent or less for 20

Table 3.1 *Generic characteristics distinguishing services from goods*

Goods	Services
Are manufactured	Are performed
Made in premises not open to customers (separable)	Performed on the producers' premises with customer participation (inseparable)
Goods are delivered to places where customers live	Customers move to places where services are delivered
Purchase means right of ownership to use at will	Purchase confers temporary right to use at a fixed time and place
Goods possess tangible form at the point of sale; can be inspected	Services are intangible at the point of sale; often cannot be inspected
Can be stocked, physically	Perishable, cannot be stocked physically

Note: These characteristics are those which apply generally to most services and most goods

weeks in the year. Seasonal closure of many leisure tourism businesses is still common.

On a weekly basis, city centre restaurants may fluctuate from 80 per cent occupancy on Thursdays to 20 per cent (if they open) at weekends. On a daily basis, seats on a scheduled air flight may be 95 per cent full at 0800 hours, while seats on the following flight at 1000 hours may be only 45 per cent occupied. These demand variations are all the more acute because of the factor of perishability discussed previously, and it is always a major preoccupation of marketing managers to generate as much demand in the troughs as market conditions permit.

Interdependence of tourism products

Most visitors combine in their travel purchase decisions not one service or product but several. A vacationer chooses attractions at a destination together with the products of accommodation, transport, and other facilities such as catering. Tourist accommodation suppliers at a destination are therefore partly influenced by the marketing decisions of tour operators and travel agents, attractions, transport interests and tourist boards, which together or separately promote the destination and its activities and facilities.

Over time there is a relationship underlying the capacity of different travel and tourism products at a destination, and a potential synergy to be achieved in their marketing decisions if the different suppliers can find ways to combine their respective efforts. There will often be opportunities for joint marketing of the types discussed in Part Five of this book.

Interdependence can best be understood when a new resort, e.g. a ski resort, is being planned. The basic capacity estimated is the number of skiers per peak hour who can be accommodated comfortably on the slopes. With an estimate of skiers and non-skiers, and of day and staying visitors, it is possible to determine the optimum capacity of ski lifts, the number of beds needed, and the required restaurant facilities, car parks and so on. Each visitor facility in the resort is functionally related to other facilities and, even if they are separately owned, their fortunes are certainly linked. This vital interdependence was designated 'complementarity' by Krippendorf (1971). The same concept appears as 'partnership' in the USA (Morrison : 1989, p. 175).

High fixed costs of service operations

When the profit and loss accounts of businesses in the travel and tourism industry are analysed, it is generally the case that they reveal relatively high fixed costs of operating available capacity, and relatively low variable costs. A *fixed cost* is one that has to be paid for in order for a business to be open to receive customers; a *variable cost* is one that is incurred in relation to the number of customers received. What this means in practice may easily be understood in the case of a visitor attraction, in which the following main costs must be incurred in order to be open to receive visitors:

● Premises (capital costs and annual maintenance costs).
● Rents, leases and rates.
● Equipment (including repairs, renewals, and servicing).
● Heating, lighting and other energy costs.
● Insurances.
● Wages and salaries of full time employees.
● Management overheads and administrative costs.
● The bulk of marketing costs.

The point to note is that these fixed costs, mostly committed ahead over a 12-month period, have to be met whether the attraction draws in 50 visitors, 500 or 5,000 on any day. While a significant element of variable cost arises in operating catering and shops, and in the numbers of part-time staff employed, the variable cost of admitting one additional visitor is virtually nil. The same basic fact of operations is true for room sales in hotels, seats in transport operations, and all forms of visitor entertainments.

To illustrate the same point with a transport example, consider an airline that operates a particular flight with either 20 per cent or 80 per cent of seats occupied. Its aircraft maintenance costs are the same, its airport dues are the same, it pays the same wages to cabin and flight deck staff and to its airport and other personnel, and its fuel charges vary only marginally. In other words, to perform the service at all calls for a high level of fixed cost regardless of how many passengers are carried. Although operating costs are mainly fixed regardless of seat occupancy, the revenue side varies dramatically. For a seat price of say US$200 (average), sales of forty seats produce a basic gross revenue contribution of $8,000. If 200 seats are sold, contribution is $40,000. If the fixed costs of operating the flight are $20,000, then forty occupied seats produces a loss of $12,000 and 200 occupied seats produces a surplus of $20,000.

The facts of high fixed costs of operation focus all service operators' attention on the need to generate extra demand, especially *the additional, or marginal sales*, a very high proportion of which represents revenue gain with little or no extra cost. Kotas, for example, defined the connection between the high fixed cost structure of hotel and restaurant businesses and their need to be market- rather than cost-orientated (Kotas: 1975: p. 18.). The same point is even more important in some of the other sectors of the travel and tourism industry.

It is worth stressing that most large-scale businesses are obliged through competition to operate on a very narrow margin between total costs and total revenue. Plus or minus one percentage point in average load factors for airlines (seat occupancy) or room occupancy for hotels may not sound large. But over a year it means the difference between a substantial profit on assets employed or a significant loss. Imagine the atmosphere in boardrooms of large hotels in England in 1991 as they faced up to an average 10 percentage points fall in room occupancy during the Gulf War crisis period, January to April. Imagine it again when in the same four months in 1992 they faced a further 7 percentage points fall as a result of economic recession in the UK and elsewhere.

Such shifts in demand are unusually severe, and they impose very daunting tasks for marketing managers as the principal revenue generators.

The marketing response to the characteristics of supply

In reviewing the distinctive characteristics of service operations generally and of travel and tourism in particular this chapter has focused on six very important structural aspects of supply, summarized below. These aspects strongly influence the attitudes and decisions of management in all sectors of the travel and tourism industry as they seek to respond to and influence prospective customers' demand for their products - the marketing response. Further reference to these structural influences will be found in all parts of this book, especially in Part Five, which considers the application of marketing in each main sector of the industry. The six aspects are:

- Inseparability.
- Perishability.
- Interdependence.
- Seasonality.
- High fixed costs.
- Fixed in time and place.

This chapter also stresses that these characteristics are found in an industry in which the supply of products by large-scale organizations is taking an increasing share of total demand, and increasingly dominating customer expectations of products, prices and satisfaction. The larger an organization is, the more vulnerable it is to any shortfalls in demand, and the more emphasis it puts on ways to influence its customers – in other words, on marketing.

Simply put, the marketing response to the six characteristics is to *manage or manipulate demand*. The more an organization knows about its customers and prospective customers – their needs and desires, their attitudes and behaviour – the better it will be able to design and implement the marketing efforts required to stimulate their purchasing decisions. The marketing response has strategic, long-run implications, and a tactical, short-term role.

To understand the enormous continuous pressure which the six characteristics impose on operators in all sectors of travel and tourism, students in particular will find it helpful to consider operations in terms of daily capacity. To illustrate this point, if the task is to organize marketing for a hotel of, say, 150 rooms, the first step is to express its total capacity over the year. Thus, 150 rooms × 365 days × 2 (average beds per room) ×, say, 65 per cent (target bed occupancy average over a year) = 71,175 bednights to be sold. The marketing task is to break up that total into the estimated number of bookings to be achieved per day of each week, and by the different groups of customers with which the hotel deals, e.g. customers for business or leisure.

If the task is to market an airline, one jumbo jet represents, say, 450 seats × 350 days (in operation allowing for routine servicing) × 3.4 (average seat utilization per 24-hour period, assuming optimum number of hours in the air) × 70 per cent (target seat occupancy average over a year) = 374,850 seats to be sold. The marketing task is to break up that total by the estimated number of bookings to be achieved on a daily basis, and by the different groups which the airline serves, e.g. first class, club class, and economy class passengers.

It cannot be stressed too often that the role of marketing in the travel and tourism industry in response to the six factors noted in this section is to manage or manipulate sales, (customer purchasing behaviour) on an orderly, continuous, daily and weekly basis, (a) to utilize the regular daily flow of available, inseparable capacity, (b) to generate the extra or marginal sales, which produce revenue at very little extra cost. The better the product is designed to meet customers' needs and expectations, the easier the task will be. The greater the knowledge of customers, the more effectively the demand management task can be carried out.

How does marketing in travel and tourism differ from other forms of marketing?

Students of travel and tourism often find it difficult to appreciate the way in which the marketing of travel and tourism differs from other forms of consumer marketing practice. Standard texts on marketing principles are not much help. Generally speaking, however, it appears to be common ground that the *principles* of the body of knowledge about marketing, and its main theoretical elements, can be applied in all industries and in commercial and non-profit sectors of an economy. Differences occur in the *application* of the theory.

To the extent that there is an internationally recognized theory of marketing, its principles should hold good for all types of product. In other words, the basic or core principles of marketing must be relevant to all products, whether they are based on services or manufactured goods. Marketing managers at senior levels of responsibility can, and frequently do, switch between industries with little difficulty. This is only possible because of the integrity of the body of knowledge. In travel and tourism in particular many marketing managers have been 'imported' from manufacturing and other service industries to bring their expertise to bear as firms grow faster than the level of expertise available from within their own sector of business.

Against this evidence of common ground, however, experience convinces many in the industry that there are some characteristics of travel and tourism services that are so dominant in their implications that standard marketing principles must be considerably adapted to ensure success in an operational context. If this is true, it is clearly a very important consideration indeed.

This author believes that the body of knowledge about marketing in travel and tourism must be based firmly on five aspects of demand and supply in the industry, each of which has important common characteristics that combine to give marketing practice its particular approach and style. These are:

● Nature of demand (see Chapters 4 and 5).
● Nature of supply (discussed in this chapter).
● Products and prices, which respond to 1 and 2 (see Chapters 8 and 9).
● Characteristics of promotion used to influence demand (see Chapters 15 to 17).
● Characteristics of distribution used to facilitate purchase (see Chapters 18 and 19).

Marketing practice, reflecting these five aspects of demand and supply, is discussed throughout Parts Five and Six of this book.

On the basis of these five aspects of demand and supply, it is possible to conclude with three propositions about marketing in travel aud tourism, that are relevant to all the forms which it takes:

1 In the context of opportunities and constraints arising from the business environment of a major national and international market, products in tourism are designed, adapted and promoted, to meet the long-run needs, expectations and interests of prospective customers. This is the common ground with all forms of consumer marketing, and the cornerstone of all marketing theory.

2 Service products have particular characteristics of inseparability and perishability, which call for a different application of the marketing mix variables. This is the common ground with those who advocate, properly, that marketing of services is different in practice from that of physical goods.

3 Marketing in travel and tourism is shaped and determined by the nature of the demand for tourism and the operating characteristics of supplying industries. The forms of promotion and distribution used for travel and tourism products have their own

particular characteristics, which distinguish their use in comparison with other industries. These characteristics form the common ground on which marketing for travel and tourism is based.

It is the *combined* effect of these three propositions that distinguishes marketing in travel and tourism from marketing in other industries. The full meaning of the propositions, and the ways in which they determine and influence marketing decisions at strategic and tactical levels, are the subject matter of this book.

Chapter summary

This chapter explains the characteristics of service production influencing marketing generally, and the importance of modern large-scale service operations in particular. The main characteristics of travel and tourism operations are noted, and the implications for demand management are stressed. While none of the aspects discussed is unique to travel and tourism, it is the combined effect of the characteristics that influences marketing in the industry.

Inseparability and perishability are shown to cause inflexibility in the supply of product capacity, which, allied to seasonality, make tourism businesses very vulnerable to short-run fluctuations in demand. Marketing managers are therefore usually preoccupied with the need to manage or manipulate short-run demand around the fixed capacity of supply. The chapter notes that the marketing task is easier if long-run strategic decisions have created products that match customer needs, and especially if marketing managers have detailed knowledge of their customers with which to undertake short-run demand management efficiently.

The high fixed costs of operating most service businesses are highlighted. The fact that additional customers can often be accommodated at the margin at little or no extra cost to the business underlies many of the short-run marketing methods used in travel and tourism, especially the widespread use of price discounting. All the characteristics together help to explain why much of travel and tourism is considered to be a high risk business, a business in which entrepreneurs with a strong intuitive understanding of rapidly changing market-place trends, and a willingness to make the difficult adjustments in capacity faster than competitors, have so often thrived in the industry with spectacular success. The equally spectacular failures are usually traceable to the effects of high fixed costs and cash flow problems when demand fails in crisis conditions.

Students of marketing will be aware that the simple distinctions drawn here between goods and services are open to dispute, and there is much evidence that many physical goods require extensive services to support their sales. For the purposes of this book, however, the distinctions summarized in Table 3.1 should be helpful in clarifying differences that profoundly influence the nature of the marketing responses discussed in Parts Four and Five.

Further reading

Cowell, D., *The Marketing of Services*, Heinemann, 1984, Chapters 1,2 and 3.

Kotler, P., *Marketing Management : Anaysis, Planning, Implementation and Control*, 7th edit., Prentice-Hall International, 1991, Chapter 17.

Lovelock, C. H., *Services Marketing: Text, Cases and Readings*, Part 1, Prentice-Hall, 1984.

4

The changing business environment: aspects of demand for travel and tourism

Chapter 2 identifies the marketing process common to all businesses and explains that a marketing orientation is an outward looking set of management attitudes, sometimes known as a corporate culture. Organized around a detailed knowledge of existing and prospective customers, outward looking means being highly responsive and proactive to the general business environment within which any organization operates. Figure 2.1, which represents the systematic marketing process, has at the start of the process an appreciation of the external environment, on which all strategy and subsequent marketing decisions are based.

The external environment contains a number of elements requiring careful analysis, some of which are also discussed in Chapter 6. First and foremost among them for any marketing-led organization must be a continuous, systematic study of market demand and customer behaviour, normally based on market research. While recognizing that total demand and many of the shifts that occur in market patterns are outside the control of individual commercial operators or tourist boards, it is the business of

marketing managers to influence demand to the maximum extent possible and to adapt their products and operations to it. Marketing is, therefore, both responsive to what it cannot control in the external environment, and proactive in adapting operations to ever changing circumstances.

Other than in tourist boards and major international organizations, most marketing managers are not usually concerned directly with measuring the factors that influence *total* market movements. But they are invariably involved with interpreting such movements and deciding how their organizations should respond. Accordingly, the discussion that follows is relevant to all engaged in marketing decisions, regardless of their actual direct involvement in market research.

Market demand and customer behaviour for travel and tourism reflect two separate dimensions, characterized by Burkart and Medlik as 'determinants and motivations' (Burkart and Medlik: 1981, p. 50). Determinants are the economic, social and political factors at work in any society that set limits to the volume of a population's demand for travel, whatever individuals' motivations may be. For reasons discussed in this chapter, a country such as India, for example, cannot generate the same level of travel demand per capita as the USA, primarily because the average personal income in India is only a fraction of that in America. Within any particular country economically depressed regions do not generate the same volume of travel as affluent ones, and so on. Motivations are the internal factors at work within individuals, expressed as needs, wants and desires, which lead some people to place a much higher value on leisure travel than others. Motivations, the subject of the next chapter, are not necessarily related to economic factors. Students, for example, may set a much higher priority on international travel than many older, more affluent people.

This chapter focuses on the main determinants of travel and tourism, and begins by noting that the factors influencing the total demand for travel and tourism are common to all countries. Eight principal factors are identified and discussed separately. A framework is provided in Table 4.1, which summarizes the factors associated with high and low propensities to engage in travel and tourism. The chapter concludes with a brief note on the implications of the determinants for marketing managers.

The determinants of demand, common to all countries and suppliers

Fortunately for students and others wishing to understand the demand for travel and tourism, the basic factors that underlie demand and determine its total potential size are common to all countries. While the demand and the particular patterns generated by the population in each region within any country are unique to the area, the underlying factors are the same.

The factors are also relatively easy to measure and the measurement methods used by researchers in all countries are essentially the same.

The same set of external determinants of market demand affect individual operators such as hotels, tour operators and airlines. The responses marketing managers make however, will certainly differ according to their understanding of the factors at any time.

Categorizing the main determinants of demand

The main determinants of demand for travel and tourism are summarized under eight broad headings, as follows:

- Economic.
- Demographic.
- Geographic.
- Socio-cultural and social attitudes.
- Comparative prices.
- Mobility.
- Government/regulatory.
- Media communications.

These determinants of demand are external to individual businesses, and changes occurring in any of them exert an influence over the size and patterns of travel markets. In the last part of the twentieth century the determinants are changing rapidly, requiring constant study by those whose job it is to understand and anticipate market shifts.

Of course demand responds also to changes in the *supply* of products, so that the capacity of supply is an important determinant of demand. For example, a significant volume of demand for leisure travel from the USA to Australia, or from Britain to Spain, could not have been developed until a supply of products was available - in these cases based on new technology of transport capable of undertaking the necessary journeys at a speed and cost that the market could afford. Such products were the result of commercial decisions taken by suppliers in the light of their appreciation of demand in countries of high tourism potential. At the level of the individual operator, making supply or product decisions in relation to estimates of changes in demand is a constant theme throughout the book, and for this reason supply based determinants are not discussed separately in this chapter.

Economic factors

Wherever travel and tourism markets are studied, the economic variables in the countries or regions in which prospective tourists live are the most important set of factors influencing the total volume of demand generated. For international tourism in the early 1990s '30 major origin countries ... account for 92 per cent of world travel spending ... The top ten alone account for some 66 per cent of spending and 65 per cent of nights' (Edwards: 1992. p8). These top thirty are those with the highest income per capita, and highly developed economies such as the USA, Japan, and West Germany.

Developed and growing economies sustain large numbers of trips away from home for business purposes of all kinds. Business meetings, attendance at conferences and exhibitions, and travel on government business are all important parts of the travel and tourism industry. In 1990, for example, the UK received 18 million overseas visits, of which 25 per cent were for business purposes, accounting for 28 per cent of all expenditure in the country (IPS: 1990).

The influence of economic variables is equally obvious in leisure travel where, in many countries with developed economies, average disposable income per capita has grown over the last two decades to a size large enough to enable two-thirds or more of the total population to take one or more holidays (staying away from home) in any year. If allowance is made for day visits from home, this proportion usually rises to over 90 per cent of the population in a year.

Using published statistics of tourist trips and of national economic trends, it is possible to trace the relationship over time between changes in real disposable income (measured in constant prices) and the volume of trips and expenditure away from home. For the bulk of the population in countries with developed economies, notwithstanding the world energy crises of the 1970s and early 1980s, steadily rising real incomes over the last two decades have led to a proportionately higher expenditure on travel and tourism. This relation between incomes and expenditure on travel and tourism is known as the *income elasticity of demand*. If, for example, in any measured group in a population there is a greater than 1 per cent increase in expenditure on travel and tourism, in response to a 1 per cent increase in disposable income, the market is known as income elastic. If demand changes less than proportionately to income, the market is known as inelastic. In travel and tourism the total demand for vacation travel has generally proved to be income elastic, while the demand for visits to friends and relatives has been relatively inelastic.

If the other determinants remain unchanged there is a very clear direct relation between the performance of a country's economy, especially the average disposable income of its population, and the volume of demand which it generates for holidays and leisure trips. For over a quarter of a century up to the 1980s travel and tourism was income elastic. The evidence noted in Table 1.2 for the USA and the UK, and projections now being made for the rest of the century, indicate that future growth of demand in the relatively mature markets of the main generating countries is more likely to change only in line with disposable income. Preliminary results linking a marked downturn in international tourism with economic recession in 1990-3 tend to confirm this view.

One important implication for marketing managers of the continuing rise in disposable incomes in countries with developed economies is that the people most likely to engage in travel and tourism are also those most likely to have increased their standards of living as expressed in their home environments. As a consequence, the quality standards of furnishings and fittings in hotels, for example, and other forms of accommodation, have had to improve to keep pace with customers' rising expectations. Soundproofing, adjustable heating and ventilation, bathroom facilities, size of rooms and lighting, are all aspects of product provision influenced by rising levels of relative affluence, to which marketing managers in the travel and tourist industry have to respond with new and modified products.

Demographic factors

The term 'demographic factors' is just a convenient way to identify the main characteristics of the population that influence demand for travel and tourism. Mostly operating much more slowly than economic variables, which can change rapidly from year to year, the main characteristics determining tourism markets are household size and composition, age, and the experience of further and higher education. The total number of people in each population group is obviously the base from which any market volume projection is calculated.

Over the last two decades, in countries with developed economies, smaller households have emerged as the norm, with fewer young children in them, and a much greater proportion of married women in full- or part-time work. The number of households including couples and one or more children in Britain is now only just over a quarter of the total, and the number of children under the age of 15 fell by over 2 million between 1971 and 1991. The growing incidence of divorce has created many single-person and single-parent households, and this is changing the nature of demand. Obviously these changes have affected producers who traditionally provided family holiday products based on the needs and interests of children. Smaller households also means more households and more reasons to visit family and friends living outside the area of residence.

At the other end of the age scale the increasing number of people over the age of 55 who are retired or near retired has been identified as a vitally important population trend, which will increasingly influence travel and tourism markets by the end of the century. In the USA there were some 39 million people over the age of 55 in 1970, 46 million in 1980, and over 50 million in 1990. In Western Europe it is estimated that one in four people will be aged 55 or over by the year 2000 (De Rooij: 1986, p. 17). Apart from the size of the market, these retired and near retired people have very different attitudes from any previous generation of senior citizens, in the sense that most of them are far more active, fit, and affluent than before. By the year 2000 many of them will have been brought up in a civilization accustomed to high levels of personal mobility, and most will have established patterns of leisure activities and holidays, which they will be able to afford to continue into their seventies and eighties. Marketing managers around the world are studying ways to develop their shares of this expanding market, and there are obvious profit prospects for those who design products that mature markets want to buy.

The influence of education as an important determinant of travel is not easily separated from associated changes in income and household composition. But it is clear that the higher the level of education achieved, the greater the amount of travel, both for business and leisure purposes. This tendency reflects a greater knowledge of what travel opportunities are available and also the experience of travel as a normal part of college and university life, especially for those living away from home.

Geographic factors

For populations living in northern climates, the weather is undoubtedly one of the principal determinants of travel demand for leisure purposes, and explains destination patterns. For the population living in northern Europe, Spain and other Mediterranean countries offer the most accessible locations for warmth and sunshine. Florida provides much the same amenity for many Americans in the north-eastern states of the USA.

Next to weather, another important geographic factor is the size of the community in which populations live. Large urban and suburban communities, reflecting also the factors of relative wealth and education previously discussed, typically generate more tourism per capita than the populations of smaller, especially rural communities. Large urban centres are also catchment areas for day visitors to attractions within accessible distance, which is typically defined in Britain as 1 to 1½ hour's drive. Beyond that distance the volume of day visits drawn from any place of origin dwindles to a small proportion, even for large, nationally known attractions.

In the nineteenth century the geography of seaside resorts in northern Europe can be explained in terms of population centres and railway journeys lasting typically no more than 1½ hours. In the twentieth century the geography of Mediterranean resorts is explained by a combination of weather factors, the location of large urban areas in northern Europe, and air transport journeys of up to around 1,000 miles, which can be accomplished in up to 2 hours' flying time.

For operators of all kinds of visitor attractions and for accommodation suppliers, the choice of location for their businesses in relation to their intended markets is usually the most important decision to be made. For hotels, for example, as for retail supermarkets, it will normally be possible to calculate with precision the probable level of business to be achieved at any given site, purely on an analysis of locational factors and their experience of demand in similar locations.

Socio-cultural factors

The term socio-cultural factors is used to describe the broad trends in any society's attitudes that influence individual motivations, but have a wider national impact in the sense that they represent commonly held beliefs and notions with which people are brought up as children. In northern climates, for example, millions of people hold the belief that there is a therapeutic value in lying on beaches exposed to the sun. Responding to such beliefs underlies much of the tourism destination capacity provided in sun belt areas around the world. Recent concerns about depletion of the global ozone layer and the toxic effects of too much exposure to unfiltered sunlight may shift this deeply held attitude, with potentially major effects on the future demand for the products of sunshine destinations.

Another belief is that holidays are necessities rather than luxuries, and that trips abroad for business or pleasure are symbols of economic and social status that serve to indicate the value of one's position in society. Related to this is the belief by many that the amount of paid holiday entitlement of those in work should increase. Supported by trade-union pressure, there was a remarkable growth in the amount of paid leave enjoyed by most British employees in the 1970s. At the start of the decade 28 per cent of British manual workers received 2 weeks' paid holiday, with only 4 per cent receiving 3 to 4 weeks or more. By the end of it none were receiving 2 weeks or less, more than nine out of ten received over 3 weeks, and a half achieved four or more weeks' paid holiday. Similar trends in increased amounts of paid holiday time can be observed in other countries, although not usually at such speed.

Large numbers of people in northern countries with developed economies clearly believe that second homes and sunshine holidays are important attributes of a satisfactory life style. There are many surveys confirming the strength of these beliefs, which are also widely communicated in the popular press and on TV.

The full marketing implications of the extra time available for holidays, including the most appropriate product responses, do not appear to be fully understood. Yet the change has certainly helped to encourage the development of additional short holiday products taken at most times of the year, and has made it possible for tour operators to increase the capacity of products offered in shoulder months, confident that there are sufficient people with the necessary holiday entitlement and flexibility in their arrangements to travel outside what were the traditional peak summer months of July and August. The growing number of retired people able to travel when they wish, and the decline in the number of families committed to school holiday periods, has also helped to support this new flexibility in demand patterns. Yet the pricing policies adopted by most operators towards peak and off peak periods still largely reflect the traditional summer demand patterns, which are far less relevant than they were a decade previously.

The importance of attitudes

The evidence reviewed in this chapter indicates that the *potential* market for domestic and international tourism includes a growing number of people with enough income, leisure time and mobility to generate and sustain significant market growth in the next decade. Much more important for the future than numbers, however, are the general attitudes and behaviour of the potential market towards holiday travel compared with other leisure products claiming their interest, time and money.

Attitudes are not of course based simply on facts; they are formed of ideas, fears, aspirations and beliefs, which people hold about their lives. They can be influenced by effective promotion. Attitudes to tourism do not exist in isolation; they are sub-sets of a wider view of the desired quality of life and how to achieve it. Quality of life is not simply quantifiable but it is recognized intuitively and experienced as satisfactions, enjoyment, stimulation, and through a sense of physical and mental well-being.

Effective marketing helps to generate demand but it is most effective when it works with the grain of changing social attitudes to enhance awareness and motivation and stimulate purchase. Promotion cannot alter fundamental social attitudes and beliefs, or persuade people to do things which they find to be unsatisfactory.

Changing attitudes

There are many recent examples of the strength of social attitudes and the speed with which they can change. The emergence of 'green' issues in developed countries, the revolution of attitudes in Eastern Europe, the changing attitudes to trade unions in Britain, are illustrations. A growing interest in cultural and rural tourism is noticeable in Europe.

Although it is seldom obvious, there is usually a causal link between consumers' attitudes and the products they buy. Most commercial businesses understand that and invest heavily in market research to assess the implications of attitude shifts on purchasing behaviour. The more affluent customers are, and the more 'discretionary' their expenditure, the more likely it is that purchases reflect their ideas about themselves and the lives they lead. It behoves business in travel and tourism to understand changing attitudes, especially as marginal shifts in annual tourist volume (+ or − 2 per cent) may mean the difference between profit and loss, or even survival and collapse.

Since the 1970s, in North America, Western Europe and Australia, for example, social psychologists, market researchers and business forecasters have been measuring national attitudes and life styles. Recognizing the limitations of traditional classifications of people by age, demographics and socio-economic groups, researchers have sought alternative ways to group people and explain their behaviour. Evidence of their work is most obviously seen in the world of advertising, whose business it is to define and communicate images and messages that appeal to targeted customers.

Attitude groupings for UK residents

The Stamford Research Institute in the USA pioneered the national measurement of values, attitudes and life styles (VALS) in 1978, dividing the US population into nine segments according to life styles. In the UK Applied Futures Ltd has developed a classification of the attitudes of the British population over the last 20 years based on regular measurement. Its division of the population into three basic groups is relevant to many facets of purchasing behaviour including travel and tourism. The jargon of the labels used below is unattractive, but beneath the somewhat inelegant labels there are ideas of importance for the future of tourism products and the way they are presented and promoted to the public. The terms used are similar to those developed for VALS.

Sustenance-driven groups

These are people of all ages whose attitudes and behaviour patterns are organized around fear for their future and needs for security. Many such people are old and economically disadvantaged and live in constant fear of losing income, health or what they have managed to achieve of stability and status in their lives.

Some are apparently very affluent but feel threatened by possible loss of jobs, inability to pay the mortgage or school fees, or credit card dues. It is estimated that up to a third of even the most affluent 20 per cent of the population in developed societies are in practice 'sustenance-driven'. Economic recession quickly influences this proportion.

Outer directed groups

People of all social groups with sufficient income and confidence to overcome their security worries, who strive to achieve their perceptions of social esteem and status. Typically materialistic and acquisitive in outlook, and often in their twenties to forties, members of this group organize their purchasing behaviour around the way they look and the expected effect on others of the possessions they own and the holidays they take. Purchasing the 'right' holidays, the 'right' clothes, the 'right' leisure interests (such as golf and boats) – as perceived by the groups whom they seek to impress – provides them with evidence of achievement and belonging to the 'right' group. Fashion motivates this group. Its members are open to media persuasion and promotional messages.

Inner directed groups

In this group are people of all social categories and income levels, mostly educated beyond school leaving age and usually over 40, who have achieved the self-confidence, maturity of personality and tolerance to be able to live easily with themselves and social contacts. Their criteria for behaviour and purchases lie within themselves and reflect self-reliance, self-expression and self-realization. Such people seek information and control over the quality of their lives and their environment; aim to be responsible for the way they work and live, and intend to achieve the goals they set themselves. Spiritual and aesthetic values and creative aspirations are strongest in this group, which provides most of the volunteers and supporters for the work in society they consider important in its own right.

Since 1973 there has been a consistent and remarkable shift towards the inner directed groups in British society, as Table 4.1 shows. Similar trends appear to be occurring internationally. Each of the three groups noted above may be further sub-divided but the broad divisions will suffice. The groups overlap to some extent and individuals may display divergent rather than cohesive sets of attitudes. They may be *inner directed* for some activities and purchases and *outer directed* for others.

Table 4.1 *Changing composition of attitude groups in the British population (per cent)*

	1973	1984	1989	Trends to 2010	
Sustenance-driven	40	31	28	>	falling
Outer directed	35	34	29	–	plateau
Inner directed	25	34	42	<	growing

Source: Applied Futures Ltd, UK (1991)

Chapter 5 discusses individual motivations but the potential implications of the social attitude shifts noted in Table 4.1 are strong enough to merit their inclusion in this chapter, with other factors in the external environment to which marketing managers should respond.

Comparative prices

There is convincing evidence in the British market for package tours that the price of products, compared with those of competitors and from one year to the next, is the most important short-run determinant of the volume of demand. Price, which represents value to customers and is relative to their spending power, reinforces the economic determinants previously discussed and is related to socio-cultural attitudes. For international tourism, price is complicated by the combined effects on holiday prices of exchange rates between countries of origin and countries of destination, and by the comparative level of inflation in the destination area, compared with the area in which tourists live. The cost of oil, which is especially important in all forms of air transport, adds a third variable to these price complications. The concept of comparative prices is highly complex in practice and the effects are far from easy to predict with any precision, partly because customers' perceptions may differ from reality. In the short run at least price appears to be the strongest single influence on the level of demand for many forms of leisure tourism.

The influence on demand of just one of the price factors, the variability of exchange rates, is well illustrated by the following data:

Relationship of the US dollar to the British pound

  £1 = $ (US) (all rates at year end)
  1980 = $2.39
  1981 = $1.91
  1982 = $1.62
  1983 = $1.45
  1984 = $1.16
  1985 = $1.45
  1986 = $1.48
  1987 = $1.89
  1988 = $1.81
  1989 = $1.64
  1990 = $1.93
  1993 = $1.45 (March 1993)

With these changes affecting the price of travel products, it is hardly surprising that British holiday tourism to the USA, which had increased massively in 1981, fell back year by year to 1985, when it was only 40 per cent of the 1981 level. It recovered very strongly in 1986 as a result of the stronger pound, and between 1986 and 1990 the number of British visitors to the USA more than doubled. In the other direction across the Atlantic, for Americans visiting

Britain on holiday, 1985 was a record volume year, with the number of trips recorded more than double the 1982 total. At the time of writing, £1 was worth 1.4 dollars and was affecting the volume of UK travel to the USA. Effective marketing of course aims as far as possible to work with the grain of external events affecting demand, and to exploit all the opportunities that occur.

In Europe the growth of British holidays abroad, which increased by 50 per cent between 1982 and 1986, was largely influenced in that period by the comparative strength of the pound against currencies in tourist destination countries, and the beneficial effects of a fall in the price of fuel oil. In the case of Spain, the largest destination for British holiday makers travelling abroad on package tours, the number of packages fell by just over 1 million in 1985 (nearly 30 per cent of the total) when prices for that year were increased relative to other destinations. The following year, with substantial price reductions (estimated at 15-20 per cent), Spain recovered more than a million extra holidays in the third quarter alone (Middleton: 1986, p. 17).

Personal mobility factors

The personal mobility provided by cars has become a prime determinant of the volume and nature of tourism for many producers over the last two decades, especially those primarily concerned with domestic tourism. In the USA the private car has for decades been the dominant holiday transport choice. Between European countries sharing land frontiers the car is the preferred mode of transport for leisure tourism, and for much of business travel too. Car ownership is highest in the USA (1990 data) with some 600 cars per 1,000 population; West Germany has 500, and the UK and other northern European countries around 400 cars per 1,000 population.

Ownership and access to cars has increased significantly in Europe over the last decade. In the 1990s most hotels, nearly all self-catering establishments, most tourist restaurants and the great majority of visitor attractions and entertainments, are highly dependent on travellers by car for their business. Looking toward the end of the century, although growing traffic congestion and air pollution may force some destinations to restrict the usage of cars, there is currently no reason to anticipate any lessening of the demand for personal mobility and the convenience and comfort it provides. It appears probable, however, that the growing experience of extensive road congestion will cause changes to travel and tourism patterns. Day visits from home at weekends appear to be especially vulnerable to such changes. Traditional arrival and departure days for holidays may no longer favour Saturdays in July and August.

The use of surface public transport invariably declines as car ownership increases. Apart from non-leisure travel, such as much of inter city transport by rail and air, there remain some important segments of the travel and tourism market that use public transport on longer journeys for economic reasons, or through preference. Accordingly, transport operators have responded with a wide range of marketing schemes to provide attractively priced products for target market segments, such as those over 60, or students still in full-time education. Coach and bus operators have found many niches to exploit, especially for international tourists and groups, in the private hire market as well as for the more traditional holidays based on coach tours. Such schemes are likely to develop if traffic congestion grows as predicted and regulations favour public transport.

Government/regulatory factors

Government and regulatory factors are rather different in kind from the other determinants discussed in this chapter. They are, however, crucially important in understanding the national and international framework within which demand evolves for travel and tourism. Although most such laws and regulations are aimed at influencing supply rather than demand, their influence over demand is significant.

Virtually all governments impose laws and regulations to safeguard the health and safety of their populations and the use of land; and most impose penalties for non-compliance. Such regulations are important but typically influence all forms of industry and are not referred to in this section, which is specific to travel and tourism. Governments also intervene in markets for three principal reasons that directly influence demand and supply and often have a particular impact on travel and tourism, which marketing managers have to understand:

- The first is regulation to ensure fair competition between suppliers. This is usually intended to prevent the formation of monopolies and cartels or oligopolies, which may otherwise be able to prevent new competition from entering their markets or to determine capacity and prices in their favour, and not in their customers' interests.
- The second is regulation to ensure that customers have choices and rights against suppliers, which may be enforced.
- The third, which is relatively new but expected to have a particular impact on travel and tourism, is regulation to ensure that project developments and business practices do not damage the environment. Rural, coastal and heritage environments will be targeted for special protection.

Reflecting changing political aspirations to which businesses have to respond, in the 1980s and early 1990s there was a remarkable international shift away from traditional forms of direct intervention and regulation undertaken by or on behalf of governments. The trend was towards encouraging more commercial sector competition but with close supervision by government-appointed monitoring bodies,

whose duty it was to intervene for one or more of the reasons outlined above.

The subject of regulation is vast and warrants a book in its own right. For the purposes of explanation in this chapter some of the key factors are summarized below:

Transport regulation

For air transport, regulation may determine or influence the routes that can be flown, the number of flights, the capacity of seats on routes, and often the prices that can be charged. Traditionally closely regulated by governments on the basis of bilateral treaties between countries, transport in the 1990s is shifting towards more open international competition. Led by the USA in the late 1970s, deregulation is being enforced in Europe under EC directives in the 1990s. It is likely to have a major impact on the prices of travel products.

Other forms of transport are also closely regulated, e.g. the influence the UK government exercises over cross-Channel ferries and the nature of the competition they may wage with the Channel Tunnel. The issue of rights to sell 'duty free' items has been controlled by governments, and the revenue it earns influences the price that customers have to pay for transport. It has also been a strong motivation for choosing to travel by sea.

Tour operation and hotels

The European Community's Directive on Package Travel, implemented in 1993, is a recent example of direct regulation in the interests of customer protection (see Chapter 24).

The imposition of statutory hotel registration in some countries and the control over classification and grading systems in others, typically influences the type and price of hotel products and thereby changes the nature of demand.

Computer reservations systems (CRS)

Both the USA government and the EC are well aware that manipulation of the large airline owned international CRS systems, such as SABRE, WORLDSPAN, GALILEO and AMADEUS (see Chapter 18), could inhibit competition. Regulations in both continents are expected to limit the possible bias inherent in prioritizing the sales of the system owners' products.

New regulation for the environment

The rapidly expanding influence of environmental legislation now affects most sectors of the travel and tourism industry. Examples are the legal requirement, enforced in North America and by the EC, that all new large projects shall be submitted to environmental impact assessments. Such assessments certainly influence the economic viability of locations evaluated for tourism purposes, and are likely to become more stringent in the 1990s. To date there are no formal requirements for businesses to undertake a detailed environmental audit of their operations, although, since about 1990, many organizations do. Among leading examples are American Express, British Airways, and Inter-Continental Hotels. The trend to more environmentally responsible businesses is likely to continue and be reinforced as the legislation and regulatory provisions following the Earth Summit Conference at Rio de Janeiro in June 1992 are implemented in the 1990s. The trend is likely to be supported by the new but growing use of attaching personal legal responsibility to the directors of companies failing to comply with regulations. (See also the Epilogue.)

Mass media communications

The last of the factors in the business environment to be discussed in this chapter also has a powerful and relatively recent influence over the demand for travel and tourism. The principal influence is that of television, especially colour television, to which the populations in countries with developed economies are by now virtually universally exposed. Television watching emerges as the most popular leisure-time pursuit in many countries, with an estimated 35 hours a week per household in the USA and around 19 hours a week for the average adult in Britain (the figures are not directly comparable). No other leisure activity occupies more time than the number of hours spent in front of the small screen.

Over the last decade cable-based and space satellite transmitters have provided instantaneous international images of places and events, as well as a continuous stream of films identifying places and standards of living, and promoting activities such as golf and tennis, patterns of behaviour, and exotic resorts. The cumulative effect of television over the years in shaping travel and tourism expectations in the major demand-generating countries cannot be overestimated.

Television is of course also a main medium for advertising many products in travel and tourism, and sometimes the two influences come together, as in the promotion of Australia in the USA in the mid-1980s. Initially, considerable impact was scored by Paul Hogan commercials for Australia as a destination, which were followed by massive exposure of Australia during the America's Cup races of 1986-7. At the same time, initially in the cinema, the Hogan films *Crocodile Dundee* and its sequel became major box office draws. The combined effect of all this publicity on travel from the USA to Australia is impossible to quantify, but is known to have had a considerable impact on general attitudes and awareness of a previously little known destination. The media coverage of visits by the British Royal Family to the USA has had an equivalent impact on attitudes to travel to Britain.

The cumulative impact of thousands of hours of TV watching must have a major social influence on travel demand. No generations before the 1960s ever had such massive, continuous exposure to events, people and places outside their normal places of residence and work. In the year following the Chernobyl nuclear disaster in Russia and the American punitive raid against Libya (1986), and again during and after the Gulf War in 1991, one can only speculate on the full effect the massive exposure had on the travel plans of Americans in 1986, 1987 and 1991/2.

Not least of the influences exerted by the mass communication media is the effect achieved by regular TV travel programmes, which review and expose a wide range of tourism products on offer and provide critical evaluations of their quality and value for money. Such programmes achieve a level of authority and exposure that no individual organization's advertising budget could match. For individual products covered, the programmes have the power to reduce demand for the businesses or destinations that are criticized, or create it for those they approve.

At a lower level in terms of mass impact, the exposure of prospective travellers to books, films, newspapers, magazines and radio, contributes to awareness and attitudes in addition to TV programmes. But the other media cannot reproduce the sense of colour and action conveyed by TV or command the same hours of attention.

The ability of TV to expose and draw attention to the things that go wrong for tourists is also part of the effect on demand. It includes, for example, the coverage given to airline disasters, the stories of muggings of British tourists in Florida in 1993 or the disaster to the Townsend Thorenson ferry that sank in the Channel in 1987. Where the majority of a population participates regularly in travel and tourism, the industry is of great interest to the media, and is certain to generate stories the public wish to see and read. The full effect on demand of wide media coverage is still not well understood in the early 1990s but there can be no doubt of its importance.

Characteristics associated with high and low demand for tourism

Because the underlying factors determining the volume of demand for tourism are common to all countries, it is possible to summarize the influence of the main determinants in a *scale of propensity* to travel away from home, which applies for all purposes. Propensity is a useful term, frequently used in the study of travel and tourism to define the extent of participation in travel activity in a given population. From national tourism surveys of trips taken, it may be broadly quantified.

Holiday propensity is a measure of the proportion of a population that takes holidays in a year. Of course some people take one holiday only, while others take three or more. Accordingly, it is useful to distinguish between gross propensity and net propensity, defined as follows:

● Net propensity is the proportion of a population that takes at least one holiday in a 12-month period.
● Gross propensity is the total number of holidays taken, expressed as a proportion of a population (proportion taking any holidays multiplied by the average number of holidays taken).

To illustrate, in 1990, 59 per cent of British people aged 16 or more were estimated to have taken at least one holiday of four or more nights away from home to any destination in Britain or abroad. Net propensity is therefore 59 per cent. On average, those travellers took 1.6 holidays each, so gross propensity was $59 \times 1.6 = 94.4$ per cent.

Measured annually over a decade or so, it is possible to assess the extent to which a market for travel and tourism is increasing its size due to increased penetration (more of a population taking trips away from home) or because of increased intensity (the same people taking more trips in a year). Both of these are important measures for marketing managers, especially when related to specific market segments, e.g. to measure the holiday propensity of people aged 55 or more, or of a particular social class. For countries with highly developed economies, such as Switzerland or Sweden, net propensity already exceeds 75 per cent and gross propensity exceeds 150 per cent.

Table 4.2 is based on the main determinants of demand discussed in this chapter, especially the socio-economic aspects. The determinant effects of comparative prices, government/regulatory and communication factors are not separately identified in the table, but each would have the effect of accelerating or retarding the propensities established by the other determinants.

The response of marketing managers

The role of marketing managers in response to the determinants of travel and tourism can be put simply. First, it is their business to research and monitor the external factors that influence movements in the particular markets with which they are concerned. Second, based on this

knowledge, it is their business to forecast the direction and speed of change in the determinants, and the implications of such forecasts for the travel patterns in their markets. The techniques for monitoring change for marketing purposes are aspects of marketing research discussed in Chapter 11.

Research is used to identify opportunities and threats emerging in the business environment, and the demand determinants are always a vital element. Both opportunities and threats require a management response through products and promotion, and the other elements, known collectively as the 'marketing mix' (discussed in Chapter 6).

In the long and short run, investment and operating decisions in marketing-led organizations will always be based on an understanding of the business environment. This is true in all circumstances, but especially true where markets are no longer growing rapidly, and are changing structurally. In British tourism in the 1980s, for example, there was a massive structural shift away from traditional 1- and 2-week summer seaside holidays taken within Britain. The shift is largely explained by the effects of the determinants discussed in this

Table 4.2 *The scale of propensity to engage in travel and tourism*

Low propensity characteristics	High propensity characteristics
Low income per household	High income per household
Single parent household	Two parents (employed) household
Rural community dweller	Large-city dweller
Educated to minimum age	High level of qualifications
Older people (75+)	Younger people
No private transport	2 or more cars in household
3 or less weeks' paid holiday	6 or more weeks' paid holiday

Note: In cases where all the determinants combine, such as a 75-year-old retired farm labourer living alone without an occupational pension, the propensity to engage in any form of travel and tourism in a year may be zero. At the other end of the scale, a young, professional couple without children, both working, and living in a city apartment, may well generate ten or more leisure trips of one night or more away from home, over a year. Such a couple would be likely also to make several business trips in a year.

chapter, to which tour operators offering holidays abroad reacted with great speed and energy. At the time of writing traditional air package tours for the British abroad using hotels in Mediterranean resorts were rapidly losing share of market to other forms of holidays; the reasons for the decline may be found in the determinants, especially social attitudes, discussed in this chapter.

Chapter summary

This chapter focuses on the marketing implications of eight variables in the economic, social, and cultural environment. They are common to all the countries with developed economies currently generating the bulk of the world's tourism. It has been stressed that such variables are part of the external business environment within which all firms operate; they are not under the control of any commercial organization and are only partly influenced by government decisions.

Some of the determinants, such as income per capita, geographic factors and population changes, have long-run implications for marketing. Such factors tend to produce fairly stable relationships with demand, e.g. income elasticity ratios, and they are the basis of most of the forecasting models used to project tourism flows. These long-run determinants are summarized in Table 4.1 in the scale of propensity to engage in travel and tourism.

Other determinants, such as exchange rates, regulatory changes and the impact of the mass media, have a much more immediate effect on the volume of tourism demand and market patterns, which it is often impossible to predict.

Socio-cultural factors are also seldom predictable in econometric forecasting models but their influence may be dominant in shifts of market behaviour. A lesson of the past decade has been the remarkable speed at which social attitudes have changed and more such changes appear certain in the 1990s. Changing attitudes in society to watch for in the 1990s are likely to affect:

● Use of motor cars for international and long-distance travel in an era of congestion and pollution, especially for same-day visits from home.
● The perceived attraction of beach-based/sunshine products if further evidence of skin cancers emerges.
● Reaction to the environmental deterioration attributed - rightly or wrongly - to over-development for tourism purposes as in Venice, Hawaii, Barrier Reef and other coral areas, or cities such as Oxford.

Marketing-led organizations will always base their strategic decisions on a carefully researched analysis of the determinants of demand and their associated market patterns, and will adjust those decisions tactically in the light of changing trends. The larger the organization, especially if it is multinational, the more important such analysis becomes. The importance of understanding the determinants underlies the commitment of marketing organizations to market research, as discussed in Chapter 11.

In a chapter of this length it is only possible to highlight the nature of the determinants affecting travel and tourism markets. Students may find it helpful to draw up their own specific lists of determinants and their effects on particular tourism businesses of which they have some knowledge, using this chapter's contents as a framework.

Further reading

Baker, M. J., *Marketing: An Introductory Text*, 4th edit., Macmillan, 1985, Chapter 3.

Burkart, A.J., and Medlik, S., *Tourism: Past, Present and Future*, 2nd edit., Heinemann, 1981, Chapter 5.

Kotler, P., *Marketing Management: Analysis, Planning, Implementation and Control*, 7th edit., Prentice-Hall International, 1991, Chapter 5.

5

The changing business environment: travel motivations and buyer behaviour

The previous chapter discussed the elements of the social, economic and political environment that are essentially *external* influences on individuals but collectively tend to determine the volume and patterns of travel and tourism generated within any country. The determinants of demand certainly explain why residents of countries such as Germany, the USA and Sweden have high propensities to participate in travel and tourism, whereas others, such as India, Egypt and China, have low propensities. In discussing determinants it is generally assumed that customers in large numbers respond in predictable ways to variations in income, leisure time, price and other factors discussed in Chapter 4. Indeed the study of macroeconomics could not be sustained if these cause and effect linkages did not operate with reasonable consistency within an economy.

High propensities to participate in travel and tourism, however, are also strongly correlated with the propensity to purchase hi-fi equipment, theatre and opera tickets, fashion goods, eating out and purchases of a whole range of non-essential goods and services, which compete for shares of disposable income. A discussion of

motivations is required to throw light on why consumers choose to spend significant amounts of their disposable income on travel and tourism, rather than on other forms of purchase.

Importantly, within a context established by the largely external determinants, it is necessary for marketing managers to understand how *internal*, psychological processes influence individuals to decide the choice of a particular vacation destination, and a particular type of product. These internal, psychological processes are known within marketing as aspects of *buyer behaviour*. Behavioural concepts lie at the very heart of marketing theory, and have been the subject of extensive literature in recent years. The understanding that marketing managers have of how consumers make their product decisions influences all the subsequent decisions in the marketing process.

This chapter deals therefore with issues that are fundamental to modern marketing, defined as centred on customer needs and behaviour. The chapter covers the main issues in three parts. First, the internal, personal influences and motivations affecting buyer behaviour are introduced and summarized in a classification of travel motivations. Next, a simple input–output model of the buyer behaviour process is explained with a diagram shown in Figure 5.1. The diagram explains the relationship between the influences that are brought to bear on buyers (inputs); the personal factors that reflect an individual's position in society, his personality, attitudes and needs, wants and goals (buyer characteristics); and the outputs shown as purchase decisions. Figure 5.1 also illustrates how buyers process inputs to arrive at their decisions.

The chapter concludes with a discussion of the way in which all products can be placed on a spectrum or scale reflecting the complexity of the buying decision seen from the customer's viewpoint. In travel and tourism there is a wide range of products, some of which require only routine decisions; others, such as annual vacations, customers see as complex and demanding purchases. The place a product occupies on the scale greatly influences the way in which it is marketed.

Behaviour influenced by internal processes

The internal, psychological influences affecting individuals' choices are commonly known as 'motivations'. Motivations operate on individuals' purchase choices within the framework already set by the determinants of demand. For marketing managers, a working knowledge of the motivations affecting behaviour will usually be more important than measuring the determinants, because marketers are directly concerned with choices buyers make between competing products. They can influence those choices through promotion and other marketing decisions.

To illustrate the important distinction between the external and internal influences on buyers, consider the vacation decisions of a young, professional, unmarried person, living in a rented apartment in New York, with 2 vacation weeks to plan. The choice is wide, because disposable income is high; the time is available; distance by air is no problem for a relatively affluent New Yorker; and the technology of air transport and travel organization is sophisticated enough to make Europe, the Far East, or anywhere in North or South America, easily accessible. In terms of demand determinants discussed in Chapter 4 this prospective travel buyer has one of the highest propensities to travel.

What motivating factors will influence the choice, for example, between a Club Mediterranée Village in the Caribbean, culture seeking in Thailand or Bhutan, an adventure holiday in Canada, or a vacation at a sports resort in Florida? What will be the conscious and unconscious influences on the decision that is made? How far will this prospective traveller make his or her own decision or be influenced by the preferences of possible companions for the trip? Even more basic, why should, say, $3,000 be spent on a vacation when it could be spent on furnishings or equipment for the apartment? No marketing manager has anything like a full or satisfactory answer to all these questions or their equivalents affecting any form of vacation decision. But the more he finds out about what sort of people choose particular products, what needs they seek to fulfil through each type of vacation, and their activity preferences once in a resort, the better he will be able to formulate an appealing product and communicate its benefits and attractions to a target audience of prospective visitors.

Before listing the wide range of possible motivations that exist in travel and tourism, we stress that the customer decision or buyer behaviour process in travel and tourism is likely to be highly complex.

Classifying travel motivations

To illustrate the wide range of possible travel and tourism motivations, it is possible to draw on the work of others. What are listed below, however, are not motivations for individuals in the sense that psychologists and authors of behavioural marketing texts would understand them, but simple groupings of the reasons for different types of travel that share some common characteristics. A more precise discussion of individual motivation has to be related to needs and personal goals, and will be found later in this chapter. The groupings below provide a broad structure within which buyer behaviour operates and may serve a useful function as an introduction to behavioural models.

Many authors of tourism books provide a classification of the basic motivations to be found worldwide in travel and tourism. Variations on such classifications are also widely used in numerous commercial market research studies. The following list draws on contributions by Valene Smith (1977), Murphy (1985) and McIntosh and Goeldner (1990). It is broadly compatible with the classification of travel purpose being developed by WTO for use in surveys of travel and tourism internationally.

The main motives for travel and tourism

Business/work related motives

● Pursuit of private and public sector business, conferences, meetings, short courses.
● Travel away from home for work-related purposes, including airline personnel, truck drivers, service engineers.

Physical/physiological motives

● Participation in indoor sport and active outdoor recreation such as golfing, walking, sailing, skiing.
● Undertaking activities in pursuit of health, fitness, recuperation.
● Resting/relaxing/generally unwinding from stress of everyday life.
● Finding warmth/sunshine/relaxation on a beach.

Cultural/psychological/personal education motives

● Participation in festivals, theatre, music, museums - as spectator, player, or volunteer.
● Participation in personal interests, including intellectual, craft and other leisure-time pursuits.
● Visiting destinations for the sake of their cultural and or natural heritage (including ecotourism).

Social/interpersonal and ethnic motives

● Enjoying the company of friends and relatives.
● Undertaking social duty occasions - from weddings to funerals.
● Accompanying others travelling for other reasons, such as business or social duty.
● Visiting the place of one's birth.

Entertainment/amusement/pleasure/pastime motives

● Watching sport/other spectator events.
● Visiting theme parks/amusement parks.
● Undertaking leisure shopping.

Religious motives

● Participating in pilgrimages.
● Undertaking retreats for meditation and study.

Any visit to a large travel agency and a look through the brochures will confirm the wide range of primary reasons for leisure travel and tourism currently catered for by producers.

Stimulus and response concepts in buyer behaviour

The broad groupings of motivations noted in the previous section serve a purpose in outlining the wide range of possibilities, but they do not indicate the reasons why individuals have such motivations, nor how their travel decisions are made. To throw light on this, it is necessary to put the individual, metaphorically, under the microscope, drawing on the analysis originally developed in the study of economics and more recently in other behavioural sciences.

Classical economic models of buyer behaviour operate on the well-tested assumption that buying decisions (demand) are primarily governed by price. Other things being equal, the lower the price, the higher the volume of demand, and vice versa. Economic concepts of price response and price elasticity of demand are still highly relevant in travel and tourism, but from a marketing management standpoint other behavioural influences are equally important considerations in making marketing mix decisions.

For those considering buyer behaviour for the first time it may be helpful to imagine that in some important ways consumers' minds work rather like microcomputers. Every computer has a given range of functions determined by its designed characteristics; every buyer has a personality that is partly inherited at birth and partly developed by experience. Computers can perform certain tasks very rapidly through built-in programmes, while other tasks require extensive additional programming in order to produce the required output. Buyers perform some buying decisions very rapidly by habit and with hardly any conscious thought, while other purchases require careful consideration and extensive information-gathering.

Both computers and consumers' minds can only process information that has been fed into their decision systems at the right time, working within the limitations of their design (or personality constraints) and memory capacity. If an operator fails to input vital data to a computer, then for that computer the information simply does not exist. Similarly, if an 'ideal' product exists and is available to a prospective purchaser, but the purchaser is not aware of it, then for that consumer the product does not exist. In other words, computers and buyers' minds receive inputs which they process

according in their inbuilt capacities and programmed 'states'. Both produce outputs that are a resolution of all the input variables. Obviously machines are totally predictable and consistent in their outputs, whereas people clearly are not. But the basic principle of inputs, information-processing, and outputs, is to be found at the heart of all models of buyer behaviour.

Marketing is very much concerned with supplying prospective buyers with factual and persuasive inputs of information about specific attributes of particular products. To be effective, it is necessary for marketers to have some understanding of how and to what extent that information is likely to be received and processed and how the purchasing decision is made. In the next section a simple input–output model of buyer behaviour is explained.

A buyer behaviour model for travel and tourism

The stimulus–response concept discussed in the previous section is shown diagrammatically in Figure 5.1. The diagram has four interactive components, with the central component identified as 'buyer characteristics and decision process', which incorporates motivation. The first two components are inputs, most of which can be manipulated by marketing managers, while the final component represents the purchase output, i.e. the customers' response. The four components within the diagram are explained below. The communication filters, shown in the shaded part of the diagram, are discussed separately towards the end of the chapter.

Product inputs

These comprise the whole range of competitive products and product mixes that are made available to the prospective customer. In Britain, for example, there are dozens of tour operators

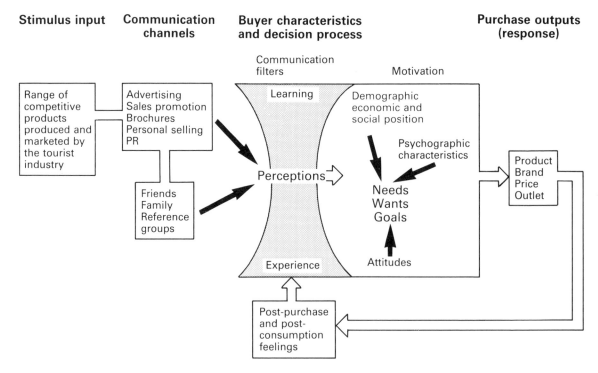

Figure 5.1 *A stimulus-response model of buyer behaviour*

offering holidays abroad to potential vacationers, and dozens of domestic British destinations and operators also seeking the travellers' purchase. Across the USA a prospective tourist is faced by a similar choice, amounting to literally thousands of possibilities, if they could all be counted.

Communication channels

These are in two parts. There are the formal communication channels or media, aimed at persuading prospective buyers through advertising, brochures, sales promotion techniques and public relations (PR) activity. There is also information accessible to individuals through their family, friends and the groups of people with whom they interact at work and socially. Much research suggests that these informal channels of information, noted in Figure 5.1 as 'friends, and reference groups', are

at least as influential on purchase decisions as the formal channels, and are sometimes referred to as 'word of mouth' communications.

Buyer characteristics and decision process

Grouped around the central focus of needs, wants and goals, there are three main interacting elements, which determine an individual buyer's disposition to act in certain ways. These three elements act sometimes as constraints upon purchase decisions and sometimes to provide or reinforce the motivation. The three elements are discussed below; communication filters are discussed later in the chapter:

1 *Demographic/economic/social position.* These are the easily quantifiable characteristics such as age, sex, occupation, region of residence, household size and social class, some of which were dealt with under determinants in

Chapter 4. They are also relevant here since they act as constraints or limits within which individuals' motivations and buying behaviour take place. Included in these characteristics is stage in the life cycle, meaning whether a person is a child, young adult living at home, adult married but without children, retired person, and so on. These aspects are developed in Chapter 7 on segmentation.

2 *Psychographic attributes* or 'personality traits' as they are often referred to, indicate the type of person the buyer is and strongly influence the types of product that are bought. These attributes also determine the sort of advertising and other communication messages to which buyers respond. Psychologists and marketing researchers measure people's psychographic character-istics, using dimensions such as confident or diffident, gregarious or loner, conscientious or happy-go-lucky, assertive or submissive, neurotic or well-balanced, tense or relaxed, adventurous or unadventurous. These dimensions can be used in product formulation and in promotional messages.

3 *Attitudes.* All people adopt conscious and unconscious attitudes towards ideas, people, and things, affecting their lives. An attitude was defined by Allport as 'A mental state of readiness, organized through experience, exerting a directive influence upon the individual's response to all objects and situations with which it is related' (Allport: 1935). Attitudes extend to beliefs and knowledge of products as well as to people and events. Attitudes also cover feelings, such as likes and dislikes aroused, and a disposition to act or not because of such beliefs and feelings. The broad grouping of attitudes into 'life styles' was discussed in Chapter 4.

It should be noted that there is nothing necessarily right, wrong, or rational about attitudes, and also that people do not have to have direct experience of products in order to form an attitude. Consider, for example, Club Mediterranée. There are those who consider the Club offers an ideal holiday for discriminating young people, while others consider the idea of being in close proximity to hundreds of others a daunting and disagreeable prospect. For some people cruise ships are an ideal form of vacation, whereas others prefer fishing and hunting in the wild. Some like casinos and gambling, but others find them repellent and morally wrong.

Modern marketing research methods and the power of computer processing have made a considerable contribution to the measurement of attitudes and their relation to product purchasing. While this is far from an exact science, most large organizations in air transport, accommodation, and tour operating, as well as national tourist organizations, have had at least some experience of attitude measurement in recent years, and the research techniques are improving. The understanding of attitudes is also an essential aspect of product positioning, which is discussed in Chapter 8.

Needs, wants, goals

Individuals have a range of needs and aspirations extending, in the well-known hierarchy established by Maslow in 1943, from immediate basic physical needs for food, warmth, shelter and sleep, through safety and social needs for affection and love, to self-esteem and status needs, and the most sophisticated level of self-development needs (self-actualization in Maslow's terms). Self-development needs relate to people's striving for personal fulfilment of their potential as individuals. Of course self-development needs are unlikely to become very important until most if not all the lower order needs are satisfied on a reasonably regular basis. Individuals with a high propensity to participate in travel and tourism, as measured by the determinants discussed in Chapter 4, are also those most likely to be in a position to focus on their own self-development.

For centuries travel has been associated with a broadening of awareness and self-recognition, through added knowledge and exposure to other cultures and human circumstances. Vacations in particular, and their associations with rest and recreation (in a literal sense of being renewed in mental and physical ways), have a stimulating effect upon people's minds and are clearly linked with self-development. The tensions of living in the late twentieth century are often associated with a longing to escape for a while into forms of self-indulgence as well as self-development, usually with family or chosen companions. The increasingly frequent links between travel and personal hobbies, sport and other recreational activities, may combine to associate leisure travel and tourism with the fulfilment of self-development needs. It is this powerful association that helps to explain why vacation travel tends to be regarded, among those who can afford it, as more of a necessity than a luxury. As a 'necessity', travel and tourism clearly competes for disposable income with other goods and services. It is essential for marketing managers to recognize that their products are valued only to the extent of satisfying underlying needs, wants, and goals, many of which are highly sophisticated.

Personal goals influencing behaviour patterns include, for example, the respect of friends, the influencing of peer groups, the achievement of a happy domestic life, or achievement and status in employment or voluntary work. Travel and tourism can be used, in part at least, as a means of achieving personal goals. See also the section on 'the importance of attitudes' in Chapter 4.

Motivation, the dynamic process in the model

Psychological theory holds that needs, wants and goals generate uncomfortable states of tension within individuals' minds and bodies, tension that cannot be released until the needs are satisfied. States of tension, including hunger, fatigue, and loneliness, as well as the drive for self-development, are thus the motivators that produce actions to release tension states. Motivations therefore are the dynamic process in buyer behaviour, bridging the gap between the felt need and the decision to act or purchase. Most readers will recognize in themselves many less important needs, which are not satisfied primarily because the felt motivation is not strong enough to overcome the inertia against decision choices. A powerful motivator is one that triggers urgent action. In a marketing sense motivation bridges the gap between a general interest in a product, and a decision to go out and buy it. It is in this sense that products can be designed and marketed as *solutions* to customers' needs (tension states). A marketing manager who has taken the trouble to understand customers' needs and attitudes will clearly be more able to trigger their decisions by targeting communication on their motivating influences.

Purchase choices/decisions/outputs

The final stage of Figure 5.1 lists outputs of the decision process of most direct concern to producers, including which type of product, what brand, what price, at what time, and through what distribution outlet. These decisions are all related to the individuals' personal circumstances and are systematically monitored by many large companies through the marketing research procedures discussed later in this book. The point to be understood here is that action on purchases is linked directly to motivations, which in turn are linked to the buyers' characteristics defined earlier. Motivations may be influenced through marketing decisions, especially product design and the ways products are presented to prospective purchasers.

Filters in the buying decision process

Experience, learning, and perceptions, influenced strongly by attitudes, are shaded in Figure 5.1 to draw attention to the fact that the information shown as inputs to buyers is not necessarily received by individuals as its marketing originators intend. All inputs pass through a sieve, or series of filters, which serve to suppress most of the available information and to highlight specific parts, very probably distorted in the reception process. Perception is the term used to cover the way individuals select and organize the mass of information they are exposed to, and perception is a function of attitudes. The exact way in which information is received and processed remains the most obscure area of all behaviour models. Knowledge of an individual's demographic, psychographic and attitudinal characteristics will obviously enable a producer to communicate in suitable terms with prospective buyers. But it will not enable that producer to predict how far, or how accurately, his information messages will penetrate the filters and stimulate action.

Perception is influenced by personal attitudes, by motivations, knowledge, and interest in products; it may also be influenced by experience, advertising and hearsay. It changes over time through a constant learning process. While no advertiser is ever likely to gain the ultimate secrets of perception and manipulate prospective customers against their will, there is obviously scope to make improvements to communications and product design aspects at the margin. If the perceived positive aspects of product design and promotion can be enhanced, and the perceived negative aspects can be reduced through consumer research that throws light on perception processes, more cost effective marketing expenditure should result.

Post-purchase feelings

If, having found a specific product considered likely to satisfy his needs, a consumer is sufficiently motivated to buy it, the experience of consumption will affect all future attitudes towards it. If the product is highly satisfactory, the probability of repeat purchase will be high,

the likelihood of good 'word of mouth' is high, and the customer will have 'learned' that satisfaction is associated with that product. If the experience is highly unsatisfactory, the opposite will occur, and, depending on the importance of the purchase, the consumer may never buy that product again. For example, a good experience of an airline, with a punctual flight and friendly service, is highly likely to influence future choices. A long delay, surly service or an overbooked flight can create tensions and frustrations, which are observable on any day at any large airport. In other words, it is not enough to secure a sale. Good marketing aims to achieve subsequent sales through harnessing product satisfaction as often the most powerful means of influencing future buyer behaviour. It achieves this through the learning process that conditions an individual's perceptions.

Personal and situational variables in buyer behaviour

Thus far, travel and tourism buying decisions have been treated as though they all occupied equal significance in the minds of customers. In practice of course this is obviously not true. It is necessary to consider a classification that makes it possible to distinguish simple purchases, such as routine car rental or motel accommodation, from complex purchases, such as a 2-week vacation abroad or a world cruise.

In marketing texts the basic distinction between *convenience* and *shopping* goods, originally drawn in 1923 by Copeland, is a standard element of marketing theory. A convenience good is a manufactured item that typically has a relatively low price, is bought frequently, is widely available and satisfies basic routine needs. A typical shopping good has a relatively high price and is bought infrequently, and it may be necessary to travel some distance and make some effort to buy it. Shopping goods usually satisfy higher order needs in the Maslow hierarchy noted earlier in this chapter. Exactly the same distinction can be applied to service products, which may be categorized on a scale or spectrum, with simple convenience items at one end and extensive shopping items at the other. The terms *routinized* and *extensive problem-solving* were used by Howard and Sheth in one of the seminal papers on buyer behaviour models in 1967. They are clearly relevant to the buyer behaviour process explained in Figure 5.1.

Figure 5.2 shows a spectrum of buyer behaviour characteristics for both goods and services. The type of products (goods and services) is also shown. This author summarized the spectrum of behaviour as follows:

> The place a product occupies on the spectrum of buyer behaviour will tend to determine the way in which it is marketed. For example, both car rental and city hotel accommodation are essentially convenience products for many American business travellers, who comprise the principal buyers for these products. They involve, therefore, only routinized behaviour and a secretary or a travel agent may make the purchase so that the user has only to collect his key. Car rental in this context matches every one of the convenience characteristics listed. For European vacationers on the other hand, hotel selection and car rental are often shopping products, and a quite different marketing approach is needed (Middleton: 1983).

The essential point to note is that it is customer perception which determines where on the spectrum of convenience/shopping a tourism product lies. It is not primarily a characteristic of the product itself.

Convenience products	*Shopping products*
mainly low unit value/price	mainly high unit value/price
mainly perceived necessities	mainly non-essentials

◀--▶

low problem-solving; routinized/low information search	high problem-solving high information search
low customer commitment	high customer commitment
high purchase frequency	low purchase frequency
high brand loyalty	low brand loyalty
high speed decision process	low speed decision process
high rapidity of consumption	low rapidity of consumption
extensive distribution expected	limited distribution expected

This spectrum of behaviour characteristics may be applied equally to goods and services and some examples of both are shown below.

Spectrum of products associated with the spectrum of buyer behaviour

Convenience products	*Shopping products*

◀--------------------   --------------------▶

urban bus transport	holidays
commuter train transport	hotel accommodation
bank services	air transport
post office services	private education
take-away foods	motor cars
washing powder	freezers
cigarettes	carpets
branded chocolates	furniture
beer	

Figure 5.2   *Spectrum of buyer behaviour characteristics – goods or services* *Source*: Middleton, VTC in *Quarterly Review of Marketing*, Vol 8, No 4, 1983

Chapter summary

Chapter 2 notes that one of the three key elements in the marketing system 'comprises the attitudes and decisions of consumers concerning the perceived utility and value of available goods and services according to their needs and wants and ability to pay'. This chapter has sought to justify that statement, and to provide some practical indications of how to achieve a better understanding of buyer behaviour. An understanding of consumer motivations and behaviour lies at the heart of all modern marketing theory and practice. It underlies the techniques of market segmentation discussed in Chapter 7.

While the behaviour model included in this chapter is descriptive rather than predictive, its principal practical value lies in explaining the range of variables likely to affect any travel and tourism purchase decision, and the linkages between them. The model may serve also as an aide memoire in drawing up marketing programmes, and as a framework for organizing marketing research.

Complicating any simple classification of travel motivations is the fact that within the total market for travel and tourism many customers perform more than one role as buyers. The businessman in the executive suite this month may be a vacationer in 2 weeks' time using budget accommodation; the hang-gliding expert may also be a regular business class traveller, or a back-packer seeking the cheapest range of accommodation; the hamburger eater at lunchtime may be visiting a top restaurant in the evening, and so on. Often the buying decision in travel and tourism is not made for an individual's sake, but for the sake of others, such as family or friends.

Finally, there is the difference to consider between buyer behaviour that is 'routinized', calling for little conscious decision effort, and that which is 'extensive problem-solving', and may take weeks of careful deliberation and information searching and analysis before a decision is made. Such differences have great significance for the way in which marketing is undertaken.

If, notwithstanding the attempt to simplify the explanation of buyer behaviour, the reader concludes this chapter somewhat alarmed at the enormous range of the subject, that is no more than a measure of its significance. It is all too easy to say that marketing is about understanding consumers' needs and matching them. Achieving it in practice is both difficult and uncertain, but the rewards to those who achieve even marginal improvements can be great in terms of marketing efficiency and added profitability. Effective marketing in competitive conditions is impossible without some understanding of buyers' motivations and decision processes.

Further reading

Baker, M. J., *Marketing: An Introductory Text*, 4th edit., Macmillan, 1985, Chapter 4.

Chisnall, P.M., *Marketing: A Behavioural Analysis*, 2nd edit., McGraw-Hill, 1985, Chapters 2, 3, 4 and 5

Kotler, P., *Marketing: Analysis, Planning, Implementation and Control*, 7th edit., Prentice-Hall International, 1991, Chapter 6.

Part Two

Understanding the Marketing Mix in Travel and Tourism

6

The four Ps: focus of the marketing mix

This chapter introduces the four principal variables with which marketing managers are concerned in their efforts to manage consumer demand in relation to perishable, inseparable products (see Chapter 3). Known collectively as the 'marketing mix', these four variables reflect and express in practical decision terms the second of the three elements in the marketing system, referred to in Chapter 2, as 'the attitudes and decisions of producers concerning their production of goods and services for sale, in the context of their business environment and long-term objectives'.

This chapter is in two parts. The first part explains the meaning of each of the four core variables in the marketing mix, and provides examples of the marketing decisions noted in Figure 6.1. The second part explains where the mix decisions fit within the marketing system for travel and tourism organizations, which is represented diagrammatically in Figure 6.2.

The marketing mix concept is central to understanding modern marketing, and the key variables discussed in this chapter are subsequently developed and referred to throughout this book. In particular the planning of the marketing mix is discussed in detail in Chapter 14.

Marketing mix defined

The marketing mix may be defined as 'the mixture of controllable marketing variables that the firm uses to pursue the sought level of sales in the target market' (Kotler: 1984, p. 68).

The concept implies a set of variables akin to levers or controls that can be operated by a marketing manager to achieve a defined goal. By way of illustration, the controls may be likened to those of an automobile, which, to reach a chosen destination, has four main controls. There is a throttle or accelerator to control engine speed, there is a brake to reduce speed or stop, there is a gear shift to match the engine speed to the road speed required or to reverse direction, and there is a steering wheel with which to change the direction of travel. As every driver knows, movement of the controls must be synchronized and used in ways that respond to constantly changing road conditions and the actions of other drivers. Progress from one point to another is, for the driver, a continuous manipulation of the four basic controls.

In commercial organizations marketing managers are also 'driving' products towards chosen destinations. The four controls are *product formulation*, which is a means of adapting the product to the changing needs of the target customer; *pricing*, which in practice tends to be used as a throttle to increase or slow down the volume of sales according to market conditions; *promotion*, which is used to increase the numbers of those in the market who are aware of the product and are favourably disposed towards buying it; and *place*, which determines the number of prospective customers who are able to find convenient places and ways to convert their buying intentions into purchases. These four controls are manipulated continuously according to the market conditions prevailing, especially with regard to the actions of competitors.

While it is not sensible to push the car driving analogy too far, the central concept of continuously adjusting and synchronizing the controls according to constantly changing market conditions is the important point to grasp about marketing mix decisions. Continuous in this context could mean daily decisions, but in practice is more likely to mean weekly or monthly adjustments in the light of market intelligence about progress being achieved. Marketing is always a dynamic process.

The destinations or goals towards which products are being 'driven' by the four controls, are set by strategic decisions taken by organizations about their desired futures (see Chapter 12).

It will be noted that the four variables all begin with the letter 'p', hence the name 'the four Ps' originally used to describe the marketing mix in 1960 by McCarthy (1981, p. 42).

The four Ps

As the focus of marketing management decisions, each of the Ps, *product, price, promotion* and *place* warrants a separate chapter in this book. Here the object is to introduce and explain them in an integrated way, which also serves as an introduction to market research and planning for marketing strategy and tactics.

Product

Product covers the shape or form of what is offered to prospective customers; in other words, the characteristics of the product as designed by management decisions. Product components include:

● Basic design, such as the size and facilities of a hotel.
● Presentation, which for service products is mainly a function of the atmosphere and environment created on the producer's premises.
● The service element, including numbers, training, attitudes and appearance of staff engaged in 'delivering' the product to the consumer.
● Branding, which identifies particular products with a unique name and image and is a synthesis of all the product elements as well as the focus of promotional activity.

In a modern marketing context products in travel and tourism are designed for, and continuously adapted to match, target segments' needs, expectations, and ability to pay. Most organizations produce and market not one but several products. For example, tour operators provide a range of products within their brochures, and large hotels may have up to a dozen separate products ranging from meetings and business class rooms to short break packages for the holiday market. See also Chapter 8.

Price

Price denotes the published or negotiated terms of the exchange transaction for a product, between a producer aiming to achieve predetermined sales volume and revenue objectives and prospective customers seeking to maximize their perceptions of value for money in the choices they make between alternative products. Almost invariably in tourism there is a regular or standard price for a product, and one or more discounted or promotional prices reflecting the needs of particular segments of buyers, or particular market conditions, such as seasonality or short-run over-capacity. See also Chapter 9.

Promotion

The most visible of the four Ps, promotion includes advertising, direct mailing, sales promotion, merchandising, sales-force activities, brochure production, and PR (public relations) activity. Promotional techniques, explored in detail in Part Four of the book, are used to make prospective customers aware of products, to whet their appetites, and stimulate demand. They also provide information to help customers decide, and generally provide incentives to purchase, either direct from a producer or through a channel of distribution. The range of promotional techniques is so wide that the term 'promotional mix' is frequently used in practice.

In this introductory chapter it is important for the reader to appreciate the relation between this P and the other three Ps to which it is integrally linked in the marketing process. However important and visible it is, promotion is still only one of the levers used to manage demand. It cannot be fully effective unless it is co-ordinated with the other three. See also Part Four.

Place (or distribution)

For marketing purposes, place does not just mean the location of a tourist attraction or facility, but the location of all the points of sale that provide prospective customers with *access* to tourist products. For example, 'place' for Disney World in the USA is not only Orlando, Florida, but also the numerous travel agents located in the north-east of the USA (and elsewhere inside and outside the USA) selling products that include Disney World admission. As a result of marketing decisions, prospective visitors to Florida can obtain promotional information and buy a range of products that either include Disney World admission, or make such visits probable in terms of vacation locations and motivation. Travel agents are of course only one of the ways in which 'place' or access is created for Disney World customers, or

indeed for most other products in travel and tourism

Place for a self-catering operator, for example, would include computerized and other reservation/booking systems that provide access to products for repeat or loyal customers targeted by direct mail. See also Chapter 18.

Mixes multiplied and sometimes confused

Because each of the four Ps includes within it so many important sub-elements, it is not surprising that subsequent authors have developed many variations of the original four, especially for service products. Cowell (1993, p. 69) for example, reviewing recent American contributions and drawing in particular on work by Booms and Bitner, recommends a 'revised marketing mix' for services, which comprises:

● Product.
● Price.
● Promotion.
● Place.
● People (numbers, training, attitudes).
● Physical evidence (furnishings, colour, lighting, noise).
● Process (customer involvement, procedures in service delivery).

Closer scrutiny suggests that the proposed additional three mix elements are in fact all integral elements of travel and tourism *products*. It is of course a matter for judgement whether or not it adds to marketing understanding to sub-divide the product elements as shown. Certainly the nature of service products compared with those based on physical goods heightens the importance of the sub-divisions. But product design decisions that do not incorporate these elements explicitly make little sense in practice. A similar approach to the marketing mix is adopted by Morrison (1989, p. 175), whose definition comprises:

- Product.
- Price.
- Place.
- Promotion.
- Packaging.
- Programming.
- People.
- Partnership.

Once again, people and packaging are integral aspects of the product. Partnership is always a relevant consideration in promotion,

and programming is one of the ways in which the mix may be co-ordinated and marketed to target segments.

This author remains convinced that it helps the understanding of a central marketing concept to focus on an unambiguous, easy to understand, four Ps. Readers will also encounter terms such as 'product mix', 'communication

	Hotel	Scheduled airline	Museum
Product Designed characteristics/ packaging	Location/building size/ grounds/design/room size/facilities in hotel furnishings/decor/ lighting/catering styles	Routes/service frequency Aircraft type/size Seat size/space Decor, meals, style,	Building size/design/ facilities Types of collection Size of collection Interior display/ interpretation
Service component	Staff numbers/uniforms/ attitudes	Staff numbers, uniforms/attitudes	Staff numbers, uniforms/attitudes
Branding	e.g. Holiday Inn, Savoy, Meridien	e.g. American Airlines British Airways, Virgin Atlantic	e.g. Tate Gallery (London) Metropolitan Museum (New York)
Image/reputation/positioning	e.g. upmarket, down-market	e.g. reliable, exotic food, badly managed	e.g. dull, exciting, modern
Price Normal or regular price Promotional price (for each product offered)	Rack rates Corporate rates Privileged user rates Tour operator discount rate	First class/business/ tourist fares APEX Standby Charter Consolidated fares	(assuming charge made) Adult rate, senior citizen rate Group/party rates Children rate Friends of the museum rate
Promotion (solo and collaborative) Advertising (TV/radio/ press/journals) Sales promotion/ merchandising Public relations Brochure production and distribution Sales force	Examples not provided since these are generally self-evident and specific to individual organizations (See Parts Four and Five)		
Place Channels of distribution including reservation systems	Computerized reservation systems (CRS) Other hotels in group Travel agents Tour operators Airlines 800 telephone lines	Computerized reservation systems (CRS) City offices Airport desks Travel agents Other airlines 800 telephone lines	Other museums Tourist information offices Hotel desks Schools/colleges

Figure 6.1   *Examples of the marketing mix in travel and tourism*

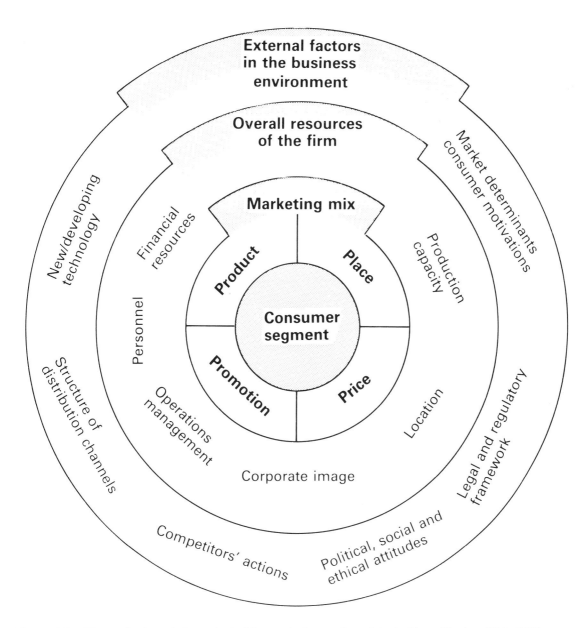

Figure 6.2   *The marketing mix in context of the marketing system. Adapted from Stanton, W.J., 1974*

mix', 'promotional mix', 'presentation mix', and 'distribution mix'. There is no recommended definition or agreed usage of these terms, but, provided the central concept of designing a marketing mix around the needs of identified customers is clearly understood, the variations and extensions should not create difficulties. The practical use of the mix concept is most clearly seen in the way in which marketing campaigns are planned and executed (see Chapter 14).

The four Ps, with illustrations drawn from hotels and airlines, are further explained in Figure 6.1. Readers may find it a worthwhile exercise to complete their own illustrations for visitor attractions, tour operators, a cruise ship or a car-rental operation.

Marketing mix cost and revenue considerations

It is important to understand that all marketing mix decisions represent costs to an organization, and have implications for sales revenue. Consideration of Figure 6.1 demonstrates that three of the Ps require significant expenditure, which has to be *committed in advance* of the revenue it is expected to generate. Changes to the product, advertising, sales promotions, brochure production, and the organization and servicing of distribution channels, all represent financial commitments made in the expectation of future sales. While pricing decisions do not cost anything in advance of sales, they obviously determine the level of revenue achievable, and in the case of price discounting to sell unsold capacity they represent revenue forgone.

To illustrate this important point, if a tour operator decides to develop its existing product range by adding new destinations, there will be set-up costs in investigating the options available and contractual obligations to be made, months before the first customers make full payment. Advertising and brochure costs will also be committed months ahead of the first sales. To give a different example, a decision by a hotel group to provide improved access for customers by investing in a new, on-line computer reservation system, may be made up to 3 years before the advantages of the new system secure additional customer bookings, and contribute revenue to pay back the cost and add to profit.

Marketing mix in context of the marketing system

Figure 6.2 expresses the marketing system for any organization in three concentric rings, which is an *alternative* way to represent the marketing process. Readers should compare this diagram with Figure 2.1 in Chapter 2. The two diagrams are completely compatible, but illustrate the same process from a different standpoint. Figure 6.2 is designed to demonstrate how marketing mix decisions operate around the core focus of selected consumer segments.

As discussed earlier in the chapter, the four Ps in the *inner ring* are under the direct control of marketing managers, but subject to the other resources and management functions of an organization shown in the middle ring.

The *middle ring* functions are influenced by, and influence marketing decisions, but are not usually under the direct control of marketing management. For example, initial choice of location and capacity for a hotel, as well as its general corporate image, will be heavily influenced by marketing inputs to project appraisal, but thereafter these aspects will be difficult or impossible to change in the short run. The management of personnel and operational systems, e.g. in an airline, will place constraints or limits for manoeuvre on marketing management. The size and scope of marketing budgets in all organizations will be governed by financial resources.

In the *outer ring*, summarized under six headings, are the factors external to a business, which are not controlled by, or even much influenced by, marketing managers of any one organization. The powerful effect of some of these external factors on business decisions has already been made clear in Chapter 4, dealing with market determinants, and in Chapter 5, on buyer behaviour. The combined influence of the six factors in Figure 6.2 provides the context of opportunities or threats, within which strategic and tactical marketing-mix decisions have to be made. Brief notes are provided below to explain what is meant by legal and regulatory framework, political, social and ethical attitudes, new and developing technology; structure of distribution channels, and competitors' actions.

Legal and regulatory framework covers the whole range of statutory and voluntary rules within which decisions on the four Ps are made. Both advertising and brochures, for example, are surrounded by detailed consumer protection legislation covering the way in which products may be communicated to customers. Legal requirements for price notification in travel and tourism affect pricing decisions and limit the room for manoeuvre. Much of the regulatory framework is common to all consumer industries, but some is specific to sectors of travel and tourism, such as the deregulation provisions for airlines noted in Chapter 4. Other examples can be seen in the legal or voluntary requirements for registration, classification and grading, which in many countries are applied to hotels and other forms of tourist accommodation.

Political, social and ethical attitudes normally take years to evolve, but rapidly growing concern for the future of the global environment and for 'sustainable' development has emerged internationally in the years since the 1987 Brundtland Report. Such concerns were focussed in 1992 in the *Earth Summit* in Rio de Janeiro. The external pressures exerted by environmental issues are expected to become more urgent in the 1990s, not just for travel and tourism but for all forms of economic activity and especially for new developments. Environmental concerns are expressed both as social and ethical attitudes, as well as part of political pressures before becoming reflected and absorbed in legal and regulatory frameworks.

Less dramatic but relevant to marketing managers are, for example, modern European attitudes to nude bathing, which have provided marketing opportunities for so-called naturist resorts, such as Cap d'Agde in Southern France. The traditional concepts of non-charging museums in North America and Britain are presently changing fast in the face of cost pressures and evident opportunities for revenue generation from visitors. Skilled marketing requires a careful assessment of political and other social attitudes in order to take advantage of and exploit emerging trends ahead of the competition.

New and developing technology in travel and tourism applies in different ways to all sectors of the industry. For example, when the first generation of Boeing 747 and other 'jumbo' jets appeared in the early 1970s, they made a significant difference to airline seat/mile costs and, through their influence on speed of journeys as well as prices over long distances, opened the markets for long-haul leisure travel in ways previously not possible. New information technology, e.g. international computer networks for hotel reservations, linked by space satellites, has provided powerful new marketing tools. These were first exploited by Holiday Inns in the late 1970s, and, now developed by all chains, are linked or merged with the international reservation systems owned by airlines. At a different but still highly significant level for marketing in the sector, the nature and quality of the tourist products provided by the caravan park sector of accommodation has been transformed in recent years by the production technology applied to new caravans and trailers, and also to the provision of facilities such as swimming pools and other leisure equipment.

The structure of distribution channels may appear relatively stable on first consideration, but, taken over a decade or so, the changes are considerable. In the USA, for example, the number of travel agency outlets more than doubled from just over 12,000 to over 30,000 between 1976 and 1990. In Britain the rapid regrouping of many retail agencies into six large, national, multi-site networks took place over less than a decade, and has altered the structure of distribution channels and distribution strategies for most large producers in the tourism industry. The combination of changes in information technology and organizational structure in distribution channels is one of the most important developments for marketing in travel and tourism, which will influence marketing mix decisions significantly over the remaining years of the twentieth century.

The actions of competitors provide the most immediately powerful of all the external factors affecting marketing managers' decisions. With very few exceptions, commercial organizations in travel and tourism are locked in continuous 'battle' with their competitors, many of which offer very similar products, at similar prices, and use the same distribution channels. Where non-commercial organizations are engaged in marketing to achieve additional revenue, e.g. national museums or public sector heritage sites, they are inevitably engaged in a similar competitive struggle. In terms of long-run strategies as well as short-term tactics competitors are engaged, quite literally, in a battle of wits. The principal weapons or tools available for use are the four Ps. The prizes in the struggle are expressed as market share, sales revenue, and profit.

Chapter summary

In this chapter the essential components of the marketing mix are introduced as the four Ps. They are discussed as the main levers or controls available to marketing managers in their continuous endeavours to achieve planned objectives and targets, expressed as sales volume and revenue from identified customer groups. The mix decisions are based on a combination of marketing research, marketing planning procedures, and the judgement of individual managers engaged in a battle of wits with their competitors.

This chapter sets the four Ps in the wider context of non-marketing resources within organizations, and the continuously changing external influences to which marketing managers have to respond. This very important concept of marketing response is succinctly summarized by Stanton's view that:

> A company's success depends on the ability of its executives to manage its marketing system in relation to its external environment. This means (1) responding to changes in the environment, (2) forecasting the direction and intensity of these changes, and (3) using the internal controllable resources in adapting to the changes in the external environment (Stanton: 1981, p. 32).

In terms of this quotation there is no difference whatever in principle between what is required of marketing managers in travel and tourism and those in any other industry selling products to the general public. Such differences as do occur in marketing practice are based on the nature of the products offered, the particular implications of price manipulation in an industry distinguished by highly perishable products, and the nature of the distribution channels available. These differences are fully discussed in later chapters of this book. Because of their special influence in travel and tourism markets, two of the principal factors external to the business - determinants and motivations - are the subject of separate chapters (4 and 5).

Finally, it is stressed that marketing-mix decisions mostly imply significant costs, which have to be met or committed in advance of the revenue such decisions are expected to achieve. Later chapters will emphasize the need for integration and co-ordination of marketing-mix decisions, in which even small improvements in the effectiveness of marketing expenditure can make a significant difference to profitability.

Further reading

Kotler, P., *Marketing Management: Analysis, Planning, Implementation and Control*, 7th edit., Prentice-Hall International, 1991, Chapter 3.

7

Segmenting travel and tourism markets

Chapter 3 stresses that the role of marketing managers is to manage and influence demand. 'The more an organization knows about its customers and prospective customers – their needs and desires, their attitudes and behaviour – the better it will be able to design and implement the marketing efforts required to stimulate their purchasing decisions'. As explained in this chapter, market segmentation is the *process* whereby producers organize their knowledge of current and potential customer groups and select for particular attention those whose needs and wants they are best able to supply with their products. In other words, since it is usually impossible to deal with all customers in the same way, market segmentation is the practical expression in business of the theory of consumer orientation. It is arguably the most important of all the practical marketing techniques available to marketing managers in travel and tourism. It is normally the logical first step in the marketing process involved in developing products to meet customers' needs. Segmentation is also the necessary first stage in the process of setting precise marketing objectives and targets, and the basis for effective planning, budgeting, and control of marketing activities.

In practice, apart from national tourism organizations (NTOs), no individual producer is ever likely to be much concerned with the whole of any country's tourist markets. They will usually be closely concerned with particular

sub-groups of visitors within the total market, or 'segments' as they are known, which they identify as the most productive targets for their marketing activities. NTOs also find it necessary to segment the total market of potential tourists in order to carry out marketing campaigns, although they may have to provide facilities, such as information services, for all visitors.

This chapter is in three parts. The first part introduces the wide range of segments that typically exist for most producers of travel and tourism products. The second part defines the process of segmentation and outlines the criteria to be applied to any grouping of customers. The third part describes the principal ways used in travel and tourism to divide up markets for marketing purposes. The meaning of segmentation for a tour operator is illustrated in Figure 7.1.

Multiple segments for producers in travel and tourism

Before considering the techniques used to segment markets, it may be helpful to indicate the range of sub-groups with which operators in the different sectors of the travel and tourism industry are concerned. For each of the main sectors identified in Chapter 1 (excluding destination organizations that tend to deal at least indirectly with every segment), five broad consumer segments are listed below:

Hotels
1 Corporate/business clients
2 Group tours
3 Independent vacationers
4 Weekend/midweek package breaks
5 Conference delegates

Tour operators
1 Young people 18-30
2 Families with children
3 Retired /senior citizens
4 Activity/sports seekers
5 Culture seekers

Transport operators
1 First class passengers
2 Club class passengers
3 Economy class passengers
4 Charter groups
5 APEX purchasers

Destination attractions
1 Local residents in the area
2 Day visitors from outside local area
3 Domestic tourists
4 Foreign tourists
5 School parties

The segments listed above are not comprehensive but simply an illustration of the range of possibilities that exist for each sector. Readers may find it a useful exercise to extend these lists to around fifteen segments for each sector, using the analysis discussed later in this chapter.

Even the minimum list above should make clear a very important point: *most businesses deal not with one, but with several segments*. Some segments are largely dictated by the location in which a business operates; others may be attracted by products designed for identified customer groups and marketed to them.

A marketing and operations view of segmentation

At first sight it may appear obvious that managers work together to create a range of products and market them to identified customer groups or segments. In practice there is often a real conflict between the needs of operations management and the view of marketing managers.

From an operational standpoint it is usually most cost-effective if a single, purpose-designed product, such as a standard airline seat, or a standard bedroom, can be marketed to all buyers. In that way unit costs can be cut to the minimum and operational controls can be standardized and more easily implemented. In such conditions segmentation is still relevant as the basis for separate promotional campaigns, but it does not interfere with the smooth operation of production processes. Some marketing-led organizations, most notably McDonald's family restaurants, major theme parks, and other attractions, do provide standard products for their customers. But they tend to be the exceptions in the tourism industry rather than the rule. Increasingly, under competitive market conditions in which several producers are competing for shares of the same markets and aiming their products at more than one group of the same prospective customers, the need to create and deliver *purpose-adapted products* for each group is becoming more urgent. For reasons discussed in earlier chapters, the essence of a marketing approach is to adapt an organization's operations to satisfy identified customer requirements. If groups of prospective customers are found to have different needs, wants and motivations, competition makes it essential to design products that meet those needs, and to promote and distribute them accordingly.

In an ideal world each separate customer would receive special personal service or a custom-built product. They may still do so in travel and tourism if they are able to pay the necessary price, as in luxury hotels. It may be possible also in very small businesses, such as farmhouses taking in a few visitors to stay, in which the level of personal contact between visitor and host is very high. In the real world of large-scale marketing of quality-controlled, standardized products, however, such individual attention is not possible at the prices most customers are willing and able to pay. There is therefore often a considerable level of tension between the interests of marketing managers in offering products designed to cater for sub-groups in the market, as the best way to secure their custom, and the interests of the operations managers responsible for holding down or reducing unit costs, and controlling the quality standards of product delivery.

If significant product differentiation is required to meet the needs of different market segments, there are also likely to be management problems in servicing the needs at the same time on the same premises. To provide an example, a hotel may find it difficult or impossible simultaneously to meet the needs of business people and coach parties of packaged tourists in the same restaurant; museums have similar problems with noisy school parties and older visitors requiring peace and quiet to achieve their satisfaction with a visit. The problems are very clear in the case of conference halls, which may be separately marketed as the venue for a pop concert one day, a political meeting next day, and a sales conference on the day after. In each case a different segment with different needs is dealt with, but they are not compatible on the same premises on the same day. Considerable strain and careful sequencing imposed on those who manage such operations.

Management concerns with reconciling the requirements of segmentation and product differentiation with economies of scale is not a new problem. As Alderson put it some 30 years ago, marketing is to be seen essentially as a multi-phase sorting process, which 'makes mass production [standardization] possible first by providing the assortment of supplies needed in manufacturing [production] and then taking over the successive transformations which ultimately produce [deliver] the assortments [products] in the hands of consuming units [to customers]' (Alderson, 1958, p. 59). By inserting the words in brackets as shown, it is easy to adapt Alderson's original sorting concept, intended for manufacturing industry, to a travel and tourism context. As such, the sorting concept neatly explains the essence of a segmentation approach to marketing today.

In other words, the task of marketing management, in close liaison with operations management, is to identify compatible products that meet the needs of compatible target segments. This has to be achieved on the same premises in a way that permits economies to be achieved in both operational and marketing processes, so as to achieve optimum income from the selected customer and product mix. Such optimization is never easy to achieve in service businesses, and readers should be aware of the conflicting management interests often existing in practice. This author expects these issues to be better resolved in the 1990s through closer integration of management structures to link marketing more closely with operations.

Segmentation defined

Segmentation may now be defined as a process of dividing a total market such as all visitors, or a market sector such as holiday travel, into sub-groups or segments of the total for marketing management purposes. Its purpose is to facilitate more cost effective marketing, through the design, promotion and delivery of purpose-designed products, aimed at satisfying the identified needs of target groups. In other words, segmentation is justified on the grounds of achieving greater efficiency in the supply of products to meet identified demand, and increased cost-effectiveness in the marketing process. In most cases travel and tourism businesses will deal with several segments over a 12-month period but not necessarily simultaneously.

In the tourism industry most established producers will often have no practical choice but to deal with certain segments because of the location and nature of their business. Usually there will be other segments that can be chosen as targets if they meet the producer's needs. These new or optional segments are likely to change over a period of, say, 5 to 10 years, as the determinants of travel and tourism change. For example, as a normal part of monitoring market trends and observing competitor's actions, a tour operator may decide to develop a range of specific products for segments of people over the age of 55. If the operator is successful, the over-55s product may grow from a small base to, say, 20 per cent of total turnover over a period of years. The operator will have changed its segment/product mix as a result of a marketing decision.

Most businesses will have scope and opportunities for altering the current mix of their business generated by the existing structure of segments, through manipulating the marketing mix to target new segments. The criteria for choosing new segments for marketing development will stem either from the producer's needs to utilize assets, e.g. to develop off-season business, or from attractive characteristics of the segments themselves, e.g. high relative expenditure per capita of some groups compared with others.

Actionable market segments

Drawing on the contributions of Kotler (1991) and Chisnall (1985) it is possible to focus on four main criteria that must be applied to any segment if it is to be usable or actionable in marketing. Each segment has to be:

- Discrete.
- Measurable.
- Viable.
- Appropriate.

Discrete means that the selected sub-groups must be separately identifiable by such criteria as purpose of visit, income, location of residence, or motivation, as discussed later in this chapter.

Measurable means that the criteria distinguishing the sub-groups must be measurable by means of available marketing research data, or via such new data as can be obtained within acceptable budgets. Research is normally expensive, and segmentation must be affordable within available budgets. Segments that cannot be adequately measured on a regular basis cannot be properly targeted. If targeting is not measurably precise, it will be difficult or impossible to evaluate the effectiveness of marketing activities over time. At the risk of being flippant, one might add 'if a segment cannot be measured, it doesn't exist, except as wishing thinking'.

Viable means that the long-run projected revenue generated by a targeted segment exceeds the full cost of designing a marketing mix to achieve it, by a margin that meets the organization's objectives. In the short run it may be necessary to ignore segment viability in order to achieve other organization objectives. Viability therefore is a function of the costs of designing products for segments, promoting to target groups, and ensuring that prospective customers can find convenient access to such products, once they have been persuaded to buy.

Appropriate, reflecting the inseparability of service product delivery (see Chapter 3), means it is essential that segments to be supplied on the same premises are mutually compatible and contribute to the image or position in the market adopted by a producer. An economy car with a Rolls-Royce label would be absurd, even if the company wished to make it. Similarly, down-market coach tour business to the Savoy Hotel in

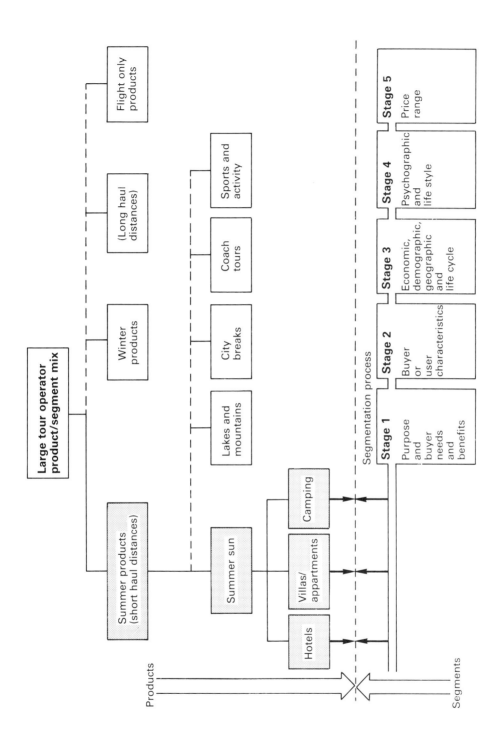

Figure 7.1 *Typical tour operator product/segment mix for summer and sun holidays*

London or to Crowne Plaza hotels could only damage those companies' reputations for exclusiveness and luxury at a price that maintains the expected standards.

To summarize thus far, market segments are identified target groups within a total market, chosen because they are relevant to an organization's interests, skills and particular capabilities. In other words, selected segments have particular needs and a profile a producer feels especially competent to satisfy with relevant products.

To be actionable in marketing, segments must meet the four criteria noted in this section; they are as relevant to service organizations as to producers of manufactured goods. The next section discusses the ways, sometimes known as 'modes', by which target groups may be identified and measured.

In considering the modes, it may be found helpful to relate them to the context of a product/segment mix for a large tour operator, shown in Figure 7.1.

Methods used to segment markets

There are seven main methods or ways of dividing up markets for segmentation purposes, all of which are used in practice in the travel and tourism industry. These methods are usually based on some form of marketing research, and a commitment to segmentation normally implies a commitment to market research.

The methods are listed below and subsequently discussed. The sequence in which they appear is not the sequence commonly found in marketing texts but it reflects an order of priority which this author believes to be most relevant to travel and tourism markets.

The main methods of segmentation are by:

1 Purpose of travel.
2 Buyer needs, motivations, and benefits sought.
3 Buyer or user characteristics.
4 Demographic, economic, and geographic characteristics.
5 Psychographic characteristics.
6 Geodemographic characteristics.
7 Price.

These seven methods are not to be seen as alternative choices for segmentation. They are overlapping and complementary ways by which it is possible to analyse a consumer market in order to appreciate, and select from it, the range of segments it comprises. Many businesses in travel and tourism will use at least three of the methods for any particular segment; all of them could be used if the segment being analysed is important enough to a business.

Segmentation by purpose of travel

For most producers in travel and tourism, practical marketing segmentation should always begin with a careful analysis of the purposes for which customers travel and use their (and their competitors') products. For example, if the purpose of travel is mainly for business, this obviously requires a range of business orientated travel products. Within the broad category of business travel there are many aspects of purpose, which determine the nature of the products offered and the promotional approach to be used. For example, conference markets require different products to those supplied to other business travellers, meetings for groups of different sizes may require special provision, some travellers may require secretarial services, and so on. The range of segments noted under the main sectors of travel and tourism earlier in this chapter reflect some of the more obvious purposes. A little thought will indicate a broad range of possibilities. Provided the customer groups associated with any purpose meet the four essential criteria for effective segmentation, a detailed understanding of each purpose of visit will always be useful in practice. For smaller businesses in travel and tourism, segmentation by simple analysis of purpose may be all that is needed for practical or actionable purposes.

For a tour operator, customers' purposes and product needs will differ according to whether they are looking for:

- Main summer holidays.
- Additional summer holidays.
- Winter sun.
- Winter sports.

Within the broad categories of main and additional summer holidays, typical subsidiary purposes would include beach holidays (with and without children), city breaks, rural holidays, lakes and mountains, and cultural tours. For larger operators, the products designed to appeal to such markets would usually have a separate brochure or separate sections within a brochure. The provision of different brochures is therefore an obvious sign of segmentation in practice.

Thus, for an established tour operator with a successful business, the grouping of products currently provided is likely to be an accurate reflection of customer purposes served. In other words, and this is an important point, *market segmentation and product formulation are opposite sides of the same coin if they are correctly matched.*

The other segmentation methods discussed below are ways to develop a clearer, more precise understanding of segments, that already exists in outline through the identification of travel purpose. Figure 7.1, which shows an example of segmentation for tour operators, will help to make this point clear.

Segmentation by buyer needs and benefits sought

Within purpose of travel, and obviously an aspect of it, the next logical consideration for segmentation is to understand the needs, wants and motivations of particular customer groups, as discussed in Chapter 5. For reasons that are developed in the next chapter on products, it is generally accepted in marketing that customers tend to seek particular benefits when they make their product choices. In the case of the tour operator example, motivations may relate to opportunities to meet and mix with particular types of people, young or mature; or to indulge in gastronomic pleasures; or to be highly active or take pleasures sedately, and so on. For organizations dealing with business markets, some business travellers may identify luxury and high levels of personal service as the principal benefits they seek when travelling away from home. Others may identify speed of service and convenience of particular locations as their principal benefits. Some business travellers, if they are paid a fixed sum of money for their travel expenses, may seek economy products, especially if they are able to retain the difference between their travel allowance and the actual cost they pay. Some travellers prefer to stay in large, modern, international hotels, while others choose older, more traditional establishments, which may offer a more interesting environment or a more personalized service.

In the case of visitor attractions the benefits sought by family groups may relate to children's interests rather than those of the adults who purchase the admission tickets. In the case of museums the benefits sought by most visitors are likely to be understood in terms of an hour or two's general interest and amusement, since they have only a limited knowledge of the subject matter's intrinsic merit. Many a museum has been misled by its own enthusiasm for its precious collection into believing that average visitors are also very interested in the subjects displayed. Usually they are not, and their threshold of patience is very easily crossed if the collections are not displayed in ways designed to appeal to general interest.

In most sectors of travel and tourism the range and perceived importance of the benefits sought by customer segments are not necessarily apparent to marketing managers. Usually they may be discovered only through market research among identified target groups, and they change over time. Segmentation by benefits makes it possible for marketing managers to fine-tune their products within the broad requirements of purpose noted earlier. Promoting the benefits sought is a logical objective for brochures and other advertising materials.

Segmentation by buyer or user characteristics

Within purpose and benefits sought there is ample scope for refining the segmentation process according to the types of behaviour or user characteristics customers exhibit. One obvious example is the frequency of usage of products. Business users may be very frequent users of hotels, with perhaps twenty or more stays in hotels in a year, and even more frequent users of airlines and car rental companies. Frequent users may represent only 10 per cent of individual customers in a year but up to 60 per cent of revenue for some hotel groups and airlines. As such, they are always a key segment for marketing attention. The benefits sought by frequent users for particular purposes are an obvious focus for marketing research.

Visitor expenditure per capita, not necessarily directly associated with levels of income or socio-economic status, is another dimension of behaviour or user characteristics that is highly relevant to segmentation decisions. For example, many British holidaymakers in Spain outspend German and Swedish visitors, although their per capita income is very much less. Other things being equal, high expenditure segments are seen as attractive targets in all sectors.

Some buyers tend to use the same hotel group, airline or travel agent on each or most occasions, a buyer characteristic known in marketing as 'brand loyalty'. Others may choose their purchase on each occasion according to price, convenience and availability. 'Loyal' customers are highly attractive to producers for obvious reasons, and a combination of high

spending, high frequency and high loyalty would be the best of reasons for designing products and promotional campaigns aimed at securing and retaining such valuable buyers.

A little thought will soon indicate that there are a wide range of user characteristics that could be relevant for identifying particular segments. The characteristics may be divided according to the timing or sequence of buyers' decisions, before, during, or after using any travel and tourism product. Table 7 .1 explains this point in a context relevant to accommodation businesses or tour operators.

Table 7.1 *Buyer behaviour/usage characteristics by sequence of purchase and usage*

Before booking	Booking process	In use/ consumption pattern	After use
Previous usage/ experience	Package/ independent arrangements	Utilization of facilities available	Customer satisfaction level and perceived value for money
Frequency of usage	Credit terms required	Expenditure per head	Communication to friends/contacts
Media habits	Via travel agent	Length of stay	
Awareness/use of brochures	Via central reservation office	Party size and composition	
Sources of travel information used	Booking direct with producer	Transport mode	

The aspects of behaviour noted in the table, are not fully comprehensive but they cover main aspects that can be adapted to the specific context of any producer in travel and tourism. Pre-booking characteristics, for example, would be less important to museums (but still relevant for group visitors), whereas details of visitor circulation patterns, exhibits visited, division of time within the museum during the visit, would be highly significant in management terms.

Measuring and monitoring the user characteristics noted in Table 7.1 is the basis of many surveys of customers and prospective users (see Chapter 11). In their various forms user surveys are the most widely practised type of market research used in all parts of the travel and tourism industry.

By the late 1980s the increasing availability of powerful low cost computers with extensive memory capacity made it possible for growing numbers of marketing managers in travel and tourism to input and retain information about their customers and their user characteristics in databases. Databases utilizing a unique record number for every buyer (or enquirer) are capable of recording and linking most aspects of customer profile and purchase patterns as they are revealed from coupons requesting information, booking forms, invoices etc. Such databases (see also geodemograhphic segmentation) can to some extent replace traditional market research methods based on sample surveys of customers and provide better and cheaper ways to segment markets than was possible previously. The direct contact with customers on the producers' premises provides access to customer information in travel and tourism that is not generally available to manufacturers of goods using retail distribution systems.

Segmentation by demographic, economic, geographic and life-cycle characteristics

If producers begin their segmentation process with an analysis of customer needs and benefits sought, within purpose of travel, they are likely to have a very clear understanding of the type of products their chosen customer groups want. If that understanding is backed up by information obtained by user surveys of the type noted in the preceding section, and/or database analysis, their knowledge of target groups will already be considerable. For the purposes of efficient promotion and distribution of products, however, especially to prospective new customers rather than existing ones, they will also need to know the demographic and other physical characteristics of their target segments.

At the simplest level of analysis, familiar to most readers, customer segments may be defined in terms of basic facts about their age, sex, occupation, income grouping, and place of residence. Known collectively as *customer profiles*, such facts are often easily obtained for existing customers in travel and tourism as a by-product of booking records, registration procedures, and regular customer surveys such as the in-flight studies undertaken by airlines and tour operators. Descriptive information about buyers of travel products generally is usually also available in many countries from various forms of national tourist office and commercial surveys of travel and tourism markets. These are commonly available for purchase in countries with developed tourism industries. In the UK the *UK Tourism Survey* (monthly and yearly), published by national tourist boards, provides a wealth of standard demographic data. In the USA the US Travel Data Center in Washington is the source of similar data.

Simple descriptive profiles have their uses in segmentation, at least in deciding which media to choose for advertising purposes. Many producers in travel and tourism go no further. But on their own, without the prior analysis of purpose, benefits and user characteristics, basic demographic profiles are not an adequate basis for organizing effective marketing campaigns. Producer organizations that rely solely on such simple data run the risk of being out-manoeuvred by their competitors.

At a slightly more complex level of analysis of customer profiles it is possible to group together a number of physical characteristics of people to form what is usually termed 'life-cycle analysis'. This is based on the stages through which all people progress in life, from infancy, through adolescence and child-rearing to old age. The travel behaviour of many people aged 18 to 35 may not vary much according to whether they are single or married, but it is likely to vary enormously according to whether or not they have children. Those with young children under the age of 4 have different travel needs from those with older children between the ages of 10 and 15. At the other end of the age scale the travel activities of those aged between 50 and 70 will vary enormously according to whether or not they are retired or still at work. All developed countries have market research organizations that will analyse markets by life-cycle categories.

Segmentation by psychographic characteristics and life style

'Psychographics' is a term used to denote measurement of an individual's mental attitudes and psychological make-up. It is clearly distinguished from demographics, which measures the objective dimensions of age, sex, income and life cycle, noted in the preceding section. Dependent on sophisticated marketing research techniques, psychographics aims to place consumers on psychological rather than physical dimensions. The reason for segmenting buyers on psychological dimensions is the belief that common values among groups of consumers tend to determine their purchasing patterns. For example, some individuals are mentally predisposed to seek adventure, enjoy risks and active vacations. Their values and goals are those of competitive people for whom measures of achievement, such as winning races or gaining proficiency certificates, are important. Others are risk-avoiders, and choose passive and unstressful vacations, often at familiar destinations unlikely to present any unknown threats.

The measurement of consumer attitudes and values has been a preoccupation of market researchers on both sides of the Atlantic for decades. The methods of measurement, usually asking consumers to make complex ratings of items included in multiple choice questions, were greatly enhanced by the availability of computers in the 1960s and 1970s. A range of computer programmes is now available to measure the extent and strength of any correlations that exist between people's attitudes

and values, and their behaviour patterns as buyers of travel and other products. Such measurements may be further refined by including questions about attitudes to, and perceptions of, individual companies in the industry, and the products they supply. This type of research underlies the modern concept of *product positioning*, discussed later in this book.

Related to their demographic characteristics and stages in the life cycle, the links between attitudes, perceptions and actual buyer behaviour, combine to determine the *life style* which individuals adopt. An understanding of the life style of target customers has obvious advantages when formulating new products or creating messages designed to motivate such people. Among international operators in travel and tourism, Club Méditerranée, for example, clearly understand and have singlemindedly adopted a life-style segmentation approach, as any consideration of their product brochures will confirm.

Life-style segmentation reflects an understanding of individuals' needs, benefits sought, and motivations. It normally requires significant expenditure on marketing research, and it is used within the basic segmentation by purpose of visit noted earlier.

Geodemographic segementation

In Britain since the early 1980s, and there are equivalent techniques, for example, in several other European countries and in the USA and Canada, a very interesting and powerful segmentation tool was developed through the combination of census data with the postal area (zip) codes used to identify every group of households in the country. Allied to the power of modern computers to store and analyse data, the major development was the classification of household types into a total of thirty-eight different groups in the UK, more usually summarized under eleven groups, each with clearly defined characteristics of housing types, which in turn correlate closely with population characteristics of age, family structure, life cycle and income. The housing types include, for example, *modern family housing, higher incomes; better off council estates*; and *affluent suburban housing*.

Known in the UK as ACORN, which stands for *a classification of residential neighbourhoods*, the census data can now be supplemented by data from major commercial surveys of purchasing patterns, including travel behaviour. By the late 1980s, provided that producer organizations recorded the names and full addresses of their customers, it was possible for research companies to locate and map the typical household types in all the areas in which buyers with similar characteristics could be found throughout Britain.

The geographic aspect of geodemographics was greatly enhanced in the late 1980s when new computerized mapping techniques were introduced, based on satellite technology. The best known software system, GIS (Geographical Information System), was developed in the USA. GIS is expected to develop considerably in the next decade in all countries, and will provide improved linkages between mapping techniques and customer databases generally. This ability to combine mapping software with customer databases provided by census and market research survey data explains the generic title 'geodemographic'. Geodemographic segment-ation tools are now capable of targeting individual buyers and households with great precision, and they clearly have 'particular relevance to direct marketing, leaflet distribution, and local media selection' (Chisnall: 1985, p. 280). Since 1986 the ACORN targeting techniques have been increasingly used by tourist boards in Britain, and appear to offer great scope for cost-effective direct-response marketing. (See also Chapter 19.)

To illustrate the usefulness in practice of the demographic, economic, geographic, and life-cycle analysis of segments, it is interesting to consider one of the typical target customer groups for weekend and mid-week package holidays in hotels in Britain. These products enjoyed a significant growth market in the 1970s and 1980s. The target groups of buyers are typically married, professional people, college-educated, living in their own homes (not rented) in cities or suburbs, in the age range 35-60, either without children living at home or with children over the age of about 10 who can be left with friends or relatives. It is also possible to define the typical distance in miles such couples are prepared to drive to reach their destinations, so that the catchment areas of target customers can be mapped for the location of any hotel. With such a profile, which draws on most of the descriptive characteristics referred to in this section, supplemented by the geodemographic tools, it would not be difficult to develop a broadly relevant promotional campaign and choose the type of media best calculated to reach the target audience. To refine the segmentation further, market research would be needed to assess customers' reasons for taking breaks, their personal motivations, and benefits sought, for any particular hotel and its location.

Segmentation by price

In general buyer behaviour in travel and tourism markets in all countries appears to be highly price-sensitive, and many operators act on the assumption that price is a key segmentation variable. In other words, there are segments of customers to be identified and located who respond to different price bands. In practice this would appear to be mostly true when major new tourism developments are planned, e.g. a new Center Parc holiday village of the type found in several countries in northern Europe. In such cases feasibility studies are required to identify the ability and willingness of sufficient customers to pay the prices that will generate the level of revenue required to pay back investment, cover fixed costs and create targeted profits. One may conclude that this is a form of segmentation by price, but it will still rank second to purpose, benefits sought, and user characteristics in the hierarchy of segmentation modes. Feasibility studies are not an exact science, however, as the first years' trading results for Euro Disney show in 1992-3, and willingness to pay is dependent on other variables.

For established businesses there will nearly always be some room for manoeuvre within broad price ranges in the short run, and price is often the major tool for promotional tactics. But limits are set by the strategic marketing-mix decisions and the costs of operating the business and satisfying existing customers. Thus, although there is no doubt that price motivates very large numbers of customers, it is not a segmentation variable of the same kind as the others outlined in this chapter. As noted earlier, segments to be mixed on the premises of a producer organization such as a hotel must be broadly compatible to sustain consumer satisfaction.

Chapter summary

This chapter focuses on the role of market segmentation as a set of techniques. They enable marketing managers to divide total markets into component parts, in order to deal with them more effectively and more profitably for marketing purposes. As Chisnall puts it, 'market segmentation recognizes that people differ in their tastes, needs, attitudes, lifestyles, family size and composition, etc. ... It is a deliberate policy of maximizing market demand by directing marketing efforts at significant sub-groups of customers or consumers' (Chisnall: 1985, p. 264).

The more that people differ, and the greater the level of competition between producers seeking to maintain or increase their shares of the same market, the more important segmentation becomes to business success. It is usually impossible in practice to promote to, and satisfy, all customers in the same way. The case for segmentation increases as markets grow in total volume and sub-groups are identified, around whose particular needs it becomes cost-effective (viable) to focus particular marketing activity. For some producer organizations, for operational reasons, the basic product is essentially the same for all customers. This is usually the case for many visitor attractions. But there are always different ways to promote to sub-groups in the market, and opportunities to enhance the basic product around a segment's needs. The promotion of special group facilities for educational visits to museums, and the creation and use of special information materials for school visitors, illustrate this point.

'There is no single way to segment a market. A marketer has to try different segmentation variables, singly and in combination, hoping to find an insightful way to view the market structure' (Kotler: 1984: p. 254). This chapter outlines seven variables in the order of importance considered relevant to most producers in travel and tourism. In particular, this chapter emphasizes the importance of segmentation by purpose of travel, and of understanding the benefits that different groups of customers seek. The implications for segmentation of researching user characteristics before, during, and after purchasing travel products, is also stressed.

Segmentation in a rapidly changing business environment is a dynamic process. New segments emerge as some older ones disappear or are no longer viable as a result of market change. At any point in time most organizations in travel and tourism will be dealing with several different segments. All of them are likely to be in a state of continuous change, partly in response to shifts in the external market determinants, and partly to changes in customers' needs, attitudes and motivations. In almost every case there will be opportunities for marginal improvements in what a business knows of its customers, and therefore how best to promote to them and satisfy their product needs marginally better than the competition.

For these reasons, except for the smallest of

businesses, segmentation normally justifies a considerable and continuous commitment to marketing research - an important consideration developed in Chapter 11. For a growing number of larger organizations in the 1990s, it will also mean a commitment to the development of customer databases for research and marketing purposes and the development of geodemographic techniques.

Further reading

Baker, M. J., *Marketing: An Introductory Text*, 4th edit., Macmillan, 1985, Chapter 6.

Kotler, P., *Marketing Management: Analysis, Planning, Implementation and Control*, 7th edit., Prentice-Hall International, 1991, Chapter 10.

8

Travel and tourism products: product formulation

The ways in which products are put together (product formulation) are the most important responses marketing managers make to what they know of their customers' needs and interests. The process of identifying customer segments is covered in Chapter 7. Product decisions, with all their implications for the management of service operations and profitability, reflect all aspects of an organization's management policies, including long-term growth strategy, investment, and personnel policy. They largely determine the corporate image an organization creates in the minds of its existing and prospective customers.

To a great extent the design of products determines what prices can be charged, what forms of promotion are needed, and what distribution channels are used. For all these reasons, customer-related product decisions are 'the basis of marketing strategy and tactics' (Middleton: 1983a, p. 2). As the most important of the four Ps in the marketing mix, product formulation requires careful consideration in any branch of marketing. Because of the particular nature and characteristics of travel and tourism, the subject is especially complex in the tourism industry.

This chapter is in four parts. The first part introduces the existence of two different dimensions for understanding tourism products, one of which is the product as perceived by customers, and the other the view of products taken by marketing managers of individual producer organizations. Products are explained in terms of their component parts and the benefits they offer to customers. The second and third parts discuss these two dimensions of products separately, and the fourth part introduces *product positioning*.

A components' view of travel and tourism products – from two standpoints

It follows from the definitions discussed in Chapter 1 that any visit to a tourism destination comprises a mix of several different *components*, including travel, accommodation, attractions and other facilities, such as catering and entertainments. Sometimes all the components are purchased from a commercial supplier, e.g. when a customer buys an inclusive holiday from a tour operator, or asks a travel agent to put the components together for a business trip. Sometimes customers supply most of the components themselves, e.g. when a visitor drives his own car to stay with friends at a destination.

Conveniently known as a 'components' view', the conceptualization of travel and tourism products as a group of components or elements brought together in a 'bundle' selected to satisfy needs, is a vital requirement for marketing managers. It is central to this view that the components of the bundle may be designed, altered and fitted together in ways calculated to match identified customer needs.

The overall tourism product

Developing the components' view from the standpoint of the tourist, Medlik and Middleton noted (1973) that, 'As far as the tourist is concerned, the product covers the complete experience from the time he leaves home to the time he returns to it'. Thus 'the tourist product is to be considered as an amalgam of three main components of attractions . . . and facilities at the destination, and accessibility of the destination'. In other words, the tourist product is 'not an airline seat or a hotel bed, or relaxing on a sunny beach . . . but rather an amalgam of many components, or a package.' The same article continued, 'Airline seats and hotel beds . . . are merely elements or components of a total tourist product which is a composite product.' This original concept of the product was used subsequently by Wahab *et al.*, (1976), and Schmoll (1977), and has been widely accepted and used internationally.

The product of individual producers

Without detracting in any way from the general validity and relevance of the overall view of tourism products noted above, it has to be recognized that airlines, hotels, attractions, car rental and other producer organizations in the industry, generally take a much narrower view of the products they sell. They focus primarily on their own services. Many large hotel groups and transport operators employ product managers in their marketing teams and handle product formulation and development entirely in terms of the operations they control. Hotels refer to 'conference products' for example, or

'leisure products'; airlines to 'business class products'; and so on. For this reason, the overall product concept sets the context in which tourism marketing is conducted but it has only limited value in guiding the practical product design decisions that managers of individual producer organizations have to make. A components' view of products still holds good, however, because it is in the nature of service products that they can be divided into a series of specific service operations or elements, which combine to make up the particular products customers buy. Thus for a visitor to a hotel (business or leisure), the hotel product is a 'bundle', which may be itemized as:

● Initial experience and reactions in selecting from a brochure.
● Experience of the booking process.
● First impression on entering the hotel.
● Reception process on arrival.
● Standard of room and any en suite facilities.
● Experience of customer–staff interactions.
● Provision of meals and any ancillary services.
● Checking out process on leaving.
● Any follow up, such as direct mailing, received subsequently.

This is not a comprehensive list but it serves to stress the point that any individual product is composed of a series of elements that combine to satisfy the purchasers needs. Understanding, unravelling, and fine-tuning the elements, provide ample opportunity for marketing managers to increase their knowledge of products and improve their presentation and delivery to prospective customers.

It is usually highly instructive to analyse any service producers' operations in terms of the full sequence of contacts between customer and operator, from the time that they make initial enquiries (if any), until they have used the product and left the premises. Even for a product such as that provided by a museum, there is ample scope to analyse all the stages of a visit and potential points of contact that occur from the moment the customer is in sight of the entrance until he leaves the building, say 2 hours later. Putting the components' view in slightly different terms, individual service producers designing products 'must define the service concept in terms of the bundles of goods and services sold to the consumer and the relative importance of each component to the customer' (Sasser *et al.*: 1978, p. 14).

To bring the two distinctive aspects of tourist products together – the *overall* view and that of *individual producer* organizations – it is possible to consider them as two different dimensions. The overall view is a horizontal dimension in the sense that a series of individual product components are included in it, and customers, or tour operators acting as manufacturers (Chapter 24), can make their selection to produce the total experience. By contrast, the producers' view is a vertical dimension of specific service operations organized around the identified needs and wants of target segments of customers. Producers typically have regard for their interactions with other organizations on the horizontal dimension, but their principal concern is with the vertical dimension of their own operation (this point is developed later in this chapter).

A benefits view of products

Before discussing the two dimensions of travel and tourism products in more detail, it is important to keep in mind the customers' view of what businesses of all types offer for sale. Levitt's statement is succinct; 'People do not buy products, they buy the expectation of benefits. It is the benefits that are the product' (Levitt: 1969). Developing this point, Kotler noted 'the customer is looking for particular utilities. Existing products are only a current way of packaging those utilities. The company must be aware of all the ways in which customers can

gain the sought satisfaction. These define the competition' (Kotler: 1976, 3rd edition, p. 25).

Researching targeted customers' perceptions of product benefits and utilities, and designing or adapting products to match their expectations, lie of course at the heart of marketing theory. There is no difference in principle between a benefits view of products applied to travel and tourism or to any other industry producing consumer goods.

Components of the overall tourism product

From the standpoint of a potential customer considering any form of tourist visit, the product may be defined as a bundle or package of tangible and intangible components, based on activity at a destination. The package is perceived by the tourist as an experience, available at a price.

There are five main components in the overall product, which are discussed separately below:

● Destination attractions and environment.
● Destination facilities and services.
● Accessibility of the destination.
● Images of the destination.
● Price to the consumer.

Destination attractions and environment

These are elements within the destination that largely determine consumers' choice and influence prospective buyers' motivations. They include:

● *Natural attractions:* landscape, seascape, beaches, climate and other geographical features of the destination and its natural resources.
● *Built attractions:* buildings and tourism infrastructure including historic and modern architecture, monuments, promenades, parks

and gardens, convention centres, marinas, ski slopes, industrial archaeology, managed visitor attractions generally, golf courses, speciality shops and themed retail areas.

- *Cultural attractions:* history and folklore, religion and art, theatre, music, dance and other entertainment, and museums; some of these may be developed into special events, festivals, and pageants.
- *Social attractions:* way of life of resident or host population, language and opportunities for social encounters.

Combined, these aspects of a destination comprise what is generically, if loosely, known as its *environment.* The number of visitors the environment can accommodate in a typical range of activities on a typical busy day without damage to its elements and without undermining its attractiveness to visitors is known as its *capacity.* Between the 1960s and 1980s tourism marketing managers were mostly able to plan their strategies without much if any regard to capacity issues. This is changing, however, and the development and practice of responsible marketing conducted in context of the sustainability of destination environments appears certain to be a key issue in the 1990s (see Epilogue).

Destination facilities and services

These are elements within the destination, or linked to it, which make it possible for visitors to stay and in other ways enjoy and participate in the attractions. They include:

- *Accommodation units:* Hotels, holiday villages, apartments, villas, campsites, caravan parks, hostels, condominia, farms, guesthouses.
- *Restaurants, bars and cafes:* ranging from fast food through to luxury restaurants.
- *Transport at the destination:* taxis, coaches, car rental, cycle hire (and ski lifts in snow destinations).
- *Sports/activity:* ski schools, sailing schools, golf clubs.

- *Other facilities:* craft courses, language schools.
- *Retail outlets:* shops, travel agents, souvenirs, camping supplies.
- *Other services:* hairdressing, information services, equipment rental, tourism police.

For some of these elements, the distinction between attractions and facilities may be blurred. For example, a hotel may well become an attraction in its own right and a prime reason for selecting a destination. Nevertheless, its primary function of providing facilities and services remains clear.

Accessibility of the destination

These are the elements that affect the cost, speed and the convenience with which a traveller may reach a destination. They include:

- *Infrastructure:* of roads, airports, railways, seaports, marinas.
- *Equipment:* size, speed and range of public transport vehicles.
- *Operational factors:* routes operated, frequency of services, prices charged.
- *Government regulations:* the range of regulatory controls over transport operations.

Images and perceptions of the destination

For reasons outlined in Chapter 5, the attitudes and images customers have towards products strongly influence their buying decisions. Destination images are not necessarily grounded in experience or facts, but they are powerful motivators in travel and tourism. Images, and the expectations of travel experiences are closely linked in prospective customers' minds.

For example, of the millions of people in America and Europe who have not so far visited Las Vegas, there will be few who do not carry in their minds some mental picture or image of the experiences that destination provides. Through the media and through hearsay, most people have already decided whether they are attracted or repelled by the Las Vegas image. All destinations have images, often based more on historic rather than current events, and it is an essential objective of destination marketing to sustain, alter or develop images in order to influence prospective buyers' expectations. The images of producer organizations within destinations, e.g. the hotels in Las Vegas, are often closely related to the destination image.

Price to the consumer

Any visit to a destination carries a price, which is the sum of what it costs for travel, accommodation, and participation in a selected range of services at the available attractions. Because most destinations offer a range of products, and appeal to a range of segments, price in the travel and tourism industry covers a very wide range. Visitors travelling thousands of miles and using luxury hotels, for example, pay a very different price in New York than students sharing campus-style accommodation with friends. Yet the two groups may buy adjacent seats in a Broadway theatre. Price varies by season, by choice of activities, and internationally by exchange rates as well as by distance travelled, transport mode, and choice of facilities and services.

Some marketing implications of the overall product concept

With a little thought it will be clear that the elements comprising the five product components, although they are combined and integrated in the visitor's experience, are in fact capable of extensive and more or less independent variation over time. Some of these variations are planned, as in the case of the Disney World developments in previously unused areas around Orlando, Florida, or the purpose-built resorts along the former mosquito-infested coastline of Languedoc

Roussillon in France. In both those cases massive engineering works have transformed the natural environment and created major tourist destinations in recent years. Center Parc holiday village developments in the UK illustrate recent forms of destination engineering, since they provide covered, climate-controlled attractions within a central facility, as well as outdoor attractions, and capacity-controlled accommodation in carefully landscaped surrounding areas. Center Parcs are planned to protect and in places enhance the environment. In such cases all five product components are integrated under one management.

By contrast, in New York, London, or Paris, the city environments have not been much altered for travel and tourism purposes, although there have been massive planned changes in the services and facilities available to visitors. Many changes in destination attractions are not planned, and in northern Europe the decline in popularity of traditional seaside resorts since the 1960s has been largely the result of changes in the accessibility of competing destinations in the sunnier south of the Continent. Changes in the product components often occur in spite of, and not because of, the wishes of governments and destination planners. They occur because travel and tourism, especially at the international level, is a relatively free market, with customers able to pursue new attractions as they become available. Changes in exchange rates, which alter the prices of destinations, are certainly not planned by the tourism industry, but have a massive effect on visitor numbers, as the movements between the UK and the USA since 1978 have demonstrated.

It is in the promotional field of images and perceptions that some of the most interesting changes occur, and these are marketing decisions. The classic recent example of planned image engineering may be found in the 'I Love New York' campaign, which, based on extensive preliminary market research, created a significant improvement to the 'Big Apple's' appeal in the early 1980s. At a very different level, industrial cities in Britain such as Glasgow, Manchester and Bradford are working hard on their image projection to achieve the same type of change in visitors' perceptions.

The view of the product taken by customers, whether or not they buy an inclusive package from a tour operator or travel wholesaler, is essentially the same view or standpoint as that adopted by tour operators. Tour operators act on behalf of the interests of tens or hundreds of thousands of customers, and their brochures are a practical illustration of blending the five product components discussed in this section (see also Chapter 24).

The overall view is also the standpoint of national, regional and local tourist organizations, whose responsibilities usually include the co-ordination and presentation of the product components in their areas. This responsibility is an important one even if the destination tourist organizations are engaged only in liaison and joint marketing, and not in the sale of specific product offers to travellers.

In considering the product, we should note that there is no natural or automatic harmony between components, such as attractions and accommodation, and they are seldom under any one organization's control. Even within component sectors such as accommodation there will usually be many different organizations, each with different, perhaps conflicting, objectives and interests. Indeed it is the diversity or fragmentation of overall control, and the relative freedom of producer organizations to act according to their perceived self-interests, at least in the short term, which makes it difficult for national, regional and even local tourist organizations to exert much co-ordinating influence, either in marketing or in planning. Part of this fragmentation simply reflects the fact that most developed destinations offer a wide range of tourism products and deal with a wide range of segments. In the long term, however, the future success of a destination must involve

coordination and recognition of mutual interests between all the components of the overall tourism product. Achieving such co-ordination is the principal rationale for much of the marketing work undertaken by NTOs (see Chapter 20).

Specific products – the producer's view

The overall view of tourism products is highly relevant to the marketing decisions taken by individual producers, especially in establishing the interrelationships and scope for co-operation between suppliers in different sectors of the industry, e.g. between attractions and accommodation, or between transport and accommodation. But in order to design their product offers around specific service operations, there are internal dimensions of products for marketers to consider; these are common to all forms of consumer marketing and part of widely accepted marketing theory. Marketing managers 'need to think about the product on three levels' (Kotler: 1984, p. 463).

Using Kotler's terminology, which is based on earlier contributions by Levitt, these three levels are:

● The *core product*, which is the essential service or benefit designed to satisfy the identified needs of target customer segments.
● The *tangible product*, which is the specific offer for sale stating what a customer will receive for his money.
● The *augmented product*, which comprises all the forms of added value producers may build into their tangible product offers to make them more attractive to their intended customers.

Although the labels applied to these three levels of any product are unattractive marketing jargon, the value of the thought process is potentially very great indeed. The thought process can be applied by producers in any of the tourism industry sectors, and is equally applicable to large and small businesses. It will repay careful thought and application in particular operations.

The following example of an inclusive weekend break in a hotel will help to explain what the three levels mean in practice. The product offer is a package comprising two nights' accommodation and two breakfasts, which may be taken at any one of a chain of hotels located in several different destinations. Because of the bedroom design and facilities available at the hotels, the package is designed to appeal to professional couples with young children. The product is offered for sale at an inclusive price through a brochure, which is distributed at each of the hotels in the chain and through travel agents. It is in competition with the products of other very similar hotels, which are promoting to the same market at similar price levels. Products of this type are now widely available in many parts of North America and Europe, and the total market for them grew substantially in the 1970s and 1980s. The example reveals the three product levels.

Core product is intangible but comprises the essential need or benefit as perceived and sought by the customer, expressed in words and pictures designed to motivate purchase. In the example under discussion, the core benefit may be defined as relaxation, rest, fun, and self-fulfilment in a family context.

It should be noted that the core product reflects characteristics of the target customer segments, not the hotel. The hotel may, and does aim to, design its core product better than its competitors, and to achieve better delivery of the sought benefits. But all its competitors are aiming at the same basic customer needs and offering virtually identical benefits. Customers' core needs usually tend not to change very quickly, although a hotel's ability to identify and better satisfy such needs can change considerably. Since customer perceptions are never precisely understood, there is ample scope

for improvement in this area.

Tangible product comprises the formal offer of the product as set out in a brochure, stating exactly what is to be provided at a specified time at a specified price. In the example under discussion, the tangible product is two nights and two breakfasts at a particular location, using rooms of a defined standard, with bathroom, TV, telephone, etc. The provision (if any) of elevators, coffee shops, air-conditioning and swimming pool are all within the formal product and the name of the hotel is also included.

In the case of hotel products generally, and certainly in the example cited, there is often very little to choose between competitors' tangible product offers, and price may become a principal reason for choice. Blindfolded and led to any one of say twenty competitors' premises, most hotel customers would not easily recognize the identity of their surroundings. The brochure description of the tangible product forms the basic contract of sale, which would be legally enforceable in most countries.

Augmented product. Both tangible and intangible, augmentation is harder to define with precision. It comprises the *difference* between the contractual essentials of the tangible product and the totality of all the benefits and services experienced in relation to the product by the customer – from the moment of first contact in considering a booking - to any follow-up contact after delivery and consumption of the product. The augmented product also expresses the idea of *value added* over and above the formal offer. It represents a vital opportunity for producers to differentiate their own products from those of competitors.

In the example under discussion there may be up to twenty 'add ons' – some fairly trivial, such as a complimentary box of chocolates on arrival, and some significant, such as entrance tickets to local attractions or entertainments. Some of the added benefits are tangible as indicated, but some are intangible, such as the quality of service provided and the friendliness of staff at reception, in the bars and so on. Also intangible is the image or 'position' the product occupies in customers' minds. In the case of a hotel group this will be closely related to the corporate image and branding of the group. In the example under discussion the augmented elements would be purpose-designed and developed around the core product benefits in ways calculated to increase the appeal to the target segment's needs.

There is, inevitably, an area of overlap between the tangible and augmented elements of the product, which cannot be defined with any precision. For example, if only one hotel group offers jacuzzi pools, that is a form of product augmentation. If all hotels offer jacuzzis, the pools are simply part of the tangible product.

Competitive product formulation

To stay ahead of the competition, proactive marketing managers are constantly looking for product innovation. There are clearly no secrets once brochures are published, but there is normally considerable scope for creative innovation and for experimentation in the area defined as product augmentation, and strong advantages in being first with product developments. One augmented element, which cannot be easily copied, is the image a hotel creates in prospective customers' minds, and image is therefore often one of the principal reasons for choosing between alternative products.

In order to define the core product, the formal product, and to identify the scope for product augmentation with some precision, frequent research into the perceptions and purchasing characteristics of segments is a necessary aspect of consumer orientation in the travel and tourism industry.

In the example used to illustrate the three levels of the product it is interesting to note the degree of overlap between the particular accommodation product offer discussed (vertical dimension) and other components of the overall tourism product (horizontal dimension). Attractions at the destination in which the hotel is located may be part of the hotel users' total experience, whether or not the hotel forms links with the attractions as part of an augmented product. Similarly, hotel users may use public transport links to the destination, whether or not the hotel forms links with transport operators to include fares as part of the tangible product.

Product positioning

In this chapter image, as perceived by customers, is identified as one of five components in the overall tourism product and as a vital element within the augmented product developed and marketed by individual businesses in the industry. In common with most services, the benefits provided by travel and tourism products are essentially intangible and, for vacationers in particular, products are strongly identified with personal goals and aspirations at levels which Maslow termed 'self-actualization' (see Chapter 5).

Accordingly, the image or identity chosen for the purposes of promoting tourism products is a matter of the greatest importance to marketing managers. As Ries and Trout put it, 'knowing what the customer wants isn't too helpful if a dozen other companies are already servicing his or her wants' (Ries and Trout: 1981). In such circumstances producers are not just concerned with satisfying customers' needs, but doing so in ways which are recognized as unique or very strongly identified with a particular organization, and which cannot be easily copied by any other producer. Images provide identities both for products and for the organizations (or destinations) that produce them.

The modern approach to product positioning is based on the well-tested hypothesis that products, companies and tourist destinations have images or perceptions with which they are identified in the minds of existing and potential customers. Appropriate positions are also segment-related. For example, one hotel may be identified as good for business travellers, another as good for families, another as the place to stay for the best food and wine; another as offering the highest standards at the top end of the market, or offering specific sports facilities such as golf. By measuring these perceptions and images, it is possible to compare one company's image with that of its competitors. It is equally possible to compare different organizations or different destinations in terms of what customers believe about them, and to identify image strengths and weaknesses. By tackling any weaknesses that emerge among key segments – using the product formulation methods noted in this chapter – or focusing on strengths, it is possible for organizations to 'steer' their products via the techniques of the marketing mix. For airlines and hotel groups especially, the positioning of products and corporate images has emerged at the centre of marketing management decisions in recent years.

The measurement methods used to identify images and positions call for relatively complex statistical techniques and are usually handled by market research agencies acting on behalf of marketing managers. Product positioning is a strategic issue and it is discussed further in the chapters on marketing strategy and advertising (Chapters 12 and 15).

Chapter summary

This chapter emphasizes a components' view of travel and tourism products at two separate but related levels. At both levels the components' view implies an ability, given adequate marketing research and product knowledge, to 'engineer' or formulate products to match the identified needs of target segments. Because needs are continuously shifting and competitors' abilities to supply needs are constantly changing, product formulation is a continuous process. This holds good for new, purpose-built products, which may be designed years before they are in operation, and for existing products, which may be adapted over time through rearranging product components.

Product formulation has two sides, reflecting concerns with demand and supply. In terms of demand, the approach requires market research focused on customer needs, behaviour and perceptions, in order to define target segments and to identify strengths and weaknesses of product images. In terms of supply, product formulation requires an analysis of product components and elements and identification of the range of existing and potential products that could be improved or developed profitably to meet customer needs. These demand and supply implications apply equally to tourist destinations and to individual producers. Matching supply to demand is of course the cornerstone of the modern marketing approach. Integration between the two levels of the product is often an essential part of the matching process in travel and tourism.

There is always a danger in tourism marketing that the ability to 'engineer' intangible service products on paper, and to promise satisfactions in brochures and in advertising, exceeds a destination's or a producer's ability to deliver the satisfaction at the time of consumption. Because tourism products are ideas at the time of purchase, it is relatively easy to oversell them, especially to first-time buyers. Any significant dissatisfaction experienced during consumption may destroy the vital word of mouth recommendations and decisions on repeat purchase, on which long-term business profit and survival are likely to depend.

Most tourism destinations and individual producers provide several products to match the needs of their several segments. Some of their products are likely to be relatively new and growing in market share, some will be well established or 'mature', and some are likely to be relatively old and may be declining in popularity and market share. The idea that organizations have a mixture of products and segments – usually known as a 'market/product portfolio' – is a very important one in travel and tourism. Portfolio analysis is the basis for much of marketing strategy and this point is developed in later chapters.

This chapter stresses the concept of the marketing mix in its most important dimension - that of the product in the context of market segmentation and customer motivations. Marketing is nothing if not an integrated approach to business and students in particular should note the overlapping structure of the chapters thus far.

Further reading

An understanding of product concepts in travel and tourism is crucial to effective marketing in the industry. Accordingly, the limited space in this book is allocated deliberately to tourism aspects in preference to other important, widely used, standard product concepts, which are fully explained in most textbooks of marketing principles. For an understanding of the concepts of product life cycles, product-mix decisions and product classifications, the following reading is recommended:

Baker, M. J., *Marketing: An Introductory Text* 4th edit., Macmillan, 1985, Chapters 3 and 12.

Kotler, P., *Marketing Management: Analysis, Planning Implementation and Control*, 7th edit., Prentice-Hall International, 1991, Chapters 11, 13, and 16.

9

The role of price

In Chapter 6, dealing with the 'marketing mix', price is introduced as one of the four Ps. Price denotes the terms of the voluntary exchange transaction between customers willing to buy and producers wishing to sell. Through the agreed terms of exchange, customers are attempting to maximize their perceptions of benefits and value for money as they choose from competing products on offer. Producers are aiming to achieve targeted sales volume, sales revenue, market share, and optimize their return on investment.

This chapter aims to show the significant and complex role that pricing plays in the marketing-mix decisions that marketing managers in commercial travel and tourism organizations are required to make. The contents focus first on the crucial role of price in manipulating demand, and therefore sales revenue. The characteristics of travel and tourism influencing pricing decisions are then outlined, followed by a discussion of pricing strategy and tactics. The latter half of the chapter identifies the main influences on pricing decisions and comments separately on each of them.

Manipulating price in order to manage demand

It is easy to appreciate that the volume of products sold × average price paid = sales revenue. It is also easy to see that the potential influence on profit of relatively small changes in price may be massive. For example, if a hotel of 150 bedrooms operates at 70 per cent room occupancy, with an average price across its segments and products of $150 per room night (room rate achieved), 150 rooms × 365 nights × 70 per cent × $150 = $5,748,750 (annual room sales revenue). If, by more effective use of marketing techniques, the same hotel could increase its average room rate by 5 per cent to $157.50 without loss of volume, the annual sales revenue would be 150 × 365 × 70 per cent × $157.50 = $6,036,188. The difference is $287,438, which, if fixed costs were held constant, would certainly represent a significant percentage of gross operating profit earned by this hotel. The role of a marketing manager in achieving such an average increase in room rates through more effective deployment of the marketing mix to stimulate demand would reflect many separate decisions spread over the whole year. Continuous judgement would be required as to the price each of the hotel's segments could bear at a given time.

While most businesses in travel and tourism publish standard prices, and many are required by law to display them, there are usually many opportunities to vary the published price in practice. The reasons for this are made clear in this chapter. Over a year's trading, the sales revenue generated in any except very small businesses is a function of many decisions on the optimum price to be charged to the range of segments involved, on a daily or week by week basis. For some businesses, such as visitor attractions, average prices are relatively stable over a year, but for others, such as tour operators and scheduled airlines, prices may vary widely as managers seek to optimize their short-run revenue. The use of price changes to manage demand is common throughout the industry, and is often a daily concern for many marketing managers.

Yield management and market segmentation

What is simply expressed in the preceding section as the 'use of price to manage demand and revenue' is rather more complex in practice. First, most travel and tourism businesses deal with several segments at the same time, and there are usually different prices for different segments. Second, there are multiple products with different pricing implications, leading to a *product–market* mix in which the range of prices even for a medium-sized firm is extensive. Third, there are often unpredictable daily and weekly fluctuations in business, which require a tactical pricing response.

In its marketing sense the term *yield management* is increasingly used to describe the process of managing revenue against demand in travel and tourism. The implications of this will be clearer in Part Five of the book, but in principle any hotel, airline or attraction has a potential revenue achievable for a given number of customers on any day. *Yield is the actual revenue achieved*, compared with the potential revenue if all the capacity is optimally used at the published prices. For example, two hotels of equivalent standard and with the same rack rate may each be 70 per cent full as measured in room occupancy. But hotel A may be discounting heavily to achieve volume through tour operators and hotel B may be more successfully marketing itself direct to customers. In this example, for the same room occupancy, hotel B would have a far higher yield than A. In the case of an airline a shift of, say, 10 per cent of passengers from business class to economy class greatly lowers the yield from the same number of passengers. For a museum, if two-thirds of all visitors are admitted at less than full adult price (i.e. at special group rates), the yield is much lower than it would be if, say, half the visitors paid full price.

In an era of excess capacity for the available demand the concept of yield management on a daily basis is relevant in all sectors of travel and tourism. It is the business of marketing managers to balance the segments they deal with in ways best calculated to improve yield, not just to increase the number of customers.

The characteristics of travel and tourism services that influence pricing

While price is a vital decision in the marketing of all types of goods and services, the characteristics of travel and tourism products explain the industry's particular preoccupation with price. The main characteristics of services, introduced in Chapter 3, are summarized below from a pricing viewpoint and discussed later in this chapter.

- High price elasticity in the discretionary segments of leisure, recreation and vacation travel markets.
- Long lead times between price decisions and product sales. Twelve months or more are not uncommon lead times when prices must be printed in brochures to be distributed months before customer purchases are made, as is typically the case for tour operators.
- No possibility of stockholding for service products, so that retailers do not share with producers the burden and risk of unsold stocks and tactical pricing decisions.
- High probability of unpredictable but major short-run fluctuations in cost elements such as oil prices and currency exchange rates.
- Near certainty of tactical price-cutting by major competitors if supply exceeds demand.
- High possibility of provoking price wars in sectors such as transport, accommodation, tour operation and travel agencies, in which short-run profitability may disappear.
- Extensive official regulation in sectors such as transport, which often includes elements of price control.
- Necessity for seasonal pricing to cope with short-run fixed capacity.

- High level of customers' psychological involvement, especially with vacation products, in which price may be a symbol of status as well as value.
- The high fixed costs of operation, which encourage and justify massive short-run price cuts in service operations with unsold capacity of perishable products.
- High level of vulnerability to demand changes reflecting unforeseen economic and political events.

A major tour operator such as Thomson, for example, has to cope with each of these characteristics in its pricing policies. Traditionally, in the British market, Thomson has also established itself as the first large operator to publish its summer prices in the preceding autumn. As such, it has tended to establish price leadership for much of the rest of the British tour operating industry, a position that has disadvantages as well as advantages.

Strategic and tactical prices

A very important way in which travel and tourism businesses respond to their highly complex pricing circumstances is to operate prices at two levels.

The first level, which corresponds broadly with marketing strategy, is the price an operator is obliged to publish months in advance of production, in brochures, guides, on admission tickets, and so on. For hotels, this price is the so-called rack rate; for airlines, it is the published fare structure. This price structure reflects strategic marketing decisions concerning product positioning, value for money, long-run return on investment requirements, and corporate objectives such as growth, market share, and profit levels set for the operation.

The second level, which corresponds to marketing operations or tactics, is the price at which an operator is prepared to do business on a weekly, daily or hourly basis. It changes as the date of production approaches and in the light of bookings and expectations at the time. This often may be many weeks or months after the published price decisions were made. The tactical price may be widely known, advertised and published, as are the 'sale' offers regularly put out by tour operators as they seek to achieve additional last-minute bookings. Alternatively, the price may be a closely guarded commercial secret, as happens when tour operators undertake deals with hoteliers facing cash-flow crises or bankruptcy unless they can generate additional revenue from otherwise empty rooms. Unofficial 'dumping' of airline tickets for sale at heavily discounted prices is commonly practised around the world, and frequently criticized but not stopped because discount fares provide a tactical, daily service of great value to the airlines. In Britain the daily and Sunday press regularly publish pages of unofficial discount fares, well below published rates. Members of the public willing to bargain with half empty hotels in the late evening will often find they can achieve significant reductions from the published room rate.

Travel and tourism sectors are not alone in practising these two-level pricing approaches. Heavy discounting, e.g. of new car sales or computer equipment, is also frequent and undertaken for the same reason – to secure additional sales which it is believed would not otherwise occur. In the case of manufactured goods, discounting is used also to release money tied up in expensive stocks so that the fixed costs of operation can be paid.

The role of price in strategy and tactics

Chapters 12 and 13 discuss the meaning of strategic and operational planning. In this chapter it is necessary only to distinguish between the role of price as a management tool to achieve strategic business objectives, and as a tactical tool to manipulate short-run demand. In pricing, as in all other elements of the marketing mix, the tactical or operational decisions have to be made within a strategic framework, that steers the business toward its chosen goals.

The main distinctions can be summarized as follows:

Strategic role (regular or published prices)

- Reflects corporate strategies such as maximum growth or maximum profit.
- Communicates chosen positioning and image for products among target segments.
- Communicates expectations of product quality, status, and value to prospective customers.
- Reflects stage in the product lifecycle.
- Determines long-run revenue flows and return on investment.
- Determines the level of advance bookings achieved.

Tactical role (discounted/or promotional prices)

- Manipulates marginal (last-minute) demand through incentives, which may be general or more often restricted to particular segments.
- Matches competition by the quickest available route.
- Promotes trial for first-time buyers.
- Provides a short-run tool for crisis management.
- Determines short-run cash flows.
- Determines daily yield.

At the strategic level, growth strategies in price-sensitive markets are often based on relatively low or 'budget pricing' in order to make a rapid impact on a large number of potential buyers. Such strategies usually aim for a high volume of sales at low profit margins per unit sold. The life-cycle stage of a product is also

very much a strategic consideration, and older, mature products will often be more price-sensitive because of the competition they face from newer, developing products in high demand. Because many service products cannot be seen or easily evaluated before purchase, the product's image and implications of quality have added significance for prospective buyers. Price is a highly relevant symbol in signalling or communicating what buyers should expect in terms of product quality and value for money.

The strategic decision of an organization to operate in the de-luxe end of a market rather than the budget end immediately commits it to a relatively high cost structure, which can only be met by relatively high prices. In this sense the decision to occupy a certain price band in the market precedes and determines the other three Ps of the marketing mix. The strategic price band decision is therefore also an operational decision. For hotels, restaurants and airlines especially, it determines the level of investment required for buildings and equipment. For all these reasons, strategic price decisions have implications beyond marketing, and necessarily affect the other senior managers of an organization. It is of course the role of marketing managers to research and interpret what price levels are realistic and achievable among the consumer segments whose needs an organization aims to satisfy.

Important as pricing decisions are in a strategic sense, they play an even more dominant role in a tactical sense. This is because of the inseparable and perishable nature of service production and consumption, and the inability of service producers to carry over unsold stocks as a buffer to cope with future demand. Thus, while a hotel with 150 rooms in the budget end of the market has a capacity of 54,750 room nights to sell in a year, the marketing requirement is to organize budget level demand in 'blocks' of 100–150 room buyers per night. To achieve this feat, requires what amounts to a continuous obsession with demand manipulation, in which tactical price cuts are usually the most important and often the only available tool. Surplus capacity in any market heightens this obsession.

The typical seasonal and daily variation in demand for most travel and tourism products, and the seasonal pricing structure devised to respond to it, also heighten the concern with tactical pricing decisions.

Figure 9.1   *The network of influences on pricing decisions*

The influences on price-setting

From the foregoing discussion it should be clear that there are many influences determining price-setting in practice. Figure 9.1 shows the range of influences that marketing managers in travel and tourism have to take into account in setting prices, especially at the strategic level. At the tactical level, discussed above, the considerations focus more narrowly on day-to-day demand management in relation to competitors' actions. The remainder of this chapter comments on each of the influences separately.

It should be noted that there are two circles of influence surrounding pricing decisions. The *inner circle* reflects primary influences:

- Corporate strategy and positioning.
- Marketing objectives for the period over which prices are set.
- Segments with which a business is concerned.
- Operating cost constraints.
- Competitors' actions.

The *outer circle* reflects wider influences of:

- Characteristics of products and capacity.
- Non-price options.
- Legal and regulatory constraints.

Corporate strategy and positioning

The first and dominant influence on product pricing is that of strategic business decisions concerning image and product positioning (such as de-luxe or budget) and strategies for growth, market share, and return on investment. These decisions set the context for marketing operations over a 3 to 5 year time span or longer, and effectively set realistic upper and lower limits within which product prices are likely to move.

Marketing objectives

In modern, marketing-led organizations in any industry, business strategy has to be implemented systematically on a week by week basis, through operational decisions focused on specific targets for sales volume and sales revenue. Price is a highly influential component of the marketing mix, which is adjusted to meet particular short-run objectives for each product/market sector of a business. For reasons developed in Chapters 13 and 14, objectives for particular campaigns will be a critical input to price setting decisions.

Market segments

Since marketing in practice revolves around an understanding of consumer behaviour and profiles, it follows that every pricing decision has to be realistic in the context of the expectations and perceptions of chosen market segments, and their capacity and willingness to pay. Through consumer research and experience gained from results of previous price changes, marketing managers are expected to know what price level each segment can bear, and to what extent price signifies value for money and product quality. Knowledge of segments also reveals practical ways in which pricing may be made relevant to one group of customers but inaccessible to others. Senior citizen rail cards designed to promote cheap travel on railways outside commuting times, or hotel weekend prices designed to appeal to non-business segments, are examples. In the context of airline travel, Shaw provides an excellent illustration of the principles of pricing by segments (Shaw: 1982, p. 153). Pricing by segments is developed to maximize yield and minimize the dilution of revenue caused by offering cheaper prices to segments able and willing to pay more.

Operating costs

As noted earlier, in order for a business to survive over the long run, the average prices charged must be high enough to generate sufficient revenue to cover all fixed and variable costs and provide an acceptable return on the assets employed. Operating costs, expressed as average costs per unit of production, are therefore a primary input to pricing decisions.

Many catering establishments, hotel restaurants and bars, still fix prices according to the basic cost of production per unit sold, plus a mark-up percentage to cover return on investment and profit. Unfortunately for tourism businesses with a significant volume of turnover from leisure segments, such as airlines, tourist attractions, accommodation suppliers and tour operators, the so-called 'cost plus' methods are not very useful in practice. This is partly because most tourism markets are highly competitive and price-sensitive, so that operators are often forced for tactical reasons to accept prevailing market prices regardless of mark-up. It is also because of the influence on operations of high fixed costs and low variable costs. It costs an airline very little extra, for example, to operate an aircraft with 60 per cent seats occupied rather than 50 per cent. In principle, at least, it would be preferable to charge a fare of say $50 one way across the Atlantic than to forgo the revenue and fly empty seats. The $50 would be much less than average seat cost but it would at least provide some revenue to help offset an otherwise certain loss. Obviously there are dangers of upsetting regular customers with very low prices not accessible to all. One common way around this for airlines is to offer 'stand by' seats with last minute availability and no guarantee that customers will fly.

Average unit of production costs typically provide a target floor for prices, below which they should not fall except in the short-run circumstances previously noted. Sometimes, however, long-run average operating costs of businesses become too high for the prices that can be charged in competitive markets. One dramatic illustration of the irrelevance of cost-plus pricing approaches can be seen in the decision in 1981–2 of British Airways to reduce its costs in order to prepare for privatization. The airline could not be privatized unless it could convince investors of its profitability, and in the depressed markets of 1981–2 it was making massive losses and was technically bankrupt. To make a profit from achievable revenue (available demand × the average ruling prices) meant a major cost-cutting exercise and increases in efficiency. As there was no option to raise average prices, 23,000 staff from a total of around 57,000 lost their jobs, but the airline was successfully privatized in 1987. Productivity was increased and targeted profit was achieved at ruling price levels which were to drive some competitors from the market (Reed: 1990, p.47).

Competitors' actions

It is at the level of tactical marketing that price competition becomes a dominant influence. For example, for summer 1985, reflecting increased costs of hotels abroad and unfavourable exchange rates, the average published price of package tours from Britain to destinations abroad rose by around 15 per cent over 1984. The result was tens of thousands of unsold holidays, massive late price-cutting between competitors, and a flood of last minute bookings stimulated by very low prices. For 1986, with more favourable exchange rates, falling oil prices and reduced hotel prices, Thomson Holidays reduced its average prices by over 15 per cent and increased its capacity significantly. As a result, Intasun immediately matched its main competitor and most other smaller operators were forced to follow suit. By July 1986, both Thomson and Intasun, with over 3 million package holidays between them on offer, achieved sales volume increases of up to 50 per cent above 1985 levels.

Five years later, in 1991, after two difficult years for UK tour operators, projected summer bookings failed to materialize in the critical period between January and March. The first quarter of the year roughly coincided with the Gulf War, which, with the effects of an unexpectedly severe economic downturn in the UK, totally disrupted normal cash flow for tour operators. Traditional discounting could not influence a crisis of this magnitude and International Leisure Group (ILG), the owner of Intasun, went into liquidation. It was unable to sustain its operational costs and persuade banks to fund the rising cost of its existing extensive borrowing for expanding its airline. As a result of the sudden withdrawal of a significant proportion of capacity from the UK package tours market, prices firmed and provided large windfall profits for the survivors in that year.

In all countries generating or receiving tourist flows the travel trade press is likely to contain frequent examples of competitive, tactical pricing decisions. It is a useful exercise for students to select some of these examples for examination and discussion. Students should also consider how far most of these decisions are planned or simply forced by market circumstances permitting no alternative.

Characteristics of products and capacity

When products have close substitutes and producer organizations have surplus capacity, it is highly likely that price will be the dominant consideration in marketing tactics. Many resort hotels find themselves in this position. In Britain sea ferries operating across the channel are similarly placed, and airlines in deregulated conditions also are forced into price competition. Across the travel and tourism industry generally the close substitutability of many products, coupled with the need to secure daily customer purchases, heightens the level of marketing dependency on pricing tactics.

Substitutability of products is one of the reasons why leisure products in travel and tourism demonstrate high price elasticity. Other things being equal, a small increase in the price of one product provokes a considerable shift in demand to other similar products, which are then relatively less expensive. Analyses of price against volume of sales data confirm that many travel and tourism markets do respond in accordance with traditional economic models of 'price-elastic' demand and supply. Most managers are well aware of the effects of price-elasticity, although they can rarely predict exactly how any given market will respond in a forecast period. In practice, therefore, likely market responses to changes in price have to be guessed at, managers relying heavily on judgement and market intelligence to interpret any forecasting models that may be used. Even where price/response models exist, they are mostly based on historical data and cannot cope with unpredicted events. Moreover, prices are usually set with only limited knowledge of competitors' actions, which, when known, may require a matching response, regardless of the revenue consequences in the short run.

On the other hand, some products, even with large capacity, are able to secure a unique niche or position within the minds of potential customers, which reduces perceived substitutability and lessens their sensitivity to price. For example, the Ritz or Savoy hotels in London, Disney World in Florida, and Center Parcs in northern Europe, have developed product concepts which, for marketing purposes, are unique. Marketing managers have a primary responsibility for creating and sustaining such product niche positions, unless of course an organization's strategy is deliberately based on lowest prices.

Non-price options

From the foregoing discussion of the main influences on price setting decisions it should be obvious that the principal requirement for marketing managers is to understand fully what the influences are and how they work. Often, especially as a result of competitors' actions, the initiative in pricing may be lost in the short run. Ideally no business aims to be a price follower, responding to what the market place dictates; but in practice it often happens in many travel and tourism markets, and cannot always be avoided.

There are, however, other marketing ways in which it is possible to limit the intensity of price competition by reducing the effects of substitution between products. Most of these ways are aspects of adding value to the services offered through product augmentation, which was described in detail in Chapter 8. Through augmentation focused on target segments, it is possible significantly to enhance the benefits that products provide, and therefore the reasons for choosing according to product attributes rather than lowest price. For example, to meet the needs of frequent business customers, many privileged-user or frequent-user card schemes have been designed and promoted by major hotel groups since the early 1980s. Such cards sometimes provide price discounts but almost invariably offer attractive services such as rapid check-out facilities or credit billing, or up-grades when capacity permits. The holder of a card may use it, in preference to simple price switching to a competitor, for reasons of convenience, familiarity and the status of recognition and special treatment on arrival. These card schemes are of course designed to promote loyalty among targeted business visitors, and represent an excellent and cost-effective marketing method for securing additional sales revenue often at, or very near, the strategically determined price level.

There are also numerous ways of disguising price cuts as consumer benefits, in the guise, for example, of offering spouse accommodation (but not meals) 'free', or one 'free' night for every three paid for at the full rate and so on. The link between sales promotion and tactical

pricing considerations is an interesting one, and is further discussed in Chapter 16.

For hotels, the advantages of a particular location, such as city centres for business persons, may confer a benefit in the minds of users that justifies a premium price. For an airline, the careful cultivation and promotion of a particular image for service and efficiency may constitute a benefit, for which customers are willing to pay a premium price. For visitor attractions, most of which are already unique in their own intrinsic qualities, the route out of price substitutability lies in enhancing the quality of their sites or the enjoyment benefits conferred by a better presentation of the experiences offered. The Jorvik Viking Exhibition in York, for example, offered a new way to present historic artefacts in the 1980s. As a result, the visitor interest in what was offered made it possible to charge relatively high prices for a relatively short but intense experience. All these are consumer orientated marketing routes to avoid head-on price competition between products that may otherwise be seen by customers to be close substitutes.

Legal and regulatory constraints

While pricing is essentially a decision based on commercial influences, travel and tourism prices are often also subject to government regulation. For reasons of public health and safety, and to ensure competition between suppliers and achieve consumer protection, governments in all countries frequently intervene in or influence pricing decisions. For example, for many international scheduled air routes, air fares are still ratified by official agreements between governments and may be subject to investigation to prevent predatory pricing. In some countries, in which accommodation is officially registered and classified, price categories are fixed annually and can be varied by individual businesses only within given limits.

The 1980s, in former communist countries as well as in the developed economies of the western world, witnessed a marked shift in the dismantling of state-run enterprises in favour of commercially owned and managed companies. This shift, combined with the development and growing power of national, transnational and global corporations (see Chapter 2), makes it inevitable that regulatory bodies will find it increasingly necessary to intervene in market decisions. In developed countries the law provides for regulators to ensure fair competition and prevent the operation of monopolies or oligopolies against the public interest. As Wheatcroft puts it in the context of world airlines, 'There certainly could be abuses of dominant market positions and it is highly desirable that there should be powers, such as those given to the EC under the competition rules, to prevent anti-competitive behaviour' (Wheatcroft: 1992, p. 19).

Administrative friction

Not an influence in the same context as those included in Figure 9.1, an important argument against frequently changing prices is the administrative problems which arise, as well as possible inconvenience and irritation caused to customers and retailers. Shaw notes in relation to the bewildering array of airline fares, 'Simplicity – or rather the lack of it is becoming a major concern of pricing . . . complexity in the tariff will involve airlines in costs of staff training, and costs of staff time and passenger delay whilst fares are worked out and the details of the different price options explained' (Shaw: 1982, p. 154). If one adds to this the difficulties of communicating changes to retailers as well as consumers, the problems of administrative friction are clear. To some extent this friction may be eased by the use of modern computer systems, but confusion for customers is still a factor. In practice the imperative need to generate revenue often overcomes longer-run concerns about harmful effects upon consumers, but the dangers of over-frequent fluctuations cannot be ignored.

Chapter summary

Managing relatively volatile demand around a relatively fixed capacity of highly perishable product supply is identified in previous chapters as one of the principal characteristics of travel and tourism marketing. The use of price, as one of the four main levers in the marketing mix, is particularly important in managing demand and revenue. But its successful use means reconciling customer interests and operational constraints within a strategic framework of business objectives. As stressed in Chapter 6, price must be integrated with the other three Ps to achieve the most cost effective results.

Two levels of pricing – strategic and tactical – are discussed, and these are themes developed in Chapters 12 and 13. Summarized in Figure 9.1, this chapter identifies and discusses the main influences taken into account in setting prices in practice and introduces the concept of *yield management* which measures the success achieved in pricing policies and balancing the earnings from customer segments. The chapter lays particular stress on the importance of non-price marketing options in tourism markets, the use of which enables marketing managers to reduce the sometimes dominating effects of price-elasticity and product substitution.

Price is a central concern in marketing all types of goods and services. It is often an obsession in many travel markets, especially those concerned with leisure segments, and it is essential that it should be kept in its proper perspective. It may often be the dominating influence in the short run, but it is one of four levers to be co-ordinated, not the only one. The implications of strategic and tactical pricing are further developed in Part Five of this book.

Further reading

Baker, M. J., *Marketing: An Introductory Text*, 4th
   edit., Macmillan, 1985, Chapter 14.
Kotler, P., *Marketing: Analysis, Planning,
   Implementation and Control*, 7th edit., Prentice-
   Hall International, 1991, Chapter 18.

Part Three

Planning Strategy and Tactics for Travel and Tourism Marketing

10

Organization for marketing: the role of marketing managers

Successful marketing requires skilled managers to plan marketing strategy and tactics, implement the marketing mix, and evaluate results. But marketing is only one part of business operations and it will not be effective in practice unless it is well-organized and integrated with all other business activities.

Effective marketing decisions in travel and tourism have to be integrated and co-ordinated with the management of service production operations, with personnel management, and with financial management and control. Because customers are present on the premises of service producers, even greater attention has to be given to the co-ordination of marketing and operations than is necessary in the production of physical goods manufactured by staff in factories away from the customer's gaze and participation.

It is because marketing is involved with so many aspects of corporate strategy and co-ordination with other departments of a business, that effective organization for marketing extends well beyond the simple internal aspects of how best to arrange the work load and reporting structure of the marketing and sales team. Marketing organization extends into the management structure as a whole. As Medlik expressed it for hotels, 'Organization is the framework in which various activities operate. It is concerned with such matters as the division of tasks within firms... positions of responsibility and authority, and relationships between them' (Medlik: 1989: 73).

For small businesses, such as guesthouses, small hotels or visitor attractions, marketing is the responsibility of the proprietor or general manager. Larger businesses will normally employ a marketing manager or director with one or more executive staff, according to the size of the operations. Special considerations apply where a large, multi-site organization, such as a chain of hotels, employs a head office marketing team as well as marketing and sales executives in each of the individual hotel units.

This chapter first identifies the tasks that are undertaken by marketing managers and have to be integrated with the other common business tasks (or functions as they are known), such as operations, finance and administration. It notes two dimensions in organization and describes how businesses have been traditionally organized according to *functions*, a pattern still found in many sectors of travel and tourism. The main problems with traditional ways to organize are noted from a marketing viewpoint, and the modern need for splitting businesses into manageable components, usually grouped around customers and their needs, is explained. A modern form of matrix organization for effective marketing is shown in Figure 10.2. The chapter discusses the personal qualities of successful marketing managers and ends by noting some of the marketing implications of organization for larger, multi-site groups with headquarters marketing staff.

Summary of marketing tasks to be organized

Undertaking successful marketing programmes for any size of business calls for management and executive actions, which may be grouped into three areas. The object of the list below is to identify the main tasks but not to discuss them, since each is covered later in the book:

- *Planning and control tasks*: marketing research, including undertaking or commissioning studies, gathering marketing intelligence, and interpreting the results (see Chapter 11); marketing planning, including strategy, tactics, and marketing mix decisions (Chapters 12 and 13); planning product presentation and promotion; planning marketing campaigns and budgeting; monitoring performance and evaluating marketing results (Chapter 14).

- *Implementation tasks*: attending workshops and exhibitions, conducting direct marketing operations, making and following up sales calls, briefing agencies, and undertaking the functions of advertising, PR, print, and sales promotion, (these tasks are discussed in Chapters 15–19).

- *Co-ordinating tasks*: liaison with operations, personnel, financial and other management to ensure that the delivery of products in terms of quality, timing and costs, is matched with promotion and presentation.

If a company markets only one or two products to one or two segments, the needs of marketing organization are minimal. But the tasks must still be carried out and co-ordinated in a logical sequence. Where there are several products for multiple markets, the problems of organizing the many tasks increase. It becomes essential to find ways to *group* operations and other business functions, in order to plan and control them effectively and achieve efficient marketing.

For large national and international corporations there is always an organizational issue in how best to inject marketing orientation, policy and strategies at board level so that marketing thinking is absorbed and implemented throughout the organization. When Sir Colin Marshall was appointed to British Airways, for example, in 1983, a traditionally organized airline 'underwent a dramatic and fundamental sea-change, becoming market-led – that is with the marketing department making the innovatory running – rather than planning and operations-led as had traditionally been the case'. A key organizational mechanism for achieving this was the formation of a board level Marketing Policy Group with a brief 'to spearhead the sweeping alterations in the airline's internal organization' (Reed: 1990, p. 79). In 1992 operations and marketing were combined under one director.

Two dimensions of marketing organization

As noted in the introduction to this chapter, there are two levels of marketing organization that have to be put together in practice.

At the lower level, organization means establishing a framework of responsibilities for undertaking the tasks summarized in the previous section. This is essentially an internal problem for the marketing team. At the simplest it may concern just one person, whose main problem is how best to organize his or her time.

At the higher level, organization means establishing a much wider framework of responsibilities, designed to ensure effective co-ordination links between marketing and the other essential business functions of a firm. This requires some consideration of what the other business functions are. At its simplest, Kotler notes, 'all companies start out with four simple functions. Someone must raise and manage capital (finance), produce the product... (operations), sell it (sales), and keep the books (accounting)' (Kotler: 1984, p. 717).

To these four basic functions it is necessary to add some refinements in order to bring the discussion up to date. Larger businesses in the travel and tourism industry have a personnel or human resource management function to recruit, train, pay and manage staff in accordance with legal requirements. Many have a properties/capital equipment management function, to purchase, develop and maintain the capital assets and ensure compliance with their own and externally regulated environmental policies and controls. Most have marketing functions extending far beyond the narrow concern for sales. These functions can be represented in a simple chart, relevant in principle to most large service businesses in travel and tourism. See Figure 10.1.

The traditional, functional structure of business organization

In Figure 10.1, in each of the four main functions including marketing, there are managers, executives and operational staff who are specialists in their particular roles, e.g. in purchasing, in finance, and in personnel. In larger firms the specialists are generally represented by a senior manager or a director for each of the functions, and they report through a chief executive to a board of directors. Co-ordination may occur informally in this organizational structure through consultation and meetings between managers, and formally

through scheduled co-ordinating meetings and the board. As commercial firms and public sector bodies increase in size, the need for specialists tends to increase. The specialist focus is denoted in Figure 10.1 by the vertical arrows under each main function.

Understandably, the operations division of service businesses (the equivalent of manufacturing production for makers of physical goods), has traditionally tended to be seen as the most important of the management functions. Operations produce the products, handle the customers, maintain quality controls and receive the revenue. Operations are also responsible for most of a firm's costs. The efficiency of the operations division is therefore often perceived as the basis of business success or failure. An operations focus is, of course, just another way of describing production orientation (see Chapter 2). For a hotel, production processes include food and beverage management, front of house operations, housekeeping, and room services. For a managed visitor attraction, production processes include reception and ticket issuing, cleaning and maintenance of exhibits and buildings, operation of shops, cafes, cloakrooms, provision of information, and security services. When markets are growing, operations are understandably the principal focus of management attention. If the growth in demand levels off, competition increases and the focus of attention shifts to sales and then to marketing. Such a shift of focus usually forces changes in the organization of companies.

Figure 10.1 reflects a traditional orientation in service companies, in which sales and marketing are typically perceived and used as a service function required to support the operations division. As the most recent of the four business functions to emerge, and it is still emerging in many parts of the travel and tourism industry, sales and marketing are too often seen as an extra or 'bolt on' specialist service, not an integral part of the business. Marketing people in production-orientated firms tend to be treated

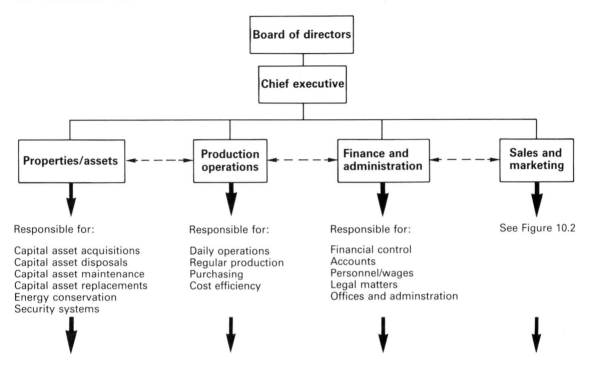

Figure 10.1 *Traditional functional organization of a service business in travel and tourism*

primarily as specialists in various processes (or functions), such as advertising, sales promotion, and marketing research. In such a traditional structure the value of marketing people is often only understood in a tactical, reactive sense of generating customer demand when it is needed. But, even if the essentially proactive and strategic role of marketing outlined in this book is recognized in such firms, its full potential is unlikely to be achieved, because traditional organization structures are not conducive to it.

Because the concept of a formalized marketing function is still relatively new to most service businesses, it is often difficult to define where marketing specialists should be positioned in the organization structure, what their responsibilities and authorities should be, and precisely what should be expected of them beyond a somewhat reactive advertising or public relations role (Lovelock: 1984, p. 413).

The need to divide and group business operations into manageable components

As businesses grow and become more competitive, senior managers normally have to examine the efficiency of their production processes and other business functions more closely. Often the most effective way to do this in practice is to divide a total business into its component parts, or 'mini-businesses'. This is normally done by identifying particular groupings of operations having costs and revenues that can be separately calculated. Cost and revenue 'centres', as they are normally known, are usually associated with particular products aimed at particular market segments (see also Chapter 12).

For a tour operator with winter and summer products, it is usually possible to split the costs and revenues associated with the operation of summer sun packages from the equivalent data for winter sun products. Analysis of the figures may show that summer business is far more profitable per unit of staff, marketing, and office overheads, than the operation of winter packages. Examining the specific winter business in terms of all its direct costs and revenues may reveal areas of weakness that can be rectified, possibly with a different approach to marketing. Such analysis is only possible once the relevant costs and revenues have been clearly identified.

Although it may appear simple, it is often far from obvious how best to define the cost and revenue centres of a total business. Analysing the main customer groupings or segments provides a logical basis for dividing most service businesses. It is customer orientated and thus provides the basis for a marketing rather than an operation-based grouping. An alternative method is to divide a business up into logical groups of products, provided that adequate research is available for the consumers and segments that support the products.

Dividing businesses by purpose

Of the various ways in which businesses may be sub-divided and organized by purpose, Baker notes the three main groupings which are alternative to the traditional organization by functional specialisms (1979, p. 104). These are:

- *Product-based*: business operations are grouped into the main products provided, but this type of grouping does not necessarily imply *production orientation*.
- *Market-based*: business operations are grouped around the main markets which a business serves; this type of grouping is also a traditional approach to selling and does not necessarily imply *marketing orientation*.
- *Area-based*: business operations are grouped around the regions, territories or countries a business serves.

To give brief examples, a large hotel may organize its production operations according to products such as banqueting, conferences, exhibitions, executive suites, or short-stay leisure packages. Each of these groupings represents one or more products offered to one or more customer segments.

A tour operator may organize its operations according to the types of customer it serves, such as winter-sports enthusiasts, senior citizens, families with children or young people in the age group 18–35. Each of these is a segment to which may be offered one or more products.

A national tourist office, or an airline with an overseas network, will usually tend to organize its operations according to the geographical areas it serves. Within each of the areas it may identify several segments for each of which one or more products will be required.

Dividing up businesses, as described above, leads logically to a conclusion that separate marketing activity is required for each of the cost/revenue centres identified. Effective marketing has to be organized around the needs of product/market groupings, and may not easily be provided as a functional specialism on the centralized basis noted in Figure 10.1. If the organization is large enough, separate marketing personnel may be needed for each product/market group.

Potential conflict between grouping by segments and grouping by business operations

For reasons set out in Chapter 7, it is usually impossible for a large organization to market a single product to customers. It is necessary to identify segments, which become the basis for developing targeted marketing campaigns. The delivery of products in travel and tourism means putting together particular bundles or groupings of service operations (see Chapter 8).

Thus segment/product groupings are a logical consumer-orientated basis for the conduct of businesses, and provide a logical framework for organizing operations and business processes generally, including marketing. In due course the cost-effectiveness of campaigns is measured against segment and product-specific objectives, and the financial rewards of managers are often geared to the level of success achieved.

Thus there are two sets of interests to be served by an organizational structure: those of managers responsible for *operations* or business processes, and those of managers responsible for *customer groups*. In discussing these interests Piercy suggests that the critical problem facing any large organization is how to achieve 'a compromise between grouping [business activities] by purpose ... and grouping by process ... in an attempt to retain the advantages of a functional specialism at the same time as gaining the strengths of a sharper focus on the market segment'. He identifies 'purpose' with market segments (or products, or projects); he sees 'processes' as functions, specialisms or disciplines (Piercy: 1985, p. 159).

This brief discussion of the underlying reasons why businesses are increasingly being split up into manageable components can only hint at a most important management debate. Around the world, large commercial organizations and others in the public sector are finding it more efficient to manage and control their operations on the basis of cost/revenue centres, rather than through centralized headquarters' planning and control. For transnational corporations with bases in several countries, organization by cost/revenue groupings is the principal way to achieve efficiency and flexibility. This change of emphasis amounts to a managerial revolution that goes much deeper than marketing and draws on all aspects of modern management techniques. In the last decade the process of decentralization and sub-division has been greatly facilitated by the emergence and sophistication of information-processing technology, which creates the continuous information flows needed for managers to identify and control the new groupings. Since the new divisions of business usually have marketing origins or implications, marketing managers are at the forefront of this modern managerial revolution. The sub-division of businesses has strategic and tactical implications for marketing, which are discussed in Chapters 12 and 13.

Modern customer-based organizational structure for marketing

Earlier in the chapter Figure 10.1 noted a traditional function or process-based organizational structure, in which marketing is seen as a set of specialisms providing services to the other major business functions. By contrast, Figure 10.2 shows a modern customer-based organizational structure, in which all the business functions, including marketing, are grouped around particular market (or product or area) groupings; these groupings are cost/revenue centres, shown as A, B, and C.

Figure 10.2 is a matrix organization, so called because it highlights the interaction between columns (management functions and specialisms) and rows (groupings of the business, which cut across all columns). The lateral arrows in Figure 10.2 illustrate how the management of the sub-groups of the business (including marketing) extends sideways, through co-ordination, across the responsibilities of the main operational functions. It can be seen that they cut across the specific specialisms within the marketing function, too.

To illustrate what this matrix organization means in practice, consider the case of an international airline that has decided to split its total operations into cost/revenue centres for first class travel, business-class travel, economy products, and charter operations. A management group responsible for business travel will have responsibility for the costs and revenues of that sector of operations and draw the functional skills of different managers together within a team in which marketing must have a key role to play. The marketing manager appointed for business travel, for example, is directly responsible for all the tasks noted at the beginning of this chapter, summarized as planning, implementation and co-ordination. The job comprises researching into the market, forecasting business traffic flows, agreeing the seat capacity to be operated (in the context of all other operational constraints), and agreeing the levels and quality of service to be provided to the customers by the cabin staff. He will also help negotiate the size of the budget to be spent on marketing business travel, and the way in which that budget is spent. The marketing manager reports both to the manager of the business-travel group and to a marketing director, who has to co-ordinate the budgets and activities of the other marketing managers and

resolve any conflicts that may arise with operations and other functional divisions.

At the end of the budget year a marketing manager is expected to evaluate the results of marketing efforts in detail and to account for the success or failure of the programmes that were recommended. He may well have salary bonuses tied to results achieved.

Davidson notes that the 'marketing department is the link between the firm and the market place. It represents the views of consumers to the company, and works out, with other departments, how to transfer these views into profitable products' (1975, p. 79). Davidson and others stress that, without marketing managers to represent the customer point of view internally within the firm, there is no natural process whereby this happens automatically. In market conditions in which customer needs, attitudes and expectations change very rapidly, as is often the case in travel and tourism, this internal function of customer

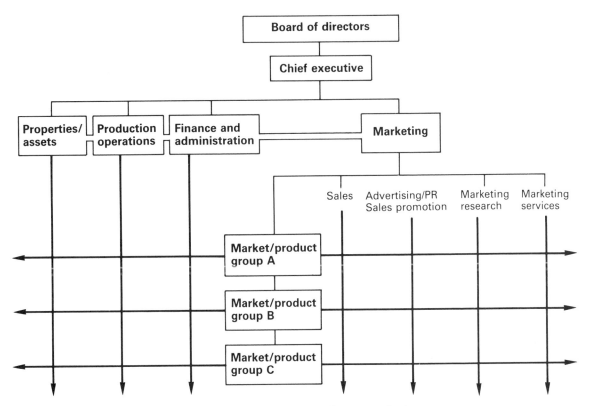

Figure 10.2 *Modern customer-based matrix organization for effective marketing*

representation is vital in achieving fast, effective responses on the part of general management.

Product, brand or marketing managers?

It creates much confusion, but there is no agreement in practice on the job titles given to marketing executives. There are three basic choices used in travel and tourism:

- Brand manager.
- Product manager.
- Market or marketing manager.

In hotels in particular, job titles often incorporates sales, as, for example, 'sales and marketing manager'.

It is possible to attribute to each of these titles a separate meaning, and many marketing texts do so. This author finds the distinctions drawn are largely irrelevant in travel and tourism practice, where titles often reflect traditional practice or current fashion. All that matters for the purposes of understanding what a job entails is whether the marketing person (by whatever title) carries out the tasks of marketing set out in this chapter or not. In particular, is the marketing person responsible for the tasks of co-ordination and implementing marketing programmes in collaboration with others? If the answer is yes, it is simpler to use the generic title of marketing executive or marketing manager than to worry about the niceties of product, brand or market management. In this author's experience there is many a so-called advertising manager or sales manager who is responsible in practice for the full range of marketing functions, and many a so-called brand or product manager who is not. If a manager or executive is responsible for only one of the functions, such as advertising or sales, then it is better to use the functional title, as in sales manager.

Apart from disagreements over the titles, there is a continuing academic debate over the extent to which marketing managers actually 'manage', and are less relevant in the 1990s than they were in the 1960s–1980s. Certainly it is incorrect to see a marketing manager as necessarily having executive power over the specialists who manage operations processes: his primary role is one of persuasion, liaison and co-ordination rather than one of control. But as long as it is necessary to split up large businesses into smaller components for management and marketing purposes, and over that issue there appears to be no disagreement, it will be necessary to find adequate arrangements to plan, implement and control marketing programmes. That means marketing managers acting as generalists rather than specialists, and their future role, whatever their titles, appears likely to become more, rather than less, important.

Personal qualities for successful marketing managers

As many readers of this book are likely to be, or aspiring to be marketing managers (by whatever job title their employers use), it may be helpful to indicate the principal qualities which are common to successful practitioners. These qualities are not specific to travel and tourism, but applicable to any form of marketing. They are as follows:

- *Energetic*: very active, competitive, and aggressive rather than passive by nature.
- *Creative*: in thought processes and in seeking out opportunities to develop and exploit, especially at the margins of revenue generation so vital to the profitability of service businesses. Artistic creativity is not an essential attribute, since this is normally achieved through the use of advertising and other promotional agencies.
- *Good communicator*: (a) as an advocate for his product (or market) interests, at meetings, in presentations and in documents, and (b) in securing vital co-operation and goodwill among managers whose actions he may influence but cannot control.

- *Numerate*: not necessarily competent in statistical methodology, but very confident and intuitive in analysing and appreciating meaning from the mass of data that flows continuously across marketing desks.
- *Good administrator*: able to handle and organize the numerous administrative and progress-chasing details associated with managing any marketing programme.

Finally, to this list of desirable characteristics should be added the quality of judgement. Impossible to define with precision, judgement is an ability to weigh the many imponderables in any marketing decision and decide on a course that is bold in the context of evaluated risks but not unnecessarily risky. Judgement is also an intuitive sense of knowing when to change previous decisions, either to limit the damage caused by inevitable mistakes or to back a hunch. Because so many marketing decisions have to be made ahead of the customer decisions that are their only final validation (you don't know if it works until the customers pay or stay away), the ability to make balanced judgements of events is crucial.

The reader may observe many military analogies in the language of marketing: strategies, campaigns, tactics, pre-emptive strikes (against competitors), targeting, loss leaders, logistics, and so on. Not for nothing does Davidson describe product managers as the 'storm troopers of marketing' (Davidson: 1975, p. 95). The qualities of successful marketing managers are certainly akin to those of successful military leaders. Good judgement, confidence, and steady nerves are as essential in generals as they are in marketing directors of large companies, and for much the same reasons.

Organization for group marketing of multi-site corporations

Any individually owned business, such as a car-rental firm based on one garage, a proprietor-

owned hotel, or a retail travel agent with one office, will be solely responsible for organizing and implementing its own marketing activities. But if a business such as a hotel group contains many individual units, totally different organizational considerations for marketing apply. For example, Avis, in car rental, Holiday Inn in hotels, and Thomas Cook in tour operation and travel retailing, all have corporate marketing staff at their headquarter offices, and they are responsible for group marketing policy. To operate effectively as a group, products and operational processes – including marketing – have to be standardized as far as possible, so that customers can purchase the same reliable products at any of the group's locations under the same corporate image.

Co-ordinated marketing programmes for groups are usually designed to cover the promotion of group images and the deliberate 'branding' of group products. Brochures and other sales literature tend to be identical, or at least clearly identified with group logos and themes; sales promotions are often the same and co-ordinated between units; and prices, product presentation and customer services are as closely harmonized as possible.

Obviously, group policy restricts the room for individual units to exercise their own marketing discretion, and it is not unusual for unit managers to have very little influence over the external marketing of the units for whose profits they are nominally responsible. In group hotels the unit manager's discretion may be limited to promoting functions in the local catchment area of the hotel, liaising with local businesses to promote the use of the hotel, undertaking local public relations, and direct-mailing particular product offers to addresses of existing customers. Unit managers retain principal responsibility for 'in-house' promotions, but even these may be organized with materials provided by head office. While the percentages vary from one unit to another, it is unlikely that many unit managers in nationally promoted groups are responsible for generating more than about a fifth of their unit's total sales revenue. The balance of marketing power has shifted from the unit to the group, increasingly organized around cost and profit-centred groupings of products and segments. Achieving better synergy in marketing between group HQs and individual units remains an important issue to tackle in the 1990s.

Chapter summary

Organizing for effective marketing in larger businesses means establishing a framework in which marketing managers and executives can use their skills to best effect. This framework has two levels, of which the most important is that which facilitates integration between marketing functions and the other business functions of any commercial firm or public sector body. Unfortunately there are no simple answers to optimum organization structures, partly because organization has to fit within the ruling 'corporate culture', partly because it reflects ways in which different personalities at senior level are able to work together, and partly because the market/product groupings are usually in a state of constant internal and externally caused change. Most managers will be aware of confusion in the best-run organizations – no doubt it is part of the human condition – but there are some underlying principles based on marketing, as this chapter explains.

The traditional type of function-based organization often encountered in travel and tourism is shown in Figure 10.1. In such an organizational structure, 'although marketing has assumed greater importance in recent years, the operations function still dominates line management in most service industries' (Lovelock: 1984, p. 415). Traditional organizational structure is contrasted with a modern form of matrix organization, summarized in Figure 10.2. This latter type of structure enables marketing to play its full role in the conduct of business operations. It is especially relevant where large businesses are split into cost/profit centres, usually reflecting particular groups of products and segments.

Successful marketing requires skilled professionals who need the special blend of personal characteristics noted in this chapter. Because many marketing managers are managers in title only, it is stressed that the skills of persuasion and co-operation are always important.

Further reading

Baker, M. J., *Marketing: An Introductory Text*, 4th edit., Macmillan, 1985, Chapter 7.

Kotler, P., *Marketing Management: Analysis, Planning, Implementation and Control*, 7th edit., Prentice-Hall International, 1991, Chapter 25.

11

Marketing research: the information base for effective marketing

What marketing managers know of market trends, consumer segments, buyer behaviour, product performance, and consumers' response to all aspects of marketing campaigns, is mostly derived from one or more aspects of marketing-research activity. The planning processes at both strategic and operational levels, discussed in Chapters 12 and 13, are research-based. This chapter, therefore, focuses on techniques that are essential in successful marketing practice.

In relation to computer programmes, most readers will be aware of the maxim, 'garbage in, garbage out'. In other words, if the information or data fed into a computer is inaccurate or inadequate, one cannot hope for useful results. There is a marketing-research parallel because the whole of marketing strategy and operations are also calculated responses using information input. The lower the quality (or absence) of information used for marketing decisions, the higher the risks of marketing failures, especially in strongly competitive markets.

Some authors draw distinctions between market research, consumer research and marketing research. But for all practical purposes, the term *marketing research* can be used to include all research based information used in making marketing decisions.

Commencing with an initial definition, this chapter identifies the six main types of marketing research. It next describes ten kinds of marketing-research activity, widely used in travel and tourism, which readers can expect to find in practice. The next section explains a typical 'menu' of marketing research choices available to operators, and illustrates it in a travel and tourism context. The final part of the chapter indicates how to use a market-research agency, and comments on test marketing and monitoring for travel and tourism products.

Marketing research defined

Marketing research is an organized information process, which 'has to do with the gathering, processing, analysis, storage and dissemination of information to facilitate and improve decision making' (Seibert: 1973, p. 128). The value of this definition is that it is sufficiently broad to encompass the whole range of systematic information inputs. This ranges from regular analysis of customer databases, 'intelligence' gathered by a sales force, or cuttings taken from the travel trade press, up to full-scale sample survey research on a national or international scale.

Most authors stress that marketing research

cannot, as is commonly supposed, provide solutions to management problems. Research can seldom ensure correct decisions. What it can do is reduce the amount of uncertainty and risk associated with the results of marketing decisions, and focus attention on the probable implications of alternative courses of action. As Luck *et al.*, put it, 'Imagination, judgement and courage remain important qualities for the successful decision maker. Research is the handmaiden of competent management but never its substitute' (Luck *et al.*: 1970, p. 8).

From observation of the way that travel and tourism businesses are conducted in many countries around the world, it appears to be a distinctive feature of the industry that the use of marketing research is weaker than in any other major industry dealing with consumer products. Of course there are exceptions, although they are mainly the very large international corporations in air transport, tour operations, car rental, and some hotel groups. The reason for this weakness appears to be rooted in the increasingly irrelevant assumption that research is not needed when producers and customers meet face to face on the producer's premises; that through such contact, managers 'know' their customers without the need for expensive research. This may still be true for guesthouses and individual neighbourhood travel agencies but it is increasingly untrue for larger businesses, especially those with multi-site operations. The presence of customers on the premises is, however, a most important marketing asset to be exploited systematically by producers, and this point is developed at the end of the chapter. The reasons for using marketing research, and the techniques available, are essentially the same for travel and tourism as for any other form of consumer marketing.

Judgement or research?

In practice it is nearly always the case that managers have to take most decisions with less than adequate information. The cost of obtaining additional information has to be measured in time as well as money, and must always be relevant to the prospective gain or loss at risk in the decisions that are made. For example, faced with a decision between two alternative designs for a brochure cover, a marketing manager for a tour operating company has either to exercise judgement or commission a survey to evaluate target customers' responses to the two designs.

Where millions of brochures are to be printed, a 10 per cent better customer reaction to one of the designs could pay off in thousands of additional bookings. Research in this case would be justified if waiting for results did not delay production and distribution. For smaller operators the expense would rarely be justified by the potential extra business, and close attention to the print design brief (itself research-based) would have to suffice, together with experience and judgement gained with other brochures.

By contrast, a strategic decision by a business such as a theme park to restructure its product by major investment in new facilities would always justify marketing research studies at a cost related to the size of the investment. Such research would be needed to inform decisions about the scope and range of the new facilities, and the design of the new product in terms of identified market needs, behaviour patterns, and visitors' capacity to pay. For example, if research indicated that visitors would spend only 2 hours at a new attraction and not 4 hours, the implications for car parking, prices, display and content, would be critical. In practice there is always a requirement to balance the need to know against the cost in time and money.

Six main categories of marketing research

It would be possible to draw up a list of several dozen different types of research. Such a list would not be helpful to the student of marketing, however, and an understanding of

Table 11.1 *Six main categories of marketing research*

Research category	Used in	Typical marketing use
1 Market analysis and forecasting	Marketing planning	Measurement and projections of market volumes, shares and revenue by relevant categories of market segments and product types
2 Consumer research	Segmentation and positioning	(a) Quantitative measurement of consumer profiles, awareness, attitudes and purchasing behaviour including consumer audits (b) Qualitative assessments of consumer needs, perceptions and aspirations
3 Products and price studies	Product formulation, presentation and pricing	Measurement and consumer testing of amended and new product formulations, and price sensitivity studies
4 Promotions and sales research	Efficiency of communications	Measurement of consumer reaction to alternative advertising concepts and media usage; response to various forms of sales promotion, and sales-force effectiveness
5 Distribution research	Efficiency of distribution network	Distributor awareness of products, stocking and display of brochures, and effectiveness of merchandising, including retail audits and occupancy studies
6 Evaluation and performance monitoring studies	Overall control of marketing results and product quality control	Measurement of customer satisfaction overall, and by product elements, including measurement through marketing tests and experiments

the six main categories of marketing research noted in Table 11.1 will be adequate for most purposes. The six categories correspond exactly with the information needs required to make efficient decisions for marketing-mix programmes, and the strategic and operational plans within which they are implemented. The categories in Table 11.1 are common to any marketing organization dealing with consumers, although the uses noted are specific to travel and tourism.

Ten kinds of marketing research commonly used in travel and tourism

Because marketing research has become a large and complex sector of economic activity in its own right, it has inevitably produced its own technical vocabulary. This chapter makes no attempt to cover the full range of technical terms but ten commonly used in practice to denote different research methods, will be found helpful and are discussed below. They are:

● Continuous and *ad hoc*.
● Quantitative and qualitative.
● Primary and secondary.
● Omnibus and syndicated.
● Retail audit and consumer audit.

Continuous and *ad hoc*

Commercial organizations are finding it increasingly necessary to measure certain key trend data on a regular, or 'continuous' basis. 'Continuous' in this context may mean daily, weekly or monthly. Data covering sales volume, market shares, customer satisfaction, hotel bed occupancy and booking patterns, are typical examples of 'continuous' marketing-research measures in travel and tourism. For reasons developed later in Chapter 19, continuous information may be integrated within a database, which provides a fertile source of information for marketing-mix decisions generally.

There are also many specific problems in marketing that require research relevant to a particular circumstance. For example, could a redesigned guide book at a visitor attraction, with a print life of say 3 years, produce extra sales revenue? Would the introduction of a buffet style instead of full service lunch reduce customer satisfaction or increase it? Does market size warrant investment in a new hotel, and what size and level of service is justified? To inform such management decisions a specific or *ad hoc* investigation would be needed.

Most marketing-research programmes are a mixture of continuous research to monitor trends and *ad hoc* surveys to illuminate identified problems or opportunities as they occur.

Quantitative and qualitative

Traditionally, most consumer research studies depend on questions asked of random samples of existing or potential customers. They are used to establish the relevant segments possessing particular characteristics of interest to marketing managers. For example, a coach-tour operator may need to know that 60 per cent of adults took a holiday in a given year, of whom a third travelled abroad, stayed an average of ten nights away from home, and spent £400 per capita. The operator would also want to know what proportion used coaches and cars, and how that proportion varied year by year, month by month, by type of client, and so on. All these are quantifiable dimensions which, with due allowance for statistical variation, can be projected into the tens or hundreds of thousands of people comprising total market volume: hence, quantitative research, meaning studies to which numerical estimates can be attached. Quantitative research is always based on 'structured' questionnaires in which every respondent is asked identical questions. Mostly the range of possible answers is also printed on questionnaires, based on previous experience, and variations to suit individual respondents are not possible.

Quantitative methods are less suitable for exploring consumer attitudes, feelings, desires or perceptions, because often the researcher cannot predict the ways in which people think about different products. It is always possible to construct hypothetical answers and ask people to agree or disagree, but these may not get at what really matters to prospective buyers. For example, Wales as a destination has many surveys quantifying likes and dislikes in terms of scenery, heritage, villages, beaches, weather etc. To dig deeper, the Wales Tourist Board in 1984 commissioned group discussions of target travellers, who were invited in groups of six to eight to talk informally about holidays in general and Wales in particular. The discussion leader, trained in social psychology, was responsible for introducing the subjects for discussion and encouraging views, but did not impose her own preconceived ideas. What emerged, recorded for analysis on tape, was a discussion in consumers' own words concerning what mattered to them. This is qualitative research.

In the case of Wales a fairly widespread concern emerged among prospective visitors that possible dislike of the English by the Welsh could create a negative, cold, or even hostile atmosphere, which is obviously not conducive to holiday motivations. Other research among people who had recently visited Wales indicated that in fact the welcome they received was generally warm and friendly. Responding to this perception problem became an aspect of WTB communications. The research was also used as the basis for communicating the need for more friendly attitudes by the tourism industry in Wales. By definition, such surveys cannot be quantitative, because the ideas are not tied down to structured questionnaires or based on adequate samples of the target group. They can be used to structure subsequent quantitative surveys, or they can be used in their own right to help marketing managers understand the ways in which travellers think, and what matters to them.

In recent years, given adequate quantification of the main patterns of visitor behaviour, qualitative studies have been more widely used. They are especially useful in designing advertising messages and brochure contents, in ways best calculated to communicate with prospective customers in their own terms.

Primary and secondary

Primary data is a label applied to marketing research specifically commissioned by a business to contribute to its decisions. It requires the gathering of data not available from any other (secondary) source. For example, a survey commissioned by one airline to study business travellers' current attitudes towards other airlines competing on the same route would be primary data.

Secondary data is information gathered originally for a purpose not related to the specific needs of a business, but which may be used by it as part of its information search. All published sources, including government statistics, trade association surveys and commercial publishers' market surveys, represent secondary data.

It is common sense that it will always be quicker and cheaper to obtain and use secondary rather than primary data. For any decision requiring research information, initial investigation should always begin at the secondary level before proceeding, if necessary, with primary research.

Omnibus and syndicated

Not only in travel and tourism, but in consumer markets generally, there has been a growing tendency for market-research companies to operate their own regular (continuous) sample surveys and sell space in them to a range of customers. Such surveys are known technically as 'omnibus' surveys, because they are potentially open to all users. Where an organization seeks answers to say four or five key questions, it may be possible to get access to a nationally representative sample of 2,000 adults for a tenth of the cost of commissioning its own survey. For the price, a client would not only get answers to his questions but also fully cross-tabulated data, using profile characteristics, such as age and readership of media, which are a standard part of any 'omnibus'. The United Kingdom Tourism Survey (UKTS) is probably the best known survey of UK tourism. It is in fact a series of questions regularly asked on an MAI Research Ltd omnibus survey. There are many other omnibus surveys available, covering not only adults but many segments, such as motorists, doctors, business travellers, frequent users of hotels, and so on.

Syndicated surveys serve much the same purpose as omnibus surveys but are usually commissioned by a group of clients on a cost sharing basis. Frequently one major user draws in others on the basis, for example, of dividing costs by the number of questions asked. The British National Travel Survey (BNTS) is a syndicated survey commissioned annually.

Both syndicated and omnibus studies provide cost-effective research, especially for smaller businesses, for whom the costs of an *ad hoc* survey would usually be prohibitive. By using such studies, firms can also obtain technical assistance from research agencies with the wording of questions and interpretation of results. The omnibus method is especially suitable for achieving quantified results much faster than would be possible with *ad hoc* surveys.

Retail and consumer audit

In many sectors of consumer-goods marketing, but to a much lesser extent in travel and tourism, the most common forms of continuous marketing research are consumer and retail audits. It is no accident that two of the largest international marketing research companies, AGB Ltd and A C Nielsen, have built their multinational operations on such audits.

Initiated as long ago as the 1930s for manufacturers of products sold through grocery/chemist retail outlets, retail audits are based on visiting shops and physically checking and analysing product stocks, purchases from wholesalers, and consumer sales in a sample of retail outlets selected to represent the national pattern. Such audits, carried out at regular monthly or 2-monthly intervals in grocery and chemist outlets, for example, measure the volume of sales by product type, the average sales price, the volume of stocks, and the proportion of outlets with stock on display. Of course much of the data is now audited by computers rather than physical checks. The results collected in the sample of audited outlets are then used to project the estimated sales in the total number (universe) of outlets from which the sample was selected. In travel and tourism various agencies have audited holiday bookings and brochure display for tour operators, using samples of travel agencies. For hotels and other forms of accommodation, occupancy studies in samples of accommodation units perform the same 'audit' function for the accommodation sector, and have been used reliably for many years.

Consumer audits follow the same basic principles of regular reporting from nationally representative samples, based in this case on panels of consumers who keep specially designed diaries, in which all purchases are recorded. Since the profile of the samples is known in detail, recorded purchases can be analysed by segmentation data. The use of diary panels on an experimental basis to record travel and tourism behaviour has been tried in the UK in recent years, e.g. to measure day visits from home. But the results produced have not thus far proved reliable. In the Netherlands the Central Bureau for Statistics has used diary panels since 1980 to measure holidays of 4 or more nights away from home, and is satisfied with the reliability of the methodology for that purpose.

A menu of marketing research methods

Drawing together the different categories of marketing research noted earlier, and the types of approach that are commonly used, it is possible to present the wide range of methods available to any operator as a 'menu'. 'Menu' simply means an available listing of research techniques, from which it is possible to make a selection according to need and circumstances. Each technique is available at a price. The menu, in a form relevant to producers of travel and tourism services, is shown in Figure 11.1. The menu concept is developed from papers originally presented at a UK Market Research Society training course. It is important to stress that the 'menu' means prospective users can select items according to their needs and budget. Only the largest organizations, with research staff and budgets in excess of say £100,000 per annum, are likely to need or be able to use all the items over a period of 12 months.

A Desk research (secondary sources)

1 Sales/bookings/reservations records; daily, weekly, etc. by type of customer, type of product, etc.
2 Visitor information records e.g. guest registration cards, booking form data.
3 Government publications/trade association data/national tourist office data/abstracts/libraries.
4 Commercial analyses available on subscription or purchase of reports.
5 Previous research studies conducted; internal data bank.
6 Press cuttings of competitor activities, market environment changes.

B Qualitative or exploratory research

1 Organized marketing intelligence, such as sales-force reports, attendance at exhibitions and trade shows.
2 Group discussions and individual interviews with targeted customers/non users – to identify perceptions and attitudes.
3 Observational studies of visitor behaviour, using cameras or trained observers.
4 Marketing experiments with monitored results.

C Quantitative research (syndicated)

1 Omnibus questions of targeted respondents.
2 Syndicated surveys, including audits.

D Quantitative research (ad hoc and continuous)

1 Studies of travel and tourism behaviour and usage/activity patterns.
2 Attitude, image, perception and awareness studies.
3 Advertising and other media response studies.
4 Customer satisfaction and product monitoring studies.
5 Distribution studies amongst retail outlets.

Figure 11.1 *The marketing research menu*

Using the 'menu' – a holiday-park operator

To help explain the possible selective use of the menu in travel and tourism practice, consider a holiday-park operator in England with eight parks comprising some 2,000 caravans and chalets for let on a weekly or part weekly basis. A turnover of around £7 million would be realistic for such an operator, with a marketing budget of, say, £500,000, of which say £30,000 is allocated for research (all in 1992 prices). Such a

budget could be deployed as follows:

Use of menu items in Figure 11.1

A1 A computerized record system would show bookings for each park on a weekly basis, with analyses of areas from which bookings flow, type of caravan/chalet most or least in demand, size of party, etc. Many of these data would be required for producing business accounts and customer invoices.

A2 On a continuous or a sample basis, customers checking in on arrival could be asked to complete a short form establishing, for example, the incidence of repeat visits, how they heard of the park, whether the park brochure was seen, and distance travelled from home.

A3 Published results of tourist board surveys, e.g. UKTS and BNTS, would throw useful light on trends for the self-catering market nationally and by region. Occasional other inexpensive analyses of the market would be available from time to time (**A4**). Several journals for the holiday parks and caravan industry provide valuable insights into current events and trends in the market (**A6**).

A5 Previous years' records (as in **A1** and **A2**) would provide valuable benchmarks against which to view current patterns on a weekly or monthly basis.

B1 There are numerous trade shows and travel workshops available for the caravan/chalet park operator, as well as national conferences. All provide opportunities to see what others in the industry are doing, especially in terms of park design, accommodation-unit design, product presentation in brochures, and so on.

In terms of the foregoing uses of marketing research, assuming that management time is excluded from the cost and that business records are a by-product of essential accounting procedures, the total expenditure would be measured in hundreds rather than thousands of pounds. To proceed beyond this point calls for more significant expenditure, to be set off against the expected value of results.

B2 Not affordable on an annual basis in this example, the decision to renew the main brochure could repay discussion of alternative covers, contents, and formats conducted with small groups of prospective clients. Such group discussions would also generate ideas and concepts for advertising. With 2,000 units to let, this operator might distribute 300,000 brochures per annum at a cost of say £150,000 (including distribution via retail travel agents), so that up

to £15,000 on group discussions could be productive spread over a 3-year brochure life-span, assessed against sales revenue achievable.

B3 If, for example, the capacity of showers and laundry facilities is open to review at one or more of the parks, cameras or simple observation of queues and their reactions would be a cheap but effective form of research.

B4 In terms of pricing, different advertising formats, and product developments, e.g. mini-breaks, this operator is perfectly placed to engage in systematic test marketing and monitoring (see later in this chapter) at low cost.

C2 Park owners of this type in Britain may be able to purchase packs of printed, standardized, self-completion questionnaires designed by a commercial market research agency. Owners would be responsible for distributing and ensuring completion by samples of visitors, and collecting questionnaires. The price per thousand of these standard questionnaire forms (similar in concept to those used by tour operators to measure customer satisfaction at the end of a holiday) would usually be less than 10 per cent of the cost of conducting surveys with trained interviewers on site. These forms are designed for electronic scanning by machines, so that the costs of manual coding and checking are reduced. Understandably, commercial research agencies would aim to syndicate this type of research across several parks to make it a profitable exercise for themselves. A standard provision of basic cross-tabulations would be included within the price, with extra cost for additional analysis.

D4 Of the **D** options, **D4** would be particularly important for this type of operator.

Administered as part of a syndicated (**C2**) survey, or as a separate entity during, say, six selected weeks of the operating year, measuring satisfaction would probably account for the largest portion of annual marketing research expenditure in this example. Analysed by type of product, type of customer, time of year, and in association with any test marketing initiatives, the value of this research in marketing planning would be considerable.

Using a market-research agency

While the great majority of marketing managers can expect to use marketing research data regularly, relatively few will be also engaged in organizing and conducting surveys. Large organizations such as airlines, tourist boards and major hotel corporations have their own research departments, but most survey work will be commissioned from specialist market-research agencies. There were over 400 in the UK in 1990 with an estimated turnover of around £400 million. It is therefore important that marketing managers should be aware of what agencies do and how to get the best response from them.

In the UK the Market Research Society (MRS) is the professional body for all individuals using survey techniques for market, social and economic research. With some 6,500 members, the MRS claims to be the largest body of its kind in the world (MRS, 1990) and it has developed and published sophisticated codes of professional conduct over many years. These codes are designed to protect and enhance the integrity with which research is practised, and to safeguard the interests of the general public and clients as well as the interests of agencies offering research services. Similar codes exist in several other European countries.

In research, as in most of marketing practice, the best way to achieve cost effective work is to specify the problem with as much precision as possible, setting it in its wider marketing context. Unless a client and an agency have worked together on a regular basis, it is unlikely that agencies asked to quote for surveys will be experts on the client's business. Unless the budget is unusually large in travel and tourism terms, there will not be many hours available for the agency to absorb the key details of the

clients' marketing programmes and analysis (expressed as 'diagnosis' and 'prognosis' in Chapter 13 on use of research data in marketing planning). Time spent learning about the business will be time not available for developing the research approach.

'Problems' in marketing are seldom clear cut. They are frequently matters of perception and judgement, and two managers may well see the same problem in different ways. Time spent systematically analysing the problem therefore is seldom wasted. It focuses managers' minds and often changes the way the problem is perceived, or switches attention to a different problem area not at first sight apparent. Part of the process of thinking through the problem is a consideration of how survey results may be used. For example, if a survey of visitors to a visitor attraction is required to reveal ways to achieve higher spending in shops on site, the agency must be given details of current sales policies and trading results before they design their research methodology and the questions to be asked. The expected use of results also determines the nature of the questions to be asked, but surprisingly few research buyers recognize this basic truth when defining the 'problem'.

Problem specification, together with other information noted in Figure 11.2, should always be put in writing and filed for future reference. At this stage, with a clearly expressed 'research brief', clients can approach agencies and invite them to tender for the work. Where an agency's work is well-known to a client, competitive tendering may be unnecessary. Where it is not, it is usual practice to invite three or four agencies to submit tenders, informing them that others have been approached. The commercial market research world is highly competitive, and tendering is the usual route to new business.

Preparing tenders is a costly process for agencies, taking several hours of work even for small projects, and several days' work on larger projects. Unless otherwise agreed, the cost of research tenders is not charged but absorbed as

---

The client brief

● Identifies the marketing context and perceived problem to be researched
● Specifies expected use of results
● Indicates time scale for completion
● States approximate budget limits

The agency tender

● Defines or redefines the problem in research terms
● Proposes a methodology relevant to the problem
● Specifies a realistic programme for completion including client liaison
● Recommends a reporting format and procedure
● Sets out terms and conditions of business, including costs and timing of payments
● Specifies personnel involved, their qualifications and experience, and their respective involvement in the proposed study
● Indicates agency experience relevant to the problem, including reference to previous studies and clients whose needs were broadly comparable

---

Figure 11.2   *Basic requirements of client and agency in commissioning market research*

a business overhead. In preparing a tender the agency would normally expect at least one meeting to clarify and interpret the way the problem is expressed in the client's brief. Through experience with similar problems, agencies may well be able to restate the problem or illuminate it in ways not obvious to the client. They may have access to secondary data, not known to clients, which can reduce costs.

Tenders should cover all the points noted in Figure 11.2, and clients will often find broad similarity in the methods and costs proposed by competing agencies. Accordingly, selecting which agency to use will normally be based on the extent to which each one demonstrates comprehension of the problem, and the effectiveness and creativity of the proposed methods of tackling it within stipulated budget limits. Proven track record in travel and tourism research may be important, but more vital is the quality of the rapport between client and agency. This will be evident from the first meeting and reflected in the tenders. It will always be wise for clients to meet the research executive directly

responsible for their job, as well as the agency director or senior researcher who is likely to produce and present the tender. If meetings are necessary, visiting the agency's premises will often reveal much more about the nature and quality of its operation than the usual glossy brochure, with its predictable claims of all-round excellence and deep expertise.

Successful research depends on trust between client and agency akin to that which develops between advertising agency and client (though on a smaller scale). Reputable agencies will normally reveal names of previous clients, and it is quite usual for prospective clients to talk in confidence to previous clients about their experiences with particular agencies.

Customer access – priceless asset of service businesses

A massive potential advantage inherent in marketing most service products in travel and tourism is the presence of customers on producers' premises. In this author's view it is a grossly underestimated advantage.

Anyone who has owned, worked, or been brought up in a small business, such as a hotel, travel agency, restaurant, pub or caravan park, will recognize the powerful immediacy of customer contact, and the ease with which it is possible to detect (or impossible to avoid) customer needs, behaviour and satisfactions. Such businesses hardly need market research surveys, because, in a very real way, their customer knowledge and 'feedback' are better, more natural, and more continuous than any clipboard-carrying researcher could ever provide.

However, once a business grows large enough to have multiple branches, or is run by managers with limited customer contact, direct customer–management communication is lost. The board directors of an airline or large hotel company may not speak at all to customers for months or years, and if they do, may so intimidate them as to negate any research value of the contact. In these management circumstances systematic research is necessary, but it can still be based on the inherent advantages of customer/product inseparability and the relative ease of communication 'on site' or 'in-house'.

By contrast, producers of most consumer goods usually have either no contact at all with their customers, who purchase anonymously in retail outlets, or at best have access to names and addresses provided for warranty or servicing purposes. In travel and tourism all hotel customers sign registers and/or enter details on a hotel registration card. Airline customers spend many hours waiting in terminals and in planes for their journeys to start or to end. Visitors to attractions stroll around reception areas and car parks; travel agencies have many opportunities to seek out and record customers' needs and interests, and so on. In the 1990s it is quite extraordinary, that with the exception of some large tour operators and a very small proportion of other large companies, these opportunities for research are for the most part still overlooked and underutilized.

Researching customer satisfaction

Large tour operators in Britain typically hand out self-completion customer satisfaction questionnaires to all travellers returning from holidays abroad, generally on the flight home. Such questionnaires request rating of all aspects of the holiday, using scales such as 4 = excellent, 3 = good, 2 = fair and 1 = poor, which can be communicated by words or sketches. The responses can then be computer-processed to produce numerical ratings or scores. From this information, if plotted on a week by week basis, it is possible to detect comparative satisfaction with individual resorts and hotels, or check the performance of specific flights, or particular aspects of products such as food, excursions or the service provided by resort representatives (see also Chapter 24).

Because 'profile information' is included in the questionnaire, it is possible to analyse satisfaction by age of respondent, region of origin, cost of package and so on. These questionnaires, mostly scanned and processed by computers, can provide a vast range of continuous management information, which is both a control tool for service operations and a fertile database for marketing decisions, such as product formulation and pricing. Airlines use in-flight survey questionnaires in the same way for the same purposes, usually on a sample basis. So do some hotel companies and major attractions. In the UK Thomson Holidays first used customer satisfaction questionnaires in 1972, well ahead of their competitors. By 1990 they had processed some 12 million forms over the years, and as a commitment to research perhaps this illustrates part of the reason why Thomson have been market leaders. Club Méditerranée was processing around 250,000 questionnaires of a similar type in the early 1990s, and there is every reason to suppose their use will continue to grow.

Researching marketing innovations

Especially with multi-site operations, the possibility for managers to innovate and test market service products is endless. A hotel corporation might, for example, vary menus and prices, vary the formality of food service, offer new facilities for business or leisure customers, change room furniture and decor, or promote a particular type of inclusive weekend-break product. Provided always that the results in sales and satisfaction are monitored, there are many opportunities to carry out 'live' market research through conducting controlled marketing tests. Through a process crudely but accurately dubbed 'suck it and see', service producers can often test, learn and modify product developments on a limited scale before wider implementation in other sites or premises.

Tour operators can offer new destinations, or new product types, in the pages of an existing brochure. If the development is popular and sells well, it can often be extended quickly and modified as necessary by evidence gained from customer satisfaction questionnaires. The 'learning' opportunity available to producer organizations in services, who can set up and read the results of marketing tests at low cost, is usually not available to manufacturers of physical goods, especially where powerful retailers control distribution outlets and the shelf space allocated to producers. Test marketing of physical goods is generally a far more costly and time-consuming process than test marketing of services.

If they approach the issue systematically, most businesses in travel and tourism can create opportunities to experiment and monitor. Above all, they can build up their marketing knowledge of buyer behaviour by obtaining relatively inexpensive feedback from the customers using their premises. These are powerful opportunities for cost-effective marketing research, which other industries must envy.

Chapter summary

This chapter identifies the role of marketing research and its value as the information base for marketing decisions. It explains the six main types of marketing research that practitioners in travel and tourism are most likely to encounter, and describes ten of the commonly used technical terms applied to research methods. In particular, it draws a distinction between continuous and *ad hoc* research, 'continuous' implying the creation and use of a database for marketing purposes, a very important development, which is explained further in Chapter 19.

A market-research menu is offered in Figure 11.1, which may serve with Figure 11.2 as a useful checklist for those who have to commission research to fulfil particular purposes. The section on using research agencies is also relevant in this connection.

Emphasis is put on the scope for innovation in the marketing mix, which, combined with detailed monitoring of results, is a particular form of marketing research likely to be highly relevant to all organizations in travel and tourism. Carefully designed tests may be used to exploit fully the advantages of having customers on premises or sites owned or managed by producer organizations.

The chapter stresses that marketing research throws light on marketing decisions and reduces the level of risk and uncertainty associated with them. But it cannot provide simple answers or remove the essential quality of judgement from managers. The use of marketing-research data is most obviously seen in practice in the process of marketing planning, which is discussed in detail in Chapter 13.

Further reading

Baker, M. J., *Marketing: An Introductory Text*, 4th edit., Macmillan, 1985, Chapter 11.

Kotler, P., *Marketing: Analysis, Planning, Implementation and Control*, 7th edit., Prentice-Hall International, 1991, Chapter 4.

12

Marketing planning: strategy and operations

This chapter and the next focus on the planning process by which organizations decide and communicate the goals and objectives they seek to pursue. The key word here is 'decision', because at any given time organizations are likely to be faced with a wide range of choices, whose implications can never be fully clear. Ultimately the objectives an organization sets and pursues are the most important decisions it makes, because these determine all other operational decisions.

It is necessary to deal with objectives at two levels. The first level is a strategic level covering the whole business over the long term, and the second level is an operational or tactical level covering specific markets and products in the short term. In practice, as described in this chapter, a hierarchy of decisions exists within any organization. Students of marketing must learn to recognize the differences.

By definition, in a *marketing-led* organization customer orientation will always be a focal concern for senior management and part of corporate culture. But marketing decisions will be only one of the core business functions to be planned at strategic level. Marketing strategy is a dominant element, because of its focus on sales-revenue generation, and the responsibility of marketing management for achieving it.

This chapter deals with marketing at the strategic level, while Chapter 13 develops a step-by-step approach to operational planning, which is the basis of organizing effective marketing campaigns. As Hussey puts it, 'the planning of marketing is really a divided activity. One portion falls squarely under the heading of strategic planning ... a second portion can easily be seen as the task of the operating manager in planning and developing existing markets' (1979, p. 159).

The need for planning

In order to provide an orderly and agreed basis on which to conduct business in an ever-changing competitive market environment, all organizations are obliged to plan their activities. The larger the business, and the more products and markets with which it has to deal, the greater the importance of effective planning and the need for systematic procedures. The more volatile a market is in terms of annual fluctuations in customer demand, the more important it is to work within a framework of agreed objectives. Years of market growth tend to obscure and lessen the need for planning, while recession and market decline, with inevitable failures of some businesses, bring planning issues sharply into focus.

In essence, any plan comprises a statement of goals and objectives and a programme of activity intended to achieve them. The statement of goals usually involves market research and analysis, and the programmes of activity have to be costed and monitored in some way to work out how well the objectives are actually achieved. All planning is conducted on the assumption that the effort in time and money will produce more profitable results over a period of years than the alternative of constant reaction to market conditions and the opportunist use of business hunch. This assumption is more likely to be valid for organizations run by committees of managers than those run by individual entrepreneurs. Managers will recognize how these simple truths tend to disappear in the complexities of planning analysis and techniques, but students should hold on to this simple definition in understanding this chapter.

Strategic marketing planning

Stripped of its mystery and technique, strategic corporate planning attempts to answer three outward looking questions:

- Where are we now?
- Where do we want to be in 5 or more year's time?
- How do we get there?

The three questions lead naturally to the idea of a *position*, meaning the 'place' that an organization occupies compared with its competitors and in the eyes (minds) of customers and prospective customers (see later in chapter). The three questions also help to explain three concepts in corporate planning (adapted from Davidson: 1975, p. 109):

- Goals and objectives (chosen destinations).
- Strategies (chosen routes for achieving goals).

- Plans (action programmes for moving along the route).

In these simple terms strategic planning is as relevant to small businesses as it is to large ones.

For marketing purposes, strategic planning may be defined as the process whereby an organization analyses its strengths and weaknesses in its current and prospective markets, decides the position it seeks to attain, and defines strategies and costed programmes of activity to achieve its aims.

Strategic decisions are always focused on the longer run, usually defined as 3 or more years ahead. Included in the marketing process are:

Goals and objectives	The position or place in its chosen markets, which an organization seeks to occupy in a future period, usually defined broadly in terms of target segments, volume of sales, product range, market shares and profitability. Marketing strategy reflects corporate mission statements.
Images and positioning	Where the organization seeks to be in terms of customers' and retailers' perceptions of its products and its corporate image.
Strategies and programmes	Broadly what actions, including product development, are required to achieve the goals and objectives. Strategies are noted as 'level 1' in Figure 12.1.
Budget	What resources are needed to achieve its goals.
Review and evaluation	Systematic appraisal of achievement of goals in the context of competitors' actions and the external environment.

Larger organizations with multiple products in multiple markets, such as hotel chains or international car-rental companies, also require strategic planning to achieve effective relationships and allocation of resources between the component parts of their businesses. Strategy in this context is discussed later (see portfolio analysis).

Strategy is essentially proactive in the sense that it defines and wills the future shape of the organization as well as responding to market conditions and perceived consumer needs.

Tactical marketing planning

Tactics are always associated with decisions focused on the short run, in which specific marketing campaigns are planned, implemented and evaluated. Short run may be a year, 18 months, or only weeks. Tactics are responsive to market circumstances and particularly responsive to competitors' actions.

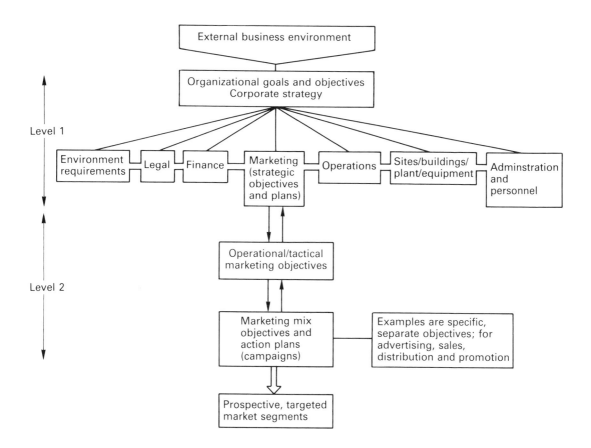

Figure 12.1 *Elements involved in a corporate business strategy, and hierarchy of objectives*

Tactical, or operational marketing plans, include:

Objectives	Specified, quantified, volume and sales revenue targets and other specific marketing objectives to be achieved.
Mix and budget	Marketing mix and marketing budget decisions.
Action programmes	The implementation of marketing programmes and co-ordination of promotional activity to achieve targets.
Monitoring and control	Monitoring the results of marketing on a regular or continuous basis and applying control systems.

A hierarchy of objectives

Figure 12.1 shows the two levels of business objectives, and serves also to put marketing strategy and objectives into the wider context of planning organizational goals and objectives. Corporate planning specifies objectives and targets for all the business functions in an organization, which combine to get it from where it is at the present time to the position it seeks to occupy at some future date.

In the first level of the hierarchy of objectives, and influenced by the external business environment, Figure 12.1 notes seven common elements, that are systematically planned and integrated in most corporate strategies. Marketing, as explained earlier, is one of the elements; it is shown in the centre of the figure with a separate input below it to demonstrate the linkages with operational marketing planning shown as Level 2.

A brief description of six of the seven strategic elements is provided below, and explained in the context of a large international airline. All seven have specific implications for decisions at a tactical or operational level but,

marketing strategy excepted, the other elements are not the subject of this chapter and are not referred to further.

While hierarchies of objectives may not appear relevant to small proprietor-run businesses, the thought process and principles discussed in this chapter are fully appropriate to any size of operation. It is often the failure to think strategically that causes so many smaller businesses to decline and founder.

Corporate strategy in an airline context

In the context of a major scheduled airline with an international network of routes, the decisions to be brought together in a strategy can be explained briefly in the following questions:

Environment	What changes to aircraft and other operational developments are needed to meet regulations concerning noise, emissions, waste control, night flights and energy consumption? What implications for conducting environmental audits and impact assessments for major new projects?
Legal	What agreements between countries are required to maintain and develop services on the agreed route network? How far and how fast might deregulation proceed? Legal implications of possible mergers and acquisitions. Compliance with legal requirements.
Finance	What asset and loan structure is needed by the airline? What returns on capital are required to service the investment, meet the stakeholders' interests and fund new investment in aircraft and facilities?

Operations What number, type and size of aircraft are required to perform agreed services, on which routes at what times? How to optimize the scheduling of the fleet?

Sites, buildings, plant and equipment What ground facilities are required at airports and operational bases? What servicing (engineering) facilities are needed for aircraft, etc?

Administration and personnel What facilities for management, buildings, equipment and general organization are needed to service the airlines' current operations and assist it to develop according to planned goals and objectives? What numbers, remuneration levels, qualifications, organization, training and career structure are required for employees, to provide and sustain an effective quality assured service across the network?

Marketing strategy

For any marketing-led organization, marketing strategy must be the most important single element in business strategy. It identifies and largely determines future sales-revenue generation by specifying the segments, products and associated action programmes required to achieve sales and market share against competitors. Each of the other elements in the strategy requires expenditure out of projected revenue. However vital these elements are to the conduct of the business, they are ultimately conditioned by the organization's ability to persuade sufficient customers to buy enough of its products to secure a surplus of revenue over costs in the long run. While it is obviously incorrect to conclude that business strategy is only about marketing, it is not difficult to establish that all strategy for commercial organizations has its bottom line in sales revenue, and that marketing managers are employed to achieve revenue targets through their specialist knowledge of market needs and circumstances.

To illustrate the point, the decision by an airline to buy an additional aircraft, such as a Boeing 747, draws on each of the seven strategic elements, noted in Figure 12.1. But unless marketing managers can undertake on a daily basis to achieve adequate seat-occupancy levels (load factors), at average prices that exceed average costs, the decision to buy cannot be taken. In practice there is always an element of risk in the decision to buy new equipment, but the principal risk lies in projecting future customer demand and having the marketing will and competence to secure the demand against aggressive competition.

Three key concepts in competitive strategy formulation

The subject of marketing strategy has assumed greater significance since the 1970s for three important reasons. The first was the global uncertainty provoked by the major international economic crises of 1973, 1979 and 1991-2. These events destroyed previous concepts of relative market stability and disrupted many of the long-range econometric forecasting models first developed in the 1960s to plan long-term business goals.

The second was the development of information technology from the 1970s, which, amongst other contributions, facilitated the internationalization of exchange rates so that all currencies are now subject to hour-by-hour fluctuations and speculative pressures hitherto unknown. Consequently, exchange rates, which are so intimately connected to tourism prices, are highly volatile and cannot be forecast with precision.

The third was the continuing growth in travel and tourism of large, transnational and global organizations locked in fierce competition for market share and sales revenue. Their strategies have an important ripple effect in world markets.

The three reasons have affected all types of industries, but they have been especially powerful in price-sensitive international travel and tourism markets. Without strategies to guide their responses to inevitable changes in the external business environment, organizations can lose sight of their goals in the time-consuming and urgent tactical decisions called for in the day-to-day management of demand, which all service industries require. Marketing strategy has to be flexible to cope with change and sufficiently sensitive to discriminate between different components of large businesses. Old concepts of centralized head office planning for large organizations are no longer seen as efficient in the 1990s, and new models of delegated planning for separate sectors of a business (known as strategic business units or areas - SBUs or SBAs) have emerged. These new approaches call for head office co-ordination and support but restrict its direct operational involvement (see also Chapter 10). As Taylor and Harrison say:

> In the 1980s . . . planning ceased to be a staff function (as in corporate planning departments) and the responsibility was handed over to management teams in newly formed profit centres and SBUs (1990, p. xii).

A fourth strategic consideration, likely to be increasingly relevant in the 1990s, is the growing importance of environmental considerations and the identification of responsibilities for travel and tourism businesses. Pressure to conserve the global environment will move firms on from technical operational considerations, such as waste control and energy management, into the broader customer-related issues of establishing corporate positions of recognizably 'good practice' in environmental matters. Customer attitudes on tourism and the environment are not yet clear, but appear likely to repay those who adopt innovative strategies.

Within the limits of this book it is only possible to draw attention to the issues, and the sources noted at the end of the chapter must be pursued to achieve further understanding. It is vital, however, that students of travel marketing should be able to distinguish clearly between strategy and operations or tactics. Three concepts in particular, drawn from the extensive literature on business strategy, will assist in making the important distinctions. These are:

● Product-market portfolio analysis.
● Product-market growth models.
● Corporate and product positioning.

Product-market portfolios

A very large business, such as UK-based Forte, comprises a range of businesses, including fast food outlets (Little Chef and Happy Eater chains), and hotels (international and British in separate product-market groupings such as Posthouse and Travelodge). In terms of their specific products and market segments, these are essentially quite separate businesses, which share in common the strength of the corporate identity, the economies and advantages of bulk purchasing, and access to investment finance. Forte can thus be seen as a holding company with a *portfolio* of businesses or strategic business units (SBUs), each with its own management structure, profit and loss accounts and plans for the future.

The strategic planning process for a large international company therefore requires analysis of its current portfolio of SBUs and decisions on what changes are needed to secure future growth and profit in the light of international market conditions. Thus 'the end product of the strategic planning process is a future best-yield portfolio . . . taking into account risk, and short-term versus long-term trade offs' (Boyd and Larreche: 1982, p. 9).

For smaller organizations, the same concept of SBUs may be more narrowly interpreted in terms of the products and markets with which a business is involved. A large British tour operator may offer, for example:

Product	Market segments
1 *Winter sun*	Older, less active, budget-conscious buyers - long stay.
2 *Winter skiing*	Younger, active, more affluent buyers - short stay.
3 *Summer sun*	(a) Families, beach-orientated, budget-conscious; (b) young adults, activity- and entertainment-orientated, various price ranges.
4 *Long-haul destinations*	Older, more affluent, experienced travellers.

In this example the tour operator's product/market portfolio comprises at least four distinctive products (each capable of sub-division by price and by destination or by accommodation variants), and at least four distinctive market segments, which could also be sub-divided.

The tour operator may find it necessary to divide responsibility for marketing its four product-market groups between four management teams, and to operate each with its own budget and cost/revenue analysis. In this process the operator would effectively be managing a portfolio of mini-businesses, following the same principles of SBUs noted earlier. If the operator owns a retail travel chain and an airline, the portfolio concept is broader but the principles are the same.

Within any portfolio of SBUs or product-market groupings, it will usually be the case that some are growing and some are declining. Some are more profitable than others. Portfolios can be analysed over time periods according to key variables of:

● Share of market.
● Market growth.
● Cash-flow generation.
● Return on investment.
● Strength of competition.
● Product life cycle.

It will quickly become obvious from analysis that some SBUs in a portfolio have a relatively large share of expanding markets with good profitability. Such products are obviously candidates for strategic support if the general projections remain favourable. Other products, perhaps because the market sector is declining and not because the product is inadequate, will be in decline and generating little profit, especially if prices are being reduced to maintain volume.

The ideal portfolio will comprise some new product-market groupings with good shares of growth markets ('stars') and some profitable products with well-established shares of stable markets ('cash cows'). In practice portfolios will frequently also contain products with low shares of declining markets and poor profitability ('dogs'), which are candidates for liquidation. The labels (in brackets) are those created by the Boston Consulting Group in the USA, which developed one of the best known techniques for product-market portfolio analysis.

Product-market growth and development strategies

It is now commonplace in all sectors of business that no organization can afford to mark time. They cannot rest on past progress, and expect to maintain the structure of existing product-market portfolios and profitability levels, even over a period as short as 2 years. Profitable product-market portfolios will usually be under constant competitive pressure, and it will be necessary to update and augment products continuously to match changing customer needs. Businesses will also have to respond to other pressures, such as unfavourable exchange-rate movements, and to any changes in regulatory requirements or technology practices, which are certain to occur over a 5-year time span.

Accordingly, it is usual for marketing-led businesses continuously to review their portfolios, and search for ways to grow or develop in order to secure future profitability. The options for growth are wide but can be neatly summarized in an elegant model originally devised by Ansoff and much copied and developed since.

Product-market growth strategies (four basic options)

	Present products	*New products*
Present markets	1 market penetration	2 product development
New markets	3 market development	4 diversification

Source: Ansoff, *Corporate Strategy*, 1987, p. 109.

Each strategy has radically different implications for marketing.

The four numbered boxes in the model may be illustrated with typical travel and tourism examples as follows:

1 The case where a hotel group, already servicing the corporate meetings sector as its principal market, decides that it is well-positioned to expand in this market. With its existing portfolio, any expansion above natural market growth would represent an increased market share, which is known as 'penetration'.

2 The case where a British tour operator, already operating a portfolio of European inclusive tours, decides to expand its operations by developing long-haul tours to the USA, aiming at the existing British IT market. This decision represents an addition to the portfolio and is known as product development.

3 The case where an international operator originally based in the Netherlands with a largely Continental European clientele, first marketed its existing Continental villages to the UK market. In the late 1980s Center Parcs developed its holiday-village concept in two locations in England, with two more contemplated at the time of writing. This represents market development.

4 Finally, if an airline company decided to buy a hotel company through an acquisition, it would be stepping outside its existing product-market portfolio and effectively diversifying its business activities with a completely new set of SBUs.

Each of these choices represents strategic considerations, and normally would be undertaken only on the basis of a detailed analysis of potential revenues and advantages, as well as potential costs and disadvantages. The process for such an analysis is outlined in the next chapter.

Corporate and product positioning

Portfolio analysis and assessment of alternative product-market growth strategies focus on securing long-term profitability. The third concept is about securing competitive advantage through a long-term favourable image or perception among prospective customers, or other groups such as retailers on which a business depends.

The concept of positioning was introduced in Chapter 8. A useful illustration in travel and tourism is that of British Airways (BA), which in 1981-2 was recording record annual losses in the wake of the international economic crisis provoked by rising oil prices. While BA's losses were not unique, the management was well aware through research that its customer contact staff were widely perceived as unfriendly and unhelpful when compared with the staffs of competitor airlines. BA was, in consequence, not highly rated in airline-preference decisions by prospective travellers.

As a key aspect of its response, the airline developed a 'putting people first' campaign, in which, over a period of 2 to 3 years, all members of staff were required to undertake participative courses designed to make them aware of customer feelings, and to develop social skills in customer handling. The airline's objective was to improve the position and image it held in customers' minds, through better service. The strategic aim was that more customers would choose, and fewer reject, British Airways as an option when purchasing air travel. The success of this effort measurably changed customer attitudes. It was supported by promotional expenditure driving home the message that BA is the world's 'favourite airline'. The obvious success of the 'people first' programme created the perceptual climate in which BA could launch new products, achieve profitable seat occupancies and contribute to its strategic goals for privatization and a competititive return on assets employed.

A more recent illustration of corporate and product positioning comes from Hilton International. In the early 1990s this global hotel chain operated 150 hotels, with 54,000 staff, in fifty countries, handling some 7 million guests from 130 nationalities. The chain was bought in 1987 by a British company, Ladbroke Group PLC, from the ill-fated, short-lived Allegis Corporation in the USA. Ladbroke clearly recognized Hilton's strengths as a leading brand name in first-class hotels internationally. It also considered the group to be an example of a 'truly conventional and conservative service culture...with massive attention paid to the craft elements of traditional hotel keeping that typified hotel growth in the 1960s'. In other words, Ladbroke judged Hilton International to be production-orientated, and set about a radical and rapid change to the competitive, market-orientated culture needed for a global chain in the 1990s.

Setting itself the goal of enhancing and promoting Hilton's strengths as 'the world's most prestigious, business-orientated, efficient first-class hotel company', the Ladbroke Group embarked upon a major market research initiative with customers and staff as the first stage in developing a single-minded quality of service proposition promoted as 'The Hilton Promise'. All 54,000 staff, including management, attended communication and quality training sessions and endorsed a 'special commitment from every employee to give the kind of superior and distinctive service our guests would remember and come back for again and again'.

In an article outlining these developments in corporate culture and positioning, Michael Hirst, then Hilton's Chief Executive, claimed 'Our change in service culture has enabled us on a global level to differentiate a superior Hilton International style of service, by responding both corporately and as individuals, to individual guests' needs. We believe that gives us an unbeatable competitive edge' (Hirst: 1991, p. 251). Allowing for a certain element of PR in the article, it is nevertheless an interesting illustration of a global positioning exercise representing a major marketing-based strategic commitment for Hilton International. There is an obvious link between corporate positioning and product (sometimes known as brand) positioning. They require different use of marketing techniques, but the relationship is a vital one for successful businesses.

Goals down, plans up

A useful way to hold the distinctions between strategy and tactics in mind is encapsulated in the phrase 'goals down, plans up'. It means that the board of an organization will normally set goals, which its managers are expected to achieve. The goals will be based on the requirements noted earlier in this chapter, especially return on investment and long-term profit. But boardroom goals cannot be set without reference to implementation, as the BA and Hilton International examples show. It is the business of managers to plan and communicate both upwards and downwards what is realistic within budgets, time, and market circumstances, both in strategic terms, and tactically for short-run periods of 6 months to a year ahead. Resolving the differences between desired goals and achievable objectives is a normal part of the management process of any organization. This process brings together and modifies strategic and operational decision processes. Since strategic goals are intended to motivate managers and always relate to desired future states, it is normal for there to be some tension and dispute between short-term and long-term planning requirements.

Chapter summary

This chapter introduces the basic concepts of systematic planning, which are central to the efficient conduct of marketing-led organizations in travel and tourism as in other industries. It distinguishes between strategic and operational or tactical levels of planning; it further distinguishes between corporate planning as it applies to the whole of an organization's business, and planning for the individual functions of a business, of which marketing strategy and tactics are only one, however important. 'Corporate planning decisions . . . are decisions that affect the whole structure of the company many years or decades into the future – huge decisions taken in conditions of extreme uncertainty about the future' (Argenti: 1980, p. 14).

The chapter focuses on the meaning of planning and strategy for marketing as the management function most directly responsible for identifying and stimulating future customer demand and converting it into sales revenue. Drawing on an analysis of product-market portfolios (or SBUs), marketing strategy defines the future mix of products and segments that best meet the organization's long-run goals, and the position such products are intended to occupy in the minds of prospective customers. The chapter defines a hierarchy of objectives found in most businesses, but stresses the need for flexibility and continuity in the planning process.

The 'goals down, plans up' dialogue is introduced at the end of the chapter to stress the way in which the different levels of planning are integrated in practice in larger organizations. It also provides a bridge into the next chapter, in which the main focus is on the process of planning, and the tactical or operational level of marketing.

Further reading

The issues of strategic planning and strategic management are at the heart of business policy studies. Not surprisingly these issues have generated a very wide literature internationally and students are advised to refer to books by Ansoff (1987), George Day (1990), Kenichi Ohmae (1983) and Michael Porter (1985). In the recommended marketing texts for this book, see:

Baker, M. J., *Marketing: An Introductory Text*, 4th edit., Macmillan, 1985, Chapter 21.

Kotler, P., *Marketing Management: Analysis, Planning, Implementation and Control*, 7th edit., Prentice-Hall International, 1991, Chapters 2, 8 and 11.

13

Planning marketing operations and tactics

The previous chapter stresses the differences between marketing strategy and tactics, and the relation between them in the hierarchy of corporate objectives. This chapter focuses on the planning of marketing tactics or operations, which are implemented in the short run through action programmes. Corporate objectives have been described earlier as 'destinations',strategies as 'routes', and plans as action programmes for moving along agreed routes. In other words, strategy sets the framework within which tactics are planned. But most of the work in marketing departments is concerned with drawing up, implementing and measuring the effects of action plans.

This chapter identifies the seven stages of the planning process that are common to marketing in any form of industry. It emphasizes that the planning process for strategy and tactics covers the same essential stages, usually drawing on the same research sources and often undertaken by the same people. For strategic purposes, the analysis and forecasting of trends in the external business environment and the development of competitive product-market portfolios are the most important parts of planning, while for tactical purposes, the setting of precise objectives and devising action programmes are the main focus.

The chapter begins by stating why time and

resources are devoted to the marketing planning process in most marketing-led organizations. It draws some contrasts with the alternatives of guesswork, hunch and feel for the market, which are characteristic of many smaller businesses in travel and tourism. It proceeds to explain the stages in the planning process, which are summarized in Figure 13.1. The chapter ends with a note on the role of objectives as an important part of internal communications within organizations.

The particular significance of marketing plans

In its principles marketing planning is no more than a logical thought process, in which all businesses have to engage to some extent. It is an application of common sense, as relevant to a small guesthouse or caravan park as it is to an international airline. The scale of planning and its sophistication obviously vary according to the size of the organization concerned, but the essential principles remain the same.

Building on the purposes of planning outlined in Chapter 12, it is helpful to emphasize six main reasons why time and resources are allocated to marketing planning at the tactical or operational level:

- To identify and focus management attention on the current and targeted costs, revenues, and profitability of an organization, in the context of its own and its competitors' products and segments.
- To focus decisions on the strategic objectives of an organization in their market context, and identify competitive action plans relevant to the long-term future.
- To set and communicate specific business targets for managers to achieve in agreed time periods.
- To schedule and coordinate promotional and other marketing action required to achieve targets and to allocate the resources required.
- To achieve co-ordination and a sense of joint direction between the different departments of an organization, around agreed targets.
- To monitor and evaluate the results of marketing expenditure and adjust the planned activity as required to meet unforeseen circumstances.

Are there alternatives to marketing planning?

The only alternatives to the systematic common-sense planning processes outlined in this chapter are guesswork, hunch, 'feel' for the market, simple intuition, or vision. Sometimes hunches and intuition are practised with brilliant success by highly energetic and determined business entrepreneurs. Many of them dismiss systematic planning as bureaucratic, rigid, time-consuming, expensive, and often wrong. But hunch and guesswork also have their disadvantages, and the history of travel and tourism reveals many illustrations of brilliant entrepreneurs whose businesses grew rapidly and successfully for some years, only to crash spectacularly in the wake of unpredicted events. Laker Airways, Braniff Airways and International Leisure Group, are just three illustrations that are widely known.

In principle, although systematic methodical planning procedures and entrepreneurial marketing flair are usually seen as opposites, they can be mutually supportive. Planning procedures must not be allowed to become inflexible or the cause of delays, but may be used to provide a framework of objectives and an information base that support and give a sense of direction or roots for marketing judgement and flair. 'Entrepreneurial planning' may sound like a contradiction in terms but it is nevertheless a desirable goal to which most modern large businesses aspire, and which they attempt to build into their internal management procedures. There is very clearly a balance to be struck in marketing management between analytical procedures and creative flair. Both are essential qualities for long-run survival and profitability. Creative flair will always be a vital quality in aggressive marketing action. Unbridled by agreed strategies and objectives such flair can also be self-destructive.

Logical steps in the marketing planning process

There are seven logical steps in systematic marketing planning. Each step feeds into the next one, with feedback loops built into the process, as noted with arrows in Figure 13.1 and explained in the text that follows.

Explaining marketing planning as a series of logical steps runs the risk of understating the importance of the work in the decision processes of a business. As Leppard and McDonald put it: 'While the marketing planning process appears on the surface to be just a series of procedural steps, it does in fact embrace a series of underlying values and assumptions' (Leppard and McDonald: 1991, p. 213). They stress that a marketing-led corporate culture in an organization is a vital aspect of successful marketing planning. Depending on the current culture, the process should be an integral part of

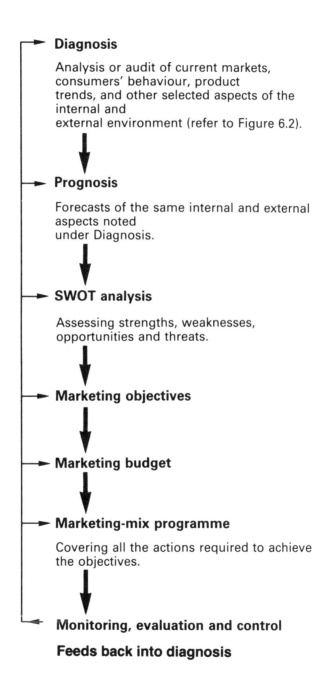

Diagnosis

Analysis or audit of current markets, consumers' behaviour, product trends, and other selected aspects of the internal and external environment (refer to Figure 6.2).

Prognosis

Forecasts of the same internal and external aspects noted under Diagnosis.

SWOT analysis

Assessing strengths, weaknesses, opportunities and threats.

Marketing objectives

Marketing budget

Marketing-mix programme

Covering all the actions required to achieve the objectives.

Monitoring, evaluation and control

Feeds back into diagnosis

Figure 13.1 *The marketing planning process*

corporate decisions and communication. At worst it may be no more than a 'bolt-on' procedure, scarcely recognized outside the marketing team.

Diagnosis

Described in some texts as part of a 'marketing audit', the first stage in the planning process is based on marketing research, drawing on available published and unpublished data for analysis of trends under four main headings:

1 Sales volume and revenue trends over at least a 5-year period, to identify total market movements and market shares for particular segments and for own and competitors' products. A tour operator would, for example, compare its own sales data with Civil Aviation Authority data for charter airline passengers, and with government and tourist authority survey data for travel and tourism volume and value.
2 Consumer profiles for own customers and competitors' customers, including detail of demographics, attitudes and behaviour, as outlined in Chapter 7. This information usually comes from business records and through market surveys.
3 Product profiles and price trends for own and competitors' products, identifying product life-cycle movements and in particular noting growing and declining product types. Such information comes from analysing internal business records and through trade press and trade research.
4 Trends in the external environment (as identified in Chapter 4), such as changing technology, changing regulatory requirements, exchange-rate movements or changing distribution structure. This information also derives primarily from trade press and trade research sources, although some aspects may justify undertaking marketing research studies.

Under the four headings above, *Diagnosis* represents a factual platform, which is the basis for all marketing plans at strategic and tactical level. Since the travel and tourism industry has access to data from many sources, the way in which data are selected, organized and presented for decision purposes, is an important management skill.

The level of detail in the diagnosis is a matter for each individual business, reflecting its size and the range of its operations. Diagnosis is likely to extend beyond the products and markets of immediate concern to a business, into adjacent markets. For example, a budget-priced hotel chain would expect to diagnose budget-sector accommodation markets and products in full detail. It might also need to monitor trends in the de-luxe end of the market in order to assess relative changes in the sectors which could have future strategic implications. A tour operator without a long-haul programme might monitor long-haul market trends in case developments suggest an entry into that sector at some future point.

Prognosis

Described in many texts as 'forecasting', the second stage in the planning process is also market research based but future-orientated. It relies on expectations, judgement and forecasting for each of the four headings already covered under Diagnosis. Because the future for travel and tourism products is subject to volatile, unpredictable factors, the prognosis is not expected to be highly accurate, and must be updated regularly as new events alter expectations. The purpose of prognosis is not accuracy but careful and continuous assessment of probabilities and options. It recognizes that most marketing mix expenditure is invested weeks, months or even years ahead of targeted revenue flows. Since marketing planning is focused on future revenue achievement, it is necessarily dependent upon realism in prognosis.

As with the diagnosis stage, much skill exists in developing relevant predictions for key variables affecting an organization's business. They must be presented in ways to which marketing and other managers are able to respond in their strategic and operational decisions.

SWOT analysis

Equipped with relevant information through the process of diagnosis, and the best indications of developing trends through prognosis, the next task is to assess what the information means for marketing strategy and tactics. A useful framework for this assessment is contained in the acronym SWOT, which stands for strengths, weaknesses, opportunities and threats.

Strengths are normally expressed as inherent advantages, whether by design or historic good fortune, in the organization's market-product portfolio, and its operations in relation to competitors.

Products with increasing shares of growing markets are obviously strengths. Dominance of key market segments is another strength. For hotels and visitor attractions, location may be a major strength. Strength may lie in historic artefacts or architectural style and it may reflect a particularly favourable consumer image. Strength may lie in the professional skills of a marketing team or a distribution system, or in customer service staff with an especially helpful and friendly approach.

It is impossible to indicate all the possible dimensions of an organization's strengths, but such dimensions are identifiable characteristics that an organization has more of, or does better, than its competitors. Once identified, strengths are the basis of corporate positions (see Chapter 12) and can be promoted to potential customers, enhanced through product augmentation, or developed within a strategic framework.

Weaknesses, ranging from ageing products in declining markets, for example, to surly customer contact staff, must also be clearly identified. Once identified, they may be subject to management action designed to minimize their impact or to remove them where possible. Weaknesses and strengths are often matters of perception rather than 'fact', and may often be identified only through consumer research.

If, for example, a historic hotel in a market town is perceived by many of its customers as old-fashioned, noisy and uncomfortable, it may be possible to highlight its strengths by repositioning it to stress old-world charm, convenience of location, and atmosphere. Such a repositioning may necessitate extensive refurbishment, including double glazing and refurnishing, but it could provide a strategic route to turn a weakness into strength. If a modern competitor hotel were to be built on the outskirts of the market town, the historic hotel would probably lose some of its clients and might be forced to reposition its products and develop new markets in order to survive.

It is common practice in marketing-orientated businesses for managers to conduct regular *audits* of their current strengths and weaknesses, or to commission consultants to carry out such work from an independent and unbiased viewpoint.

Opportunities in a marketing context may arise from elements of the business under direct control, such as a particular product or process. They may also arise from shifts in the external environment, which a firm may exploit. Club Méditerranée, for example, strongly exploiting its island and enclosed resort destinations, and its concepts of freedom and activities, extended its operations throughout the world during the 1970s. It seized an opportunity to develop its particular holiday concepts with a powerful image in a way no other operator matched at that time. A different type of opportunity arose for Australia when the USA was defeated in the America's Cup and it was agreed to stage the 1987 event at Fremantle, near Perth, Western Australia. With 4 years' notice, Perth did everything possible to use the opportunity to develop a modern tourist industry around this major event, which was the focus of the world's attention for several months. Perth was assured of film, TV, radio and press coverage beyond the dreams of any conceivable advertising budget. It is a classic example of opportunistic marketing, appropriate to its time.

Threats may also be presented by internal elements within the business's control, or by external events such as exchange-rate changes, rising oil prices or acts of international terrorism. In Britain the traditional seaside resorts offering beach-based summer holidays have been under heavy threat from seaside resorts along the Mediterranean coastline. The competition has severely eroded their customary markets and forced a strategic reappraisal of their futures.

Although it is not easy to justify the point theoretically, practical experience of marketing proves that the time and effort spent in a systematic and creative SWOT analysis is invariably productive. It is much more than routine analysis of market statistics. There is ample scope for creative interpretation, judgement, and lateral thinking, both at the strategic and tactical levels of planning. There is also ample scope for marketing managers to bring other managers into this process to draw out their expertise and perceptions.

Marketing objectives and targets

Marketing objectives and targets derive logically from the previous stages of the planning process. Targets express what managers believe can be achieved from a business over a specified time period.

To be actionable in practice, objectives must be:

- Relevant to corporate goals and strategy.
- Precise and quantified in terms of sales volume, sales revenue and, if possible, market share.
- Specific in terms of products and segments.

- Specific in terms of the time period in which they are to be achieved.
- Realistic in terms of market trends and in relation to budgets available.
- Agreed by and acceptable to the managers responsible for the programmes of activity designed to achieve results.
- Measurable directly or indirectly.

If these seven criteria are not fully observed, the objectives will be less than adequate in determining the success of the business, and make the marketing programmes harder to specify and evaluate. The more thorough the diagnosis, prognosis, and SWOT, the easier the task of specifying precise objectives.

To give an example, consider the case of a medium-size British tour operator with a capacity of say 500,000 packages sold in the previous year and a strategy to grow through market penetration. Assuming that favourable market circumstances are revealed by diagnosis and prognosis, and starting from a good competitive position, the operator might look for a 15 per cent increase in volume in the following year, e.g. *to achieve sales of 575,000 tours over the next year.*

Even if revenue and share were added to this statement, it could not be considered fully actionable in marketing terms. To meet the seven criteria previously noted, and drawing on a notional analysis of the operator's business for the sake of the example, the same objective would have to be developed as follows:

To achieve sales of 575,000 tours between April and September, at average 95 per cent occupancy, to achieve a gross contribution of £7 million, with an overall market share of 6 per cent:

(a) by sales of 355,000 Summer sun tours in Europe (+2 per cent on previous year)

(b) by sales of 115,000 lakes and mountains tours in Europe (+ 15 per cent on previous year)

(c) by sales of 30,000 coach tours in Europe (+ 5 per cent on previous year)

(d) by sales of 75,000 tours in USA (+25 per cent on previous year).

The figures in brackets represent target increases on previous years' sales, reflecting the prognosis stage of planning as well as a strategy, in this case to develop into the USA.

This level of precision would facilitate the task of planning weekly capacity for airports of origin, resort destinations, flight and bed capacity, and contracting for the necessary seats and rooms. In tour-operating practice the process of targeting numbers is built up on the basis of aircraft flight capacity and schedules, so that the operational implications of targeted increases for contracting purposes are immediately apparent to managers (see Chapter 24).

From these quantified capacity targets, the promotional and other marketing tasks in achieving the targeted volumes can be drawn up and costed for budget purposes. Subsequently, the marketing effort can be evaluated in terms of bookings against target sales on a weekly basis.

It should be apparent from this brief consideration of setting objectives that precision cannot be achieved without prior analysis (diagnosis and prognosis). In every case, except for very small operators with one product and one segment, it will be found necessary to *disaggregate* the objectives into specific products and segments. Once this is achieved, the specification and costing of marketing-mix tasks becomes easier.

Marketing budget

The marketing budget (discussed further in Chapter 14) determines the amount of money, that has to be spent *in advance* of bookings, reservations or purchases, in order to secure targeted sales volume and revenue. In the tour-operator example noted earlier, costs of brochure production, distribution and of advertising, would be committed months before the full payments or even most of the deposits are received from customers.

The budget represents the sum of the costs of individual marketing-mix elements judged necessary by marketing managers to achieve specified objectives and targets. There can never be total precision between costs and results for reasons discussed in Chapter 14, but this does not alter the principle of allocating money to specific tasks in order to achieve targeted results.

Because the budget is required to achieve volume and revenue objectives through expenditure on a marketing-mix programme, there is a vital feedback loop between target-setting and marketing management agreement on what can realistically be achieved with affordable budgets (see Figure 13.2).

Figure 13.2 demonstrates the essential dialogue or systematic interaction that takes place in marketing planning between goals, objectives, budgets and programmes. The proposed objectives reflect business goals and strategy, as previously described. The marketing resources include the numbers and skills of staff to undertake programmes. Also in resources are the size and structure of the distribution channels available to the business, its links with advertising agencies, etc. If an evaluation of objectives demonstrates that planned resources are inadequate, then additional budgets will be needed *or* the objectives must be amended.

For each marketing objective there will normally be a range of options as to how it will be achieved - more or less advertising, more or less price discounting and so on. Marketing managers are required to consider these options and the associated costs, using judgement, experience and analysis of previous results. If the preferred options cannot be met within budget, more money will be needed or the objectives must be modified.

Over the space of several days or weeks, each of the interlocking elements in Figure 13.2 will be modified until an agreed marketing mix programme is finalized for implementation. In describing targeting for the Thomas Cook Group, Davies comments, 'The essential features

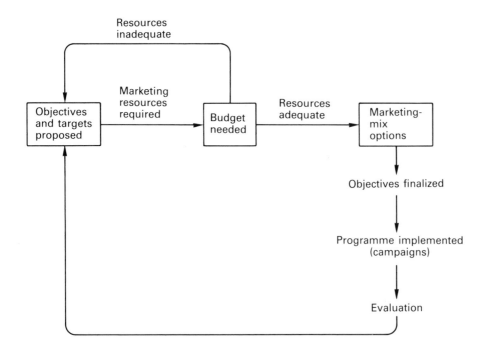

Figure 13.2   *Co-ordinating operational marketing objectives, budgets and programmes*

of targets are that they should be meaningful and that they should be acceptable to those responsible for striving to achieve them' (Davies: 1990, p. 213).

Marketing-mix programmes

Action programmes comprise the mix of promotion, distribution and other marketing activities that are undertaken to influence and motivate buyers to choose targeted volumes of particular products. These include:

● *Advertising.*
● *Direct response marketing.*
● *Sales promotion and merchandising.*
● *Personal selling.*

● *Promotional literature.*
● *Public relations.*
● *Distribution and sales staff support.*
● *Price discounts.*
● *Commissions to retailers.*

A marketing-mix programme, which is also known as a *marketing campaign,* expresses exactly what activities will take place in support of each identified product–market sub-group on a week by week basis. Since brochure production, distribution, advertising, and merchandising in retail travel agencies have different time-scales, there is a considerable management art necessary in scheduling programmes of work to make the best use of the marketing department staff's time.

Monitoring, evaluation and control

One of the important reasons for insisting on precision in setting objectives is to make it possible to measure results. In the case of the tour-operator business discussed above under 'marketing objectives and targets', it would be possible to monitor results for *each market/product sector* under at least six headings:

- Weekly flow of bookings against planned capacity.
- Sales response related to any advertising activity.
- Customer awareness of advertising messages measured by research surveys.
- Sales response to any price discounts.
- Sales response to any merchandising efforts by travel agents.
- Customer satisfaction with product quality measured by customer satisfaction questionnaires.

Evaluation and control is a complex subject, further discussed in Chapter 14. It is sufficient here to stress that efficient evaluation is vital to the diagnosis process, and that it is impossible to have efficient evaluation without first establishing precise targets against which to measure results.

The communication role of operational objectives

Involving as many staff contributions as possible in the process of setting objectives and drawing up plans is an important aspect of securing willing, enthusiastic participation in implementation. It is a subject of increasing attention in many travel and tourism organizations; it is especially important for service businesses, in which so many staff have direct contact with customers on the premises. It is possible to arrange the stages in marketing planning so that managers, and as many staff as

possible in all departments (or jobs), take part in initiating and/or commenting on draft objectives and plans. It is common sense that those who have to carry out plans should identify themselves with their success and not see them as impositions laid down by senior managers who may not have recent practical experience of what can be achieved within known constraints. Where target-setting and evaluation are linked with some form of performance incentives, the motivation of staff may be easier to secure.

Many managers will be aware of the damaging effect on staff morale of working within an organization where the objectives appear to change according to management whim, or where directives are issued by planning departments and there is no opportunity to debate their practicality in operation. While marketing planning is conducted primarily to achieve more efficient business decisions, its secondary benefit is to provide a means of participation and communication, vital in creating and sustaining a high level of organizational morale.

Marketing planning for strategy and tactics compared

Earlier in the chapter it was noted that the process of marketing planning is the same in principle for both strategy and tactics. Strategic planning usually focuses mainly on diagnosis, prognosis and the SWOT analysis, and is likely to look backwards over the trends of several years as well as forward to the extent that projections are sensible. Strategic planning is much broader in its approach than tactical planning, and strategic goals are normally not expressed in precise, quantifiable terms. Strategic goals usually state where an organization wishes to be with regard to its markets, expressed in broad terms that can be turned subsequently into short-term operational plans. Examples of strategic objectives for the

Wales Tourist Board In 1989 illustrate the point:

- To shift existing [customer] perceptions of Wales towards that of a year-round destination.
- To place greater emphasis in promotional terms on higher quality products which respect Wales' environment.
- To extend and develop joint marketing activity with commercial operators and others willing to demonstrate new initiatives to promote their products, areas, festivals and events.
- To assist the development and marketing of inclusive product offers, especially those for sale through travel agents, and those developed by marketing cooperatives.
- To develop customer databases for marketing purposes.

Strategic goals may be expressed in terms of projected growth and profit, or organizational structure, or in relation to competitors. Strategies may be expressed in terms of the four Ps of the marketing mix, or any other aspect influenced by marketing managers and ultimately measurable in customer attitudes and purchase behaviour.

Marketing strategies usually require considerable organizational commitment and effort. 'Strong, offensive strategies do not come easily. They are usually the result of prolonged and painstaking analysis of the market, competitors and the trend of change' (Davidson: 1975, p. 115).

Operational marketing planning is a 'practical exercise in deciding what a business is to achieve through marketing activity in the year ahead. It is a logical thought process and an application of common sense. It provides a basis of objectives around which marketing tasks are set, budgets drawn up and results measured' (Middleton: 1980, p. 26). Operational plans express in precise, quantifiable terms what an organization is seeking to achieve in relation to its portfolio of products and segments over a particular time period.

Chapter summary

In the early 1990s, most medium to large organizations in travel and tourism undertake some form of marketing planning; most smaller ones still rely on 'feel for the market' to guide their decisions on objectives and the routes by which they intend to get there. In this author's experience, only very large organizations have established systematic planning processes comparable to those in manufacturing industries. For most organizations there is great scope for significant improvement in the time, effort, and expertise that is employed to undertake what is perhaps the most important single aspect of conducting any business.

Understood as the systematic process whereby objectives, strategies and plans are devised and adapted to changing circumstances, marketing planning – for strategy and tactics – is essential for effective marketing action. Planning does not replace flair and judgement, but provides a fertile base of information and broad strategic direction within which imagination, flair and vision can be harnessed to produce their best results.

Organizations vary as to the headings and labels used in their marketing plans; they may not be same as those used in this chapter. Readers should note that it is not the words that matter, but the logical stages and thought processes which they describe.

In all cases the current marketing plan represents the sum of the knowledge and judgement an organization has built up over time about its products, markets, and competitive strengths and weaknesses. Students should not be surprised if commercial organizations are unwilling to provide access to such plans.

Further reading

Kotler, P., *Marketing Management: Analysis, Planning, Implementation and Control*, 7th edit., Prentice-Hall International, 1991, Chapter 3.

14

Planning marketing campaigns: budgeting and measuring performance

This chapter draws the other chapters of Part Three together in a practical focus on the meaning and nature of *marketing campaigns*. The broad, unifying concept of campaigns is explained here and developed subsequently throughout Part Four of the book. Campaign is not a term widely used in marketing texts, except in the specific contexts of advertising or public relations. For travel and tourism products, in which production operations, service delivery, and marketing are so closely interlinked, the campaign concept is considered to be especially valuable for the practical insights it provides into organizing and controlling marketing tactics and programmes. It is strongly recommended to readers.

The word campaign, with its connotations of military action, is well-suited to the activities of marketing managers aggressively promoting their organizations' interests against competitors. Marketing managers, or product managers responsible for undertaking campaigns, have been aptly described as the 'stormtroopers of marketing' (Davidson: 1975, p. 95).

The chapter begins with definitions relevant

to the whole of Part Four. It identifies the techniques marketing managers deploy in their campaigns to influence consumer demand. It proceeds with an outline of basic methods used for budgeting in marketing, and explains them by working through typical campaign budgets. The final part of the chapter defines the approaches used to measure performance, and includes practical ways to monitor results.

Marketing campaigns are action programmes

'Campaign' describes any co-ordinated programme of marketing activities in the general field of promotion and distribution designed to influence and mould customers' behaviour. In marketing practice and in texts the term is often used in a restricted sense of advertising, sales promotion, or public relations. In fact the term is not used by Kotler, but Stanton defines a campaign as 'a coordinated series of promotional efforts built around a single theme or idea and designed to reach a predetermined goal . . . we should apply the campaign concept to the entire promotional programme' (Stanton: 1981, p. 391).

Without challenging Stanton's definition, this author believes it makes sense to broaden it further and to tie it specifically into the implementation phase of the marketing planning process. Thus:

A marketing campaign is a planned, integrated action programme designed to achieve specific marketing objectives and targets, through the deployment of a budget on the promotion and distribution of products, over a specified time period.

Campaigns may be aimed at consumers direct, or indirectly through a distribution network, or both. The focus of a marketing campaign is a short-run action programme and several campaigns would normally be necessary to achieve particular strategic objectives.

The 'menu' for marketing campaigns in travel and tourism

The full range of marketing techniques to be woven into campaigns is set out in Table 14.1 as a 'menu'. Each of them has its own implications for action. The implications are mainly promotional, but price is included in its discounted sense, product augmentation is included where it overlaps with sales promotion, and distribution is both a target for

Table 14.1 *The principal marketing campaign techniques used in travel and tourism*

Activity	Notes
Paid for media advertising	Includes TV, press, radio and outdoor. Also includes tourist board and other travel related guides, books and brochures that accept advertising.
Direct mail/door to door distribution	Including general sales literature or print items specifically designed for the purpose.
Public relations (PR)	All media exposure achieved as editorial matter, not paid for as advertising space. Also influence over target groups.
Sponsorship	An alternative form of media for specific target groups.
Exhibitions/shows/ workshops	Important alternative forms of distribution and display for reaching retail, wholesale and consumer target groups.
Personal selling	Via meetings, telephone contact, workshops. Primarily aimed at distributors and intermediaries purchasing for groups of consumers.
Sales literature	Especially promotional brochures and other print used in a servicing role.
Sales promotion	Short-term incentives offered as inducements to purchase, including temporary product augmentation. Covers sales force and distribution network as well as consumers.
Price discounting	A common form of sales promotion; includes extra commissions and bonuses for retailers.
Point of sale displays merchandising	Posters, window dressing, displays of brochures and other materials both of a regular and temporary incentive kind.
Familiarization and educational trips	Ways to motivate and facilitate distributor networks through product sampling. Also used to reach and influence journalists.
Distribution networks and commission	Organized systems or channels through which prospective customers achieve access to products; includes computerized links between principals and distributors (CRSs).

campaigns and part of the promotional process. The menu represents choices from which marketing managers will select according to their particular targets and market circumstances.

Campaigns in travel and tourism have two dimensions:

(a) Promotional techniques designed to motivate and move prospective customers towards a point of sale and also to provide incentives to purchase (includes promotion to distributors).
(b) Facilitation of access techniques designed to make it as easy as possible for motivated people to achieve their intended purchase, especially at the point of sale (access is defined in Chapter 6).

Marketing texts, even when dealing with service products, generally exclude access facilitation from discussions of campaigns and focus only on aspects of promotion, especially advertising. In the context of travel and tourism products this exclusion is not helpful. Where products are normally purchased ahead of consumption, as is the case, for example, in accommodation, transportation, tour operation or car rental, it makes sense to programme and include the full cost of access facilitation in the total campaign budget. Where distribution channels are highly diverse, as again is the case for much of travel and tourism, creation of consumer access for products is much closer to what is conventionally discussed as promotion than it is to what is conventionally described as distribution.

In other words, campaigns include all four variables of the marketing mix (four Ps), where their use is designed in the short term to influence and facilitate buyer behaviour to achieve targeted campaign objectives.

The marketing campaign menu is shown in summary form in Table 14.1. This summary is not intended to be a description of each technique but an indication of what lies within a spectrum of choice. The main techniques are discussed in some detail in Part Four of the book.

Marketing campaign budgets

The marketing budget may be defined as *the sum of the costs of the campaign action programme judged necessary to achieve the specified objectives and targets set out in the marketing plan.*

In practice the most difficult decisions in a marketing manager's year lie in estimating and agreeing the budget. The budget, usually drawn up on an annual campaign basis for each major product–market in an organization's portfolio, represents money which has to be spent 'up front', or ahead of the targeted volume and sales revenue it is expected to generate. Every £1,000 spent on campaign action programmes has to be paid for out of reserves, current cash flows, or by borrowing. It is money that can only be recovered at some future point from the projected surplus of income over operating expenditure, i.e., gross operating profit. On the other hand, as marketing managers are expected to demonstrate, if the money is *not* spent, revenue targets will not be achieved. Perhaps the hardest decision to justify is that of borrowing thousands or millions of pounds to spend on promotional campaigns, not to secure a projected operating surplus but to reduce the probable size of an expected loss. Such decisions have had to be taken by most airlines and many hotels in the international economic crises of the early 1990s in various parts of the world.

In practice, setting campaign budgets depends on finding answers to three fundamental questions.

1 How much money must be spent *in total* on a marketing campaign, in order to achieve objectives? This amount will usually be expressed as a percentage of total sales revenue or as a ratio. Thus a £50,000

marketing budget on a sales turnover of £1 million will be 5 per cent or a ratio of 1:20.

2 How will the total be *split between the products and segments* included in the campaign? In practice it is essential to divide a total budget between the specific sets of targets it is expected to achieve. The process for analysing product-market groupings, discussed in Chapters 10 and 12, provides a logical basis for such division. Naturally, if an international organization such as an airline is marketing itself in several countries, then the budget also has to be divided between the targeted countries. In larger organizations each product-market grouping will have a separate campaign budget.

3 How will the total be *divided between the component parts of the action programme.* The component parts of the action programme are the marketing tools or techniques shown in Table 14.1. The choices and the costs will be different for each of the targets within a campaign and for each of the countries included in a campaign.

With a few moments' thought, it should be clear that the apparently simple tasks implied in the three fundamental budget questions become very complicated in practice for businesses marketing their products to a range of segments in different countries.

Budgeting methods

Kotler (1984, p. 621) notes four common methods of setting both the total budget and any sub-division of it:

● Affordable method.
● Percentage of sales revenue method.
● Competitive parity method (matching competitors' spending).
● Objective and task method.

The first three of these methods are in fact quite closely related and rely primarily on historic information (previous budgeting levels), and marketing intelligence about competitors' actions. In essence, they are all 'rule of thumb' methods, which commence with some fairly broad notion of an appropriate marketing expenditure considered affordable, expressed as a proportion of sales revenue or turnover, such as 5 per cent. This aggregate percentage often becomes a norm, which sets an expenditure ceiling not to be exceeded unless a company is forced to do so to match or defeat the competition, or to respond to other unforeseen events. Although they are widely used in practice, these are aggregate or top-downwards methods, and shed little or no light on how total expenditure should be allocated between product-market groupings or divided between campaign elements, two of the three basic questions posed earlier.

The objective and task method is quite different. It begins with a specification of what is to be achieved (objective) and proceeds by stating and costing the techniques (tasks) required to achieve it. This method, which is closely related to so-called zero-budgeting methods, is obviously the one most closely associated with the systematic marketing planning approaches discussed in this book. If there are precise objectives for each product–market grouping, the objective and task method can be used to construct a budget from the bottom upwards through specification of tasks, so that all three budget questions posed earlier are answered. Objective and task methods are, however, time-consuming, and the procedures for costing are often dependent on marketing judgement. The tidy logic of the textbook may not be easily implemented in practice, especially for organizations with multiple objectives and several product–market groupings.

The next section explains and illustrates how these methods work in practice.

Budget summary	**Year (000s)**	**%**
Total turnover @ £350 (arsp)[1] on 1,000,000	£350,000	
Less cost of contracted tour components,[2] say	−280,000	80
= gross trading surplus	70,000	
Less targeted operating profit before tax @ say 3% of turnover	−10,500	3
= maximum sum to cover all administration and marketing costs	59,500	17
Specific costs of administration, operations and marketing		
Committed costs of operation (fixed)	6,000	⎫
Reservation system and overheads[3]	3,000	⎪
Non marketing administration costs[4]	3,000	⎬ 4.3
Marketing staff and overheads (UK)	3,000	⎪
Overseas support costs	15,000	⎭
Marketing campaign costs (fixed and variable)		
Advertising	2,000	0.6 ⎫
Sales promotion	1,000	0.3 ⎪
Brochure and distribution	5,500	1.6 ⎬ 11.3
Other[5]	1,000	0.2 ⎪
Sales commission to retail agencies (@ average 10%)[6]	30,000	8.6 ⎭
Contingency reserve[7]	5,000	1.4
	59,500	

Notes
1 arsp = average retail sales price, per package tour sold.
2 Accommodation, transport, transfers.
3 Includes computer systems, staff and all communication costs and depreciation.
4 Office expenses, rates, staff equipment etc., including general administration.
5 Workshops, PR, familiarization visits etc.
6 Assumes 90 per cent of all sales commissionable, others booked direct.
7 Held in reserve especially for tactical discounts to promote unsold capacity.

Figure 14.1 *Marketing budget calculations for a British tour operator. Adapted from Middleton, V. T. C.,* The Marketing Implications of Direct Selling *(1980); updated in 1992 with advice from a leading tour operator*

Affordable and percentage of sales revenue methods

An illustration of a notional British tour operator's budget is shown in Figure 14.1 to indicate how budgeting methods often operate in practice. The example assumes sales are achieved at targeted load factors (typically over 90 per cent) and the items, representing a typical trading, profit and loss account, have simplified headings for the sake of presentation. The budget is based on hypothetical figures but it broadly represents British tour operator cost structures of the early 1990s. See also the explanatory notes accompanying Figure 14.1.

While the percentages noted in the budget would fluctuate from year to year, the broad orders of magnitude hold good over time and the following points can be made:

● Of the total sales revenue, some 80 per cent is absorbed in contracted product component costs and a further 4.3 per cent is committed in fixed costs of operation. Of the remainder, the brochure commitment is inescapable, and so also is the retail agency support system to achieve the given volume of sales. In other words, a total approaching 90 per cent of sales revenue is, to all intents and purposes, committed in advance of any revenue received.

● In Figure 14.1 advertising, sales promotion and other discretionary campaign costs to be decided by the marketing manager, represent just 1 per cent of total turnover. Since it is most unlikely that in practice such costs would be either halved or doubled in any one year, the real level of budget discretion is probably under 0.5 per cent of sales turnover.

● In this example the contingency reserve for tactical discounts at £5,000,000 is already 50 per cent of the itemized discretionary expenditure, although it represents only £5 per tour package. In practice, if bookings fell seriously below targeted levels, the

contingency reserve would be increased by a factor of two or more but the money could only come from the £10.5 million targeted gross operating profit. In the early 1990s no large UK tour operator averaged anything near 5 per cent gross profit on trading operations, because of the need to spend contingency money on marketing, especially tactical price discounting. The illustration is based on 3 per cent.

● There is no common agreement as to what items should be included or excluded from a marketing budget. There is a strong case for including retail commission, since it is money paid out to ensure effective distribution and sales of products, the fourth 'P' of the marketing mix.

From Figure 14.1, it should be clear that the so-called affordable and percentage of turnover methods of budgeting are relevant and practical. Apart from establishing upper limits to expenditure, however, such methods do not provide any guidance whatever as to how best to apportion the affordable sums. For that, it is necessary to use the objective and task method discussed next.

The objective and task method

To illustrate this method, consider the hypothetical but realistic case of a hotel consortium comprising 100 individually owned hotels with a combined capacity of 6,000 rooms. Assume that, through careful diagnosis and prognosis, the consortium has set itself a marketing objective to sell 45 per cent of its aggregate capacity (2,700) rooms as weekend packages over 20 selected weekends between October and April. For ease of calculation, assume that each package lasts for 2 nights and covers two people. The average price, published in the consortium's brochure, is £85 per person/package, which includes breakfast and dinner for the 2 nights.

The sales revenue target is, therefore:

2,700 (rooms) × 20 (weekends) × 2 persons
× £85 per person = package sales
revenue =   £9,180,000

2,700 (rooms) × 20 (weekends) × 2 persons
× 2 (days) × £8 per day = additional
revenue in bars, etc. =   £1,728,000

Total sales revenue =   £10,908,000

Because the fixed costs of hotel operation are already committed, the hotel consortium stands to achieve a gross contribution (additional revenue over variable costs) of around 45 per cent on this business, say £5 million.

The question to resolve is how much should the consortium spend on marketing in order to achieve the £5 million additional revenue? By applying conventional ratio methods, it is easy to calculate (using rounded figures) that:

5 per cent of total sales revenue including additional spending is £545,000
10 per cent of total sales revenue including additional spending is £1,100,000
20 per cent of total sales revenue including additional spending is £2,200,000

Even beyond the 20 per cent level of expenditure on marketing, the consortium would still find it advantageous to invest – assuming that without marketing effort, the potential £5 million gross contribution would not be achieved.

With clear objectives set, which in practice would be split by area of the country and the projected profile of target buyers, the next step is to itemize and cost the tasks in an effective marketing campaign.

Task-based campaign budget

The following costs are indicative of what would be spent in practice (1992 prices) by the consortium to meet the objectives noted in the preceding section:

Cost of producing say, 750,000 brochures	£150,000
Direct mail, say 200,000 pieces (via hotels' own lists and coupon response)	£80,000
Advertising, consumer media and trade press	£180,000
Advertising in tourist board guides etc.	£3,000
Point of sale material (retail agents and hotels)	£25,000
PR campaign costs	£15,000
Retail travel agency commission (assuming 35 per cent bookings via this route)	£350,000
Other, including distribution costs to retailers	£50,000
Total =	£853,000

The following points can be made:

1 Selecting the itemized tasks and estimating the expenditure required are based on a mixture of *fact* (postal costs, brochure costs, retail commission), *experience* (knowledge of which activities are most relevant for selling weekend packages and the costs and quantities of any previous campaigns), and *judgement* (especially in relation to media expenditure but drawing on advertising agency knowledge and expertise).

2 There can be no absolute certainty that £853,000 will produce the targeted bookings for the consortium. There is, however, a systematic method and framework for making decisions, within which it is possible to focus facts, experience, and judgement. Given adequate evaluation of the campaign's results, the systematic framework would also serve as a learning mechanism to refine the decision process for any subsequent campaigns.

3 £853,000 happens to be 9.3 per cent of the product package price, 7.8 per cent of the total sales revenue, and 17 per cent of the gross contribution. The advertising (paid

space in the media) is 2 per cent of the package sales revenue. In the end these ratios have little meaning except to establish that the pay-off is worth the investment. The cost of the campaign can be seen as the price for achieving the targeted business, and at that point the ratios are only of interest for control and evaluation purposes – they were not used to determine the size of the marketing budget.

4 In practice, in monitoring and evaluating a campaign of this sort, the hotel group would wish to analyse the proportion of its bookings which came from previous customers. It may be possible to adapt the components of the campaign to achieve a higher proportion of sales from repeat bookers, thereby lowering marketing costs.

5 The functional relation between marketing expenditure and targeted revenue should be clear.

Performance measurement: evaluation, monitoring and control

Kotler states that 'marketing control is the natural sequel to marketing planning, organization and implementation' (Kotler: 1984, p. 773). All marketing texts stress the importance of measuring the results achieved by action programmes against the planned targets. But, given the importance of the subject, it is surprising how little space most books offer on measurement, and there are no recognized guidelines for travel and tourism. The subject is too often seen, as in most hotel groups, as the responsibility of accountants and financial controllers. It is far too important for that.

Performance measurement provides the vital information for marketing managers to:

● Respond quickly and effectively if actual sales and other indicators vary significantly from targets.
● Learn from current experience in ways which will make the subsequent year's campaign targets and budgets more cost-efficient.

● Adjust strategic objectives in the light of current results.
● Integrate marketing decisions with those of other key business functions, especially accounting and finance, and operations management.
● Make the vital marginal adjustments to campaigns, which in high fixed-cost businesses will always have a major impact on profit or loss.

It is not too much to claim that the effectiveness and efficiency of marketing is actually determined by the quality of the performance measurement techniques used.

It is worth repeating that it is impossible for marketing managers to respond effectively to aggregate measures of the total volume or revenue. In other words, the number of airline passengers carried over a year is a useless measure in practice, except perhaps for annual reports and PR purposes; the total number of room nights sold by a hotel, or total bed occupancy, is just an academic statistic of no marketing management value. What matters is how many first-class passenger bookings were received against targets, and which of the segments were up or down; or how conference bookings for events over 100 persons responded to the action programmes targeted at conference organizers. This all-important linkage between targeting, budgeting and measuring performance *disaggregated by product–market groupings* is a theme throughout this book. It is reflected in the hotel example used in this chapter and further illustrated in Part Five.

In travel and tourism it will be found helpful to distinguish between four aspects of performance measurement that are the responsibility of marketing managers:

1 *Evaluation* – defined as the systematic periodic evaluation of achievement of stated objectives. Evaluation is usually an annual process and often a focal part of marketing audits carried out as part of the strategic planning process described in Chapter 12.

2 *Monitoring* – the systematic measurement of performance on a daily, weekly, or monthly basis, which assesses actual results against targeted sales. The results of monitoring are used immediately for marketing control and also fed into the annual evaluation.

For both of these aspects of measurement it is essential that marketing targets are specified with measurement in mind. It is a central criterion in the planning process described in Chapter 13 that no target is accepted unless the method of measuring it is defined in advance. In this sense performance monitoring is more than a 'sequel of marketing planning, organization and implementation', it is an integral part of the targeting and objective setting process. If objectives cannot be monitored and assessed by affordable methods, they should not be selected.

3 *Marketing control* – tactical marketing-management actions taken continuously in response to the information provided by monitoring. Generally this action will be funded out of contingency sums in marketing budgets, but in crisis conditions additional funding will be required. Such actions normally focus on tactical pricing, sales promotion and advertising.

4 *Innovation and test marketing* – not normally seen as part of performance measurement. This book argues in Chapter 11, however, that opportunities for systematic innovation and testing represent a massive and under-utilized asset to most marketing managers in travel and tourism. It can and certainly should be used regularly as a highly cost-effective form of both testing and measuring the effectiveness of marketing programmes for travel and tourism products, as well as in the more traditional role of product testing and evaluation. The opportunities arise because customer contact on premises or sites is a normal part of service operations; multi-site operations are able to compare responses to innovation between outlets, often very quickly.

In several parts of this book, reference is made to *marketing the margin*. It means concentrating marketing effort on the incremental percentage occupancy, or load factor, or visitor numbers, which in travel and tourism usually generate revenue at very little or no additional cost. Performance measurement must be designed to highlight those margins and the effectiveness of marketing programmes in influencing them.

Campaign plan monitoring – sales variance

The more that operational marketing objectives are made precise, in terms of volume targets, time periods, and specific products and segments (discussed in Chapter 13), the easier it is to measure results. Airlines, for example, forecast their passenger volume over a long-run period, by product type, e.g. first-class, business class, or types of economy fare offered, and by route, with projections on a daily basis. With modern computer facilities they are able to read sales results within hours of flight performance.

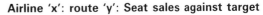

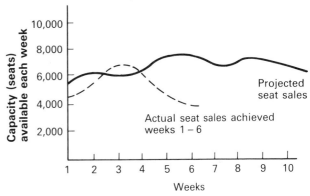

Figure 14.2 *Variance of sales against targets for an airline*

In Figure 14.2 projected sales represent weekly planning targets, based partly on previous years' operations and partly on diagnosis/ prognosis. Airline capacity and operations are scheduled on such projections, timetables are published, seats are made available through CRSs, and marketing campaigns are carried out ahead of sales. In weeks 4–6 actual sales dropped. As soon as the fall is detected, marketing managers must establish the cause of the drop and consider action to generate more sales, employing contingency reserves if necessary. This type of monitoring is known as variance analysis, and, in forms suitable to the products in question, it is the cornerstone of most marketing control. A visitor attraction would target weekly sales by segments such as school groups, holiday visitors, day visitors, and coach parties, and monitor actual sales against those targets. The management would separately plot actual shop and catering sales against their targets, to measure variance and so on.

Sometimes sales move far enough ahead of target to make it possible to reduce marketing budgets. British tour operators in early 1986, for example, drastically reduced consumer advertising expenditure partly because their pricing tactics generated massive unpaid publicity and produced booking levels well ahead of targets. It doesn't often happen.

Market share variance

In consumer goods marketing, market share analysis and variance over time is a second basic aspect of marketing monitoring. In travel and tourism, however, apart from transport operations, which are legally required to register capacity and carryings, share data is generally either not known at all, or estimated months afterwards, too late to trigger a variance response. Own sales analysis, without knowledge other than general marketing intelligence of competitors' sales, can of course provide misleading information.

When using variance monitoring, 'market-share analysis, like sales analysis, increases in value when the data is disaggregated along various dimensions. The company might watch the progress of its market share by product line,

customer type, region, or other breakdowns' (Kotler: 1984, p. 748).

Customer satisfaction variance

The third principal element in variance analysis can be achieved by regularly monitoring satisfaction, both overall and by product components. As described in Chapter 11, providers of travel and tourism service products are particularly well placed to exploit opportunities to measure customer satisfaction on a regular basis and to read any shifts from average scores. Figure 14.3 illustrates the point in the context of a tour operator monitoring the performance of one of the resort hotels included in its programme.

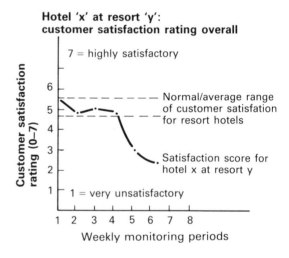

Figure 14.3   *Variance of satisfaction against targets for a tour operator*

In this illustration, based on data collected and analysed over many months, normal customer satisfaction ratings for hotels overall typically vary between 4.8 and 5.5. In that band hotels are generating good satisfaction in the judgement of customers using them. In weeks 1 to 4 satisfaction is normal. In week 5 it plunges and stays down. Why? Analysis of other scores may reveal a particular problem with food or service, and management action can be taken to rectify the problem and return scores to the average band. To be useful, such variance must be known within days of its occurrence. Modern computer technology is of increasing value in making such rapid response possible. In this case marketing-research methods to monitor satisfaction also operate as management-control mechanisms.

Ratio variance

Once the budget is agreed it is possible to calculate a series of financial comparisons between marketing expenditure and revenue targets, and they can subsequently be reviewed against actual revenue achieved. Provided that an organization divides its total portfolio of product-markets into logical groupings or profit centres for management purposes, it is possible to establish the costs and revenues attributable to each grouping (see also Chapter 10) and then calculate for each:

● Ratio of total marketing expenditure: total sales revenue.
● Ratio of total marketing expenditure: gross contribution.
● Ratio of total marketing expenditure: net profit.
● Ratio of total marketing expenditure: unit cost of production.

The comparison of current and historic ratios, and ratios between product-market groupings in the portfolio, yields very useful evaluation data. Total marketing expenditure can also be divided into its component parts to establish separate ratios for advertising, sales force, etc.

As with other variance measures, the purpose is to alert managers to any deviations from normal expectations that may require marketing action, both within the campaign period and in the longer run.

Chapter summary

This chapter defines marketing campaigns as 'integrated action programmes designed to achieve specific marketing objectives through the deployment of a budget ... over a specified time period'. Within the deliberately broad definition adopted in this chapter, campaigns can be seen as the final stage in the hierarchy of business goals, strategies and plans, introduced in Chapter 12 (see Figure 12.1).

Action programmes have to be carefully costed before implementation, and this requires marketing managers to find answers to three vital questions concerning the budget: how much to spend in total, how the total should be split between the products and segments in an organization's total product portfolio, and how it should be allocated among the wide range of promotional and other marketing-mix techniques presented as a menu in Table 14.1.

The chapter works through two different tourism related marketing budgets to explain the process and methods of budget setting, and especially to explain the important *objective and task* method. This is the budgeting method that most closely meets the needs of modern marketing-led organizations. It is relevant in its principles to all sectors of the travel and tourism industry, both commercial and non-commercial. In particular this method is the only one that directly facilitates the systematic processes for performance measurement and control defined in the chapter. The form and main aspects of performance measurement are noted and their role in *marketing the margin* is highlighted. Stress is laid on the potential value of continuous, planned innovation and test marketing for travel and tourism businesses.

Finally, this chapter serves as a bridge between Part Three, which explains the meaning and processes of planning and the role of marketing managers who are responsible for it, and Part Four, which reviews each of the main promotional techniques, and the way they are implemented effectively in practice. The marketing campaign is the coordinating framework, for all the marketing mix techniques included in action programmes.

Further reading

Kotler, P., *Marketing Analysis: Planning, Implementation and Control*, 7th edit., Prentice-Hall International, 1991, Chapter 26.

Part Four

Using the Principal Marketing Tools in Travel and Tourism

15

Advertising and public relations

Advertising and public relations (PR) are two of the most important promotional tools, or *marketing functions*, used in the implementation of marketing campaigns. As key elements of marketing communications, advertising and PR are considered together, because they are primarily concerned to influence people away from the places of production, delivery and purchase of products. This influence is achieved through the use of press, television, and other mass media discussed in this chapter, making advertising and PR the most pervasive and visible elements of what the consumer sees of marketing efforts. But in common with Baker (1979, p. 254), it is sensible to interpret marketing communications broadly, to include the other promotional activities of personal selling and sales promotion, as well as advertising and PR. In travel and tourism the special role of sales literature, which is partly advertising, partly sales promotion and partly distribution, (see Chapter 17) must also be included in marketing communications.

As a percentage of sales revenue spent on marketing, advertising and PR are less significant in travel and tourism than for many other consumer products. Even so, advertising is often the most costly element in campaign budgets and has added importance where it is used to complement the other campaign elements, such as promotional print, tactical price-cuts, and sales promotion. Advertising, and to a lesser extent PR also, are often required to make prospective customers aware of the existence of the other campaign elements.

The chapter begins by setting advertising and PR in the context of marketing communications. The barriers in the communication process are explained by way of a tourism example, and the main technical terms used in advertising practice are introduced. Advertising and PR definitions are discussed, and the objectives of PR and advertising are compared, followed by discussion of the creative role, media selection and costs, measuring results, and the use of advertising agencies. The different forms and usage of PR are outlined, and the chapter ends with a note on the reasons why advertising expenditure, as a proportion of sales revenue, is relatively low in the travel and tourism industry.

The scale of advertising and PR

The British Advertising Association estimates that over £5,500 million was spent in 1991 on display advertising (as distinct from other spending on small line entries in the press, known as classified advertising). This sum is equivalent to about 1.6 per cent of all British consumers' expenditure nationally. Expressed as a proportion of annual sales revenue, consumer advertising expenditure varies widely according to different types of product, from under 1 per cent to over 30 per cent. Approximately 4 per cent of all British advertising expenditure is accounted for by holidays, travel and transport and, with the exception of visitor attractions, very few advertisers in the tourism industry spend more than 3 per cent of their sales revenue on this form of communication.

PR expenditure in the UK is harder to define and measure than advertising. In terms of the turnover of PR agencies it is probably equivalent to well under 5 per cent of the total spent nationally on display advertising. Its total impact on consumers, however, is very much greater than this 5 per cent figure suggests, and, for some sectors of travel and tourism, PR activity is at least as important as advertising. This point is developed later in the chapter.

The purpose of advertising and PR

Both advertising and PR activity are part of the marketing communication process between producers and prospective consumers, the ultimate purpose of which is to influence buyer behaviour and manipulate demand. They are both highly technical subjects but their essential functions are easy to understand. Their principal role in marketing is to enable producers to *reach* people in their homes or other places away from where products are sold, and *communicate* to them *messages* intended to influence their purchasing behaviour. The messages may range from subtly attractive visual images and symbols designed to appeal and stimulate travel desires and needs, to simple sales announcements drawing attention to specific product offers.

With over a century of continuous development, every aspect of creating and designing 'messages', and choosing how and where to show them, has been studied and analysed in depth. But the exact ways in which both advertising and PR work on buyers' minds, and influence their purchasing behaviour are still not fully understood. In part this is because most people are continually exposed to so many advertising messages in their lives that the actual effect of any single one of them is almost impossible to evaluate beyond the level of simple memory or 'recall'.

The communication process and its barriers

Provided an advertiser knows which market segments he seeks to influence, the 'reach' part of the process is relatively simple. It requires money to buy space in the press, TV, posters, and so on, and there is a great deal of expertise in the buying process. But reach is not the principal concern for advertisers. The main problem is to design and express chosen messages in a form that is most likely to communicate with a targeted audience. If there is no 'reach', there can be no communication. But even with maximum reach and wide exposure of an advertisement, communication only occurs if the message is actually received, is understood, and is of interest to the receiver. Even then, action in response to the message may not occur.

For reasons introduced in Chapter 5, all of us have barriers and filters in our minds. The filters influence the ways in which we perceive and understand the world around us generally, including messages beamed at us by advertisers. These filters are the product of our personalities, experience of, and attitudes to, life; in many ways all of us are conditioned to see what we want to see. It is easy to demonstrate with group discussions conducted for marketing-research purposes that, in any group of people, there will be several different perceptions of the same advertising message.

In other words, a vital skill in advertising communications lies in understanding at least the main filters at work in the minds of targeted buyers, and designing messages, symbols and images, which are most likely to be well received by them.

The 'reach and communicate,' process is represented in Figure 15.1. To understand the process, consider the example of a hotel group with around 10 per cent share of the market for sales conferences. The group uses its own sales team to motivate key conference buyers in client

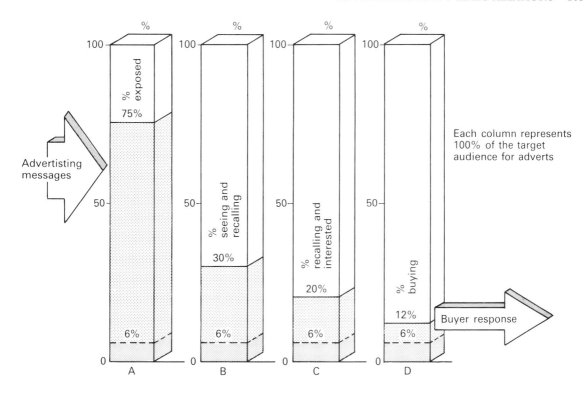

Figure 15.1 *Filters in the communication process*

companies but seeks also to communicate its advantages to the wider target audience of business people who have attended a residential sales conference at least once in the last 3 years. The hotel group has decided to use press advertising to reach its target audience. Figure 15.1 indicates how the original message works through several stages to the purchase decision. The explanation of the stages introduces some of the main terms used in advertising in a realistic context. These terms are further explained in the next section.

Figure 15.1 shows in percentage terms how the potential impact of advertising is reduced in practice. Column A represents 100 per cent of the target segment of people who attend sales conferences; their profiles as consumers would be identified in detail and quantified in the hotel group's marketing planning. With a realistic budget, the hotel group might hope to reach and

expose its message to about 75 per cent of the total target group. This means buying space in magazines and press that three-quarters of the target are likely to buy and look at at least once during the advertising campaign period.

Inevitably, not all who read the papers selected for the advertisements read all pages. Many who glance at advertising pass on very quickly to other pages and rapidly forget what they saw. Column B indicates that in this case 30 per cent of the target audience saw the hotel group's advertising and would be able to remember at least seeing it, if they were asked to do so (a commonly used method of advertising evaluation). In practice the proportion that B is of A reflects partly the size of the advertisements and the number of times they are shown, (frequency of insertion) and partly how memorable the adverts are to the target audience (creative execution).

Column C represents the proportion of the target audience who not only remember something about the advertising they saw, but are sufficiently interested to consider the hotel group's product at some time.

Column D represents those who actually participate in a sales conference at one of the group's hotels in the 12 months during which the campaign runs. The dotted line drawn through all the columns represents the 6 per cent of existing regular or repeat buyers, who would have bought the product anyway and are not converted by the advertising, although their interest may be reinforced by it.

In this example, therefore, an additional 6 per cent of target customers purchase the product as non-regular or first-time buyers during the period of the marketing campaign, including some who would be lapsed previous buyers. Adding the loyal and all the other buyers together gives a total of 12 per cent share (up from 10 per cent noted earlier). Accordingly advertising appears to have been successful, and an increased share of the conference market has been achieved. In fact of course any additional business achieved would also reflect the competitiveness of the conference facilities offered, pricing, and all the other elements of the marketing mix used to motivate additional buyers.

Simple though Figure 15.1 is, it makes it easy to appreciate that great expertise is required at each stage of the communication process, in order:

1 To purchase the spaces best calculated to reach the target (per cent of A).
2 To arrest and capture attention with appealing messages (per cent of B).
3 To keep attention through interesting information (also a per cent of B).
4 To communicate the key points that matter to buyers (per cent of C).
5 To motivate prospective buyers and turn interest into purchase (per cent of D).

At every stage there are losses in the communication process. Over time, consumers forget and have their attention drawn elsewhere by competitive offers, so that advertising messages suffer 'wear out', and have to be repeated at frequent intervals.

Modified to suit the circumstances of the other forms of marketing communication, the filters noted in this section are still applicable. Brochures and other promotional print, for example, are clearly subject to the same barriers of interest and recall.

Defining advertising and PR

Within the context of marketing communications advertising is defined by the American Marketing Association as 'any paid form of non-personal presentation and promotion of ideas, goods or services [to a targeted audience] by an identified sponsor'. The words in brackets are inserted by the author to stress that initial segmentation and targeting always precede effective advertising. 'Non-personal' implies the use of media to reach a mass audience, as distinguished from media targeted at individuals identified by name and address, such as direct mail. An 'identified sponsor' means that the advertiser's name, or that of its product, is clearly evident in the communication.

For the price of chosen media space, the advertiser has full control over the message, its size, its appearance, its content, where and when it appears, and how frequently. 'Full control' is subject in most countries to legally imposed standards designed to protect the consumer from deception and fraud. Like any other aspect of business life, advertising is controlled, constrained and, where appropriate, subject to penalties imposed by law and other regulations. It is also subject to voluntary codes of practice, succinctly summarized in the British Code of Advertising Practice, in the requirement that all adverts 'should be legal, decent, honest and truthful'.

Most travel and tourism advertising is product-focused and aimed either at consumers or the travel trade as part of marketing campaigns. But large organizations, such as airlines and hotel groups, also buy media space to communicate with other target groups, such as shareholders or politicians. They use advertising more broadly to communicate the name and corporate image of an organization as a whole.

Public-relations activity has communication functions in the wider context of corporate goals, as well as in marketing, and its budget is normally allocated out of corporate rather than marketing funds. It is defined by the British Institute of Public Relations as 'the deliberate, planned and sustained effort to establish and maintain mutual understanding between an organization and the public'. PR may be personal or non-personal but it does not involve the purchase of media space, and therefore the level of control over what appears in the media is limited. 'Public' has to be interpreted as comprising all the target groups an organization wishes to influence, from government ministers to local politicians and residents of an area in which a business is located. Although planned in its direction (like advertising), PR is more opportunist in its execution, exploiting events as they occur and maintaining good links and goodwill with the media, which can be drawn on as circumstances require.

Both advertising and PR communications are designed to operate away from the places in which the production, consumption, and purchase of service products takes place.

Terms commonly used in advertising practice

Advertising and PR are technical subjects that have generated their own jargon terms. Seventeen commonly used terms are presented in annotated form in Figure 15.2. They are intended to serve as an *aide-mémoire*.

Above and below-the-line expenditure

Students of marketing often have difficulty with the historic but frequently used distinction between 'above' and 'below' the line. Budget allocations for the purchase of media space by advertising agencies, to whom commission is paid by media owners, is traditionally known as above-the-line expenditure. By this definition, all other promotional expenditure not used in buying space is below-the-line. In the 1990s, when nearly all medium and large advertising agencies deal with above and below-the-line, and increasing expenditure is allocated to direct response marketing (see Chapter 19), these traditional terms are no longer helpful. In travel and tourism so-called below-the-line is often the largest sector of the communications budget.

The role and objectives of advertising and PR

For the purposes of marketing campaigns, the principal roles and objectives of both advertising and PR are summarized in Table 15.1. As discussed in Chapter 12, marketing objectives invariably have a strategic dimension to which the specific objectives of any campaign must be related. Both advertising and PR are used to achieve strategic objectives, especially product and corporate positioning. The role and objectives noted in Table 15.1 therefore operate at both strategic and tactical levels.

Most of the objectives in Table 15.1 are self-explanatory in terms of previous chapters in this book. 'Connections' refers to making links between a product and a target group, typically by creating visual images and through copy, with which customers can easily identify. 'Response' may be to fill in a coupon, use the telephone, or simply to feel motivated to make a visit (as for visitor attractions).

Audience	Often used generically to describe readers, viewers, listeners exposed to all forms of media. 'Target audience' describes the segments identified for communication purposes.
Message	What advertising aims to communicate. Both visual and copy elements, including images and symbols.
Media	Newspapers, TV, radio and all other mass circulation means of communicating either paid or unpaid messages to prospective consumers. Advertising media are those that sell space to advertisers as a commercial transaction.
Editorial matter	The content of the media, other than advertising, controlled by editorial policies.
Scheduling	Choice of media to be used, and the timing and frequency of insertions of adverts.
Appropriation	Conventional name for the advertising budget, also known as 'above the line'.
Proposition	The single minded, clear message of an advert, usually focused on the reason to purchase a product.
USP	Unique Selling Proposition – a particular product or company characteristic that distinguishes it from competitors, and is a main reason to buy.
Creative execution	The choice of appealing concepts, themes, ideas, pictures, situations or words, chosen to communicate the decided message.
Copy	The words included in an advertisement, normally having three components: a 'headline' to attract attention; 'body copy' to convey information, 'strap line' to conclude or sign off.
Insertion	One appearance of an advertisement.
OTS	Opportunities (by the target group) to see any particular advert. OTS is a function of coverage and the frequency of insertions, and quantified for media-buying purposes.
Coverage	The proportion of an identified audience that is reached. Coverage is related to frequency of insertions.
CPT	Cost per thousand of the target group to whom any advert is exposed. CPT is a basic cost figure used in buying media.
Threshold	The minimum level of expenditure necessary to achieve measurable impact with an advert.
Direct response	Advertising from which the intended customer response is a direct contact with the producer, by phone, letter or coupon, without going through a distribution channel such as a travel agent.
Fees and commission	Advertising agencies earn their income through commission paid on media purchases, and/or fees usually charged for smaller accounts and 'below the line work'.

Figure 15.2 *Advertising and PR terms in common use*

Table 15.1 *The principal roles and objectives of advertising and PR*

	Advertising	Public Relations
Principal role	Targeted sales-related messages, aimed at influencing prospective customers, away from the point of sale	Targeted messages, aimed at general awareness and interest, away from the point of sale
Principal objectives	Controlled messages and symbols designed to: ● create awareness/remind ● project images or 'positions' ● impart specific sales messages ● produce connections ● reassure ● alter perceptions ● stimulate desires ● generate action/response ● promote favourable attitudes	Guided messages and symbols designed to create goodwill and favourable attitudes: ● as for ads, from an 'editorial angle' ● limited extent ● very limited ● as for adverts ● limited extent ● as for ads ● limited ● very limited ● as for ads

Stages in the advertising process

Decisions on advertising objectives are geared to marketing objectives and strategies, as defined in the marketing planning process. There are six basic stages in advertising, which are common ground, well covered in most marketing texts (see recommended companion chapters). Accordingly, this section is intended to be a summary of the six basic steps, identified by Rodger (1968, p. 198) as:

1 identifying the audience to be reached (profiles of segments),
2 determining and creating . . . specific advertising messages . . . (to meet stated advertising objectives),
3 selecting the most effective . . . media to reach the audience,
4 scheduling the chosen media . . . timing, frequency and impact,
5 determining the advertising budget,
6 measuring advertising results.

Rodger stresses the need to be specific in advertising messages and in media selection, and to draw up budgets around precisely identified target audiences. This common ground fits well with the task approach to budgeting covered in the previous chapter. The four stages needing some further amplification here are stages 2, 3, 4 and 6. Stage 1 is covered in Chapters 7 and 11, Stage 5 is covered in Chapter 14.

Creating specific advertising messages

When the objectives which advertising is to fulfil have been decided in relation to an identified segment of buyers, the crucial step in the advertising process is the creative one of producing memorable pictures and words. Creative execution captures attention, expresses the essence of a product in a few words that say it all, and provides key information. Creative quality cannot be defined, but it can be recognized and measured in terms of recall. It is the factor most likely to push the message through the filters of the communication process previously described.

In travel and tourism good examples of creative executions are:

- 'That will do nicely' (American Express).
- 'We try harder' (Avis).
- 'We speak your language' (British Tourist Authority in the USA market).
- 'I love New York' (New York State).
- 'The World's favourite airline' (British Airways).

At a different, less memorable, but very creative way in the early 1980s, Holiday Inns Inc. ran a series of advertisements in the USA with the headline: *Only one hotel chain guarantees your room will be right.*

Subsequently extended to Europe, the advertising copy said, 'Everything in your Holiday Inn room will be right. Or we will make it right. Or we will refund the cost of your room for that night'. The clever aspect of this was the concept of a 'guarantee', with all it communicates about assured quality standards. In fact none of HI's competitors would be likely to refuse to make a room right, so the real product difference was only slight. But Holiday Inns created the proposition, claimed it first, and made it effectively their own concept, since no other chain could say 'we guarantee our rooms, too', without appearing to copy the original, and indirectly complimenting HI. Hilton International's 'The Hilton Promise' is a 1990s illustration of this thinking (see Chapter 12).

Doyle Dane Bernbach, the international advertising agency, quote Bill Bernbach on creativity as follows:

. . . people can't believe you if they don't know what you're saying, and they can't know what you're saying if they don't listen to you, and they won't listen to you if you're not interesting.

And you won't be interesting unless you say things freshly, originally, imaginatively.

Selecting the most effective media

As Joyce put it, 'Advertising in general can only work by being seen and heard by consumers and operating on their minds' (1967, p. 170). Finding effective, memorable ways to operate on consumer's minds is the creative aspect. Arranging to be seen and heard (reach) is the job of media selection and buying space.

Media types

The choice of media types is wide. Fifteen types commonly used in travel and tourism are noted below. Within each type, e.g. national press, there are multiple choices, such as eleven national daily papers in Britain, nine Sunday papers, and so on. As always, it is the marketing manager's job, in this case usually employing an advertising agency, to consider the options and make the selection calculated to produce the best return for the available budget.

- TV national or regional, or cable TV.
- International satellite TV stations.
- Radio, national and local stations.
- National press (daily/Sunday newspapers and magazine supplements).
- Regional and local press.
- Consumer magazines (quarterly, monthly, weeklies).
- Cinema advertising.
- Trade press and magazines (e.g. *Travel News* and *Travel Trade Gazette*).
- Outdoor – transport sites (underground, airport, rail stations – buses and bus shelters) – poster sites in general locations.
- Tourist board brochures and guides (selling space to operators), commercial consumer guides (for hotels, campsites).
- Directories and Yellow Pages.
- Exhibitions (display space on stands).
- In-house magazines, (e.g. airline or hotel magazines, selling space to other operators).
- Direct mail (using purchased address lists).
- Door-to-door distribution (an alternative to direct mail).

The professional practice of media selection, buying and scheduling, requires extensive skills, plus experience and judgement. Since the 1970s, the use of computers to aid the selection process has become widespread. The principles of the media selection process are not difficult to grasp, however, and marketing managers have to be familiar with them. The process is marketing research based reflecting the facts that:

1 All market segments to be reached through media advertising must be precisely identified in terms of numbers of people, and profiled with key demographic, socio-economic, geodemographic and psychographic variables (see Chapter 7).
2 All media owners are able to identify their reader/viewer or listener numbers and profile with considerable precision. Each of the media has a particular style and characteristics of its own.

Given precision in 1 and 2 above, media selection and scheduling are essentially a matching process for the profiles of target buyers with media options, having regard to the size of the budget available, which limits some options. For example, many travel and tourism organizations would prefer to use TV, but at around £100,000 (1990 prices) for minimum effective national coverage, most cannot consider it.

Profiling of consumers was covered in Chapters 5 and 7, and establishing the reading and viewing habits of target segments is a normal part of the marketing-research techniques covered in Chapter 11. Media profiles are provided mainly by the media owners themselves and have three main elements. First, to the owners of *The Times*, for example, the paper is a commercial product. To be successful in an editorial sense and attract readers, it must understand its customers' interests in considerable detail. To be successful in selling advertising space, *The Times* has to supply advertising agencies with a comprehensive

profile of the readers it can reach. Since over two-thirds of press revenue in Britain comes from advertising revenue rather than sales of papers, the media obviously have a vested interest in knowing their readers in great detail.

Second, the physical characteristics of the media are important to advertisers – size of pages, quality of paper, clarity of colour, and frequency of publication. TV can provide movement and images not possible in the press. Third, media also have identifiable editorial styles or 'positions', which reflect the interests of their typical readers. The *Daily Telegraph* and the *News of the World*, for example, are very different in their style of presentation. Some products are better suited to advertising in so-called 'up-market' media, and others, of 'down-market' appeal, must be advertised in the 'down-market' press.

No single choice of media coincides exactly with an advertiser's target segments, and space usually has to be bought in several media to provide a balanced coverage.

Media costs

All commercial media publish rate cards showing their regular prices for advertising spaces. The prices reflect the size of an advertisement and the numbers of readers/viewers the media reach. The standard yardstick in the industry for any given size (such as page, half page or so many column centimetres), is 'cost per thousand reached' (CPT). Thus, if a full page (four-colour) ad. in the *Sunday Times* magazine is seen by 4 million adults, and costs £55,000, the CPT for that media is £13.75. The CPT for other media may be only £3.50, but there is much more to media buying than CPT. Some British media, such as *TV Times* and *Radio Times*, are known to be especially effective in travel and tourism around December/January time. Accordingly, their CPT rates are higher than average but may still represent good value for money calculated in responses per £1,000 spent. As with any other perishable product, the rate-card prices are only indicative. Agencies are skilled at negotiating purchases at discounted rates and few advertisers pay anything like the nominal rate-card prices.

Measuring the results of advertising and PR

Mainly because advertising and PR expenditure are only two of the ways used to influence sales through marketing campaigns, it is rarely possible to isolate the sales effect of such expenditure with any precision. As Rodger put it, 'the causal relationship between advertising and sales is, generally speaking, limited, and, as yet unmeasurable' (1968, p. 216). The effect of a price-cut, or a competitor's actions, or even the weather, are all capable of distorting the relationship. A successful PR initiative, or an unforeseen change in exchange rates, can easily outweigh advertising effects in the short run. Even so, marketing managers are required to assess the effectiveness of their spending, and the following ways are used in practice.

Response measurement

Where an advertisement is designed to create a request for information, or provides a phone number for bookings, it is possible to quantify response against cost with precision. It is common practice to code advertising with letters or numbers that identify each of the media used and the date of insertion, so that replies can be assessed against the original expenditure. The use of coupons to generate responses is common in travel and tourism.

Market-research measures of communication effect

For an important advertising or PR campaign, sample surveys of target customers may be interviewed before and after a campaign to assess levels of recall and any change in attitudes. For example, if 10 per cent of a target group can recollect advertising for an airline before a campaign, while 30 per cent can do so after it, there is clear evidence of increased awareness. If the percentage of those expressing a preference for using the airline rises from, say 8 per cent to 18 per cent, there is evidence of change in attitude. Neither of these measures correlates precisely with sales, but they do indicate communication effects.

In travel and tourism, because customers arrive at the producer's premises, e.g. hotels and visitor attractions, it is often possible to organize sample surveys of customers on the premises. Visitors can be asked how they heard of the product and to state what advertising (if any) they had seen.

Pre-testing of communication effects

If a campaign is large enough to justify the cost, it is possible and normal for three or four alternative creative advertising executions to be tested on samples of the target audience, in order to assess their response. Many national campaigns are developed in this way, which helps advertisers to build on positive responses and remove any images and messages perceived to have negative connotations.

Accurate targeting

Because of the well-known problem of isolating advertising and PR effects from other influences on sales, the best route to achieving more effective advertising and PR expenditure always starts with marketing planning. Good advertising and PR require precision in stating target market numbers and profiles, clarity in deciding what messages should be communicated, and precision in assessing media audience profiles. With this precision, the prospect of achieving creative inspiration in devising memorable messages is more likely.

Without it, both advertising and PR inevitably become hit and miss affairs, in which neither the successes nor the failures can be accurately understood.

As Grahame Senior of Senior King Ltd, a UK agency specializing in travel and tourism markets, puts it:

'Fish where the fish are . . .
And use the right fly'.

The role of advertising and PR agencies

Only very small businesses, such as guesthouses or small visitor attractions, are likely to undertake their own advertising without professional help. Professional help varies from the design advice associated with printing firms all the way up to comprehensive marketing services offered by the larger advertising agencies to clients. By tradition, clients of agencies are always referred to as 'accounts'.

A medium-sized or large agency, on an account, say, spending £500,000 at 1990 prices, would attend meetings and take part in consultations on all aspects of the marketing campaign, and would often conduct marketing research. Once a campaign is agreed, the agency may be responsible for undertaking PR, sales promotion, direct mail and print, as well as traditional media advertising. Apart from full participation in marketing decisions, advertising agencies provide:

● Creative services, including original concepts and ideas, and the design of all visual material and copy, using research as necessary.
● Media assessment, selection, scheduling, purchasing services, and evaluation of response.
● Advertising production services and implementation of agreed campaign elements and materials.

The agency person who works closely and in full confidence with a client's marketing manager is known as an account director or executive, and is responsible for co-ordinating the three service elements noted above. Agencies are normally selected by competitive tender and, once engaged, may keep an account for several years, allowing a close personal relationship to develop with their clients.

Agencies are paid primarily by the commission (12-15 per cent) they receive from media owners when they buy space. If the commission is not adequate to cover the hours spent on an account, fees are payable in addition.

There is no advantage to clients in buying their own media space, since, apart from negotiating skills, media owners pay commission only to recognized agencies. PR agencies usually operate on a fee plus costs basis.

Even small accounts with only about £20,000 to spend on campaigns may find it advantageous to approach regional or local advertising agencies, which exist in most large towns and cities. Advertisers usually enjoy working on travel and tourism accounts as a welcome change from many less intrinsically interesting products, and may put in some additional effort reflecting their interest.

Advertising plays a relatively small role in travel and tourism

Buttle notes that for hotels and restaurants, 'hospitality advertising appropriations are very small compared to major fast moving consumer goods manufacturers who may budget over 30 per cent of turnover' (1986, p. 354). Certainly in terms of total sales revenue, the same is true for tour operators, travel agents and transport operators. In fact, excluding breweries, only three travel and tourism firms featured in the top 100 British advertisers spending league in

1990. For all of them advertising is well below the 3 per cent of sales turnover level. Advertising expenditure appears to average between 1 and 3 per cent of total turnover for most travel and tourism producers. For specific campaigns and particular segments, however, it may reach 20 per cent.

No reliance should be placed on these general industry averages by individual operators. Each operator must make his own decisions, having regard to current demand and other communication options provided by:

● Distribution channels available for promotional purposes (especially travel agents).
● The role of brochures and other print as an alternative to advertising.
● The availability of links with other operators for co-operative promotion.
● The scope for sales promotion, especially with clients on owned premises.
● Merchandising at all available points of sale.
● The scope for PR campaigns (see below).

These are all alternatives to expenditure on traditional above-the-line media advertising, and they are often more effective in influencing demand for many travel and tourism products than they are for most manufactured products.

Visitor attractions appear to be the exception among travel and tourism producers, generally needing to spend 10 per cent or more of admission revenue on advertising. The reasons for this are explained in a later chapter but reflect a heavy reliance on spontaneous decisions to visit and a relatively limited choice in terms of the alternative forms of communication noted above.

Uses of PR in travel and tourism

PR is often a much more important promotional tool for travel and tourism than for other categories of consumer products. This is because so much of the subject matter is intrinsically interesting. Most people are relatively unexcited about soap powders and shampoos but very interested in stories about exotic destinations, glamorous people and their travel habits, and the arts and heritage generally. These create stories of wide general interest and provide travel and tourism marketing

Press releases	To draw attention to favourable news events (real or created for publicity purposes), or to combat unfavourable publicity arising from unexpected events such as food poisoning on a cruise ship or 'muggings' in a resort.
Press launches	To announce new products, changes or developments; also used for annual reports.
Receptions	To influence and 'lobby' targeted guests with particular messages about opportunities or problems perceived by an organization.
Personality appearances	To draw general attention to a product or an organization's name.
Staged events	Ranging from major events such as Olympic Games or Australia's bi-centenary celebrations, to minor events such as ghost weekends at historic hotels, or mock battles by costumed soldiers at historic sites, which can be used to create media interest.
Product visits	Arranged for TV and radio holiday programmes, and travel journalists, especially to promote editorial comment.

Figure 15.3 *Types of PR activity used in travel and tourism*

management with frequent opportunities for good publicity. Of course the converse is also true, for there is also extensive media appetite for horror stories such as airport delays, transport disasters, violence and crime against visitors, and pollution at seaside resorts.

While all advertising is media-based by definition, PR is not. The type of PR activity that aims to influence or 'lobby' small target groups of influential people may have no obvious connection with the media at all. In practice, however, much PR work in travel and tourism tends to be targeted at media exposure, and its typical forms are shown in Figure 15.3.

At the strategic level PR may be used at the leading edge of enhancing and sustaining corporate and product images and positions, using a co-ordinated range of communications. On a scale that occurs only very infrequently, probably the most expensive corporate campaign seen in recent years was the PR blitz used to support the opening of Euro Disney outside Paris in April 1992. To have any prospect of reaching its projected 11 million visitors in its first year of operations, it was essential for Disney to make the maximim possible impact on the European public, the travel trade, and in northern France generally. In this case, leading rather than in support of a major advertising campaign, every aspect of PR noted in Figure 15.3 was employed on a massive scale, culminating with a 90-minute television spectacular launching ceremony transmitted around Europe. International interest in Disney themes was harnessed on a scale which only major global operators can use.

A second major example in which PR led the marketing mix comes from 1991. Responding to a worldwide crisis in the airline industry at the time of the Gulf War, British Airways mounted a major international PR and advertising campaign branded as 'The World's Biggest Offer'. Details of that campaign and its results are included in Part Six of the book.

A third example of a major strategic PR campaign is being mounted as this book goes to press. By mid 1994 the railway tunnel under the English Channel is due to open for business. Its opening and the early years of operation are likely to provide one of the most dramatic and sustained PR and advertising campaigns for travel and tourism to be conducted in Europe in the 1990s. The construction costs for the tunnel are estimated at over £8 billion, mostly financed by over 200 banks. At the end of 1992 the interest charges on loans alone were estimated to be running at some £2 million a day. Eurotunnel, the company operating the tunnel and its terminals at Folkestone and Calais, has the strongest possible incentive to make a massive and immediate impact on its target markets - and earn revenue for its backers. It has to divert at least 50 per cent of the traffic now carried by the long-established sea ferry companies, which have had over a decade to plan their product and marketing responses.

Eurotunnel has two core operations and multiple target segments. Some of these segments it will market to direct, others it will reach through tour operators and travel retailers. It will sell usage of the tunnel to through rail services, and operate and market its own shuttle trains between the terminals. The shuttle operation will be branded and marketed as 'Le Shuttle'. Core users will be:

● British Rail and SNCF (the British and French railway companies), using the tunnel for their through services for passengers and freight. BR and SNCF are key corporate customers for Eurotunnel and bulk-users of the facilities; they will pay fees for the tunnel, based on the number of trains they run. The three companies are logical marketing partners for the tunnel and will coordinate campaigns 40 per cent of revenues are targeted for this operation.
● Members of the public using 'Le Shuttle' to take their cars between England and France, haulage companies negotiating rates to use the shuttle trains for their trucks instead of ferries, and coach/bus companies using the

shuttle to take passengers for holiday and other reasons. These shuttle-train users are targeted to generate some 60 per cent of Eurotunnel's revenue.

Because of the national interest in this development on both sides of the Channel, there is no doubt that massive general PR coverage will be obtained. Every operational problem as well as success will be analysed and communicated. The marketing task will be to harness that PR coverage as an opportunity to deliver segmented messages through advertising and sales promotion to the target markets. Opportunities for marketing campaigns with other parties interested in the traffic generated, e.g. tour operators, will be immense. The aim will be to achieve the maximum take-up of the available capacity in the first year of operation in 1994. The competition with the ferries will probably be a media story in its own right as a war for competitive advantage is fought out by the rail and sea operators. For parts of the ferries' operations, it will be war to the 'death.'

At the tactical level, PR may be used to create and exploit opportunities to communicate selected messages to the general public, or targeted groups. Such opportunities are reflected in Figure 15.3.

A typical opportunistic use of PR would occur, for example, with the opening of a significant new visitor attraction. If it were possible to arrange for a member of the Royal Family, or another leading personality, to open it, the media would be interested to use the story in their editorial space. At the opening ceremony journalists and other guests would probably be invited to a reception, and carefully prepared information packs would be available. Press releases designed to assist busy journalists and sub-editors would be prepared, with paragraphs of important copy ready for immediate use, together with supporting photographs. Pre-opening visits might also be arranged, with perhaps, spectacular events to generate interest.

All the details of the launch would be pre-planned with great precision, using every opportunity to secure good media coverage. In recent years the use of PR surrounding the raising and restoration of the *Mary Rose* at Portsmouth Harbour created hours of air time on TV and radio and pages of press coverage over several years, which no advertising could have achieved.

On a smaller scale, another British illustration of opportunist PR work can be seen in the holding of a recent BBC TV 'Mastermind' programme at the National Motor Museum at Beaulieu. The programme-makers were invited to the museum and offered full facilities for the necessary TV equipment. The programme audience was seated in the museum among the exhibits and as cameras panned across the audience area, they picked up posters and other unobtrusive but carefully placed materials designed to communicate Beaulieu messages, including a large Beaulieu advertising poster strategically placed on a replica 1912 double-decker bus. The presenter opened the show with a brief interview with Lord Montagu, the owner of Beaulieu, and on two Sunday evenings at prime TV watching time attractive Beaulieu images were communicated to millions of homes. The invited audience included influential people in the area surrounding Beaulieu, whose goodwill the Museum values and seeks to sustain.

For most sectors of the travel and tourism industry, the range of subjects suitable for general PR coverage is wide, representing a powerful potential communication asset to be harnessed alongside advertising. As Melvyn Greene put it, writing about the hotel sector, 'Very few consumer industries are in quite such a position to obtain unpaid publicity as the hotel industry... In everyone's sales action plan it should be possible to set a specific feasible objective of, say, obtaining a free write-up in the local newspaper every month' (1987, p. 218).

Chapter summary

This chapter presents advertising and PR as two of the most important choices to be made by marketing managers when planning marketing campaigns. Both are part of marketing communications and are used primarily to influence targeted customers away from the places at which products are delivered and sold. Advertising is surrounded by its own professional jargon, and the main terms most frequently used in practice are summarized in Figure 15.2.

Both advertising and PR are used by producers to reach prospective individual buyers, and trading partners such as retailers. The purpose is to communicate messages intended to influence their attitudes and purchasing behaviour. The communication process is complex and contains several filters between messages transmitted, and messages received and acted on. These are discussed, and summarized in Figure 15.1. The purposes for which advertising is used are often specific to achieving marketing objectives, and mainly sales related; PR is more often used in a supportive role, especially to maintain awareness and favourable attitudes. Both advertising and PR have strategic and tactical dimensions, reflecting organizational objectives outlined in Chapter 12; they play a vital role in communicating the positioning strategies adopted for products and organizations as a whole. The intrinsic interest in travel and tourism products provides many opportunities for the effective use of PR. This chapter includes three international examples of major events in travel and tourism in which PR was the strategic core of marketing campaigns, with advertising in a supportive but secondary role.

The main stages in producing cost-effective advertising are noted and discussed, with emphasis on the creative aspects, media selection, and measuring results. The same stages are broadly relevant to planning PR. In travel and tourism the ancient nonsense that 'half my advertising is wasted, but I don't know which half' is still being peddled. It should be rejected. If any advertising/PR manager in travel and tourism doesn't know, they should be replaced without delay. Advertising and PR have been proven to be the most effective ways of linking product to market, time after time, and by operator after operator. Sometimes, when times are really hard and sales are falling, the only way to succeed is to increase budgets. Some of the cases in Part Six of the book show how.

For an identifiable cost, both advertising and PR provide opportunities for organizations to reach and communicate their chosen messages to selected audiences. It is worth noting that there are no willing advertisers in the commercial world, only operators who invest in advertising and PR because they do not know of any more economical way to achieve the sales targets they have set for their products.

Further reading

Baker, M. J., *Marketing: An Introductory Text*, 4th edit., Macmillan, 1985, Chapters 16 and 17.

Kotler, P, *Marketing: Analysis, Planning, Implementation and Control*, 7th edit., Prentice-Hall International, 1991, Chapters 21 and 22.

16

Sales promotion and merchandising

The previous chapter explained how advertising and PR messages are used to communicate with prospective buyers away from the place of production, consumption, and purchase of products. The main object of that communication is to move people towards purchase decisions at the point of sale, with good awareness of product offers, and with their attitudes favourably disposed.

This chapter explains how a different range of mainly tactical promotional techniques are used to provide special incentives to motivate prospective buyers, especially at the point of sale. The main object of this communication is to convert initial interest in products into actual sales.

The 'perishability' of tourism products means that marketing managers are constantly preoccupied with the necessity to manipulate demand in response to unforeseen events as well as the normal daily, weekly, or seasonal fluctuations. Sales promotion and merchandising methods are especially suitable for such short-run demand adjustments, and are vital weapons in the marketing armoury of most travel and tourism producers.

The chapter begins with the reasons for using sales promotion and merchandising. It proceeds with definitions, the meaning of 'point of sale', and the role of display. The three targets for sales promotion are identified, followed by marketing objectives attainable by sales promotion, set out in diagrammatic form, which

also indicates the range of techniques available. The chapter outlines the process of planning for sales promotions, budgeting, and evaluating results. The last section compares and contrasts the roles of advertising and PR with sales promotion.

The reader will perceive that this chapter provides more details of the purposes and types of promotion than the previous chapter on advertising and PR. This is because advertising and PR are extensively covered in standard texts, whereas sales promotion is not.

Reasons for using sales promotion and merchandising

At the stage when a marketing campaign is planned most of the elements of the marketing mix for established products have already been largely determined by previous strategic decisions. For example, in the case of a hotel chain planning a marketing campaign for the next 6 months, its products exist, the price range is broadly fixed, and the normal channels of distribution are established. In practice even some key promotional elements, such as brochures, exhibitions, and sales force are largely committed, with only limited scope for significant changes unless a crisis in demand occurs.

Against this background marketing managers are well aware that, for predictable and unpredictable reasons, daily demand for their products will be subject to surges and fluctuations. Occasionally demand will exceed supply but more often it will not, and demand manipulation is a primary requirement of tactical marketing. For example, predictable short-falls in demand for city hotels occur from Friday to Sunday and at certain times of the year. Other short-falls in demand also occur, often as a result of unfavourable political, economic or social events, and, especially in Britain, the weather. Such events affect demand, and require rapid tactical promotional responses. Some events are positive, such as favourable exchange-rate movements, and these represent opportunities to be exploited with equally rapid tactical responses.

Sales promotion and merchandising defined

Kotler (1991) offers no formal definition of sales promotion, (although the issues are fully covered) while Baker uses the American Marketing Association (AMA) definition, which is not best suited to travel and tourism. Adapting the AMA view the essential characteristics are:

> *Sales promotion is part of marketing communications other than advertising, PR, personal selling, and sales literature. It is primarily designed to stimulate consumer purchasing, and dealer and sales force effectiveness in the short-term, through temporary incentives and displays.*

The definition stresses the short-term, non-regular, incentive nature of sales promotion, and the fact that it extends beyond consumers to distribution networks and the sales force. Much of sales promotion in practice takes place at points of sale, and the term 'merchandising' is often used specifically to mean sales promotion at the point of sale. Rodger defined merchandising as the 'sum total of effort to move goods [products] at the point of sale...' (1968, p. 155).

While advertising is described as 'above-the-line' (see Chapter 15), sales promotion and merchandising are usually referred to as 'below-the-line'.

Points of sale

Having stressed the important distinction between forms of marketing communication that take place away from the 'point of sale', and other forms that focus on it, it is necessary to consider what this means in practice. At its simplest, a point of sale (POS) is *any location at which a purchase transaction takes place.*

Chapter 18 deals with distribution networks created to provide access to products at places away from the producers' premises. But 'point of sale' in travel and tourism means much more than distribution networks. It covers three very different kinds of location with different marketing requirements:

External POS	e.g. retail travel agency (for most products), ticket/booking office or desk (for transport and car rental) or tourist information centre (TIC) (especially if bookings are taken).
Internal, 'in-house' (or 'on-site') POS	e.g. reception desk (hotels and attractions); a reception desk may also operate a referral system linked with other outlets in the same organization. Locations within an operator's premises such as bars, restaurants, retail sales points (souvenirs and other items), duty free shops, etc.
Customer's home as POS	Enquiries or bookings, responding to direct mail and promotional offers by TV, radio, promotional mail, or telephone calls.

Most readers will be familiar with retail points of sale. Because the production and consumption of service products on producers' premises are simultaneous, a considerable amount of internal sales promotion also occurs 'on-site' or 'in-house'. For tour operators, the destination representative typically also acts in the same way as an 'on-site' point of sale for excursions, events etc. Such promotion aims to persuade 'captive' customers to buy specific products, or more of them, or generally to spend more once they have arrived. Because producers have full control of their premises, 'in-house' sales promotion and merchandising are vitally important to services in ways manufacturers of most physical goods must envy. Banks, post offices, and retail outlets of motoring organizations provide other illustrations of growing awareness of the value of 'in-house' promotion for service products.

In travel and tourism many producers sell at least a half their output direct to customers through guides and brochures, or in direct response to advertising. It is therefore necessary to recognize that direct booking systems, especially central reservation offices, also act as points of sale to customers in their own homes. In its way a telephone response from a guesthouse proprietor acts in exactly the same way as a sales person's response to a customer in a showroom used to sell physical goods. Pioneered by France Telecom in 1984, the well-known Minitel home-shopping system provides direct 'live' access to travel products through its provision of information and purchasing services linked by telephone lines to television sets. Some 6.5 million homes in France were in the system in the early 1990s. At the time of writing Minitel were planning an expansion into the UK in 1993, linking with British Telecom's Prestel viewdata system. If this form of home shopping, so far alien to the British way of life, takes off, it will provide a valuable new point of sale for tourism products in customers' homes.

All points of sale, external, 'in-house', or via reservation systems, offer potential opportunities for effective sales promotion and merchandising initiatives.

Three targets for sales promotion

Tactical responses designed to stimulate sales to customers have three targets:

● Individual buyers – as customer segments.
● Distribution networks (points of sale), including 'in-house'.
● Sales force.

Individual buyers

All sales promotion is designed to achieve *additional* short-run purchases by customers that producers have reason to believe would not occur without specific action. Aimed directly at buyers, the objective is to provide specific incentives or inducements to buy particular products at particular times. Much of sales promotion is restricted to chosen segments to avoid the dilution of total sales revenue, which occurs if unnecessary incentives are offered to all customers, many of whom intended to purchase without the added incentive.

Distribution networks

If an organization receives a large proportion of its sales revenue through third-party distributors, achieving customer sales objectives is likely to require their active participation. Distributors such as retail travel agents are bombarded daily by operators wishing them to provide extra display space for their products and other forms of support. Any special effort therefore usually requires special incentives and if they are not provided, customer sales are unlikely to be achieved.

Sales force

For larger organizations, sales forces are required to service and motivate distribution networks. Being human, any additional effort on top of continuous routine sales efforts often requires some additional forms of incentive or reward.

Thus sales promotions intended to influence individual buyers, often include other forms of

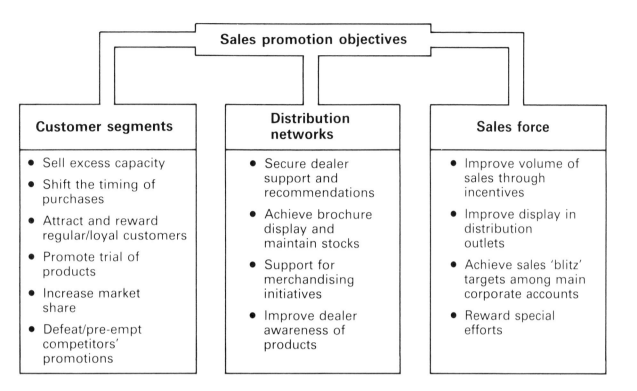

Figure 16.1 *Marketing objectives attainable by sales promotion*

supporting promotion, the objectives of which are summarized in Figure 16.1.

Marketing objectives attainable by sales promotion

The types of tactical marketing objectives attainable through sales promotion efforts are noted in Figure 16.1. In practice the objectives stem from response to a combination of factors, which may vary on a weekly basis, including:

● Sales volume targets and variance analysis (see Chapter 14).

● Problems of over- or under-capacity of production.
● Competitor actions.
● Other business environment factors representing threats or opportunities.
● Problems with the coverage, stocking, and/or display of brochures in distribution networks.

Both for distributors and for sales forces, sales promotion objectives tend to focus on aspects of display space. 'Display' denotes the availability, visibility and accessibility of products in distribution outlets, or points of sale. Every metre of counter, shelf, or rack space performs a selling role for products in a retail travel agency or other outlet. Other things being equal, more space, in more accessible parts of a shop, will sell more product because more people's attention will be attracted by the higher visibility. In much the same way a double-page spread advertisement in a magazine has more chance of being seen and read than a quarter-page one, mixed with others. If eye-catching window displays, video films and 'special offer' leaflets are added to a competitive product's display space, there is a high probability that more sales will result. In self-service outlets, where customers browse and select brochures, the amount and position of display is crucial to achieving sales volume.

Display space in retail outlets is always in short supply, and it is usually allocated, very roughly, according to a producer's market share. In other words, if tour operator 'A' has 20 per cent of a market and tour operator 'B' has 10 per cent, 'A' will normally be given around twice the available display space. One of the usual objects of sales promotion is to change these relative space allocations, but it can only be achieved for short periods. At any time, but especially in the main booking weeks, the competition to achieve prime display space for holiday products is enormous, and the costs of sales promotion incentives to distributors rise proportionately.

The objectives noted under 'distribution network' relate to the broader issues of distribution discussed in Chapter 18.

Sales promotion techniques used in travel and tourism

Figure 16.2 summarizes the main promotional techniques on which marketing managers can draw. Advertising agencies and specialist sales promotion agencies are available to assist larger companies in the choice and design of techniques. Smaller firms will have no choice but to use their judgement, basing it on previous experience of the tools that are effective in their

field, and to undertake their own research into the range of promotions on offer by competitors. The travel trade press and marketing journals are all excellent sources of information about current promotional campaigns, in all sectors of travel and tourism.

It can be seen that the incentives noted for consumers and distribution networks in Figure 16.2 have three common elements, identified by Peterson (1978, p. 62) as:

● A featured offer (outside the normal terms of trade).
● A tangible advantage (not inherent in the normal product formulation).
● Intention to achieve marketing objectives.

These three elements fit precisely with the overall definition of sales promotion noted earlier.

Some examples of customer sales promotion incentives

Price cuts for all categories of goods and services are commonly recognized as the most powerful of all consumer incentives. They are almost universally used by tour operators, for example, to sell off unsold capacity on underbooked flights. 'Sale' boards have become a common feature in travel agents' windows, with offers of large discounts on specific flights notified by the operators.

Discount vouchers, offering say 15 per cent off admission prices, or a money equivalent coupon such as '£1.00 off', are commonly used by tourist attractions on the basis that most coupons are allowable on one adult admission only, and a typical party size is nearer three persons. '£1.00 off', in the context of a high fixed price operation with spare capacity, does not undermine a very real gain in net profit terms, even before any additional on-site spending occurs.

Disguised price cuts are a popular way to maintain the regular price structure, yet offer

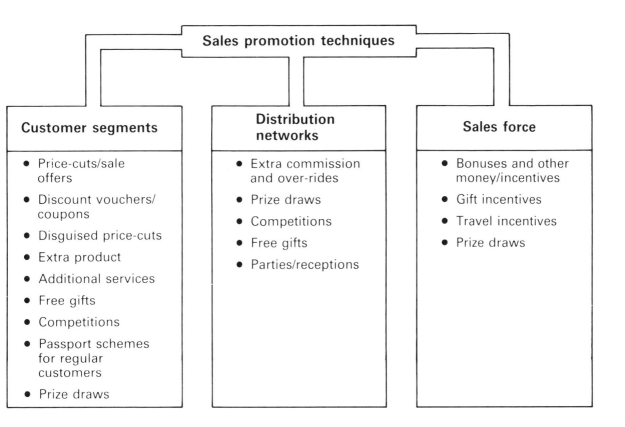

Figure 16.2 *Range of sales-promotion techniques used in travel and tourism*

added value to customers and an incentive to buy. Hotels with space to sell often offer double-room occupancy for single-occupancy rack rates, but expect to generate added revenue through meals and bars. The rather coy 'spouse free' ads put out by Cunard in the early 1980s to promote transatlantic travel by business persons otherwise travelling alone are another example of disguised price-cuts.

Extra product may be offered as an incentive, e.g. 4 nights for the price of 3; free wine on certain dates; additional features offered 'free' by visitor attractions at times of the year when they are not crowded; or additional sightseeing excursions may be added by tour operators.

Additional services may include chauffeur-driven cars from airport to town centre offered by airlines to first-class and some business-class passengers, or the welcome receptions and vouchers for beauty salons offered in some hotels to weekend visitors.

Free gifts range from tour operators' travel bags and passport wallets to badges or pens offered to children at some attractions.

Competitions are a common travel incentive, with the 1986 British Airways 'Go For it America' competition in the USA, and its Concorde competition in Britain, being two of the largest multi-million pound competitions provided by international operators in 1986.

Lastly there are *'passport'* and other membership schemes designed to reward and promote loyalty and frequency of purchase by identified repeat customers. Greatly assisted by the power of computerized databases for customer records, the history of special passport-type deals goes back to the early 1980s. At that time the now defunct airline Pan Am first offered 'reward points' for journeys performed in the USA that could subsequently be redeemed for free travel. The more journeys, the more points, and the greater the reward built up. Aimed primarily at frequent business travellers paying full fares through their companies, some of these schemes got out of hand in the late 1980s through over generous provision. But nearly all major national and international travel and tourism businesses with a core of frequent repeat travellers now offer incentives to repeat purchasers. The logic is clear. The cost of attracting a new, first-time customer through advertising and other communication far exceeds the cost of persuading an existing known customer to 'come again' or make additional purchases.

In the early 1990s most car-rental firms, accommodation chains, airlines and other transport companies are offering some form of membership club, privilege card or passport scheme to reward identified regular customers. In due course such schemes may become a regular part of product augmentation or products in their own right – such as British Airways' 'Air Miles'. But their principal aim is

to incentivize repeat travellers, typically by means of direct-response marketing methods (see Chapter 18). Names and addresses of regular buyers are invariably used for targeting short-run promotions within the scope of the definition offered at the beginning of this chapter.

From this brief review, it will be clear that the range of possible incentives is both extremely wide, and very creative. There is constant rivalry between competitors to innovate and achieve a lead in incentives, and to gain market share. Sales promotions may be greatly improved by test marketing as defined in Chapter 11. Large sales promotions may also generate sufficient media interest to gain additional unpaid coverage, supported by skilful PR activity (see Part Six of the book).

Examples of sales-promotion incentives for distributors and sales force

Although separately designed to appeal to managers and (or) counter staff, many of the incentives used to motivate distributors are the same as those offered to customers, including gifts, prize draws, and competitions. In addition, to achieve the objectives of a major promotion, it is likely that additional commission will be paid on extra sales. As Holloway puts it, 'incentive commissions of $2\frac{1}{2}$ per cent or more [are] payable by tour operators for the achievement of pre-established targets' (1985, p. 147). Additional commission payments are often known in the trade as 'over-rides', and these may be paid also for all sales above an agreed level. Because of the nature of the product, it is normal in travel and tourism for distributor incentives to include free travel to sample the promoted items.

For sales forces, the incentives are also designed to appeal to the individuals concerned, and mostly they are available in the form of money bonuses and gifts available on achieving specified additional sales targets. There is of course a large sales incentive industry, especially in the USA, which specializes in designing and supplying incentives for sales forces and distributors in all sectors of industry. Within the range of incentives offered by specialist agencies, travel products are frequently found to be powerful motivators.

How long is 'temporary' for incentives?

By definition, all sales-promotion inducements, incentives and rewards, are tactical responses of a temporary, short-term nature. If they are sustained for too long, they become perceived as part of the standard product, price, or terms of trade, and they lose their effectiveness to secure vital, additional sales. Kotler suggests that 'probably there is risk in putting a well-known brand on promotion more than 30 per cent of the time' (1984, p. 662). He also draws attention to the dangers of subsidizing existing users by over-frequent promotions. There are no precise rules, and everything turns upon the state of the market. For international airlines responding to the market during and after the Gulf War of 1991, the over-riding necessity was to stem massive daily losses as fixed costs far outweighed available revenue. In such conditions sales promotion is not an academic concept but a principal means of continuous competition and route to survival which works faster than cutting operating costs. In Part Six the massive sales promotion mounted by British Airways, 'The World's Biggest Offer' is outlined in one of the case histories. Fortunately for service producers, they can usually be far more segment and product-specific in their promotions than manufacturers of physical goods. They also enjoy more influence over much of the distribution network in which most sales promotions occur.

Another reason for limiting the extent of sales-promotion activity is that the cost, measured on a unit basis sold, e.g. one seat or one bed-night, is usually high. It is justifiable on

the grounds of recouping all or some of the high fixed costs of operation already committed, but cannot be sustained without serious erosion of profitability.

Without contradicting the limit on how long any one promotion may be sustained, it should be noted that there are often strong reasons for linking individual promotions within a theme. Themes must be relevant to the organizations and products being promoted, and can be used strategically over time to create a sense of continuity in customers' minds. McDonald's Restaurants use the character Ronald McDonald with many of their specific promotions, and so on. Some sales promotions featuring collectable items, which together form sets of linked items, are another way to build themes and continuity into sales promotions. It is also possible to build a series of merchandising initiatives into recognizable themes, especially when they are used 'in-house'.

Good examples of segmented promotions with a clear strategic dimension can be seen in the marketing work of British Rail Intercity Division. Any railway company has a major interest in promoting travel frequency outside peak hour times, and British Rail has effectively created a series of 'passport' holders through, for example, special cards now held by hundreds of thousands of students and senior citizens. Profile information on holders of these cards is retained on databases, and holders can be reached direct and cost-effectively for the promotion of travel offers. Such offers are obviously restricted to specified times of travel and calculated not to dilute normal revenue flows.

Pricing down or packaging up?

Not confined to travel and tourism, there has been a debate in marketing for years as to which of two strategies is most likely to achieve targeted sales volume. One is a strategy for low prices relative to competition, supported by additional promotional price discounting; the other is adding value to products (packaging up) to achieve targeted volume by promoting product enhancement. Packaging up means adding short-term value into one or more of the bundle of components of which travel and tourism products are comprised. The marketing issues in this are covered in Chapter 8 under the heading 'Product augmentation'.

There is no doubt that price discounting is easier to implement. It works faster and is popular with customers. But there is also no doubt that price cuts are easily matched and can degenerate quickly into price wars, which leave all producers worse off, and often result in reduced product quality. To some extent producers cannot stand aside if they are losing sales volume to a an undercutting competitor. But, wherever possible, especially with key segments, the marketing advantages of packaging up are clear, and should always be explored. Provided that a product is competitive and generating good satisfaction levels at existing prices, there is every reason to limit price cutting unless it becomes essential for survival. A commitment to product enhancement and knowledge of customer segments offers the only long-term route out of price-cutting wars, in which price becomes the primary reason for customer choice. Specific examples of packaging up are noted by Greene, who concludes that 'the hotel and airline sector have tended too often to use price reductions as the first tactic for obtaining more business when other choices could be more profitably employed' (1982, pp. 62–7). The decisions in 1990–1 of both Thomas Cook and British Airways to pull out of the lower priced end of the UK inclusive tour market appear to be indicative of changing attitudes.

Planning effective sales promotions

The process of planning and implementing successful sales promotions can be represented as six logical steps. The steps are based on the marketing planning process outlined in Chapter 13, and are undertaken in practice as part of planning campaigns (Chapter 14):

1 Calculate the volume targets and pattern of sales, which sales-promotion activity is expected to achieve over the defined promotion period. For a hotel group, for example, this would be expressed in bookings per hotel, over a specified time. For airlines it would be seat sales by route, by period of time. For a visitor attraction it would be visitor numbers. The procedure is the same, whether the objective is to gain additional business above previously targeted levels, or reduce the level of an expected loss resulting from some unpredictable external event.
2 Calculate the potential revenue gain that would arise if the volume targets were achieved in full (volume × average price of nights, seats or admission). This establishes the limits within which a budget must be set.
3 Specify the consumer profile of the segments to be targeted for sales promotion – business or leisure – and draw on details of place of origin and other profile data available from marketing research. Customer databases are an obvious source of information.
4 Choose the incentives best calculated to appeal to the target segments and cost them in relation to budget limits.
5 Draw up and implement an action programme, in co-ordination with other promotional elements in the campaign, especially advertising, PR, personal selling, and distribution arrangements.
6 Monitor and evaluate the results achieved.

Budgeting and evaluating results

By their nature, sales promotion and merchandising are task-orientated techniques. The tasks relate to identified short-falls or opportunities, which can be expressed precisely in volume terms of bed-nights, seats, admissions etc., and in the amount of sales revenue that is at risk, or achievable. It follows that *objective and task* methods are the only realistic way to calculate sales promotion budgets (see Chapter 14).

Again, because sales-promotion methods are so specifically targeted, results can be measured in sales or bookings achieved during the promotional period. Inevitably it will not be possible to separate the sales promotion effects from effects of current advertising or recent product enhancement, but short-run promotional efforts provide the best opportunity marketing managers have to measure the results of marketing expenditure with some precision.

Sales promotion or advertising and PR?

Theoretically, producers have a choice between spending most of their marketing communications budget on advertising and PR, or most of it on sales promotion. In fact, while the ultimate aim of all marketing communications is to influence buyer behaviour and generate sales, they perform essentially different tasks.

As Davidson expressed it:

In general, the purpose of advertising is to improve attitudes towards a brand [product], while the objective of promotion is to translate favourable attitudes into actual purchase. Advertising cannot close a sale because its impact is too far from the point of purchase, but promotion can and does (1975: p. 190).

Advertising and PR have an essentially strategic role in developing and sustaining awareness, positive attitudes, images, product positions, favourable associations, and knowledge of product attributes. Sales promotion, by contrast, is essentially tactical in its short-run responses, and aimed at manipulating demand around the fixed capacity of service operations. It works by providing

specific inducements in association with displays and other ways of attracting customer attention at points of sale, at particular times.

Provided that a producer has achieved accessibility and display for customers through a distribution network, that of itself may be sufficient to create awareness of sales-promotion offers. More often, especially if a purchase is made by post or phone from the buyer's own home, promotional offers have to be advertised. This is the point of overlap between the two forms of communication, but their essentially different roles must not be confused.

Where opportunities for sales promotion occur 'on-site' or 'in-house', there is generally no requirement for supportive media advertising, because producers have full control over their own premises and a 'captive' audience to influence. The opportunity for 'in-house' promotion is open to all producers of travel and tourism products because of the inseparability of production and consumption.

The conclusion is therefore that sales promotion and advertising are complementary techniques, not alternatives. For travel and tourism products, they warrant equal attention in campaign planning.

Chapter summary

This chapter defines sales promotions and merchandising in their primary tactical role of managing short-run variations in customer demand for products. Both techniques are aspects of marketing communications, and operate by providing additional incentives at the point of sale that are strong enough to 'close' the sale for the products being promoted. Advertising and PR are used away from the point of sale and serve to bring in customers whose attitudes and interest in products are already favourably preconditioned.

Because of the perishable nature of travel and tourism products, and the operational implications of high fixed costs, the use of sales promotion and merchandising in managing demand is even more important in the tourism industry than in industries marketing physical goods. In fact, although very difficult to quantify, below-the-line techniques are often more important than above-the-line for most producers. If the cost of revenue forgone (the difference between published prices and actual prices) is added into a sales-promotion budget, the true below-the-line cost will greatly exceed the above-the-line cost for most travel and tourism operators.

The existence of three different kinds of point of sale is noted, with particular stress on the merchandising opportunities conveyed by having customers 'in-house', on the producer's premises.

The difference between the marketing objectives that advertising and PR achieve, and the objectives of sales promotion and merchandising, are brought out. It is stressed that the two forms of communication are normally planned together and co-ordinated to have maximum effect in integrated marketing campaigns.

Although the desired effect is on purchases by targeted customer segments, sales-promotion techniques are aimed separately at buyers, distributors, and sales forces in order to maximize the short-run effects at chosen points of sale. The planning for sales promotion and merchandising follows systematic procedures, which will be familiar by now to readers of this book, and which are integrated in the vital marketing and campaign planning stages discussed in Chapters 13 and 14.

Finally, the core issue of *pricing down*, or *packaging up*, is addressed. This issue may well divide retailers and producers of service products. For producers, packaging up must generally be the preferred strategy for building quality and delivering value and satisfaction – especially for repeat buyers. Retailers' interests may lie in pricing down strategies because customers are attracted by low price and it shifts products in larger volume. The 1990s will produce many illustrations of this tension being worked out in the travel and tourism industry. See also Part Six (the Thomson Summer Sun Case).

Further reading

Baker, M. I., *Marketing: An Introductory Text*, 4th edit., Macmillan, 1985, Chapter 18.

Kotler, P., *Marketing Analysis, Planning, Implementation and Control*, 7th edit, Prentice-Hall International, 1991, Chapter 21 and 23.

17

Brochures and other printed materials

This chapter focuses on brochures, sales literature generally, and other forms of printed communications paid for out of marketing budgets. Known in the USA as 'collateral materials', print represents the third distinctive group of marketing communications to be planned in marketing campaigns, in addition to advertising and PR, sales promotion and merchandising.

The nature of service products, especially those that are relatively expensive and infrequently bought, confers a particular significance on printed communications as an integral part of the marketing process that has no parallel in marketing physical goods. Whereas all producers of consumer products use advertising and PR, sales promotion, merchandising and personal selling, few producers of physical goods use print to anything like the extent found in tourism. The design, distribution, and large volume use of printed items is a major distinguishing feature of marketing in travel and tourism.

Where a large proportion of sales turnover is achieved by direct sales between producer and consumer, with no intervention of third-party distributors, the role of sales literature is at its strongest. This of course is the case for the bulk of all international and domestic travel and tourism products. While many tour operators are exceptions to the reliance on direct sales, they have other important marketing reasons for focusing their efforts on brochures. For some

organizations, especially tourist boards at national, regional and local level, the design, production and distribution of printed materials accounts for the major element of marketing budgets. In such organizations the concern with and reliance on print also takes up much of the time of marketing staff.

This chapter begins by explaining why printed materials are such an important part of marketing communications in travel and tourism. It provides a definition in the context of marketing campaigns. The types of printed materials used and their multiple roles in marketing travel and tourism are identified, followed by a step by step explanation of the process of producing effective print, both 'in-house', and through external agencies. The key issue of achieving distribution to the user is discussed, followed by brief notes on evaluating the results of expenditure.

Print production and wastage – on a massive scale

The sheer volume of printed items associated with travel and tourism products is staggering. The travel world is awash with brochures and other print items paid for out of marketing budgets. The cost in trees alone to produce the necessary paper must be considerable. In the UK, the Tourism Society estimates there are some 200,000 organizations and establishments wholly or partially concerned with aspects of tourism. Nearly all of these are generating pieces of printed information, ranging from the millions of brochures distributed by large tour operators, down to farmhouses designing and distributing a few dozen leaflets for their prospective customers. There are over 750 Tourist Information Centres (TICs) acting as a major outlet and some 7,000 retail travel outlets. In the USA, although the calculation is on a much narrower basis than that noted above by the Tourism Society, the US Travel Data Center identified just under 500,000 'total firms' in the USA travel industry in 1990, including over 30,000 travel agency locations (excluding satellite ticket printer locations).

In 1989 just one distribution contractor was distributing 150 million brochures, weighing some 20,000 tonnes, to UK travel agency outlets in a year. Around the developed world travel and tourism firms are producing billions of printed items for the purposes defined in this chapter. Chapter 15 noted the filters at work to prevent much marketing communication from influencing the targeted customer. In the case of printed items it is obvious that much of the material does not even reach the first stage of 'opportunity to see', and the level of wastage should be a matter of concern for all marketing managers. In view of its importance it is extraordinary how poorly researched the print distribution process is. In now historic (1974 and 1978) surveys in the USA it was estimated that less than six out of every ten agents opened all the brochure packs they received; and about a third of all packs were 'automatically discarded'. Although the number of US travel agents has trebled since then, it is unlikely that the wastage implications of this research have changed. A later study carried out for the European Travel Commission confirmed the same massive wastage of national tourist office printed materials.

Directly comparable figures are not available for Britain but it is a strong probability that up to half of all the literature packs received by travel agency offices never reach display racks, and that much is simply dumped. The concentration of travel retailers into fewer chains in the 1980s meant that retail display policies for brochures were more tightly controlled than ever before, and they are likely to remain so. The leading UK tour operators distributing through travel agents in the early 1990s were typically producing between six and ten brochures per person booking a holiday in their main summer programmes; smaller operators would have to produce more. Since the mid-1980s, developments in print technology have kept the cost of production down compared with other marketing costs and the cost of a large summer brochure of 100 or more pages, assuming over a million were produced, averaged out at around £0.75 p per brochure in 1992 prices. Smaller operators, with much smaller programmes to communicate, would be spending less but with smaller print runs their unit cost would be around £0.25p to £0.30p. Bottomley Renshaw notes for UK coach tour operators that 'through agencies they convert only about one in every forty brochures into a sale' (1992, p. 90).

Thus the print cost of a booking for two persons, assuming ten brochures are needed at 75p = £7.50 or £3.75 per person. In the early 1990s a typical 7 night package to a Mediterranean resort might cost around £225, and tour operators would consider it a very good year if they achieved an average of 4 per cent gross profit on that price = £9.00. Allowing for brochure distribution costs as well as production, it is obvious that print cost alone could be the equivalent of nearly half the gross operating profit on a tour package – in a good year. In a bad year the print costs will far exceed profit per holiday sold. While one cannot put too much weight on such examples, the cost of print as a proportion of marketing expenditure, and as a major cost item to be paid for out of the tour operator's earnings, should be noted. The importance of achieving even marginal improvements in the effectiveness of brochures, and thus reducing print wastage, is obvious. It can only be achieved by systematic marketing and by refining the process of designing and distributing printed materials.

Defining printed materials

Print is part of marketing communications. It may be defined as comprising:

> *Any form of printed materials paid for out of marketing budgets, designed to create awareness among existing and prospective customers and stimulate demand for specified products, or facilitate their purchase, use and enjoyment.*

This definition covers not only the familiar promotional use of print, such as tour operator and hotel brochures, but also 'facilitation' - a useful word in travel and tourism marketing to describe the ways in which producers assist customers to decide between, and to purchase particular, products, and achieve full benefit and enjoyment from using them. Leaflets provided on admission to visitor attractions, to inform and 'orientate' visitors to the experience they will receive, are one illustration of print designed to facilitate use and enjoyment.

While travel and tourism is a market of obvious interest to a wide range of commercial publishers, the definition above includes only print that is part of a communication mix intended to achieve marketing objectives. *Excluded* from the definition are all commercial publications, such as directories, maps, guidebooks, and timetables, which are sold through bookshops and other outlets, and for which the object of production is to achieve profit for the publisher through the cover price, and/or advertising revenue. While maps, for example, may be elements of promotional print for tourist boards, the criterion for inclusion in the definition is whether or not their production is geared to marketing objectives. Occasionally, printed items within the definition may also be

sold at a cover price. But if so, it is always seen as a contribution towards marketing costs and not a main reason for production. Similarly, in the UK it is normal for the production and distribution costs of some tourist board brochures at national and regional level to be fully covered by advertising revenue received from producers. Some achieve a surplus on brochure production, but since it is typically set against marketing budgets, such brochures are included within the definition.

The bulk of all printed items are aimed at consumers, but they are also produced to achieve promotional and facilitation objectives targeted at a distribution network. Printed materials may be designed for use in consumers' homes, or at 'in-house' points-of-sale on a producer's premises or site.

Types of printed material used in marketing travel and tourism

From the previous discussion it will be obvious that the range of printed materials is wide. The lists below summarize typical items used in practice to influence travellers.

Promotional print

● Tour operators' brochures.
● Hotel, holiday centre, caravan park, campsite, and other accommodation brochures.
● Conference centre brochures.
● Specific product brochures (e.g. activity holidays, theatre weekends).
● Attraction leaflets (theme parks, museums, amusement parks).
● Car rental brochures.
● Sales promotion leaflets (specific incentive offers).
● Posters/showcards for window and other displays in distribution networks.
● Tourist office brochures (general and product-specific).
● Printed letters/inserts for direct mail.

Facilitation and information print

- Orientation leaflets/guides (attractions).
- Maps (mostly provided free out of marketing budgets).
- 'In-house' guides and 'In-house' magazines (accommodation and transport).
- Menus/tent cards/ showcards/ folders, used 'in-house'.
- Hotel group (and equivalent) directories.
- 'What's on' leaflets (such as those provided out of resort marketing budgets).
- Timetables produced by transport operators.

The marketing role of printed materials

Drawing on reasons outlined in Chapter 3, it is possible to restate briefly the characteristics of travel and tourism products that underlie the need for effective print, and explain its importance in the conduct of marketing campaigns:

- Products are produced and consumed on producers' premises and cannot be inspected and assessed directly at points of sale away from the place of production. There are no physical stocks of tourist products as there are for manufactured goods, and brochures are used as product substitutes.
- While service production and consumption are simultaneous, the production process is often separated by weeks or months from the act of purchase. Inevitably, many products are ideas and expectations only at the point of sale. Printed materials provide a tangible focus for expectations.
- Especially where infrequently purchased, expensive products such as holidays are concerned, most customers seek full information and consider several options before making choices. Retailers of holidays are well aware that every minute spent answering

questions costs money; they have a powerful incentive to distribute literature in order to reduce customer contact time.

- Producers' interests are best served by the widest possible distribution of their product offers. This means securing continuous communication at points of sale, which cannot be achieved through advertising alone.
- There are many marketing reasons for communicating with customers during the production/consumption process, partly to 'facilitate' the experience and inform, and partly to generate a greater level of 'in-house' expenditure.

To explain these points, consider two hypothetical examples illustrating the role and use of promotional print. A prospective vacationer in Manchester in January may be contemplating a 2-week holiday in Ibiza in July. Probably it will be his most expensive single purchase decision of the year. Assume he has no previous experience of the Balearic Islands. A travel agent may suggest, friends may recommend, an advertisement or travel feature may arouse his interest, but in the cold gloom of a Manchester January a choice must be made between, say, four alternatives. Tour operators' brochures are designed to make that sort of decision possible without promising more than can be delivered in July.

Consider another traveller who arrives for 6 nights at a resort hotel in which his booking covers the room, breakfast, and one other main meal (Modified American Plan). On arrival, he will check in and receive a room number card and possibly a 'welcome' leaflet. From that moment on he represents a spending opportunity not only for the hotel but for many other tourist businesses accessible to the resort. The skill and tact with which a 'spending opportunity' is converted into sales, without at the same time damaging perceptions of enjoyment and good value for money, are reflected in the range of printed items the traveller will encounter during his stay, 'in-house', and in the resort.

The multiple purposes of printed materials

It is obvious from the definition and the range of items included that marketing print performs a wide range of functions in travel and tourism. They are summarized below:

- Creating awareness.
- Promotional (messages/symbols).
- Promotional (display/merchandising).
- Promotional (incentives/special offers).
- Product substitute role.
- Access/purchasing mechanism.
- 'Proof' of purchase/reassurance.
- Facilitation of product use and information.
- Providing education.

Creating awareness

Some prospective first-time customers will become aware of products through advertising and PR (see Chapter 15). Many others in travel and tourism will gain initial awareness through marketing print first seen in a hotel, at an airport, or a travel agent. The battle for awareness is fierce, and the design of front-covers of all marketing items is a matter of immense importance. The role of front-cover designs can be compared with the role of the packaging of products in a supermarket designed to attract the attention of people passing along the aisles.

Promotion

Brochures such as those provided by tour operators are designed to stimulate customers and motivate them to buy. They identify needs, demonstrate in pictures and words the image

and positioning of products and organizations, and carry the key messages. In this role they act in the same way as advertising. They also perform a vital display function in the racks of distribution outlets, such as retail travel agents, where they serve in lieu of physical products. In the typical self-service shops run by most travel and tourism retailers the display role, and the customer appeal of brochure covers and contents, are vital to marketing success. Supplementary brochures and purpose-designed leaflets are also typically used to communicate and promote special offers, and the other sales-promotion incentives discussed in Chapter 16.

Access/purchasing mechanism

Many product brochures contain booking forms to facilitate purchase, and these contain the basis of the contract to provide services. Some of these forms may be over-stamped and filled in by travel agents, but all are designed to specify the purchase details. Information in carefully designed booking forms can also be put into databases and used by operators as a source of basic marketing research data, providing valuable customer profile information such as area of origin, party size and type. The addresses can be analysed by ACORN methods to provide a detailed profile of typical buyers.

Product substitute role

Above all, for travel and tourism operators whose business depends on bookings or decisions made away from the place of production, brochures perform a product substitute role, the marketing importance of which it is impossible to over-emphasize. The brochure *is* the product at the point of purchase, especially for first-time customers. It establishes expectations of quality, value for money, product image and status that must be matched when the product is delivered.

Proof of purchase/reassurance

The brochure also substitutes for the product in the period between purchase and consumption, which in the case of vacations may extend to several months. It becomes a document to be read several times as a reminder, to stimulate expectations, and to show friends and relatives. In Europe, under the terms of the 1993 EC Package Travel Directive, the contents of brochures are covered by precise regulations setting minimum standards. Dissatisfied customers are given rights to claim compensation, and failure to provide required information may be a criminal offence for operators.

Facilitation of product use and information

Once customers arrive 'in-house' or on the producer's premises, it is normal for them to be provided with a wide range of printed materials. Some may be found in rooms (hotels) or seat backs (airlines), at information desks (attractions) or on tables (restaurants and bars). The literature is designed to explain and promote what is available:

● To promote awareness and use of ancillary services/products.
● To assist customers to get the most value out of their purchase and enhance satisfaction.
● To feature special offers (sales promotion).
● To provide basic information which may be useful.

Producers can, and do train staff to communicate with customers, in order to achieve all these things. But staff are usually busy and often forget. Printed items are the main way to provide standardized, 'user-friendly' messages to all travellers, in exactly the same way.

Carefully designed print can do much to create a sense of welcome from an establishment to its customers. It can communicate the message that an organization understands and cares about customer needs and interests. An illustration is the choice that visitor attractions have, either to provide a simple admission ticket, or a leaflet of welcome and user advice. At Beaulieu in Hampshire, at the National Motor Museum, admission is by tokens that are dropped into turnstiles and every visitor receives a leaflet and brief spoken information. The system is similar to that at Disneyland and other USA theme parks. Compare this approach with the bus or cloakroom style tickets still used in so many visitor attractions in the 1990s.

Providing education

Although the role of education is certainly not yet widely associated with marketing, except perhaps for enlightened museums and galleries, there is every reason to consider it an important and growing role for the 1990s. For example, where the impact of tourism on the environment is an issue in a destination such as a national park – social, cultural as well as physical – producers have a powerful motivation to create customer awareness, 'orientation' and understanding of the issues. It is in their long-run interest to help create and sustain an attractive and healthy environment, and destination capacity may depend more on *how* customers use a destination than on the number of visitors. Education is not confined solely to leisure tourism. Many hotels, especially in the USA and Canada, have developed sophisticated programmes to contribute to the environment, and they need to tell their customers, many of whom are on business. Of course the word 'education' will not be found in marketing print. But education it is, and education is a communication business. The professional skills of marketing managers have a potentially important educational role for the future, and printed communications will be its primary focus.

Stages in producing effective printed materials

The six stages noted below are presented in a logical decision sequence, relevant to all managers responsible for producing printed materials for marketing purposes. Although the distribution of printed materials has special considerations (see later in the chapter), the other stages are similar to those used for designing any form of marketing communication, and they are marketing-research-based for larger organizations. Print planning is normally carried out as one of the elements in the campaign plan, and it draws on data used for planning marketing strategy and objectives. The budget required for print production is best calculated by the 'objective and task' methods outlined in Chapter 14.

1 *Determining the size, profile and needs of the target audience*. Information about target customers is derived through market segmentation; print volume is related to the quantified objectives in the marketing plan. The target profile for advertising (media selection), sales promotion and for print production, will normally be identical.

   It is worth stressing that all print is designed to serve the customers' needs, not those of the producer. Print must convey the messages that target customers are known to want and respond to, on the basis of marketing research.

2 *Marketing strategy and positioning*. Here also advertising and print are likely to be planned together, with co-ordinated messages, images and positioning. If print is the larger part of the budget, it may take the leading role in expressing product images. It will certainly take a leading role in communicating specific product messages to the target audience.

   Paper quality, choice of colours, density of copy, graphics, and the style and density of photography, are varied in practice to match chosen images to selected target audiences. Up-market target groups respond better to heavier quality paper, lower density per page, pastel colours, and thematic photographs. Down-market target groups are more influenced by bold colours, direct and straightforward copy, and are not put off by greater density per page.

3 *Specifying brochure objectives*. The essential task is to clarify and state concisely what the brochure is expected to achieve in the campaign, especially in terms of the specific products it covers. A list of specific messages, rank ordered according to perceived customer priorities, should be drawn up within the context of the agreed marketing objectives. These statements will be crucial in briefing designers (see also the 'multiple purposes of print' in this chapter).

4 *Deciding the method of distributing print*. The distribution of print to its intended recipients is perhaps the most vital of the six stages, because communication can only work if sufficient numbers of prospective customers receive it. The cost of distribution per unit of print may easily exceed the unit cost of its production, and most producers in travel and tourism will have to choose between several distribution options. This vital decision is discussed later in this chapter.

5 *Creative execution*. As for advertising, the way in which product concepts and images are presented in print will strongly influence the way in which consumers receive and respond to messages. In particular, the appearance and appeal of the front cover, especially of items to be displayed in self-service racks, will be crucial in establishing eye contact and initial visual interest. Without the initial appeal, a leaflet or brochure is unlikely to be picked up and looked through. Maas notes that 'the cover of a brochure is just like the headline of a print advertisement: four out of five people never get beyond it. For these readers, you must get your selling message across on that page (or waste 80 per cent of your money)' (1980: p. 23). From research into the influence of pictures in advertising in Britain and the

USA, Haines concluded that 'a majority of advertising pictures are not projecting their intended message; some are so misconceived as to be counter-productive or even damaging to the advertiser's interest' (1984, p. 20).

While creative execution will usually be the business of designers (see below), marketing managers must accept full responsibility for the designer's brief and any marketing research associated with it.

6 *Timing*. Most travel and tourism print is required to fulfil its roles at particular times. Tour operators and other producers, for example, must have their material available for distribution when customers are making their travel decisions. Print production and advertising normally require carefully co-ordinated phasing. Since it usually takes several weeks from an initial brief to final production of print, it is vital that print requirements are carefully programmed and that agreed timings are adhered to. If photographs are required, they have to be taken at the right time of the year. Many a hotel and visitor attraction has started to plan its brochure in September for production in January, only to find that the key photographs it needs should have been taken in July.

While this may seem obvious, experience demonstrates repeatedly that the bulk of all print is commissioned too late; that most brochure work is rushed, often involving mistakes and penalties of cost; and that important deadlines are missed with consequent loss of revenue. Marketing managers have only limited influence over creative execution, but they should exercise total control over timing. The scope for marginal improvements in better timing alone may have a considerable impact on revenue. This is one of the few ways in marketing to achieve marginal revenue gains and marginal budget savings at the same time.

Using agencies to produce print

In large organizations the creative aspects of print design are often handled within the organization itself, and through advertising agencies. Print production is invariably handled by specialist firms. Smaller organizations usually obtain quotes from two or three printing firms, many of which have access to designers, photographers, and copy writers.

Printing agencies will normally undertake whatever aspects of the total print design and production process clients specify, and some may only work to specific instructions. Many printers will, however, be willing to provide professional and technical assistance with all or most of the following decisions:

Creative execution of the client's product concepts
- Most effective structure, layout, content, and size of brochure.
- Design theme, and image presentation, especially of the front cover.
- Use of colours and 'atmosphere'.
- Artwork and use of photographs.
- Captions, copy, and choice of typefaces.

Print production and distribution
- Choice of paper weight (affects costs and indicates quality).
- Packing (bulk and individual copies).
- Distribution.

To get good work from any agency, especially to get the best assistance in aspects of design and layout, it is essential for the client to supply a detailed written brief. The brief should refer to all the stages in producing effective print noted in the previous section, and include extracts of the marketing plan and details of the print budget. While printers are not always concerned with the distribution of materials, distribution considerations (see later in this chapter) must be clearly explained, since they will heavily influence the creative execution.

In practice many smaller organizations fail to produce adequate briefs for print, and worse, they change their minds after the initial design, layout, and artwork have been produced. Such changes are certain to add to cost, cause delays and produce a less than satisfactory result. Where external agencies are used, the process of agreeing print production usually calls for detailed liaison at the following points:

- Agreement and interpretation of initial design brief, production schedule and costs.
- Preliminary ('rough') artwork sketches, headlines, format and content, colours and typeface.
- Photography (if necessary), finished artwork, copy.
- Printer's proofs for correction.

Distributing printed materials to target audiences

In the enthusiasm for creating an attractive leaflet or brochure it is easy to focus all attention on the design, photographs, images and copy. In practice the most important consideration for any printed material is how it will reach its intended target readers. If the answer is direct mail, there is an immediate design concern related to the cost of postage. It is not unusual for unit distribution costs of literature to exceed unit print costs. If the intention is to distribute through travel agencies, it must first be ascertained how many travel agents are willing to handle the item. For every brochure currently displayed in a British travel agent's racks, there are probably at least twenty others seeking space. Again, if travel agents are an agreed distribution source, the size of their standard display spaces will tend to dictate brochure size and page layout. These may appear obvious considerations, but experience suggests that distribution problems often come last and not first in the print decision process.

The distribution options for getting printed items into prospective buyers' hands are very wide. Where brochures or leaflets are displayed and given out 'in-house' or 'on-site', the distribution process can be fully controlled by the producer. Where a larger producer, such as an airline, hotel group or car-rental company, controls multi-site outlets, the literature distribution process is also easily controlled.

For distribution away from owned premises, there are at least ten main options for getting print into the hands of prospective buyers. These are summarized below:

- Advertisements carrying coupons to be completed by those requiring information.
- Cards or other inserts into press and magazine media, which are an alternative form of media space.
- Direct mail to previous customers, and others using names and addresses bought for the purpose from a list broker.
- Direct distribution on a door-to-door basis in targeted residential areas
- Direct distribution at exhibitions and shows open to the public, e.g. camping and caravan exhibitions, World Travel Market.
- Distribution via retail travel agencies.
- Distribution via tourist information centres and public libraries.
- Distribution via relevant third parties. For example, American Express, Access and many clubs and societies will, for a fee, include printed leaflets with their regular mailings to members; alternatively via hotel reception desks and similar relevant outlets (suitable for attractions, entertainments, car rental).
- Distribution via consortia (this is a variation of distribution via multi-site operation under one owner).
- Distribution via counter sales at newsagents/bookshops, etc. (if a cover price is charged).

Beyond these common choices, there will usually be other places, such as airports, railway-station concourses, bus-station waiting rooms, or petrol/gas stations, at which relevant opportunities to distribute literature may occur. Any controlled place that attracts a sufficient throughput of targeted prospects may be used for literature distribution purposes. The scope is very wide indeed.

The choice of distribution outlets will normally be based on experience of what has worked in previous years for the same or similar products. The scope for innovation and test marketing with new forms of distribution is, however, wide. It is strongly recommended as an essential method of learning how to improve the effectiveness of distribution at the margin.

Evaluating the results of print

Generally it will be impossible to distinguish with any precision the effectiveness of expenditure on printed communications from other elements of the marketing campaign, such as advertising and sales promotion. Bookings and sales revenue result from the marketing mix as a whole. Through marketing research, however, it is possible to reach some conclusions, and studies may be carried out:

1 To choose between alternative cover designs and content, using evidence of qualitative discussions with target groups of potential customers (see Chapter 11).
2 To measure the results of 'split-runs', in which two different brochure formats are distributed to matched samples of target recipients, and bookings compared. Using direct mail to distribute print makes this a relatively easy option for many producers.
3 To measure customer reaction through *ad hoc* telephone or postal surveys of brochure recipients, identified, for example, from completed coupons included in advertisements.

4 To measure customer recall and use of brochures in brief surveys conducted, for example, at reception desks when customers arrive on a producer's premises or site.

Tour operators, accommodation suppliers and tourist boards use all these measures, although the costs of 1 and 3 are unlikely to be affordable by any organization with a sales turnover much under £2 million (1992 prices).

In every case where printed materials are part of the marketing mix it is common sense to identify all items with code numbers or letters, which identify as appropriate:

● Through what media the print was requested.
● By what distribution methods print reached the customer (assuming more than one method).

Provided that consumer responses are analysed by the codes assigned, the use of printed materials and its distribution methods normally provide many opportunities for innovation and testing responses (see Chapter 14).

Alternatives to brochures

Current technology, including radio cassettes, video films, computerized images, video-text, and on-line communications between a principal's stock of products and a consumer's home TV set, could, in theory, replace much of the role of brochures. Improved quality of pictures accessed on television screens will clearly be helpful later in the 1990s. But the *physical* value of attractively produced print, and its ability to inspire images and dreams, appear to be critical in travel and tourism. This author, at least, does not believe that print is likely to be replaced by other forms of visual communication in the foreseeable future. Alternative forms have a complementary role to play, however, and might be used effectively to reduce existing levels of wastage in retail outlets.

In the USA in the early 1990s, initially for the selection of business hotels and cruise ships, at least two major CRS systems were providing laser disc technology capable of interfacing high quality pictures of products with reservation systems in the same PC hardware and software. WORLDSPAN uses a system known as IRIS (Integrated Reservation Imaging System) and SABRE use a system known as SABREVISION. (See chapter 18 for definitions of CRS.) At the time of writing these systems were also available in Europe but only on a very restricted basis. They appear certain to develop.

Chapter summary

This chapter identifies the vital part that printed materials play in marketing travel and tourism products, within the context of communications paid for out of marketing budgets. It notes the massive volume of items produced in the industry and the range of functions they perform, distinguishing between promotion and facilitation.

The different purposes for which print is used in marketing are discussed and the six main stages in producing effective print are explained, with reference to the roles of printing and other agencies.

The chapter emphasizes a particular need for organizations to analyse the problems of securing effective distribution for printed materials to targeted readers, and notes the choices available to producers. The *objective and task* method of costing print requirements (introduced in Chapter 14) is recommended, and makes it easier in practice for managers to measure the results of their expenditure.

In summary, it is interesting to reflect that, at least for commercial producers in the travel and tourism industry, their printed materials frequently embody all aspects of the marketing mix to the extent that they:

- State and physically represent the product in consumer terms.
- State the price and other details as the basis of a legally enforceable contract.
- Are a principal medium of promotion.
- Are part of the distribution process that represents 'place' for customers.

Given the nature of service products in general, and travel and tourism products in particular, printed communications are often the most important single element within co-ordinated marketing campaigns. Print distribution in particular provides significant opportunities for cost savings at the margin.

18

Distribution channels in travel and tourism: creating access

This chapter considers the last of the four Ps in the marketing mix – place, distribution or 'access' as it was introduced in Chapter 6, and points of sale in Chapter 16. In defining access it is important to note three points. First, that the nature of distribution systems and processes is one of the principal ways in which the marketing of services differs from the marketing of goods. Second, distribution processes vary considerably between sectors of the travel and tourism industry. Whereas there are many similarities in the methods of product formulation, pricing, and promotion for all types of travel and tourism products, this is not the case for distribution and the provision of access. Third, that 'place' and the location of an operator's business are not the same thing.

Up to the present time a widespread myth still persists that, because services cannot be inventoried on shelves and in warehouses, distribution systems or 'channels' are less important in service industries than in others. Paradoxically, the inability in travel and tourism to create physical stocks of products adds to rather than reduces the importance of the distribution process. Creating and manipulating access for consumers is one of the principal ways to manage demand for highly perishable products. Producers are willing to pay relatively high costs for the advantages of extending their points of sale.

This chapter recognizes the importance of location for businesses in travel and tourism, but stresses the need to provide access to points of sale away from the place of service production, for all but the smallest of businesses. Definitions of distribution channels and of 'pipelines' are discussed, and key terms defined. The marketing functions performed by different kinds of distribution outlets are noted, and reservation systems discussed. The chapter ends with a discussion of distribution costs.

Because of the importance of travel agents as a leading and influential sector in the industry, most texts on travel and tourism marketing deal with the distribution function from the standpoint of the retailer. Some assume (wrongly) that tourism is mainly concerned with air travel and package tours to international destinations. This author fully recognizes the importance of retail travel agencies, especially for transport and tour operators, but it has to be stressed that agencies are by no means the only channel of distribution in travel and tourism. Nor are they necessarily the most important channel for most producers and travellers. In the USA and in the UK the majority of travellers (domestic and international tourism combined, as defined in Chapter 1) do not use travel agents, and the majority of producers in the industry use more than one form of distribution channel. Most smaller businesses, which are the largest part of the industry in all developed countries, are effectively excluded from retail distribution channels because individually they are too small. Accordingly, this chapter and the next take a deliberately broad perspective of distribution in which travel agents are important but only one component within a wider context of creating and sustaining customer access.

The importance of location and access

For most small businesses with only one 'production unit', such as proprietor-owned restaurants, guesthouses, taxi firms, small visitor attractions or independent travel agents, the choice of location is the most important business decision. A well-located small business can often be sure of an adequate flow of customers to its area and past its doors.

In such circumstances consumers come to the producer. Producers expect the customer to find them, and the concept of distribution channels has little relevance, other than a telephone for reservations. Product formulation, promotion, and above all pricing remain vital marketing considerations for small businesses, but not distribution. Thus *location* is both the place of production and the primary point of sale.

For smaller businesses then, the well-known industry cliché about the three golden rules for running a successful business, *location*, *location*, *location*, is true. But, increasingly, the circumstances of small single-unit businesses do not provide useful marketing guidelines for the travel and tourism industry, and a wider focus is needed to understand access and distribution.

Location inadequate as sole point of sale

As businesses expand in size and volume of sales, the fundamental attraction of well-located sites does not diminish. The more or less

continuous search in the 1980s l hotel companies for suitable hote European cities, provides some the power of location. But location .. production units is seldom a *sufficient* source of sales volume for bigger businesses, and supplementary points of sale *away* from the locations of service production and consumption are required. The factors that focus attention on supplementary points of sale are:

● Growing size of business (production capacity to be matched with more sales).
● Increasing number of units within a group or chain (under one ownership, or linked in marketing co-operatives).
● Greater distances that customers travel to reach a unit, especially where international travel is necessary.
● The importance of drawing in first time visitors in order to grow.
● Growing competition for shares of markets, for which there is excess capacity in a location.
● The need to reduce dependence on day-to-day sales by selling capacity ahead of production, through a reservation system.

These six factors, separately and combined, tend to force the obvious marketing response, which is to generate more demand. One logical route to this is by creating additional points of sale or, in other words, moving the purchase decision away from the location of production towards other places that prospective customers find more convenient. These additional points of sale make up what is known collectively as a 'distribution system'.

As this chapter will indicate, there are other good marketing reasons for developing distribution or access systems, but the over-riding reason is to generate sales revenue additional to that which may be sustained solely by a good location. While, to some extent, additional expenditure on advertising or other communications is an alternative to creating more points of sale, in practice there is usually a balance to be achieved between promotion and place. A massive demand generated by advertising could be lost, for example, if convenient points of access were not available to turn demand into sales. Sales promotion and merchandising at points of sale are of course vital activities in travel and tourism marketing. The possibilities and requirements of such promotion both reflect and influence the choice of distribution systems.

Defining distribution or access systems – the notion of pipelines

'The concept of marketing channels is not limited to the distribution of physical goods. Producers of services ... also face the problem of making their output *available* and *accessible* to target populations' (Kotler: 1984, p. 545). Kotler adopts Bucklin's 1966 definition of distribution channels as comprising 'a set of institutions which performs all of the activities (functions) utilized to move a product and its title from production to consumption'. While Bucklin's definition is clearly based on physical goods, which move from a place of production, it nevertheless contains key elements for an adequate definition for services. Drawing on these ideas the following definition of distribution is proposed for travel and tourism:

A distribution channel is any organized and serviced system, created or utilized to provide convenient points of sale and/or access to consumers, away from the location of production and consumption, and paid for out of marketing budgets.

The essence of this definition is that channels are not in any way left to chance, but carefully planned by producers and serviced regularly by them with sales visits, literature, computer links, and in other ways. Each channel, once organized

and serviced at a cost to be paid for out of marketing budgets, becomes in effect a 'pipeline'. Through this pipeline flows a targeted volume of sales over a marketing campaign period. This definition is deliberately wider than that proposed by either Bucklin, or a decade later by Donelly, in a seminal article on channels of distribution for services, which has been much quoted. His definition states: 'Any extra corporate entity between the producer of a service and prospective users that is utilized to make the service available and/or more convenient, is a marketing intermediary for that purpose' (1976: p. 57).

Experience with travel and tourism services suggests that pipelines should not be restricted to 'extra-corporate entities', and that several of the vital pipelines for tourism do not use intermediaries. This chapter suggests therefore that a more fertile approach is to define the functions served by distribution systems, and then use functional criteria to identify the pipelines.

All the definitions noted above exclude the activities of sales representatives, who negotiate contracts with corporate clients to deliver a specified number of products, over a specified period of time, at a specified price. The essence of any pipeline is that it is a non-personal system, set up in advance to facilitate targeted sales volume, but the actual flow of sales achieved over the period of a campaign cannot be known in advance. The rate of flow may be influenced by marketing activities in the pipeline, or external to it, such as advertising.

Key words in services distribution

Because of the special nature of distribution in travel and tourism, many people experience confusion over the way in which terms are used. Rathmell suggested that, 'To facilitate integration with conventional thought, location and distribution, and channel and delivery are used interchangeably' (1974: p. 104). If readers attempt to use these terms interchangeably, confusion is certain. The following terms are defined therefore to limit semantic difficulties; they draw on the views of the principal American and British contributors to the subject and appear to represent common ground:

Distribution process	The process of creating access for potential customers in one or more places convenient for them, but away from the place and time of delivery of products being bought.
Location	The geographical location of a site or premises, at which service products are delivered to customers.
Delivery	The physical process of producing or performing the service product simultaneously with consumption.
Distribution channel or pipeline	Any organized and serviced system, created or utilized to provide convenient points of sale and/or access to consumers, away from the location of delivery.
Intermediary	Any third party or organization between producer and consumer that facilitates purchases, the transfer of title to the buyer, and sales revenue to the producer.

Principals, customers and intermediaries

In the terms used to discuss distribution in travel and tourism, a 'principal' is any producer or operator who has products to sell. For all practical purposes it is convenient to include tour operators as principals within this definition. Principals have a basic choice whether to sell direct to the customer or to achieve sales through one or more third parties, known as intermediaries. Drawing on the definitions used by Kotler (1984: p. 542) the five main choices open to any principal are presented in Figure 18.1.

From the examples provided, it will be clear that distribution channels vary according to size and types of organization, and that larger principals use more than one form of distribution. Thus a car-rental business may establish desks at airports to service travellers by air, provide direct 'pipelines' to frequent users; offer commissions on sales by travel agents, and provide allocations of cars to tour operators that include car rental in their holiday packages. A guesthouse or a small tourist attraction usually deals only direct with customers, most of whom will purchase at the location of the business. Holiday caravan parks may offer allocations to operators such as Hoseasons Holidays or Blakes Holidays, which incorporate the products of many parks into one brochure distributed direct and through travel agents.

Two main roles of a distribution system

As previously indicated, the main function of a distribution system is to extend the number of points of sale or access, away from the location at which services are performed or delivered. In this sense at least the function of distribution is the same for tourism products as it is for physical goods.

An important secondary function of services distribution is to facilitate the purchase of products in advance of their production. 'Advance' could be anything from 2 to 3 hours (for transportation products), and up to 2 or 3 years or even longer (for major conventions or exhibition venues). It is a basic law of service production that the greater the volatility of daily

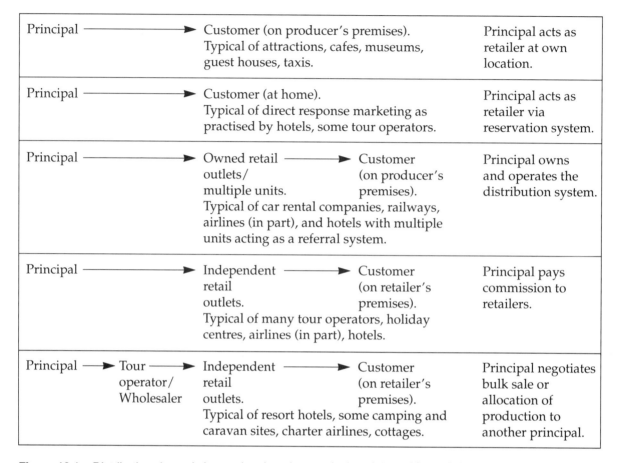

Figure 18.1   *Distribution channels in travel and tourism marketing. Adapted from Kotler: 1984, p. 542*

demand, the greater the imperative to sell forward if possible. Obviously, for an airline running shuttle routes for business commuters, daily and hourly demand is closely predictable to within a very few percentage points. For a resort hotel, contemplating July's profits in January, the daily or weekly demand is open to very wide fluctuation. The logical marketing response is to reduce risks by selling summer holidays throughout, say, January to June, so as to achieve 100 per cent room occupancy weeks, if possible, before the July visitors arrive.

Advertising, print, and sales promotion are of course geared to this pattern of advance sales,

but will not work unless pipelines are organized and an efficient reservation or advance booking system is continuously in operation to receive the flow of sales.

Advance purchase through reservations

To modern students brought up in the computer age, it must seem strange that well into the 1970s most travel reservation systems were manual, even in the USA. Teams of clerks using telephones toiled like ants around massive pegboards, blackboards, or charts that filled the whole wall space of large offices. Such charts physically represented production capacity for several months ahead. The systems were slow, inflexible, liable to failure through human error, and very costly in labour employed. By the early 1980s most manual systems had disappeared from large and medium-sized producers, to be replaced by on-line, electronic information systems, operating through each principal's main computer, through as many peripheral terminals as the flow of business could justify. It was not until 1986, however, that Thomson Holidays in the UK refused to accept bookings by telephone. Modern systems handle not only reservations but also searches for alternative products. The systems may be linked with automatic printers which produce travel documents, confirmations, and invoices, and can also be used to generate continuous marketing research data. Through the use of space satellites, modern systems operate internationally. In the 1990s, as different mainframe computers can link their databases and communicate better with each other, the implications for improved efficiency in travel and tourism distribution systems are expected to be very significant (see CRS systems, p. 209).

An important split between reserved and non-reserved services

Before considering the specific functions of a distribution system, an important distinction between reserved and non-reserved products in travel and tourism must be noted. Distribution pipelines may be a relevant consideration for principals with or without a reservations facility, but their full functions are best understood in the context of products capable of reservations or advance booking. Burkart noted that products in travel and tourism split between those for which a large excess of supply over demand exists at most times, and others for which an excess of demand over supply exists for much of

the time (Burkart: 1976, p. 240). In the first category come museums, other managed attractions, seats in most trains, touring camp sites, much of car rental, pubs, popular catering, country parks, and so on. Where reservations are not made, the point of sale is usually the reception desk at the producer's location. Pipelines may still be needed to reach particular customer segments and as points of information and display (such as tourist information centres). In the second category come most hotels and other accommodation suppliers, most airlines, inclusive tours, car ferries, theatres, and shows. In these cases advance bookings are normal and the point of sale is generally a distribution outlet away from the producer's location.

Ten functions of a full service distribution system

The following ten functions are carried out by distribution outlets offering the full range of services to tourism industry producers. Full service distributors in travel include retail travel agents, airport, rail, or coach terminal booking offices, hotel reservation companies, and tourist information offices (TICs) if they include booking facilities. All of them provide:

1 Points of sale and convenient customer access, either for immediate purchase or for booking in advance.
2 Distribution of product information such as brochures and leaflets (provide choice for customers).
3 Display and merchandising opportunities.
4 Advice and purchase assistance, e.g. itinerary planning and helpful product knowledge.
5 Arranging transfer of title to a product through ticketing and travel documentation.
6 Receiving and transmitting sales revenue to principals.

7 Possible provision of ancillary services, e.g. insurance, advice on inoculations, passport assistance.

8 Possible source of marketing intelligence for principals.

9 May supplement principal's promotional activities.

10 Receiving and assisting with complaints from customers.

Where large producers, such as hotels and airlines, have their own multiple units, each unit acts as a retailer for the others and also fulfils all ten distribution functions. Other than the lack of physical stocks to move about and maintain, the ten functions listed are identical to those carried out by the distributors of physical goods. There is one other important exception. Travel and tourism distributors do not purchase products in bulk and do not, therefore, share with principals in the financial risks of production. By contrast, distributors of physical goods purchase their stocks, take responsibility for selling them to customers, and risk losing money on unsold stocks. This process of sharing risk has led to buying in bulk and has been part of the impetus to growth of large, multi-site retail chains for physical goods in the last three decades. It has given such retailers great power over manufacturers. It has also led to the larger outlets, such as supermarkets, using their 'own labels' to sell products they have bought in bulk at factory prices. Some distributors have integrated their operations backwards by buying producer organizations to service their needs and increase their profitability.

In travel and tourism the prime responsibility for generating and managing demand has remained in the hands of the principals. It is they who have controlled product design in the industry, borne the bulk of the marketing costs, fixed prices, and generally been responsible for the volume of sales their products achieved. Although the key issue of risk-taking has not changed, the economics of operating travel agencies in the 1980s has altered the structure of the retail sector in the UK, especially the need to invest in professional management and the new CRS-linked technology. This led to the growth of a small number of large retail travel agency chains in the 1980s known as 'multiples'. The names have changed and some have disappeared but in the early 1990s six multiples owned around a quarter of retail agencies and handled about half of leisure turnover (their dominance is even greater in the business travel market). These multiples have influence over principals and some, notably Thomas Cook, have been powerful enough to impose their strategies on the operators with which they do business. Some of the large multiples are now able to secure more commission from principals, and some are beginning to produce their 'own label' products by taking allocations of capacity, as tour operators do, from producers.

Six functions of limited service distribution systems

As discussed in Chapter 17, the product substitution role of print in travel and tourism means that access, if not always points of sale, can be created wherever sufficient numbers of prospective customers can be brought to a focal point. This flexibility leads logically to limited service distribution systems.

Limited service distributors in travel and tourism include most TICs, hotel porters' desks, reception areas of holiday centres and holiday parks, and reception areas of visitor attractions. Many of these limited service outlets are to be found in tourist destinations. Most are local only with no national links for distribution purposes.

Limited services are of great value to many smaller producers, for whom they provide opportunities to merchandise their products, achieve display, and distribute their sales literature (including sales promotion offers) to prospective customers, away from their location of production.

There is wide scope for extending limited service distribution outlets, using petrol stations, roadside restaurants, newsagents' shops, and post offices, all of which offer potentially valuable ways to reach prospective customers. For small producers with no access to travel retailers, the flexibility of these limited service outlets is especially attractive.

The functions performed by these limited channels, in distributing information, and promotional print, to some extent overlap with the functions performed by advertising media. All of the channels in this section are, however, permanent locations, to be serviced by producers and maintained in much the same way as full service distribution outlets.

Limited services perform the following functions:

1 Distribute product information, such as brochures, leaflets, and sales-promotion offers.
2 Provide space for display and other merchandising activities.
3 Provide customer advice and assistance.
4 May provide supporting services, e.g. bed reservation schemes.
5 May receive and assist in following up customer complaints.
6 May act as a source of marketing intelligence for producers

Other forms of travel and tourism distribution channels

Reflecting the flexibility conveyed by the non-physical nature of travel and tourism products another group of pipelines exists which is increasingly used by airlines, hotels, car rentals, restaurants and some attractions. The channels noted below are not normally referred to as part of a distribution process, yet they can be used to fulfil the distribution functions noted on p. 205. They also meet the essential criteria included in the definitions noted earlier in this chapter. The channels listed below are strongly associated

with sales promotion and some forms of direct-response marketing. This association with other marketing functions is significant, and requires careful co-ordination in planning marketing campaigns. Each of the channels below is relevant to a specific user or segment group and is not accessible to customers as a whole. Provided that any such system is structured in advance to generate a targeted but unknown volume of business over a campaign period, it meets the 'pipeline' criteria previously noted. In an era of increasing market segmentation, these types of channel or pipeline are likely to be increasingly used:

● VIP/privileged user cards and membership clubs for frequent customers (provided by hotels, airlines, car rental firms and some visitor attractions).
● Secretaries' clubs (maintained by some hotels and airlines).
● Special links with other bodies such as schools, clubs, societies, trade associations (maintained by attractions and hotels).
● Allocations of product capacity to credit card companies acting, for this purpose, as tour operators.

Fixed and variable costs of distribution

Some of the costs of maintaining and supporting distribution systems or pipelines are fixed for the duration of any marketing campaign, in the sense that outlets must be organized and serviced in advance of any business that is expected to flow. Fixed costs in this sense include:

1 The costs of installing reservation systems, computers and programmes, and staff capable of dealing with enquiries and monitoring bookings through each pipeline.
2 The costs of brochure production, distribution and maintaining supplies to the points of sale.

3 Costs of sales promotion incentives aimed at motivating retailers and other points of sale.
4 The costs of support visits to distribution intermediaries, including any costs of merchandising efforts and display materials, that may be used at points of sale.
5 The costs of maintaining and motivating a sales force (if any) to negotiate agreements with intermediaries, in order to secure brochure distribution and display.
6 Costs of any *educationals* and workshops organized in support of distributor systems, and staff training.

The variable costs are measured in commission, which is usually paid only when sales are achieved, and any phone calls connected with bookings or enquiries and paid for by principals.

Calculating the costs of distribution channels

Because there is no physical transfer of goods, it is the experience of most producers in travel and tourism that distribution or access channels are relatively flexible and may be increased at relatively low cost, according to opportunities available. At least in theory, the only limit to creating additional channels is the marginal point at which the unit costs of providing access exceeds the marginal unit profits of bookings using that access. Up to that limit, more profit is achieved by creating more access.

In practice the margins are too difficult to measure and producers tend to balance and monitor the costs of distribution as the following example shows. Assume a small hotel group, with three hotels and 500 double occupancy rooms, for which it targets 25 per cent sleeper nights to be distributed over 12 months through three channels *other* than referral between units, and direct bookings arising from locations and repeat customers. For the sake of simplicity it is assumed that all bookings have the same unit value (eg. £40 per person-night):

- 500 rooms × 2 persons × 365 nights × 25 per cent distribution via channels = 91,250 sleeper nights.
- Channel A costs £100,000 to service and generates 50,000 sleeper nights. The average unit cost of distribution per night = £2.00 (not including commission).
- Channel B costs £30,000 to service and generates 25,000 sleeper-nights. The average unit cost of distribution per night = £1.20 (not including commission).
- Channel C costs £97,500 to service and generates 16,250 sleeper-nights. The average unit cost of distribution per night = £6.00 (not including commission).

'Cost to Service' is the calculated cost of staff, and equipment overheads, which have to be spent to sustain a channel at the targeted level of business turnover, plus brochure costs and expenditure on incentives required to secure distributor support. It does not include the cost of commission on sales (say 10 per cent) which is assumed to be standard for all three channels. If commission levels were variable in practice, it would be sensible to include them in the cost to service, since it would alter the average unit cost of distribution.

Of course the average value of bookings may be greater in one channel, or more useful in creating low season bookings in another, but these complications should not obscure the basic need to assess and compare the unit costs of providing customer access in each pipeline. Such calculations are inputs to decisions about which existing channels to develop, and essential for assessing the potential value of any new channels that might be opened up.

Provided that a hotel group or other principal is willing to apportion the costs of servicing and commission for each channel, the costs of creating pipelines for customer access can be budgeted with precision, using the *objective and task* methods described in Chapter 14.

International CRS systems – inventory management

In the 1988 edition of this book, major developments in inventory management were identified in the Epilogue.

'In all sectors of the industry except attractions . . . computerization has served to create customer convenience; improve operational productivity through speed of access to products; reduce the number of staff involved; and reduce the unit costs of making individual bookings. Through interactive computer links between different suppliers it is now common for different elements of the overall tourism product to be brought together in ways impossible until recently. Air transport can be linked with hotel and car rental inventories to produce international bookings in seconds' (1988, p. 293).

Inventory management using computer managed databases has made massive strides since 1988 through international airline-developed CRS systems, some of which already span the globe and are known as GDS – Global Distribution Systems. This is a massive topic

Table 18.1 *The top four international computer reservation systems (CRS) in North America and Europe in 1992*

Name	Countries of origin	Airlines involved	Current	Comment
AMADEUS established 1987	France, Germany, Spain, Sweden	Air France, Lufthansa, Iberia, SAS	Approx 40,000 terminals in countries of origin. Claims around 60% of European CRS business	Projected links with SABRE failed in 1992. Links with WORLDSPAN under discussion in 1992
APOLLO (Covia Corporation)	USA	United Airlines, US Air, Air Canada, British Airways, Swissair, KLM	Claims 30% US CRS market	Galileo succeeded TRAVICOM in the UK therefore is likely to become the dominant UK system. Working closely with Apollo in US, and Gemini in Canada.
and GALILEO established 1987	UK, Netherlands, Italy, Switzerland, USA, Greece, Belgium, Portugal	British Airways, KLM, Alitalia, Swissair, Olympic Airways, United Airways, and US Air.	Claims 80% of UK and 40% of European market share	The two systems were expected to merge in 1993.
SABRE established 1976	USA	American Airlines	Mainly USA outlets but growing UK presence at around 500 outlets. Claims 45% of US CRS bookings	7,000 agents in USA use SABRE VISION to communicate high quality product pictures
WORLDSPAN established 1990	USA and Far East (ABACUS)	Delta/TWA/North West Airlines and ABACUS group of 7 airlines	Approx 38,000 USA terminals; plus 5000 worldwide; 500 in UK. Claims 15% US CRS bookings	Succeeded PARS and DATAS. Links with American Express

Notes:
1. Most CRSs use AT&T/ISTEL systems to link agents with principals' computers.
2. Leading CRSs are PC-based and offer sophisticated supplementary office/business management software packages for travel agents.
3. Most CRSs have, or are forming subsidiary access systems for leisure products, eg., GALILEO LINK and LEISURE SABRE.

Source: Author's notes from travel trade press, journals, and contribution by I. Mitchell of Oxford Brookes University

and developments are occurring so fast that any book is likely to be out of date before it is published. As a record at least of the state of play at end 1992, Table 18.1 provides brief information on the four main systems in North America and Europe, noting the WORLDSPAN link with ABACUS, which links with airlines in the Far East.

CRS systems:

● Use 'intelligent' PC systems rather than 'dumb' viewdata terminals, so that other software programmes can be added and linked to CRS inventory-management software. These include automatic ticketing and invoicing of course, but also accounting and other office management systems, including word-processing and capability to link with customer databases. In the UK, however, it seems probable that up to a third of current retail outlets will be too small to make the necessary investment in equipment and staff training.
● Are 'hard wired,' mostly using AT & T/Istel systems rather than dialling through the public telephone service. This improves the speed of connections to databases and increases the volume of traffic the terminals can handle. It is needed when one considers that a system such as SABRE can already handle over 1 million bookings every day. The extension in the 1990s of digital telephone systems (Integrated Services Digital Network – ISDN) will further enhance the capacity of information processing networks.
● Are shifting from the original focus on business travel into leisure products. Initially into hotels and cruise ships, but major tour operators and agents such as American Express, Thomson and Thomas Cook have already linked their own systems with the CRS majors.
● Are capable of handling very high quality visual material, which may not replace but could help to reduce the existing costly wastage of printed brochures and other materials.
● Provide leading edge competitive advantages to CRS owners and major principals in capturing the vital marginal business that has such a massive gearing to profit – so much so that CRSs were early targets for competition policy to prevent undue bias in the use of systems to favour the owners. In 1992, in the USA and EC, competition policy regulations were under consideration to prevent possible abuse and unfair competition.
● Exploit global developments in information communications technology, which are predicted to have increasing influence over all aspects of life in the twenty-first century. In particular the systems benefit from the reducing unit costs of creating, accessing, and linking interactive international databases, and extending their capacity and capabilities (see the Epilogue).

At present, CRSs work on behalf of airlines directly and through travel agents. Travel agents are the logical pipeline and natural partners, especially in their roles of handling much of business travel, inclusive tours, air travel generally and car rental. But there is no reason why travel distribution systems should be limited to agents. Provided that a potential flow of business is large enough to warrant the investment necessary in the essential hardware and software, CRSs can easily cope with additional pipelines within the definitions offered in this chapter. If Minitel-style home-shopping takes off, even though it is a viewdata system, it can generate enough business to gain access to CRSs. If banks decide that travel is a business in which they wish to expand, there are no overwhelming obstacles to prevent them. Their credit-card-customer databases already give them powerful leverage as potential marketing partners for CRS systems.

An even more exciting opportunity for future marketing will exist when the customer databases maintained by large operators (see

Chapter 19) can be interfaced with customer information in CRS systems. At that point regulatory developments appear certain to limit the extent to which operators can exploit their information technology and invade individual privacy, but the potential exists. The marketing opportunities of channel flexibility are immense.

Chapter summary

This chapter explains why distribution or access systems are vital considerations in the marketing of travel and tourism products, excepting only very small businesses where location remains all important. Within the context that distribution or access is a generic difference in the marketing of goods and services, the key differences between location, points of sale, and place of delivery, are identified and discussed. The definition of principals and intermediaries in the distribution process makes clear the potential flexibility of pipelines in travel and tourism, reinforced in recent years by the growing use of leading edge information technology, especially for products requiring advanced bookings. Many principals use several different distribution channels simultaneously to create additional points of sale for their products. The marketing tasks associated with different types of channel are outlined, distinguishing between full service and limited service distribution.

While the distribution of travel products is flexible and multiple pipelines are commonly used, there are significant costs in providing access to customers and a need to balance the costs of the different channels used. Throughout the chapter the linkages between providing access and the other elements of the marketing mix are noted. Access typically acts in a supportive role by providing convenient points of sale to customers already motivated through advertising and PR, but it is also the focus for many forms of sales promotion, especially those designed to stimulate last-minute purchases. This association and synergy with other aspects of the marketing mix is most clearly seen in retail travel agencies.

Paradoxically, the inability to transfer and store products physically, which was once thought to be such a disadvantage in travel and tourism marketing, has now become a powerful asset. Product capacity can be accessed across continents and across months or years, at the touch of a button. Electronic information technology conveys enormous flexibility to producers, the full scope of which has yet to be fully developed.

Further reading

Baker, M. J., *Marketing: An Introductory Text*, 4th edit., Macmillan, 1985, Chapters 10 and 15.

Kotler, P., *Marketing: Analysis, Planning, Implementation and Control*, 7th edit., Prentice-Hall International, 1991, Chapter 19.

For those interested in the particular characteristics and development of British travel retailing, see Bottomley Renshaw, *The Travel Agent*, Business Education Publishers 1992.

19

Direct response marketing in travel and tourism versus retail distribution

As Americans express it, the 'bottom line' of all marketing is achieving sales volume and revenue targets. Within the integrating framework of the marketing mix, Chapters 15 to 18 review the individual functions of advertising and PR, sales promotion, printed materials, and distribution. All of them are key techniques in the implementation of marketing campaigns in travel and tourism; all of them are sales- and revenue-focused.

This chapter discusses the strategic choice to be made between planning the marketing mix to generate sales on a *direct-response* basis, in which the producer promotes to and deals directly with the customer, or an *indirect-response* basis. Indirect means that sales are achieved through third-party distribution channels created and maintained for that purpose, as described in Chapter 18. In practice the choice is seldom clear-cut, and a combination of both strategies for achieving sales response is common in the travel and tourism industry.

Because of the advantages of choice and flexibility in distribution channels for service products generally, the strategic choice between direct or indirect-response marketing has always been much more important in travel and tourism than for most manufactured products.

New computerized database technology, available only in very recent years for identifying individual customers by their addresses, profiles and purchasing behaviour, is altering the strategic choices facing many operators in the 1990s. On current evidence, this new technology looks likely to shift the emphasis in marketing toward direct-response strategies for all types of product, whether physical goods or services.

This chapter begins by viewing travel sales from the customers' standpoint, in a practical context of enquiries, reservations, and bookings. This is followed by key definitions, and a review of the strategic options for generating sales, using a diagram representing the marketing flows in the producer, distributor, customer triangle (Figure 19.1). The same diagram provides a framework for reviewing the tactical options in the marketing mix, once the nature of the product portfolio and prices have been decided. The chapter proceeds to review the methods available to direct-response marketers and summarizes the potential benefits achievable by those who use such methods in conjunction with new forms of computerized databases and reservation systems. The chapter concludes with a discussion of the balance to be achieved in travel and tourism between direct and indirect marketing response methods.

The characteristics of sales in travel and tourism

At its simplest, a sale is made when a customer parts with money in exchange for a promise to deliver a product. That is the bottom line. In practice there is a complex decision process at work between a customer's initial awareness and review of what is available, consideration of the options which best meet his or her needs, and the final selection and purchase. The decision process, introduced in Chapter 5, is especially complex in much of travel and tourism because of the relatively high cost of many products and the relatively high level of customers' psychological involvement with the product. Holidays are good examples of what are described in marketing texts as 'shopping' or 'speciality products', in the purchase of which most buyers are willing to invest considerable time and effort.

Because of the nature of holiday products, buyers will usually make enquiries of several producers and evaluate the choices according to their perceptions of what is offered, their interests and needs, and their ability to pay. The way in which travel brochures are laid out is an obvious illustration of producers' response to this purchasing behaviour. Accordingly, much of marketing is aimed first at generating interest and enquiries, and, second, at motivating and converting interest into sales through the provision of mainly printed promotional materials.

Putting the question

It is axiomatic in commercial marketing that there is no sale without customer interest, and no interest without awareness. All producers are therefore interested in creating greater awareness of their products and converting it into sales. In travel and tourism, however, the flexible nature of distribution channels leads to a vital question. Is it better – more cost effective – to approach customers direct? Or to do so indirectly through distribution channels? Or by some combination of the two? These are questions that should exercise all marketing managers.

Defining marketing methods of achieving sales

This section sets out the key definitions relevant to this chapter. It deserves careful reading because the loose usage in practice of terms such as 'sales', 'selling', 'personal selling', 'direct selling', 'direct marketing', 'direct-response marketing', and 'database marketing', is the source of great confusion to students of marketing. To judge from the travel trade press this confusion is as deep if not deeper among practitioners and it reflects changes that are occurring in the travel and tourism industry. It is worth the effort to use the main terms with some precision. Three important clarifications can be made at the outset:

1 Distinguishing reservations or bookings from in-house sales.
2 Distinguishing bookings by the general public from bulk or group sales.
3 Distinguishing marketing methods from those that are sales-orientated.

The first clarification is to stress that this chapter is concerned only with product sales, which are bookings or reservations made by customers either from home or through a distribution channel. It is *not* concerned with any aspects of in-house or on-site selling, which were described in Chapter 16. The focus on reservations means that this chapter is more relevant to all forms of accommodation suppliers, transport operators, and tour operators than to visitor attractions, although the principles are applicable to all sectors.

The second clarification is to distinguish between sales to the general public, and sales that are group bookings or bulk purchases negotiated between a sales force or a head office staff and buyers who represent a group. This chapter is about the methods used to generate bookings from the general public and is not concerned with the techniques of using a sales force. The use of a sales team to generate group bookings is of course very important in the travel and tourism industry, especially for hotels. The techniques used to achieve such sales are widely known as personal selling, because they usually comprise a form of face-to-face negotiation between buyer and seller, which may take hours, or weeks in the case of a large contract such as a major conference. Important as personal-selling skills and managing a sales force are, however, the techniques have been practised and developed over many years and they are fully covered in general marketing literature. New techniques for generating sales direct from the general public in travel and tourism are not well-covered, and for this reason they are the focus of this chapter.

The third clarification is to draw a distinction between traditional selling methods aimed at the general public, which are older than this century, and modern sales techniques integrated within a marketing system. In the former case selling is the dominant element in achieving revenue targets, typically within a sales-orientated business philosophy of selling the products designed by production-orientated organizations. In marketing-led firms selling is one element in an integrated marketing mix employed by organizations that put knowledge of customers needs at the centre of their business philosophy. Hotels and holiday centres, for example, have for many years used cut-out coupons with their advertising in order to generate enquiries. The regular mailing of brochures and leaflets direct to previous

customers to encourage repeat purchases is another technique of considerable vintage. Modern direct-response marketing employs many of the traditional techniques. But fundamental differences lie in the way they are used, especially the databased learning process about customers, and the continuous adaptation of the product around the identified needs of customers.

Direct sell or direct-response marketing?

It follows from the three clarifications noted above that the main focus of this chapter is on two-way direct communication links between producers and prospective customers. In its traditional form it was usually known under the generic title of *direct selling*, defined as 'selling of goods and services, which involves direct communication between the producer and customers, without the use of retail outlets, distributors, wholesalers or any other type of middleman. Often includes direct mail and telephone selling' (Medlik: 1993). In the 1960s and 1970s the typical direct-selling techniques practised by producers used direct-mail colour catalogues of consumer goods, often targeted at housewives. Names and addresses of prospective buyers were obtained by advertising that incorporated coupons to complete, or telephone numbers to ring, and were added to lists of previous customers. This form of selling is much more significant in the USA than in Britain, although it has significantly increased its share of total consumer sales in both countries over recent years.

In travel and tourism the shift from direct selling to direct-response marketing began in the 1980s. It reflects three important changes in the business environment:

● The growing need to know more about customers' profiles and needs, in line with all forms of modern marketing.

- The growing ability to research, store, retrieve, and analyse data on hundreds of thousands of individuals, made possible at relatively low cost by new forms of computerized database technology.
- The need to establish competitive advantage in marketing methods.

In the UK, ACORN and other geodemographic analysis systems available since the 1980s have revolutionized the ability of producers to obtain and exploit a detailed knowledge of customer segments. As this chapter explains, this new technology opens routes to more cost-effective generation of enquiries. It combines with better design of materials sent to convert enquiries into bookings, which appears especially well-suited to the requirements of producers in travel and tourism.

The essence of a marketing approach to achieving sales by direct response is expressed succinctly by Gater; he uses the term 'database marketing', which he defines as 'the building of a continuous relationship between principal and customer. That means not always selling when a communication is made and not always demanding a response . . . It means . . . obtaining loyalty through customer service and care, by building a relationship centred around the customer rather than the product' (Gater: 1986, p. 41).

What distinguishes the marketing approach from traditional direct selling is a planned system for developing a detailed knowledge of customers, and of the effectiveness of the response packages used to convert awareness into sales. Direct response marketing is a highly cost-effective tool for market research, segmentation, and market innovation and measurement, as well as a means of making sales. The new direct-response methods offer possibilities for improving marketing efficiency that were only just being realized at the end of the 1980s. In Britain expenditure on this form of marketing is growing faster than on the other ways of communicating with customers.

Key definitions

Four important, frequently used terms are defined below, and recommended to readers to avoid communication problems based solely on semantics. In a developing topic such as this readers will certainly encounter other usage of the terms and will have to make their own interpretations of what is meant. The following explanations should be useful:

Personal selling (group sales)	Achieving group or bulk sales through direct negotiation normally face to face with group buyers. Telephone selling to the general public, or tele-marketing as it is known in the USA, is *not* included in this definition. Door to door sales (not common in travel and tourism) are also excluded from this definition of personal selling focused on group buyers.
Direct selling	Selling to the general public using direct communication between producer and customers. Direct mail, and telephone selling are included in this definition. Direct selling is characteristic of sales-orientated businesses.
Direct-response marketing	*Direct-response marketing links producers with their customers in a two-way communication, using individually addressable media (such as mail and telephone). Interaction is organized through a computer database recording unique details of actual and prospective customers, including their geodemographic profile, product purchasing behaviour, and their responses to different communications media.*

The development and use of customer databases also facilitates the selection and specification of mass-communication media such as television, radio and press (individual responses to which may be recorded through enquiries and bookings). But the primary objective of direct-response marketing is to achieve more cost-effective use of marketing budgets based on a deep and evolving knowledge of customers, and their behaviour, and direct communication with them. It is this objective which distinguishes direct-response marketing from traditional forms of direct selling.

Subject to legal and other regulations designed to protect individuals' right to privacy, marketing in the 1990s is expected to take advantage of the development of more powerful, low-cost computerized databases. These databases facilitate marketing research and marketing innovation as well as being an integral part of measuring marketing results. The potential linkages between different individual organizations' customer databases and with other national and international databases, e.g. CRSs (see Chapter 18) suggests a technological breakthrough in achieving more cost effective marketing in the next decade. As Fletcher *et al.*, put it, database marketing 'is a customer orientated approach... and its special power lies in the techniques it uses to harness the capabilities of computer and telecommunications technology' (1990, p. 7).

Response-fulfilment package — Marketing jargon for the promotional package of envelope, letters, leaflets, brochures, gifts and other printed materials, such as prize draw announcements, which are distributed in response to enquiries generated by direct-response marketing methods.

The marketing triangle for producers: distributors: and customers

Figure 19.1 is used to represent the main transactions and flows of information in marketing that take place between producers (or 'principals', as they are often termed), distributors, and customers. The diagram is valid for the marketing implementation of all types of travel and tourism companies, whether in accommodation, transport, attractions, or tour operation.

The shape of the triangle reveals the two basic options:

- Two-way direct response between producer and prospective customer.
- Indirect response, with distribution channels as third parties.

Within the triangle, there are three types of transaction:

1 On the right-hand outer leg of the triangle, outwards from producers, is the whole of the communications mix targeted at existing and prospective customers. It includes media advertising, PR, sales promotions, personal selling (if relevant) as well as any direct mail and telephone marketing.

If customers deal direct with producers, their bookings and money transactions flow inwards on the right-hand inner leg of the

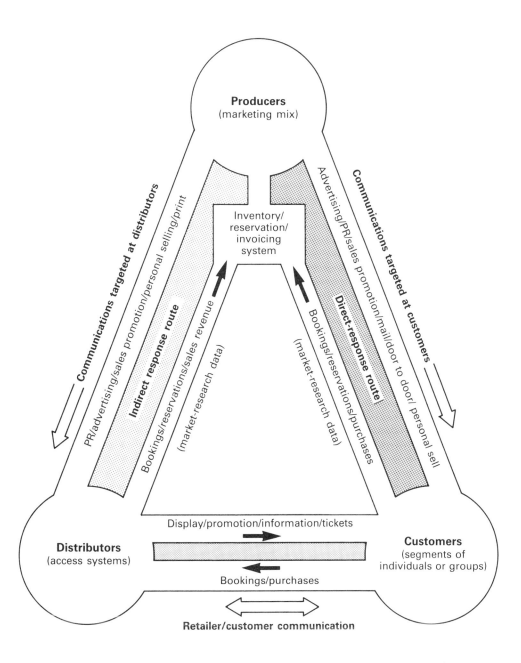

Figure 19.1 *The producer, distributor, customer triangle for travel and tourism products*

triangle to be serviced by an inventory management system, and tickets/confirmations flow back on the same route.

2 On the left-hand outer leg of the triangle, outwards from producers, is the communications mix targeted at the distribution system (all the pipelines as identified in Chapter 18).

   If customers purchase through distributors, bookings and money transactions flow inwards on the left-hand inner leg to an inventory management system, and tickets/confirmations flow outwards on the same leg.

3 The base leg of the triangle represents the two way flow of transactions between customers and distribution channels. Distributors deal directly with customers in providing access to products, information and promotional materials; they take money and supply tickets and other services. On the base leg customers do not have any direct access to producers in the purchasing process.

Because of the nature of travel and tourism operations, it will be appreciated that all inward flows of bookings and revenue are usually managed within an inventory or reservation system. Such systems are increasingly computerized for all medium-sized and large organizations, and are generally set up to handle the provision of options if the customer's first choice is not available, as well as confirmations, ticketing, and invoicing.

The inward flows in the right-hand leg of the triangle convey information about customers, which may also be incorporated into a database for recording and processing vital data for market-research purposes, such as address and purchasing behaviour (party size, date of booking, repeat bookings and so on). Depending on the recording system operated, the database may be used to identify responses from different forms of promotional techniques, such as bookings from advertising in different media. Such data are by-products of modern

reservation systems and, as pointed out in a previous chapter, they cost very little to collect once the inventory/database system has been set up to record and analyze the flows of routine information. It should be noted that database development is *not* possible through retail distribution systems, because customer profile details are not revealed to producers.

In Figure 19.1 *customers* may be one or more segments of the general public, or targeted individual buyers such as corporate clients who purchase on behalf of groups or numbers of individuals. The *distributors* are travel retailers or other pipelines, which offer display space for products and pass title on behalf of principals. The diagram is still relevant as an explanation if the distributor performs only part of the function, such as a tourist information centre acting as a display and distribution point for an attraction's leaflets, but not selling tickets (see Chapter 18).

To market direct or via a distribution system?

The triangular concept of flows makes it easier to understand the importance of the strategic question noted earlier in the chapter – whether, and to what extent, producers should distribute and promote their products direct to the customer, or aim to achieve sales through third-party channels of distribution. With few exceptions, there is rarely a simple answer to this question, and the answer may vary for different products within the same principal's portfolio at different times. Thus it may be advantageous for a hotelier to market most of his domestic business travel on a direct-response basis to corporate clients, but to market the bulk of his international business travel and weekend packages through retail travel agents.

At any point in time, according to the ever-shifting circumstances imposed by external and internal constraints, a principal has to take a judgement on the marginal revenue and the marginal costs implied by the balance between direct-response sales and indirect sales through distribution channels. The decision is mainly a financial one, reflecting the fact that any use of retailers will normally cost a minimum of 10 per cent of the sales revenue generated, usually deducted at source. Commission may be as high as 15 per cent and there are additional costs of servicing retailers with brochures, promoting to them, and possibly employing a sales force to maintain product awareness and levels of display. On the other hand, commission is a variable cost, which is not paid until sales are made, and the principal's cash flow is not affected ahead of the sale.

By contrast, many producers may be able to achieve the bulk of advance sales at a much lower average cost per unit sold than 10 per cent by using direct-response methods. But to do this, the operator has to invest large sums ahead of bookings in direct-response techniques (see Figure 19.2). Cash flow is obviously affected and there is no guarantee that the investment will succeed. If the initial investment does not produce all the required sales, further investment will be needed and, as the date of production approaches, direct-response costs rise steeply; the techniques are not cost-efficient in generating vital last-minute sales.

Although the direct/indirect choice is mainly one of cost and revenue equations, there are other implications, such as being seen to be supportive of retail travel agents or not. Where retail distribution chains command significant shares of product sales, it may not be possible for a principal to exercise his direct-response options without risking the goodwill of distributors he may need for other parts of his business. Many caravan-park operators, for example, would be glad to use travel agents to sell their spare capacity in April, May, and October, while marketing the easier and more profitable peak-season weeks direct. But this is not a practical option, as the majority of retailers would understandably refuse to handle the off-peak weeks unless they had a main season

allocation, which is easier to sell and generates more revenue and commission through higher prices.

For small businesses, there may be no alternative to direct-response marketing, because the amount of revenue they can generate is too small to interest retailers and too costly to handle. Very few small businesses operate their own computerized inventories, their telephone response systems are often too slow and inefficient and their brochures would take up too much valuable display space. Smaller firms that group together to form co-operatives with a single joint brochure and one reservation system and telephone number are a different proposition. Achieving exposure in retail-distribution systems through collective representation is, in practice, one of the main reasons why small businesses join co-operative marketing groups, and it helps to explain the expansion of such groups in recent years.

Direct response marketing methods

Figure 19.2 shows the range of direct-response marketing methods available to producers aiming at target segments of prospective customers. The techniques were introduced as elements in the marketing campaign planning process covered in Chapter 14 and need only brief additional comments here. Any direct-response marketing campaign is likely to use a combination of these methods rather than any individual one.

In terms of direct mail, the use that many hoteliers and airlines make, for example, of American Express or Access member lists illustrates the value of third-party address lists. Such lists can be accessed at a standard cost per thousand names and, although the names are not released to producers, their leaflets are distributed with routine mailings to members. An example of a joint mailing with a partner would be a country hotel group joining with, say, a manufacturer of conservatories, so that

Direct mail	● to previous customers
	● to purchased lists of targeted prospects
	● via lists owned by third parties
	● in response to enquiries/returned coupons from advertising
	● via joint mailing with relevant partners
	● to targeted households with characteristics matching those of known purchasers
Telephone/tele-marketing	● to targeted-customer lists
	● in response to enquiries
Door-to-door distribution	● to homes in targeted blocks of residential streets/roads
Travel related exhibitions	● to enquirers at stands, e.g. boat shows, travel exhibitions, and caravan and camping shows
Media advertising	● with coupons
	● with response telephone numbers, or 0800 lines
Interactive TV	● Viewdata TV terminals in customers' homes, used to make bookings direct

Figure 19.2   *Direct-response marketing methods to reach individual consumers*

two non-competing leaflets, appealing to the same group of prospective customers, could share the cost of postage.

Telephone marketing is known as tele-marketing in the USA. As indicated in Figure 19.2, it may be reactive to enquiries, or proactive to target customers. Its use for selling to the general public has undergone important development in the last 5 years, associated with computerized databases, and it may play a larger role in travel and tourism markets in the future.

Door to door distribution costs of printed materials are much cheaper per household than postal costs, but the value of such distribution depends on the ability to target appropriate neighbourhoods, e.g. using the ACORN analysis.

Media advertising covers the whole spectrum of choice noted in Chapter 15. Interactive TV for use by the general public in their own homes is already well developed in France, but it is difficult to predict the rate of growth in ownership of adapted TV sets and their use in travel marketing. The technology exists and the possibilities are clear. Producers will watch developments with interest, and the larger ones are already experimenting to see if the use of interactive TV can gain a profitable share of direct-response business. On a small scale in the early 1990s some interactive terminals are already in use in tourist information centres to display information, such as available capacity in a range of hotels. Some of these are already capable of two-way communication between customer and principal.

The potential benefits of direct-response marketing

Given the high cost of commissions and servicing in achieving access to customers through third party distribution channels, the scope for utilizing modern direct-response marketing techniques should be most carefully considered by all producers in travel and tourism.

The benefits discussed below are *potential* in the sense that they cannot be achieved without considerable effort in marketing planning. Use of a database for accurate segmentation and geographical targeting, followed by detailed attention to product presentation in advertising and to print, are all required in implementing effective direct-response campaigns. Detailed prior programming of the database to receive, monitor and analyse customer response, is essential to achieve the benefits. But if the systematic marketing procedures set out in this book are followed, the following benefits are achievable by any small business willing to invest in a personal computer:

● Detailed knowledge of the customer, not only name and address, but neighbourhood type (ACORN), and purchasing behaviour. Both telephone and coupon response mechanisms provide limited but valuable opportunities for market research questions, such as identifying new or previous customers, frequent users, and how they heard of the product.
● Ability to assess the cost and effectiveness of generating enquiries, including response by type of media, type of advertisement, type of leaflet, or timing of advertisements. Such responses can be analysed by market segments, market areas, and product variations offered. Cost per enquiry can be monitored with precision and the cost per booking can be quantified if the database is programmed to match bookings with enquiries.
● Ability to measure the effectiveness of alternative response packages sent out to enquirers, in terms of converting enquiries into sales.
● A framework for marketing innovations, whereby relatively small-scale test marketing with new or adapted products, new segments, alternative forms of media, or response packages, can be systematically evaluated at low cost.

These four groups of marketing benefits, stemming from the two-way communication process, are profound in their implications for more cost-effective marketing. They are especially useful to businesses in travel and tourism that are too small to engage in large-scale advertising, and too small to achieve cost-effective access through retail-distribution channels. Once again it is worth stressing that these benefits derive from the use of new information technology not previously available to marketing managers. The new technology appears very likely to shift the balance of advantage in marketing towards those smaller businesses willing to make the modest effort of time and cost required. Many are already using the new technology; others will be forced to follow in response to growing competition.

The cost of harnessing the potential power of computers for small businesses has dropped significantly over recent years. Gater notes, 'While a computer cost the equivalent of 20 people in 1970, by 1990 one person will cost the same as 20 computers of the same size (Gater: 1986, p. 41). While that view may be exaggerated, not to purchase the marketing capabilities of a personal computer at, say, one-fifth of the annual salary of a competent secretary, must be short-sighted in the 1990s.

The flexibility conferred by the range of direct-response marketing mechanisms is also important. Distribution networks require careful planning and organization, and continuous motivation and servicing with supplies of print (Chapter 18). By contrast, the use of direct-response techniques can be set up or changed in a matter of days as the need arises, although the time taken to generate responses and convert them into bookings will normally be measured in weeks rather than days.

And a big disadvantage

The biggest disadvantage of direct response marketing appears to lie in its limited capacity to secure last-minute bookings. For tour operators in particular, a national distribution system of retailers provides the best available mechanism for notifying and promoting their unsold capacity in the vital 4 weeks before the departure dates in their programmes. In that period all sales are likely to be marginal and their effect on profitability high. Using on-line links with an operator's inventory, agents can provide a top-up bookings service with a speed and flexibility, which direct response marketing cannot match.

By contrast, in generating advance bookings in the period before the last 4 weeks before delivery, direct-response marketing can achieve sales at a cost retailers cannot match. In addition, direct response also creates a detailed knowledge of customers, which retailers do not provide for operators. Achieving the best balance between the two advantages is discussed in the next section.

Balancing direct and indirect-response marketing in travel and tourism

Traditionally, as this author noted in 1980 in the first systematic analysis of direct response marketing in British travel and tourism, most principals before the 1960s developed their businesses through direct communication with their clients. Direct selling, as it was usually known, was the industry norm for all but a few principals, such as scheduled shipping lines (Middleton: 1980). The rapid expansion in the numbers of retail travel agents, mainly to service airline passengers, inclusive tour customers, and business travellers in the 1960s and 1970s, created a national network of some 7,000 outlets by the early 1990s in the UK. Similar trends in the USA, biased more towards domestic business travel and the USA internal airline and car-rental markets, produced over 33,000 retail outlets. As a result, retail travel outlets are conveniently situated to provide easy access for the bulk of the urban populations in both countries. Parallel developments have produced similar situations in most European countries, too, although travel-agency usage is typically lower in most continental European countries than in the UK or USA.

If they were large enough to secure display space for their brochures and able to give retailers efficient access to their reservation systems, it was entirely logical that tour operators should adapt and use these large distribution networks to sell inclusive tours to destinations abroad. In Britain traditional direct-response organizations, such as Butlins, HavenWarner and Hoseasons Holidays, made great efforts in the 1980s to adapt their marketing to travel retailers and achieve a greater proportion of their sales indirectly. Other domestic producers have followed this lead, notably hotel groups seeking maximum distribution for their weekend breaks and, in particular, to achieve vital marginal revenue.

In the 1980s, in a process of acquisition and new development colourfully known as the 'march of the multiples', six large multi-site retail chains emerged in the UK, with over a third of the total retail distribution market between them, and able to dominate the trends in travel retailing. With the support of principals investing in computer-reservation systems, they were able to achieve economies of scale and much greater operational efficiency through the rapid introduction of newly available computer technology. Their largely automated offices are now able to handle very large volumes of bookings, cancellations, surcharges and invoicing, and their computer networks have direct 'on-line' access to the larger principals' systems, which reduces the costly time spent in satisfying their customers' requirements (see Chapter 18). As a result, in the UK, the balance of advantage in producing the most cost-effective sales was seen to shift in favour of the indirect or retail outlet system of travel distribution. Many medium and smaller principals in the industry tried to secure a share of the limited display space and selling effort available through the powerful new outlets. For their part, the sophisticated new multiples were anxious to rationalize the product lines they offered and maximize revenue generated per metre of display space, techniques practised for many years in the retailing of groceries in supermarket chains.

Some tour operators in the UK, such as Tjaereborg, Portland, Martin Rooks, and the older established operators such as SAGA, retained their singleminded focus on direct-response marketing. Newer operators, such as Center Parcs, with attractive products in high demand, found that direct-response marketing was more efficient and cost-effective. Interestingly, the developments in information technology that enabled retailers to achieve greater operational efficiency in the 1980s are now assisting direct-response marketers to improve the efficiency of their own marketing efforts. In the early 1990s it is still impossible to be certain whether the future of travel and tourism sales lies more with direct, or indirect-response mechanisms. In the end it seems likely to lie in a combination of the two, with the balance of advantage constantly shifting in a competitive struggle to achieve marginal sales at least cost.

Where, as for hotels and scheduled airlines, most principals have a large proportion of frequent repeat customers such as regular business travellers, the balance of advantage must lie with direct-response marketing. It is no accident that hotel groups and airlines have been competing strenuously since the 1980s to bind their 'loyal' customers to them with a wide variety of membership or club schemes, frequent traveller awards, and special arrangements for their key accounts. Holiday Inns, for example, claimed that over a million members joined their 'Priority Club' within months of it being introduced in the USA in 1983. The operation of the Club, only possible on the basis of Holiday Inns' fully automated international reservation system, has since changed its basis of operation

but it is an interesting early example of modern direct-response marketing (TTRA: 1986, p. 52).

In the mid-1990s it appears probable to this author that for most travel and tourism businesses, especially for smaller and medium-sized operators, direct-response marketing will often yield better sales results per thousand pounds spent than the alternative indirect-response routes. For most operators, the payment of commission on retail sales produces a minimum marketing/sales revenue ratio of 10 per cent. Allowing for all the associated costs of promotion and additional incentives to third parties, the marketing costs rise to between 12 and 15 per cent. Of course, if allocations are made to tour operators by hoteliers and other principals, the cost of achieving sales by that method may be closer to 30 per cent (see Chapter 23). Each operator has to decide the balance of advantage for its own product portfolio at any particular time, but the direct route provides advantages of customer knowledge and communication, that cannot be matched by the indirect route.

Chapter summary

This chapter deals with a fundamental strategic choice concerning the method of distributing and selling products, which has to be made by all sizes and types of business. It is a choice that vitally affects the cost-effectiveness of travel and tourism marketing, and it is a matter for surprise that it is so inadequately covered in the books and journals dealing with the industry. This author advocates the evaluation and use of direct-response marketing techniques wherever possible, because they are especially suited to the common travel marketing tasks of generating enquiries, converting them into bookings, and securing repeat business. They are vital too for the majority of businesses that are too small to use retail-distribution channels, and the many others, that market themselves partly direct and partly indirectly. Direct-response marketing techniques are also easily test marketed at low cost, which adds to their attraction. In all countries, the number of organizations that sell *only* through retail-distribution channels is very small indeed and, although powerful in the industry, they appear to be a special case and provide no guidance for the majority.

The balance to be struck between direct and indirect marketing is based, first and foremost, on the financial argument of unit costs required to achieve unit sales. It is, second, a matter of adjusting to the opportunities and threats associated with rapidly changing information technology, which alter the relative costs of achieving distribution. There are certain to be shifts in the current ratios of direct/indirect sales over the next decade in all sectors of travel and tourism. Third, the balance is an issue of travel trade politics reflecting the relative power of principals and retailers within the distribution channels. Because travel retailers do not take risks by purchasing the products they sell, it appears unlikely that they will dominate travel producers in the way that supermarkets have been able to do with the manufacturers of many fast-moving consumer goods. Even so, con-

certed action by retailers against a producer of inclusive tours would be very effective, and few in the British travel trade have forgotten the months of outcry and threats that accompanied Thomson Holidays' decision to establish Portland as a direct-marketing organization in 1980. Thomson, as market leaders in the sale of inclusive tours, proved they had the power to overcome the retailers' reaction on that occasion. But that was before the recent rapid growth of the large multi-site retailers, and other tour operators do not have the same amount of market influence.

Finally, this chapter stresses the point that the choice of direct and indirect-marketing methods has great implications for the knowledge producers have of their customers. In this aspect the advantage of direct-response methods is very clear.

Further reading

Kotler, P., *Marketing: Analysis, Planning, Implementation and Control*, 7th edit., Prentice-Hall International, 1991, Chapter 23.

Part Five

Applying Marketing in the Travel and Tourism Industry

20

Marketing countries as tourism destinations

This chapter is about the marketing role of national tourism organizations, boards or offices, commonly known as NTOs. Readers will also encounter the acronym NTA (national tourism administration) used to describe the same type of organization.

NTOs are responsible for marketing countries as tourist destinations. Concern with them shifts the focus of the book away from the marketing practice of individual companies and other organizations concerned with their own products, to what are commonly public sector or government-funded organizations. The majority of NTOs are not producers or operators, they generally do not sell products directly to visitors, they are not directly responsible for the quality of services delivered, and they mostly represent only a small proportion, however important it may be, of all the travel and tourism marketing programmes carried out on behalf of their country. The principles and practice of an NTO's approach to marketing are essentially the same as those adopted by regional, state, or local tourism offices, although the scale of operations is obviously different.

Traditionally, the principal marketing role of NTOs has been seen in fairly narrow promotional terms of creating and communicating appealing destination images and messages to prospective visitors, mainly through advertising, PR and print, as a necessary basis for the product-specific marketing activities of operators. The traditional image-creation role is, however, beginning to look less credible in the remaining years of the twentieth century, especially for developed tourism destinations, such as Britain, the USA, and Spain. The objectives of NTOs are increasingly focusing on specific segments and products and on the indirect or *facilitating* roles of marketing outlined in this chapter.

The chapter begins with a definition of NTOs and their marketing operations internationally. The factors influencing NTO marketing are summarized and the nature of marketing strategy is discussed, distinguishing between what NTOs can achieve by spending their budgets mainly on promotion, and what they can achieve through various forms of facilitation. Facilitation means assisting the component sectors of the travel and tourism industry in their own country and in other countries from which visitors are drawn. Because the marketing process for NTOs is different from that for providers of accommodation, transport or attractions, the process is outlined in some detail, using two figures. The meaning of *'facilitation'* is explained.

NTOs defined: some international dimensions of destination marketing

A tourist organization, as Medlik and Burkart explain it, 'is defined by reference to the interests of a geographical area as a tourist destination, which may be a country, region, or an individual town' (1981, p. 255). Within this context, 'the term NTO is used to designate the organization entrusted by the state with responsibility for tourism matters at the national level. It may be a fully fledged ministry or a directorate general or a department or corporation or board' (a definition adopted by McIntosh: 1972, p. 86).

There are many different forms of organization an NTO may take, although the principle of government support through official recognition and funding is normal even in cases where the NTO is not part of the state administration. The scope of an NTO's marketing function is usually two-fold:

> In the first place the tourist organization can formulate and develop the tourist product or products of the destination; secondly it can promote them in appropriate markets. It can base its approach to development and promotion on market research and thus achieve a close match between the products and the markets. In doing this the tourist organization is acting on behalf of all interests in tourism and on behalf of the whole destination and is complementary to the development and promotion activities of individual providers of tourist services (Burkart and Medlik: 1981, p. 256).

In Britain, established by the Development of Tourism Act of 1969, there are four statutory bodies, each of which meets the definition of NTOs. They are the British Tourist Authority (BTA), the English Tourist Board (ETB), the Scottish Tourist Board (STB), and the Wales Tourist Board (WTB). Although its statutory powers are much wider, BTA has limited its role in practice to responsibility for marketing Britain overseas. The tourist boards for England, Scotland and Wales are each responsible for the development and promotion of tourism in their areas and STB and WTB have some powers to market themselves overseas. There are separate boards under different legislation for Northern Ireland, the Channel Islands and the Isle of Man. In the USA, at federal level, the NTO is the United States Travel and Tourism Administration (USTTA), which is responsible mainly for the promotion of tourism into the USA. Most of the US state governments have formed their own tourist offices, mainly for the promotion of US domestic tourism into their areas. All these national and state NTOs act as policy advisers to their respective governments. All have established formal and informal links for consultation and joint action with the tourism industry in their countries or regions, as appropriate.

Around the world there are some 175 NTOs of different sizes and organizational patterns. Nearly all of them are engaged in one or more aspects of destination promotion, although relatively few are practising the systematic approach to marketing developed in this book. Most of the promotional effort organized by these NTOs is aimed at international markets, but in recent years many have also been spending considerable sums on the promotion of domestic tourism, by residents within their own countries. On the international side, a report by the Economist Intelligence Unit (EIU: 1983), commenting that 'there exist no definitive statistics covering this topic', estimated that NTOs supported some 500 to 700 branch offices around the world in 1983. Larger networks, such as those supported by Britain, France or Greece, comprise over 30 offices in the main countries from which they draw their visitors, but most developing countries maintain only a few offices in key markets.

The best, although still limited source of data about the activities of NTOs, is the World Tourism Organization (WTO) based in Madrid.

WTO is an inter-governmental organization to which most but not all countries belong. From time to time WTO undertakes surveys of the activities of NTOs via self-completion questionnaires. Unfortunately, the quality of the responses and the sheer difficulty of establishing the exact size of marketing expenditure means that the results are of limited value. For example, should 'marketing' include costs of staff and premises as well as promotional budgets? Should it include research and product investment? Should it be presented as gross expenditure, or net after allowance for sales of advertising space in brochures and contributions to campaigns by commercial sector partners? Is it possible to separate marketing for inter-national tourism from domestic tourism? When these questions have been answered, it is then necessary for international comparisons to convert data into US dollars, using rates of exchange that may have altered radically by the time the results are used.

Notwithstanding these important caveats, at least it is possible for broad indicative purposes to compare declared marketing expenditure, e.g. from annual reports of NTOs, with declared receipts from international tourism as reported to WTO and OECD. Such an exercise was undertaken for a selected group of countries using 1990-1 data, and the results are shown in Table 20.1 (Lavery:1992).

From Table 20.1 it is possible to conclude that marketing expenditure as a percentage of gross receipts from international tourism to a country (excluding air and other fare payments) seems to lie in a range of 0.5 per cent and 3 per cent for most NTOs. This evidence supports earlier WTO surveys noted in the first edition of this book. Assuming an average of say just 1 per cent of the $2,500 billion estimated by WTO to have been spent on international tourism in 1990, the annual global expenditure on destination marketing is of the order of $2.5 billion in the early 1990s. This is no more than an order of magnitude, but it illustrates the scale and importance of modern destination

Table 20.1 *The indicative size of NTO marketing expenditure for international tourism, 1990–1*

Country	(a) International receipts from tourism (millions US$)	(b) Marketing budget allocated (millions (US$)	(c) (b) as % of (a)	
Australia	3,797	52.58	1.4	(1990)
Canada	6,375	21.82	0.3	(1991)
UK	15,000	55.73	0.4	(1991)
Hong Kong	5,032	14.41	2.9	(1990)
Singapore	4,362	31.84	0.7	(1991)

Source: Lavery, P., in *Travel & Tourism Analyst No. 4, 1992,* Economist Intelligence Unit

Notes: 1 International receipts are WTO published data for 1990 converted into US dollars.
2 Marketing budgets are for 1990 or 1991 as shown, extracted from annual reports of NTOs and converted into US dollars.
Caveat: Published figures are not necessarily accurate and accounting conventions used in annual reports do not always make it easy to estimate marketing expenditure. These data are therefore crude approximations for illustrative purposes only.

marketing. Expenditure aimed at domestic tourists is additional to this figure, but it is quite impossible to estimate it at the present time.

Another useful indicator of the importance of NTO marketing is the evidence, also from WTO data, that expenditure on marketing accounts for between one-half and two-thirds of the total budgets of NTOs. If full allowance is made for the overhead costs of marketing, including staff and premises, the proportion would be much higher.

It appears reasonable to conclude for all practical purposes, therefore, although the figures provide no guidance as to what *should* be spent, that an annual expenditure on marketing international tourism, of between 0.5 and 3 per cent of visitor expenditure, covers the range represented by current budgets of most NTOs around the world. The larger proportions will have to be spent by governments in developing destinations that do not have a well-established tourism industry to participate in the cost of reaching and persuading international travellers to visit their destination.

NTO marketing has influence, but limited control

The introduction to this chapter drew attention to some of the reasons why marketing for NTOs differs from marketing as practised by commercial operators. It needs to be stressed that much of the travel between developed countries is for business and other non-leisure purposes, which are not significantly influenced by the promotional expenditure of NTOs. In addition, because the average party size is generally more than two persons, it would be more realistic to relate marketing expenditure to parties rather than to individual arrivals. Third, especially for developed destinations, it is obvious that a proportion of leisure visits would continue to be made without NTO expenditure, influenced, for example, by previous visits, recommendations of friends, and of course the marketing efforts of the tourism industry as a whole.

There are serious limitations, therefore, in using the average percentages noted in the previous section. Although such important practical limitations are seldom addressed in annual reports, most NTO budgets implicitly recognize them through the process of market segmentation – in other words, dividing up marketing budgets according to specific segments at which promotions are aimed. If NTOs published information relating marketing expenditure to the receipts attributable to target segments, the NTO marketing percentage would probably reveal figures not of 1 or 3 per cent for marketing, but 20 or even 30 per cent of some targeted customer spending. The statistics of tourism demand are very seldom adequate to identify tourism expenditure by segments. Tourism data published by WTO, for example, do not even separate business from leisure spending.

In common with many other sectors of the expanding tourism industry, the development of professionalism in marketing is relatively recent in NTOs, but it appears certain to become more important over the next decade, as markets mature and competition between countries for shares of markets increases. On the broad evidence of the data above, notwithstanding the lack of precision in the available statistics, it is reasonable to expect that the application of systematic marketing techniques by NTOs could make a major contribution to cost-effectiveness measured in dollars spent per tourist arrival.

Ideally, all governments would like their NTOs to prove that for every 1,000 pounds or dollars spent on marketing in their targeted markets of visitor origin, there is a response that can be measured in the number of visits and expenditure achieved over a given period of time. If such proof were possible, governments would be able accurately to allocate larger or smaller budgets to travel and tourism, according to their policies for growth, maintenance, or other priorities discussed later. For all countries, however, apart from the size of their marketing budgets and the quality of the marketing activities in which NTOs engage, there are three main underlying factors continuously at work in determining the actual volume and expenditure of tourism generated between markets of origin and countries of destination. These factors distort the measurement of expenditure and response, as discussed below:

- Expenditure on marketing is only one of the influences which determine tourism volumes and expenditure to any country.
- The marketing effort of NTOs is only a part of the total tourism marketing effort made on behalf of a country.
- Very few NTOs sell products to prospective visitors direct. Even where they take responsibility for operating, say, hotels or transport, these activities are typically only a part of the total product supply.

Marketing is only one of the influences

Chapters 4 and 5 set out the economic, social, and behavioural factors at work in societies, which collectively determine the volume and types of travel and tourism generated by any particular country. These so-called 'determinants and motivations' of tourism include disposable income per capita, amount of leisure time available, personal mobility, availability of transport systems, the price of travel, and exchange rates. The importance of understanding the external business environment as the basis for marketing strategy has been stressed throughout this book and needs no further emphasis here.

NTO marketing must respond to, but cannot influence the external factors direct. For example, Britain derives about a quarter of its international tourism revenue from American travellers, who are its most important market. But neither the British Government nor the BTA can influence in any way the level of US incomes, the international value of the dollar, or the US overseas deficit on trade, which in the early 1990s was a major influence on that country's economy. Effective NTO marketing begins with an understanding of the determinants influencing its main markets; it aims to work with the opportunities created by favourable events, while limiting the impact of unfavourable ones. For example, if an NTO in the Pacific region had its marketing budget increased by 400 per cent in a year in which, say, the level of air fares with its main markets doubled, the number of tourist arrivals would fall. By contrast, a cut-back in a marketing budget in a year of favourable changes in external factors could be associated with a very large increase in the volume of travel. This point in no way denies the value of destination marketing, but does set it in the context of national and international events over which NTOs have no control.

NTO marketing is only part of the total effort

Heneghan, in attempting to trace the effectiveness of marketing for the Irish Tourist Board (Bord Failte) in the mid-1970s, calculated that the marketing expenditure by the Board amounted to about 15 per cent of all tourism marketing expenditure for the Republic of Ireland in the USA (Heneghan: 1976). It is difficult to calculate such figures, because records do not exist, but the proportion looks realistic having regard to what is spent by airlines, tour operators, accommodation interests and others based in Ireland, and the travel trade in the USA. For developing destinations, the proportion NTOs represent of all expenditure on marketing is likely to be higher, but rarely as much as a half. If the bulk of all tourism marketing expenditure is not controlled by an NTO but by independent third parties, it is impossible for an NTO to claim all the credit, or be blamed for failure in the fluctuations in visitor arrivals occurring over any given period of time.

Limited influence over the supply of products

In developed tourist destination countries, such as the USA or Britain, there are tens of thousands of commercial firms, and many public-sector organizations engaged in providing tourism products and services. Of these, only a small minority have any formal relation with an NTO through membership of state, regional, or area tourist boards. Thus a large number of businesses generate a very wide range of tourism products, most of which are beyond the marketing influence of an NTO with regard to volume, design, price, and promotion decisions.

One may conclude that the marketing effort of an NTO, especially in developed destination countries, will always be *partial* or even marginal in terms of the range of products it influences; *submerged* to a large extent in the greater impact of the determinants and motivations affecting markets of origin, and *outweighed* by the marketing effort of commercial interests in tourism. NTOs of developing tourist destination countries have a far greater potential influence over their countries' tourism. They are potentially better able to evaluate the success of their marketing efforts. In practice, however, they often lack the professional management skills to exploit their advantages.

These conclusions are not intended to imply that NTO marketing expenditure is necessarily ineffective or wasted. They do mean that most NTOs are not in direct control of the products they promote or the results that are achieved, as measured in annual visitor numbers and expenditure. It is therefore helpful to explain the role of NTO marketing from a perspective of *influence* rather than control, a very different perspective from that used to explain commercial practice. The influencing role is of course a two-way process. In some developed countries, such as the USA and Australia, industry associations have been formed to provide a forum within which NTOs and the travel and tourism industry collaborate. There are equivalent associations in some European countries, but not in the UK (at end 1993). The Washington-based Travel Industry Association of America (TIA), for example, draws together state and larger commercial sector bodies in travel and tourism, and supports the 'Discover America National Domestic Travel Marketing Programme' to co-ordinate marketing for US domestic tourism. The Australian Tourism Industry Association (ATIA) performs an equivalent role in that country, especially for inbound tourism. Neither of these associations are confined to marketing but they do provide a valuable forum for marketing issues and co-ordination with their NTOs.

Destination promotion role for NTOs or marketing facilitation?

From the previous discussion it can be concluded that there are two levels in marketing for any destination. The first level, concerned with the destination as a whole and tourism products, is the focus of what NTOs do. The second level covers the marketing activity of the mainly commercial operators promoting their individual products. Within the first level of marketing NTOs have to choose between two alternative strategies. One of these is reaching prospective visitors through expenditure on a promotional mix intended to promote destination awareness and influence prospective customers' attitudes; the other is concerned with exercising influence over the tourism industry.

A promotional strategy

The *promotional strategy* means implementing promotional programmes to project destination images and key messages to targeted segments of potential visitors, to encourage them to send for product brochures, or call into travel agents in their area. Using a metaphor that has been widely quoted, Burkart and Medlik summarize this strategic choice as creating an 'umbrella campaign', under which, at the second level, the various individual providers of tourist services can market their own components of the overall tourism product.

The second level of marketing thus covers the full range of mainly commercial marketing initiatives, in which 'airlines and other transport operators, hotel groups, and tour operators can market their individual services to a market of potential buyers already aware of and predisposed to the destination. . .' (Burkart and Medlik: 1981, p. 197).

The decision to invest the greater part of their budgets in promoting destination awareness and images appears to be an obvious and convincing strategy, and it is chosen by most NTOs and regional tourist offices around the world. Following the logic of the strategy, the bulk of NTO marketing expenditure and its organizational structure should reflect promotional campaign priorities. In selecting this strategy, however, it has to be assumed that the budget an NTO has to spend is large enough to implement effectively the promotional campaigns its market segmentation studies identify as necessary. To be effective, such campaigns must be of sufficient weight and impact to create the necessary numbers of potential buyers who are aware of and predisposed to the destination. But if budgets are not adequate for the task, expenditure on an image-creating strategy may in practice be a waste of money on desirable objectives that cannot be achieved. Having regard to the size of the budgets discussed earlier for most NTOs operating internationally or in domestic tourism markets, one must question the effectiveness in practice of much of their promotional expenditure.

To illustrate the point about budget size in relation to the task, in the early 1990s the Wales Tourist Board had a total budget for advertising, promotions and print of around £2 million. Expenditure by UK domestic tourists in Wales was estimated at £725 million over 12 months. In terms of promotion therefore the budget represented only a fraction of 1 per cent of total holiday tourism revenue, a sum with which it was impossible to make a major impact on national images and attitudes. The budgets for England and Scotland were proportionally similar.

Facilitation strategy

Fortunately there is an alternative strategy, increasingly employed in Wales and in other destinations, which is relevant to all NTOs. This is the strategy of *marketing facilitation*, as it is termed in this chapter. This strategy creates marketing bridges between an NTO and the individual operators in the travel and tourism industry, and a bridge between the first and second levels of destination marketing discussed above. The case for marketing facilitation is based on three considerations, commonly found around the world:

● First, that a destination country has specific government-policy objectives for wishing to promote tourism, which may be expressed in economic, social, or environmental terms as well as in marketing goals.
● Second, that the destination country possesses a range of tourist areas, products, and segments, some growing and some declining, to which it attaches differing priorities, and which have different implications for achieving government policy objectives.
● Third that budgets granted to NTOs will, in almost every case, be less than adequate to undertake all the marketing tasks identified, so that selection of priorities is required.

If these three considerations apply, the most effective marketing role for an NTO lies in:

● Establishing promotional priorities for specific markets and segments.
● Co-ordinating the elements of tourism products.
● Liaising with and influencing the tourism industry.
● Providing support for new or growth products relevant to policy.
● Creating co-operative marketing campaigns accessible especially for the hundreds of small businesses, that would otherwise be unable to participate in marketing on a national or international scale.

These processes amount to a facilitation strategy, which normally requires extensive voluntary co-operation; has implications for marketing organization and personnel; and brings the NTO and its commercial sector together in joint operations that are quite different from traditional concepts of spending money on image campaigns. It brings into sharp focus the very difficult task, which all NTOs face, of allocating available budgets between competing marketing priorities.

The strategy an NTO adopts in practice should vary according to the stage of development a country's tourism has reached. Where destinations are largely unknown in the markets they seek to promote, where existing tourism flows are small, and where the tourism industry within the country is mainly weak and fragmented, the NTO will have no choice but to take the leading role in putting its destination on the international map and playing a major role in promoting its destination's products. Even in these circumstances the available budgets will normally not be adequate to engage *effectively* in image campaigns in several markets, and the marketing support of international operators such as airlines, hotel chains and tour operators will be essential for success. For better-known, well-established destinations such as Britain and the USA, where the tourism industry has forged many of its own international links, it should increasingly be possible for the NTO to focus more of its expenditure on the strategy of support and facilitation and less on buying media space for general image advertising.

Destination positioning themes, images, and concepts

Whatever the main thrust of strategy, be it promotion or facilitation, NTOs always have a vital function to perform for their destinations in choosing the singleminded communication propositions (messages and symbols) that serve to identify and position their countries in the minds of prospective visitors, and differentiate them from all others.

BTA's Heritage themes, Scotland's Rainbow and 'Scotland's for me', Wales' Dragon, 'I love New York', Birmingham's 'Big Heart of England', and Canada's 'The World Next Door',

all serve to brand and identify their destinations with unique labels. To be successful in practice, such labels must:

● Be based on genuine product attributes.
● Make sense and be understood readily by customers.
● Involve at least the leading players in the commercial sector.
● Be incorporated into the promotional efforts of a country's regions and resorts.
● Be sustained over several years if they are to overcome the communication barriers referred to in Chapter 16.
● Be systematically exploited in a range of sales-promotion and customer-servicing techniques designed to reach existing visitors at the destination as well as prospective visitors in countries of origin.

Developing successful images and implementing them effectively requires detailed consumer research and creative flair in relation to a destination's intrinsic visitor attractions. This is usually a role that only an NTO can fulfil, and only an NTO can take on the task of communicating the chosen positioning to the tourism industry. But it should not necessarily have to spend the bulk of its own scarce resources in promoting the image to the general public in markets of origin.

It will often be possible for NTOs to develop co-operative promotional efforts arising out of the facilitation strategy, and draw on the financial support of the travel and tourism industry in mounting any advertising and publicity campaigns judged necessary to support or enhance the destination image. Working within a strategy of facilitation, an NTO will often play a tactical role with its publicity campaigns, e.g. to correct the short-run effects of negative attitudes in markets of origin, arising from news stories about prices or personal security. These tactical efforts should not be confused with highly expensive attempts to use NTO budgets to create tourist motivations

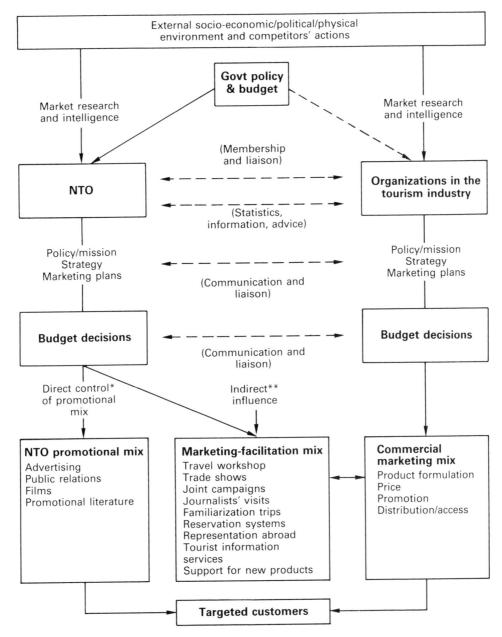

External socio-economic/political/physical environment and competitors' actions		

Govt policy & budget

Market research and intelligence

Market research and intelligence

NTO

Organizations in the tourism industry

(Membership and liaison)

(Statistics, information, advice)

Policy/mission
Strategy
Marketing plans

Policy/mission
Strategy
Marketing plans

(Communication and liaison)

Budget decisions

Budget decisions

(Communication and liaison)

Direct control*
of promotional
mix

Indirect**
influence

NTO promotional mix
Advertising
Public relations
Films
Promotional literature

Marketing-facilitation mix
Travel workshop
Trade shows
Joint campaigns
Journalists' visits
Familiarization trips
Reservation systems
Representation abroad
Tourist information
services
Support for new products

**Commercial
marketing mix**
Product formulation
Price
Promotion
Distribution/access

Targeted customers

* Expenditure mainly in the countries or areas of origin from which prospective visitors are drawn.
** Expenditure in countries or areas of origin and at the destination.

——— Line of direct responsibility.
– – – Line of liaison and communication.

Figure 20.1 *The destination marketing process for NTOs*

and attitudes through expenditure on image campaigns.

Figure 20.1 illustrates the marketing process for NTOs (on the left of the diagram), side by side with the same process for individual operators in the travel and tourism industry (on the right). The figure reveals both the similarities in marketing and the important differences that exist. Readers may wish to refer back to Figure 2.1, with which Figure 20.1 is fully compatible. The main difference occurs at the budget-decision stage, where NTOs have the choice of apportioning funds between the two routes shown as direct control of the promotional mix on the left and marketing facilitation in the middle of the diagram. Facilitation forms the important bridge between NTO and the component sectors of the industry, while the promotion strategy reflects the more traditional approach to destination marketing.

Important liaison and co-ordination links between NTO and individual operators are shown in the diagram at the policy level, at the budget decision level (industry financial participation in NTO schemes and vice versa), and between marketing facilitation and the individual marketing decisions of operators in the tourism industry. Each of the main stages in Figure 20.1 is discussed briefly below, followed by a more detailed explanation of the less familiar methods of marketing facilitation.

Researching the external business environment

As in all marketing, the process begins with researching the external environment. Only larger operators, such as airlines and hotel chains, will have the resources to undertake large-scale marketing research, especially into international markets. NTOs have a unique role to play in the travel and tourism industry in gathering and communicating market analysis and trend data, not only for their own marketing purposes but for the industry as a whole. Most NTOs publish research facts, but few appear to perform the task in a way which is easily accessible and understandable to the majority of operators in the travel and tourism industry in most countries. Provision of usable market information is an important basis for effective facilitation. Failure to communicate data effectively means that a potentially valuable method of influencing the decisions of suppliers is lost.

Government policy and tourism strategy

Where NTOs are financed by governments, there is usually a requirement that marketing objectives serve government policy. Most governments do not normally go into tourism marketing objectives in any detail, but lay down the broader strategic goals that NTOs are required to pursue. These goals, in principle, are much the same all over the world, requiring that tourism revenue should generate foreign exchange earnings and employment in accordance with national economic policy and environmental objectives.

Government policies relevant to tourism marketing strategy may be summarized as:

- To generate increased tourism revenue.
- To channel demand by season and by area of the country.
- To protect consumers' interests and enhance the quality of the product and the environment.

The first two of these policies tend to be common to most countries. The third, discussed later under facilitation, is less well understood.

The representation of commercial and other organizations on various committees and boards of NTOs is also a common feature of NTO operation. It is intended to create a productive dialogue between the main organizations in the travel and tourism industry, and the direction of government and NTO policy. Marketing strategy is an important aspect of this dialogue, and the liaison stages are noted in Figure 20.1.

Marketing planning

It follows from earlier comments about the limitations of an NTO's budget and its influence on markets that selecting priorities, and turning these into strategies and specific targets for products and segments, is a vitally important exercise. In practice marketing planning for an NTO has two separate functions to discharge. The first is in relation to any promotional campaigns it intends to carry out in its main markets of origin, and the second is in relation to guidelines, facilitation and marketing support for the industry as a whole.

For reasons explained in Chapters 11 and 13, effective planning for marketing strategy and tactics is impossible without an adequate information base. The marketing planning process for an NTO is no different in principle from any other application of standard techniques. Regrettably, the travel and tourism industry in most countries is still notorious for the paucity of its research information base compared with what is commonly available for most other manufacturing and service industries. It is a criticism of most NTOs that they have spent millions of dollars over recent years on advertising campaigns, while expenditure on basic marketing research into visitor interests, behaviour and attitudes, necessary to achieve the most effective use of the money, has been very limited.

Marketing objectives and targets

The most important output of the marketing planning process for an NTO is the identification of market/product strategies to match market trends and the resource base, and the selection of specific, broadly quantified targets for allocating marketing budgets. Figure 20.2, sets out in a format adaptable for use in any destination, a simplified model of a market/product planning matrix, comprising a number of cells, each of which represents the volume and value of target segments and products.

The segments and products to be included in the matrix are decided by marketing analysis and planning, and liaison with the travel and tourism industry. Research (and judgement) are used to estimate the volume and revenue figures to be inserted. The matrix may be used for historic data or as a framework for forecasting. With appropriate supporting statements, the model may also play a useful part in summarizing strategy, and communicating it to the tourism industry. For the UK, a matrix of this type has been used for many years (see for example, Jefferson and Lickorish: 1991, pp 140–9).

Budget decisions

It was stressed in Chapter 14 that marketing tasks must relate to objectives, and that the size and cost of undertaking specified tasks acts as a constraint on the choice of objectives. In terms of budgeting principles exactly the same considerations apply to NTOs. Possibilities of joint funding of marketing tasks exist, and these are noted later. Very few countries have successfully developed a systematic method of relating the size of budget required to the achievement of specific objectives. Precedent (what was done last year) and broad comparisons with other precedent-based budgets for public expenditure, are still the general rule in budget allocation for NTOs, adjusted more or less, by annual levels of inflation in a country's economy.

As noted earlier, the basic strategic choice for NTOs in allocating available budgets lies in the apportionment they must make between participating directly in promotional tasks, or choosing to engage in facilitation tasks.

Marketing facilitation strategies for an NTO

This section discusses facilitation strategy, neatly summarized by Jeffries (1973), who noted that an NTO '. . . can hardly run the whole of tourism, even in countries where it actually

Market areas (visitor origin) / Product types (destination)	Country A	Country B	Country C	Country D	Other market areas/ segments
	Segments 1, 2 and 3	Segments 4 and 5	Segment 6	Segments 7 and 8	Segments 9+
Resort based holidays	volume: value	volume: value	volume: value	volume: value	volume: value
Touring holidays by car					
Capital city holidays					
Business and conferences					
Other products					

Notes:
1. A developed destination country with domestic tourism and visits from several countries of origin may identify and target as many as fifty or more relevant segments.
2. The products in the matrix are those identified by marketing research, or by analysis of supply. A developed destination country may easily identify over twenty-five principal products, allowing for area and seasonal variations.
3. Where research is available, it will obviously be used to complete the cells of the matrix; where it is not, the matrix model may still be useful as a tool for summarizing managers' judgements. The process of completing the model may also serve to identify aspects of products and markets requiring new, or additional market research.

Figure 20.2 Market/product matrix model for NTO marketing planning

owns hotels and transportation. Its major role everywhere is to provide leadership and guidance; to indicate marketing opportunities and to produce a climate where all concerned will be prepared to exploit them. Having reached this point its role will be to encourage and assist'.

To assist British producers in travel and tourism to develop their overseas visitor markets, the British Tourist Authority (BTA), for example, has developed an extensive range of marketing-facilitation techniques over recent years. It distributes regularly a guide, *Marketing Opportunities*, which extended to sixty pages in 1992. It summarizes the assistance available under sixteen headings, ranging from advertising and print to travel workshops, with most headings containing more than one option. Most of these marketing services are not free, but they can be obtained at costs that few individual medium-sized or small operators acting on their own could match. For BTA, the income derived from these services achieves funding additional to that available from government sources.

Forms of Facilitation by NTOs

Twelve of the most important facilitation processes used by NTOs are discussed below.

1 Flow of research data

By providing a regular, user-friendly flow of research data to the tourism industry, through digests of statistics, short reports on market trends, and help with research enquiries, an NTO may make valuable inputs to the marketing planning processes of individual businesses in all sectors. Co-operative and syndicated research surveys also provide cost-effective ways in which an NTO can stimulate the flow of relevant data. The regular distribution of research summaries is a practical way of maintaining contacts with the industry and exercising influence over marketing strategy at the same time.

2 Representation in markets of origin

By establishing a network of offices in foreign countries generating the bulk of its international visitor flows, an NTO can create and maintain vital travel trade contacts, and act as a point of distribution for the destination's range of tourism products. By manipulating the choice of contacts and its distribution priorities, the NTO can exercise an important influence over the producers it helps, in relation to its chosen marketing objectives. The network of offices may also generate flows of vital marketing intelligence, to be fed into the NTO's information system and used in the marketing planning process.

3 Organization of workshops and trade shows

Since the 1960s NTOs have been making arrangements whereby groups of suppliers of tourist products may meet with groups of prospective buyers, such as tour operators, travel agents, and other travel organizers, at relatively low cost. Either in the market of origin or at the destination, individual hoteliers, attractions, suppliers of conference facilities, or businesses offering youth products, for example, may be able to make contact and discuss business in one or two days of intensive meetings, which on an individual basis could take weeks to organize. By choosing the theme of workshops, such as self-catering, coach tours or attractions, issuing the invitations and possibly subsidizing the costs of accommodation and travel, an NTO can make a powerful contribution to its objectives. It may of course use the workshops as an opportunity to convey information and other messages designed to promote its aims.

4 Familiarization trips

By arranging for parties of selected foreign travel agents, journalists and tour operators to visit the destination and sample the products available, NTOs can influence the effectiveness with which the travel trade in markets of origin acts in support of the destination and its products. Such trips are part of the sales-promotion process discussed in Chapter 16; they are also a method of improving the advice and information available to customers at key retail outlets and gaining better display space at points of sale. The trips also serve an important PR role and offer many opportunities for communicating key messages to influential people in distribution and media channels.

5 Travel trade manuals

With a wide variety of products available in many destinations in a country and a large number of producers, it is usually impossible for all foreign travel agents and tour operators to be serviced individually by an NTO. It is therefore customary for NTOs to produce one or more trade manuals, which serve as references and guides for use by the travel trade. A conference users manual, for example, lists the details of all the operators and their facilities, probably classified by area, particular facilities available, and prices, including commission available and how to make bookings. A different manual would be required for activity holidays, and so on. For smaller suppliers who cannot afford to establish access arrangements with an international distribution system, these manuals provide an opportunity to gain some access to foreign markets at low cost. Of course they also make the busy distributor's job easier, and they are inclined to recommend the products that are easier to deal with.

6 Support with literature production and distribution

Because printed materials are so vital an element in travel and tourism marketing (see Chapter 17), some NTOs produce brochure 'shells' for use by small businesses. These are normally full-colour leaflets containing themed photography and areas of blank space that may be over-printed by an operator's logo and product messages. Quantities of shells suitable for a range of purposes, such as activity holidays or weekend breaks, may be bought at standard prices per thousand as required, and then overprinted in one colour to produce a professional leaflet at a cost well below the price of commissioning a purpose-designed colour brochure in small numbers from a printer.

Many NTOs sell advertising space in their range of brochures, which they promote and distribute overseas. Indeed one of the main purposes of NTO brochures is to provide advertising opportunities to the tourism industry and many brochures produce a surplus of revenue over costs. Assuming the NTO's own literature distribution processes are efficient, these brochures may be very cost-effective advertising media, through which small and medium-sized businesses can reach otherwise inaccessible international markets. NTOs may also offer direct-mail distribution services for the operator's own printed material.

7 Participation in joint marketing schemes or ventures

Joint schemes or joint ventures are specific marketing projects that an NTO may be willing to support on a joint participation basis of, say, $100 for every $300 contributed by partner(s). Usually a sum of money is made available and communicated to the tourism industry – public sector as well as commercial sector – which may submit bids for the money, often in competition with others. Schemes normally require formal application procedures and scrutiny, and criteria are applied, e.g. whether or not the products concerned are likely to proceed without some financial support for their marketing, whether they potentially contribute to stated national marketing objectives, say off-season travel; and whether they have adequate backing from their originators and appear likely to succeed. Successful applicants may be granted up to half the cost of their scheme, although many receive less. Equally important, participants in an adopted scheme may draw on the professional expertise of an NTO's marketing department, and the other facilities available for production of print, overseas representation, research advice, and so on.

According to the way in which the criteria for support are drawn up, an NTO can use schemes to influence operators in the tourism industry along lines indicated through its strategic-planning process. By monitoring the success of schemes, it also develops its research knowledge of particular products, segments and markets.

8 Information and reservation systems

By using new computerized information technology, NTOs may assist sectors of their tourism industry by establishing central reservation systems in support of the brochures of product offers they distribute. Although such systems are primarily designed to facilitate commissionable bookings by retail travel agents, access to the system may also be made available separately to individual customers. Travel agents and other distributors who can access products rapidly through one central reservation operation are likely to find this the only way to deal cost-effectively with small businesses.

9 Support for new products

Through selective proactive marketing support, using criteria established through marketing planning, NTOs can help new products to emerge and establish themselves in their markets in the initial 2 to 3 years after their launch. Smaller businesses are usually unable to afford the start-up costs of national and international marketing, and 'pump priming', as this form of support is often called, is a well-established technique by which NTOs may contribute to their long-term policy goals. In Britain the development of farm tourism and activity holidays is an example of products likely to require considerable support to

establish themselves successfully. This form of assistance overlaps with the investment and development support programmes that many NTOs also operate, increasingly using marketing-orientated criteria.

10 Trade consortia

An interesting illustration of the facilitation role for NTOs exists in the support they may offer for consortia of small businesses, formed for the purposes of more efficient marketing. Aided by NTO marketing expertise and some funding of promotional activities, groups of hire-boat owners, museums, caravan parks, hotels and other facilities may be assisted. The support given in Wales to caravan parks meeting high standards (Dragon Award Parks) is an example of this type of support.

11 Consumer assistance and protection

It is well recognized that the marketing task does not end with the sale of a product. For service products, it extends into concern for customer satisfaction with the service delivery. In tourism this task includes information services, which are provided to enable visitors to become aware of and gain access to the full range of available products, about which many would otherwise have no knowledge. By creating and subsidizing a network of tourist information offices in destination areas, an NTO can extend its influence and communicate messages direct to a wide 'audience' of its visitors. In practice this may be a wider audience than many can hope to reach with available budgets through their promotional efforts in countries of origin. Whereas an NTO may not influence more than say one in four visitors in their country of origin, it may reach two out of three at information centres at destinations. By their choice of emphasis in the information provided, NTOs can expect to exert considerable promotional influence over visitor movement in destinations, and their expenditure patterns. Market research indicates that many visitors to tourism destinations, especially foreign and first-time visitors, are open to suggestion and persuasion from all sources of information, but especially those having the official endorsement and authority of an NTO and its regional bodies.

Associated with this concern for customer satisfaction are forms of consumer protection, such as the requirement that tourism prices should be clearly notified, and the operation of tourism complaint procedures, supplemented in some countries with tourism police. Finally, there is a growing concern in many countries to protect and enhance the quality of tourism products through schemes of accommodation classification and grading designed to increase customers' satisfaction with their experiences. Not normally considered a part of NTO marketing, such schemes make no sense unless they are firmly marketing-led, and designed around the identified needs of the customers an NTO seeks to promote.

Increasingly in the 1990s, NTOs are likely to define product quality standards in consultation with operators in the travel and tourism industry. These may include minimum levels of equipment to be provided in accommodation, and codes of good practice, e.g. in giving buyers full information in brochures. Adhering to minimum environmental practices is likely to feature in agreed standards in the 1990s in many countries. Once quality standards have been agreed, NTOs may limit inclusion in their brochures and display in tourism information centres to operators who comply. In this context facilitation becomes a quality control tool for marketing purposes.

12 General advisory services for the industry

Although the provision of advice to businesses is a time-consuming process, and it cannot reach more than a fraction of the tourism industry as a whole, access to information can make a very important contribution to the marketing

decisions of suppliers with limited market contacts and budgets too small to commit more than a minimum sum to market research. There are many ways in which expensive person-to-person advice can be extended. An NTO may, for example, organize seminars and conferences on marketing topics and disseminate the contributions as widely as possible through its publications. An example is Wales Tourist Board's launch of a distance-learning course in 1987, in conjunction with the national education system, which was designed to give farmers in Wales an opportunity to learn how best to provide, manage, and market farm tourism.

The destination image strategy

Earlier in this chapter it was explained that many NTOs fund and organize overall destination awareness and image campaigns. Typically these are 'umbrella' promotions, under which the specific products of operators may be marketed. This is a strategic choice, which may be implemented instead of or in addition to the alternative of marketing facilitation. As noted in Figure 20.1, an image campaign involves planning and executing a promotional mix that usually comprises advertising, public relations, sales promotion, and marketing literature. The requirements of these techniques are the same in principle for NTOs as they are for any other marketing organization, and they are covered in the principles outlined in Part Four of the book.

If the budget resources are not sufficient to implement an effective image campaign, there remains a vital role for NTOs. This is to identify and communicate to the tourism industry the integrated promotional themes, images and 'positions', judged necessary for a destination to create in the minds of prospective customers. The choice of themes is a matter for marketing research among visitors, but it must also be relevant to any inherent qualities and particular distinctions of the resources a destination offers. This is a creative process, likely to emerge out of an assessment of resource strengths and weaknesses in the marketing planning process. One of the best known examples is the 'I love New York' campaign of the 1980s.

Case studies supporting this chapter

Part Six of the book contains two cases relevant to NTO marketing. The first of these is from Canada, where Tourism Canada is the NTO with large enough budgets to practise effective promotional strategies as well as facilitation. The second is from the islands of the South Pacific, where facilitation is the appropriate strategy for co-operative marketing, led by the Tourism Council of the South Pacific.

Chapter summary

This chapter explains the scope and extent of NTO marketing worldwide, drawing attention to the large sums of money that are spent annually on persuading international visitors to choose particular destinations. It discusses three principal reasons why NTOs, especially in developed destination countries, are not likely to achieve more than a marginal influence over tourism movements. It outlines two levels of destination marketing, distinguishing between the role of NTOs and suppliers of particular products. The strategic choices facing an NTO in deciding how best to deploy its available, usually limited, budget are discussed in some detail.

The chapter outlines the stages in the marketing process for NTOs, paying particular attention to the facilitation strategy. Facilitation is defined as the unique marketing role for an NTO - unique in the sense that if the NTO does not fulfil it, it is unlikely that obviously important tasks will be undertaken at all.

Twelve facilitation tasks are described; they serve to co-ordinate the tourism industry as a whole, recognizing and strengthening industry linkages in the products that destinations provide, and devising themes and images to integrate promotional efforts. By its nature, facilitation is task-orientated and, in terms of securing value for money from promotional expenditure, it is usually easier to prove success through this strategy than through expenditure on image campaigns. The links between marketing and product formulation, which emerge naturally through the facilitation process, help to ensure that tourism development in a country is market-led.

The individual activities described as facilitation in this chapter are not new in the 1990s. But the balance in the use of NTO resources, and the co-ordinated use of the range of techniques to achieve targeted objectives is new; it results from more professional marketing in the sector. The allocation of resources is likely to be most cost-effective if it is integrated around creative images and themes judged relevant to the interests of prospective customers and the special characteristics of the destination's resources.

The principles set out in this chapter are broadly applicable to regional and area tourist boards, which have much the same co-ordinating role and strategic choices in using their resources as NTOs do. Area boards work mainly on domestic tourism and deal with smaller, mainly local operators, but they are in many ways microcosms of their larger national organizations.

Further reading

Jefferson, A., and Lickorish, L., *Marketing Tourism: A Practical Guide*, 2nd edit., Longman, 1991, Chapter 10.

21

Marketing visitor attractions

Most managed visitor attractions in the UK and in many other countries are small operations with less than 30,000 visits per annum and less than £50,000 earned revenue. Most are based on a single location and not operated as businesses for profit. Many, however, have over 150,000 visits, and the number of large commercial attractions has increased rapidly since the 1970s. Nevertheless the operators in this sector as a whole present a strong contrast to the large, multi-site commercial corporations that so strongly influence tourism markets for transport and accommodation. This chapter aims to show that the principles of marketing still apply, even in a sector of the tourism industry not distinguished by a customer-orientated culture or by its business-management skills.

As initially outlined in Chapter 8, all forms of visitor attractions are important `elements within the destination's environment, which largely determine consumers' choice and influence prospective buyers' motivation.' This chapter is concerned only with *managed attractions* based on a wide range of natural or man-made resources, which either naturally or after development have the power to draw or motivate visitors to their locations. There is ample international evidence to prove that the power of resources to motivate visitors is not an absolute but a relative quality. It may be enhanced and developed with the use of management techniques generally and of marketing techniques in particular. Although the point should not be overstated, it is easy to agree that `tourism is a resource industry' (Murphy: 1985, p. 12).

This chapter focuses only on attractions that are the responsibility of managers or owners for whom the use of marketing techniques is both possible and relevant in terms of their objectives and budgets. The term `visitor attractions' rather than `tourist attractions' is used, partly to reflect industry practice, and partly because many attractions are visited as much by the residents of an area as by its tourists. The chapter begins with a brief explanation of what the term *managed* attractions means, and proceeds to define and categorize the types of attraction to which systematic marketing techniques may be applied. Common characteristics of attractions are reviewed, followed by a discussion of the product which attractions offer, and the customer segments which they typically draw. Aspects of the external business environment and of internal operating constraints are outlined, and management responses are summarized under the headings of strategic and tactical marketing. The chapter stresses the growing importance of management and marketing links between attractions.

Modern concepts of attractions management and marketing

Increasingly since the 1960s, with the international extension of travel and tourism on a large scale, notions of unrestricted public access to natural resources in their unmanaged state have given way to concepts of resource control and visitor management, using one or more forms of management techniques. The widely used cliché that visitors tend to destroy the things they travel to see has its applications in most countries, and visitor management of natural and built resources stemmed originally from a desire to protect attractive places from the damage inflicted by too many visitors. Concepts of sustainable development and management for tourism were given a major boost in the publicity surrounding the Earth Summit in Rio de Janeiro in 1992. Students should be aware, however, that concern for the environment and biodiversity are not new. Concepts of visitor management for environmental purposes have a long history in the USA and Europe. What is new is a growing awareness and sense of urgency that natural resources are finite, that capacity matters, and that visitor management techniques must be improved.

Where management techniques are employed, marketing is increasingly fundamental to success, but it can only be practised effectively for natural resources when focused on specific areas of land or water that are enclosed or have controlled access. For example, visitor management and marketing are commonly practised in areas of national parks, or in country parks, lakes or heritage coastal areas. Other attractions based on built resources such as castles, museums or cathedrals have been subject to some form of management for decades, although here too the new forms of marketing are very different from traditional forms of information and promotion.

What distinguishes the last part of the twentieth century is the scale of visits by large numbers of people, which increasingly calls for the exercise of sophisticated management techniques at attractions. The techniques may be used simultaneously to protect the resource, to enhance the visitor experience, to promote a site and generate revenue for it in an increasingly competitive market. Associated with this new emphasis on management is a growing understanding of the ways in which visitor attractions can be developed out of resources and structures not originally thought to be of interest to visitors, or created where none existed previously. Examples are the construction of Disney World and EPCOT in Florida, which began with the purchase of some 27,400 acres of low-lying swamp and agricultural land of no obvious visitor attraction in the mid 1960s; the development of canal basin warehouses at Wigan Pier in the North of England in the mid-1980s, an example of industrial dereliction turned into an attraction; and the use of Garden Festivals in the UK to regenerate former heavy industry sites that can no longer sustain their original role.

Within this context of modern professional management, marketing techniques are emerging as the best way to develop and sustain satisfying products, create value for money, influence the volume and seasonality patterns of site visits, and generate sufficient revenue to cover the costs of operation and maintenance of the resource base.

The concept of applying systematic modern business-management techniques at visitor attractions as diverse as museums and national parks is not yet fully accepted in all countries. The idea of charging for access to the primary assets of national heritage is even less widely accepted, although charging is now common in most new purpose-designed attractions. The evidence suggests, however, that the rate of change in management and marketing awareness at visitor attractions has been rapid in the 1980s. This change is supported by the expanding educational provision for travel, tourism and recreation managers, especially in

North America and Europe, and one may confidently predict a far wider extension of modern management techniques by the end of the century.

The development of marketing thinking is of course stimulated by the pressures of competition. It is noteworthy in England that over half of all the visitor attractions available in the early 1990s were developed in the previous two decades. New attractions, often dependent on admission income for their survival, tend to be commercially orientated from the outset, in contrast with more traditional sites. In the mid-1980s, in preparation for their bicentennial celebrations, Australians travelled the world to study the latest management techniques for use in some of their major new visitor attractions in Sydney, an interesting illustration of the extent to which modern visitor management techniques are now international, even global.

The nature of managed visitor attractions

Many visitor attractions are located in environmentally sensitive areas. In such places public access may be secondary to the principal requirement to conserve a resource for its own intrinsic value, e.g. sustaining wetlands for the sake of the wildlife that inhabits them. In such cases environmental objectives will obviously take precedence over commercial interests, and the use of marketing will have to be adjusted to the dominant objective.

Allowing for this important caveat, the admission of visitors – especially the revenue they generate to contribute to environmental objectives – is generally a key element in resource conservation schemes. Managed visitor attractions as discussed in this chapter may now be defined as: *designated permanent resources that are controlled and managed for their own sake and for the enjoyment, amusement, entertainment and education of the visiting public.*

Designated means that the resource has been formally committed to the types of use and activity outlined in the definition. Designation may be either a commercial decision within the normal statutory planning regulations that apply to land and structures, a decision by a public sector body acting on behalf of community interests, or the decision of a trust acting on behalf of trust objectives. In all cases the boundaries of a managed attraction must be clearly specified – even for wilderness areas such as the upper slopes of mountains – and normally attractions are enclosed or controlled to reduce or prevent public access except at established points of admission.

Permanent is used to exclude from the definition travelling fairs, shows, temporary entertainments and any other form of visitor attractions not based on a fixed site or building. Temporary attractions have their own different forms of marketing, which are not discussed in this chapter.

Within the definition it will be obvious that there is a wide range of different types of attraction. To illustrate the range, ten different categories of permanent managed attractions are listed in Figure 21.1. The marketing principles put forward in this chapter will be found applicable to all of them.

The definition is not restricted to attractions that have an admission price, although the attractions listed in Figure 21.1 mostly do charge, and the trend is in this direction rather than for free provision. The charge for using the attraction may be made at a ticket office, barrier or a car park, or for the use of parts of the site; it may be obligatory or operated on a voluntary basis. Prices may be intended to cover the full resource cost of operating an attraction, or just to cover its current (not capital) expenditure, or simply to make some contribution to costs that are otherwise paid from some other source.

Common characteristics of the visitor attractions shown in Figure 21.1 are that they are usually small in terms of the number of visitors and the revenue they receive, many are product-

1	Ancient monuments	Typically protected and preserved sites such as fortifications, burial mounds and buildings dating up to the end of the Roman Empire
2	Historic buildings	Castles, houses, palaces, cathedrals, churches, town centres, villages, commonly termed heritage sites
3	Designated areas, parks and gardens	National parks, country parks, long-distance paths, gardens (excluding urban recreation spaces), including sites of particular scenic and resource quality
4	Theme parks	Mostly engineered as artefacts, such as Disney World, but may be associated with historic sites such as Colonial Williamsburg in the USA, or with Gardens as at Alton Towers in Britain
5	Wildlife attractions	Zoos, aquaria, aviaries, wildfowl parks, game parks and safaris
6	Museums	The range is enormous; it includes *subject*-specific museums, such as science, transport, farms, ships; *site*-specific museums, such as Colonial Williamsburg (USA) or Ironbridge Gorge (Great Britain); or *area*-based museums, with either national, regional or local collections
7	Art galleries	Most traditional galleries with collections built up over many decades
8	Industrial archeology sites	Mostly sites and structures identified with specific industrial and manufacturing processes, such as mining, textiles, railways, docks or canals, and mostly relevant to the period post-1750
9	Themed retail sites	Mostly former commercial premises, such as covered market halls, commodity exchanges or warehouses, used as speciality retail shopping malls, often themed
10	Amusement and leisure parks	Parks constructed primarily for 'white knuckle' rides, such as roller coasters, log flumes, dodgem cars and associated stalls and amusements

Figure 21.1 *Ten main types of managed attraction for visitors*

rather than market-orientated, and most have very limited marketing knowledge and marketing budgets so small as to limit what they can achieve in practice to improve their revenue performance. In the terms introduced in Chapter 2 visitor attractions do not generally have an outward looking, proactive corporate culture to guide their decisions.

For Britain, the British Tourist Authority and English Tourist Board had records of 4,840 attractions open to the public in 1990, for which they have actual or estimated visitor numbers.

Over 12 months in 1990 those attractions recorded a total of 337 million visits. Compared with a UK population of just over 57 million, plus some 18 million overseas visitors a year, the importance of attractions is clear. But only just over fifty sites making an admission charge exceeded half a million visits in 1990, many of those being in London and drawing on the large number of overseas visitors. It is unlikely that more than about 150 attractions have the staff resources to employ their own professional marketing managers, although most are engaged in marketing activities to some extent. For the rest, compared with the larger operators dominating transport and hotels, most are still in the cottage industry stage.

There are some obvious and important well-managed exceptions to the generalizations above, such as Disney World and Disneyland, and the other major operators in the USA; and Madame Tussauds, Alton Towers, the National Trust, English Heritage, Thorpe Park and Beaulieu, for example, in the UK. But the management philosophies and corporate culture at the bulk of all visitor attractions around the world are usually not strongly orientated towards marketing concepts.

In the 1900s it seems true to say that the attractions sector of the tourism industry is divided into a few that practise modern management techniques, and others that are still far from the philosophies of customer-orientation advocated in this book. In the first group come most larger operators achieving at least 150,000 visits per annum, plus some of the smaller attractions, especially where they have managed to forge links with others to operate as members of consortia for marketing purposes.

Historically, many attractions, especially those based on collections, were formed and are directed by dedicated enthusiasts and scholars. These enthusiasts usually have always been short of funds and have had to overcome great difficulties in defeating the forces of inertia to establish their collections. As a result, many attractions are located in structures and sites that are barely adequate for the purpose, having only limited facilities for display and interpretation to the general public. At the same time, the management structure of individuals, trusts, local-authority recreation departments and government agencies that control many attractions is not noted for its marketing expertise.

On this evidence, certainly in the UK, the typical site manager is responsible for one site location only, has very limited links with other sites, has never undertaken any form of market research, has had no formal management and marketing training, and has a marketing budget of under £5,000 per annum. Such a manager is likely to be more concerned with the daily problems of financial survival than with expansion and development through marketing initiatives.

There are only a few multiples established in the attractions field in Britain offering unified product standards. But the National Trust and English Heritage (with their equivalents in Scotland and Wales), do provide an equivalent to large multi-site groups, marketed with a common image and under central management control. These large groups have some smaller voluntary equivalents among the independent attractions, including, for example, the Treasure Houses of England (historic properties noted later in the chapter), Great Little Trains of Wales (steam railways), and many area co-operatives. These groupings are a logical development in the marketing of attractions, both for promotion and distribution purposes, and they are believed to point to a future in which such linkages will become increasingly common.

The attractions product

Both transport and accommodation products perform an enabling rather than a motivating role within the overall tourism product. It is also stressed that much of transport revenue still derives from various forms of business and other non-leisure travel, and from the carriage of freight. Similarly, for hotels and other forms of accommodation, a significant proportion of total sales revenue derives from non-leisure travel and from bars, catering, and functions that are geared to a local community rather than to visitors.

Some managed visitor attractions, such as museums, are also geared to local communities, but most are almost exclusively concerned with leisure travel segments and motivations. One may argue that school and other educational visits are not part of leisure, although even these fit more into a type of leisure than a business-travel category. In other words, attractions constitute part of the primary motivation for the destination choices of leisure travellers, and, as such, lie at the core of the overall travel and tourism product.

As noted earlier in this chapter, managed attractions are based on resources that may be natural or built. They often depend on collections of scarce objects as the basis of their appeal. But it is not resources or collections that are the product: it is the *visitor experience* which the resources provide. The attractions product cannot be effectively marketed unless this key point is understood. The visitor experience in each case reflects the resource the site provides. It ranges from simple aesthetic pleasure and interest, as in gardens; through 'white knuckle' thrills and excitement of amusement parks; fantasy, as at some of the Tussauds exhibitions; to serious learning and awareness, associated with new techniques for museum display and presentation, such as those found at modern folk museums. The range of experiences is very wide. What a particular experience provides to targeted market segments can usually be established only through consumer research among key market segments, not through management guesswork. But at all managed sites, the *experience* is a matter of product formulation, which can be influenced or controlled by management decisions.

Product formulation

The visitor experience at attractions begins with anticipation. It may be stimulated by effective promotion, especially printed materials, and by personal recommendation. It begins in earnest at the entrance to the site. From the moment of arrival, well exemplified by the sense of scale and quality conveyed by Disney World's astonishing motorway style entrance route and the row of parking toll booths spread across the traffic lanes, every aspect of the experience visitors undergo is potentially under management control. To some extent this is also true of transport and accommodation operations, but more so for attractions, since the purpose of being on site is not usually functional but to derive satisfaction in an awareness and enjoyment of the surroundings. In some historic buildings and sites the degree of management control is limited by planning and policy restrictions, but the essential components of the product may be summarized as follows:

- Quality of the advertising material and promotional literature, which establishes a 'promise' and influences initial expectations of a visit.
- Effectiveness of signage that guides first-time visitors to a site/building.
- First impression of a site and its perceived interest to prospective visitors – related to a pre-visit expectation. Efficiency of car/coach parking arrangements, and access to the entrance.
- Physical appearance and motivating appeal of the entrance to an attraction.
- Handling of visitors at the entrance or in a reception area including ticketing, information provided, and initial orientation at the point of sale/admission.
- Visitor circulation patterns on the site/building, managed through the logical layout of the resource elements, paths, signposting, and in other ways.
- Displays, presentation, and interpretation of the main elements of the resource, including audio-visual materials and any events or activities provided.
- Location and layout of any subsidiary attractions on the site.
- Location and layout of facilities such as toilets, cafés, and shops.

It is helpful to assess these product elements, both separately and within the overall experience, as part of a 'bundle' or package of components. The 'package' may be varied by management decisions. Since one of the prime objects of attractions management is to generate motivation, customer satisfaction, and value for money, marketing inputs into product formulation will be crucial to success.

Market segments for visitor attractions

Experience with researching attractions both in Britain and in other countries indicates that, in varying proportions, all attractions draw their customers from the same basic range of segments. Any differences between sites in the segments they attract are likely to be explained either by the motivating power of the attraction, or by locational factors such as proximity to a holiday destination.

Some attractions, such as Euro Disney in France or Shakespeare's birthplace in Stratford-on-Avon, are strong enough and sufficiently well-known to break through the normal locational influences that govern visitor flows. But for most attractions, the influence of locational factors will be at least as strong as the resource base. The reason is that, apart from specialist visitors with knowledge of the subjects covered by the resource, most visitors to attractions will have little or no knowledge of the resource at the point of entry to the site. For example, visitors to parks and gardens may well include botanists with a deep knowledge of plants and horticulture, but they will comprise no more than a very small proportion of all visitors.

Practical segmentation of the visiting public begins with user types and only then proceeds to demographic and other segmentation factors, which are covered in Chapter 7. Within most developed countries, the following segments will normally apply:

1 Local residents living within approximately half an hour's drive from the site.
2 Regional residents making day visits away from home and drawn, depending on the motivating power of the site, from a distance of up to 2 hours' driving, or more in the case of sites of national significance.
3 Visitors staying with friends and relatives within about an hour's drive from the site.
4 Visitors on holiday staying in hotels, caravan parks, and other forms of commercial accommodation within about an hour's drive from the site.
5 Group visits, usually arranged in association with coach companies or organized by direct marketing contact between groups and the attractions' management.
6 School visits and other educational groups.

Foreign visitors may be separated from groups 3, 4 and 5, and treated as separate segments for marketing purposes.

Because of the nature of attractions, their fixed location, spare capacity on most days, and need to draw as many visitors as possible, it is very rarely sensible to approach the marketing task by concentrating only on one or two of the possible segments. Where attractions charge for admission, the need to generate revenue will make it even more important to appeal to as many visitor groups as possible.

For the accommodation and transport sectors of travel and tourism, segmentation is normally an essential step in product design and adaptation. Segmentation for attractions, however, is more important for targeting promotion and distribution than for product formulation. For example, if it appears for a particular attraction that holiday visitors will be especially important in its visitor mix, the implication is not so much to design the product for holiday visitors but to focus most promotional and distribution efforts on them. The marketing approach to local residents will be quite different from that aimed at tourists. Although the length of time holiday visitors spend on the site could be important in terms of a sensible day which perhaps starts in their accommodation at 10 am and ends back there around 5 pm, the product they enjoy is not necessarily affected by their being on holiday.

Factors in the external environment

Because they mostly operate on a small scale, single-site attractions are normally less affected by the constant changes in the external environment that preoccupy the marketing managers of large-scale transport and accommodation suppliers. Four long-term factors may be stressed:

● Actions of competitors.
● Growing customer sophistication.
● Application of new technology.
● The effects of other destination organizations' decisions upon specific attractions.

So far as competitors are concerned, the most important characteristic is the growing supply and capacity of attractions that compete, often in the same locality, for the same market segments. In Britain the growth in the number of sites competing for a fairly static market demand has meant that individual sites have to work much harder in the 1990s to sustain their visitor numbers. As more localities look to tourism and recreation to generate employment lost from primary and manufacturing industry, this competition will increase. Much of the new competition will be purpose-designed or adapted to attract and satisfy visitors, and some of it may be substantially subsidized by government and its agencies and trusts. In this more competitive environment some older attractions are likely to disappear, no longer able to attract sufficient customers or adequate funding from other sources to cover their operating expenses.

'Customer sophistication' is a useful shorthand expression meaning that customers' expectations and their perceptions of satisfaction and value for money – in other words, their attitudes - are in a continual state of change and development. In all sectors of the economy there is clear evidence that expectations are rising, and 'yesterday's products' can very quickly lose their appeal if suppliers fail to keep pace with current requirements. As stated in the Old Sturbridge Village case (see Part Six) 'A continual goal is product enhancement while increasing the visitor's perceived value in comparison to the cost of visit'. For visitor attractions, sophistication also reflects the increasing exposure most visitors have to international standards, partly through their own travel, partly through television, and partly because the leading attractions in any country are continuously developing new standards of excellence against which all other sites will be judged.

New technology has opened up new opportunities which museum and other site designers can utilize in the display and interpretation of resources. Lighting, sound, film, lasers, IMAX (very wide screen effects for film displays), and new materials such as plastic, carbon fibre and fibre optics, are all involved in modern displays. Even the traditional roller coasters are giving way to new corkscrew and looping tracks, employing the flexibility of tubular steel. Computer-operated simulators, to create realistic sensations of movement and visual and aural effects, are becoming less expensive and are likely to be more popular in the attractions of the future. At a more mundane level, attractions that are not employing electronic or computerized cash tills as part of their management control systems are losing valuable market-research data about their customer profiles.

The external effects of decisions made by other suppliers at destinations must be mentioned, because managed attractions are usually only one element in the overall travel and tourism products on which the future of destinations depends. While the decisions of the Disney Organization were responsible for constructing the new resort at Euro Disney outside Paris, this is quite exceptional. Normally the demand for attractions varies with the fortunes of the host destination. In London or New York, for example, the visitor revenues of the major attractions fluctuate with the number of foreign visitors. But the attractions themselves have only a very minor role in such market fluctuations.

The net effect of all these external factors is to focus increasing attention on marketing aspects. The point made by Cossons, a leading British pioneer in the marketing of museums, can equally be applied to other forms of managed attraction: 'Museums will stand or fall not only by their competence to care for collections, but by their ability to care for people. In other words, they need to be market-orientated if they are to survive . . .' (Cossons: 1985, p. 44).

Operating constraints on marketing

As noted earlier in the chapter, attraction managers tend, by the nature of their occupations and backgrounds, to be more inwardly concerned with their resource base than outwardly concerned with customer interests. Fortunately, product formulation interpreted as managing experiences usually leaves ample scope for developing customer benefits without damaging the intrinsic quality of the resources. In practice there are fewer constraints on product formulation than might appear at first sight. However, three other constraints influence the marketing of attractions and require brief discussion.

The first reflects the by now familiar concern with the implications of high fixed costs and low variable costs of operation. This affects attractions just as it affects transport and accommodation suppliers. For example, a busy summer day at the National Motor Museum at Beaulieu, Hampshire, sees over 5,000 visitors through the turnstiles. By contrast, a day in February may produce only 150 people. Yet, if the quality of the visitor experience is to be maintained, the fixed costs of operating in February are much the same as in July. Any savings in the numbers of part-time staff are offset by the increased costs of heating and lighting. Obviously, on a simple *pro rata* basis, the museum operates at a loss in February and at other times of the year, so that the role of marketing in generating marginal extra admission income is exactly the same in principle for attractions as for transport operators. In practice large attractions have fixed costs to cover around the year, and the contribution of the February visits has to be seen as a revenue gain, that would be lost if the attraction were to be closed.

The second constraint, made worse by the fact of high fixed costs, is the effect of seasonality. A rule of thumb relevant to British attractions is that maximum capacity, or volume of demand, will be experienced on only about 20 days in the year. On each of those 20 days an average of about 1 per cent of the year's total volume will be received, and it is not unusual for attractions to turn visitors away when they are 'full'. Where the site is located near a holiday resort, over 45 per cent of the year's volume may be achieved over about 8 weeks. The role of marketing is to contribute to the generation of demand outside the limited number of peak days.

A third constraint affecting many attractions is the extent to which repeat visits to any one site in any one year are usually a minority of all visits. Some attractions have the kind of resource that encourages repeat visits, while many are designed for one visit only. But, with the competition now facing most attractions, it is probable that people making more than one visit within a 12-month span will be in the minority. Finding promotional ways to encourage new, first-time visits is therefore a primary concern for most attractions. This fact helps to explain why the successful large attractions find it necessary to spend 10 per cent or more of their admission revenue on promotion and distribution. It would be less if there were more repeat visitors. Smaller attractions spend far lower proportions, but many will be unable to grow unless they accept the logic of gearing marketing budgets to revenue targets, as explained in Chapter 14 (marketing campaigns).

Surviving on a financial knife edge

Unlike profitable businesses in other sectors of travel and tourism, it appears to be characteristic and normal for most visitor attractions that rising costs of operation tend to overtake any rise in available sources of revenue. Certainly this is true of those in the heritage sector, which usually exist to achieve non-profit-related goals. Costs rise with inflation, and because the demands of the resource for optimum conservation and refurbishment are usually far in excess of income. It is for this reason that many national museums have been obliged to charge for admission even when their organization's instinct was to provide free access.

Economic recession of the depth experienced in many countries between 1991 and 1993 reduced income from visitors and played havoc with budget forecasts. With high fixed costs committed in advance, a 10 per cent downturn in earned revenue over a year can usually only be tackled by severe cost-cutting for the year following. It is all too easy for attractions to cut costs (including marketing budgets) to the extent that the visit-experience becomes tired and worn and further falls in revenue result as customers turn elsewhere. Marketing is not a panacea. But it does offer the only strategic route to greater earnings from customers, if endowments and grants from other sources are insufficient and further cost-cutting is counter-productive of revenue.

The marketing task for attractions

It is logical to distinguish between the strategic and tactical levels of marketing decisions.

Strategic tasks

The main task of marketing strategy for attractions involves segmenting the total market and targeting the potential volume demand from each group. Segmentation is the base for forecasting maximum achievable revenue flows. Such forecasts will be essential inputs to site management, affecting both capital and operating revenue decisions. Strategic segmentation will be also the basis for creating effective campaigns for promotion and distribution, targeted on the specified groups of prospective customers. The process of analysing existing and prospective visitor groups may also identify new uses, such as opening museums in the evenings for functions and receptions.

The second, related task of strategy is to identify the nature of the experiences which the resource base is capable of sustaining, either as it is, or as it might be if enhanced. Enhancement may be achievable through development and improved presentation, display, and information techniques. Because of the obvious dangers of product orientation in managing attractions, the only effective way to ascertain the *experience*, is through research with targeted segments of customers.

Following logically from the first two aspects of strategy, the third task lies in product formulation and augmentation to provide and enhance customer satisfaction with the best quality of experience that the resource base affords. School parties, for example, will often require specific materials and facilities, both to attract them and to help them derive maximum satisfaction and perceived value for money. Product formulation is directly related to price, which for established visitor attractions is normally related to annual inflation plus a margin to help meet rising costs. In the 1980s most managed attractions were able to push up admission prices faster than annual inflation, but growing competition for visits in the 1990s appears likely to limit this option. Pricing for segments is likely to be a more productive strategy in the next decade.

Fourth, for promotional and product formulation purposes, it will usually be possible to identify one principal underlying theme, or idea, which encapsulates the resource base and the experiences it sustains. This theme will be the basis for positioning the attraction and the benefits it offers, in all marketing communications aimed at prospective visitors.

Fifth, strategy may often require the search for effective promotional and distribution linkages between the attraction and other sites of the same type, or of different types in the same location. Such links may be achieved with the support of tourist boards, or directly between co-operating attractions. Another aspect of this search for linkages may be the arrangements for promotion and distribution that can be made with transport and accommodation interests seeking to provide extra interest and motivation in their own product offers. The obvious link is with coach-tour operators, but hotels offering weekend breaks are increasingly interested to feature admission to attractions as part of an inclusive price. In this context attractions become a part of the augmentation of an accommodation product, which in turn serves as a form of distribution channel for the attraction.

Tactical marketing

Working within the strategic framework, marketing tactics will draw on the wide range of promotion and distribution techniques discussed in Part Four of the book. As with other forms of travel and tourism marketing, the main focus will be to mould demand around the fixed supply, especially to secure the vital additional admissions that represent pure revenue gain once the high fixed costs of operation have been committed. The latter point obviously applies only in circumstances where revenues have to be earned rather than provided as grants or subsidies.

The most productive promotional tools will normally be forms of targeted advertising aimed at creating and maintaining awareness and interest in the site, especially among prospective first-time users, supported by PR exploiting whatever public interest may lie in the resource base. In addition, many attractions have discovered that staging special events, such as craft fairs, demonstrations, displays and temporary exhibitions, creates interest and achieves media space other than that which has to be paid for. Events may also bring in first-time visitors, who may be persuaded to return on a 'normal' day.

On the distribution side the prime task in motivating prospective tourist visitors is ensuring that leaflets, posters and showcards are continuously available in all forms of accommodation in the identified catchment area, at tourist information centres, and through any other links which may be formed with other attractions.

There is little evidence to show that last-minute price discounting is a relevant tactic for attracting new visitors to attractions, although this is a common practice for transport and accommodation sectors. This is partly because of the difficulty of communicating temporary price changes, and also because of the relatively low level of repeat visits. Once people have made the effort to visit an attraction, provided the normal prices are realistic as measured by research into perceptions of value for money, they are unlikely to have their minds changed by discount offers at the point of admission. Of all tourism products, the motivation to visit an attraction is one of the least likely to be based on a price discount.

Experience suggests that allocating around 10 per cent of admissions revenue for marketing purposes is a realistic guideline for most visitor attractions. There may well be a convincing argument for spending more than this, especially to promote awareness of new facilities, and if the evidence achieved through visitor research indicates that the promotional efforts are paying off in admission revenue. Objective and task approaches to budgeting, outlined in Chapter 14, are particularly appropriate for visitor attractions.

Marketing and management linkages

Given the small size of most visitor attractions, it follows that there are usually only one or two managers/owners, who have to provide all the management skills needed to compete in a more sophisticated visitor market with the major operators, who have large management teams. In common with many other sectors of the economy, the only logical response to small scale is to join with others to share the management skills that cannot be achieved individually. Such a response has strategic and tactical dimensions.

Following a detailed analysis of museums in the UK in 1990, it was concluded that 'the majority of museums . . . are too small to sustain individually the range of management expertise needed if they are to respond effectively to the forces of change and competition facing them over the next decade. It is therefore strongly recommended that (they) develop functional networks with a management services focus' (Middleton: 1990, p. 70). In the UK there are many examples of successful consortia for limited promotional purposes, such as a joint leaflet, but not yet for the more important management purposes within which marketing will be one element.

Initiating consortia is not easy for small operators, and the process needs a catalyst organization from outside. There would appear to be no alternative, however, if the management of small attractions is to remain competitive. One example of a marketing consortium, which also shares management information, is noted below. The players in this consortium are large operators, although the principles are valid for smaller attractions.

The treasure houses of England

The 'treasure houses' are a group of eight attractions in England that come under the broad category of historic houses, although some of the group also feature other major visitor attractions and exhibitions in their grounds. Known until 1986 as the 'Magnificent Seven', the group was first formed in 1975 as a voluntary co-operative of fully independent owners who saw advantages in joint promotion to the overseas visitor market. The Seven, who had extended their joint marketing operations to include UK domestic visitors, changed their name to 'the Treasure Houses of England' in 1987, when they were joined by Chatsworth House. The eight are now, Beaulieu, Broadlands, Blenheim Palace, Castle Howard, Chatsworth, Harewood House, Warwick Castle, and Woburn Abbey.

At the upper end of the visitor numbers scale, these are all large attractions, which draw in around 3 million visits per annum between them and employ professional management and marketing staff. Each property has always had, and still retains, its own identity, image, name, and marketing budget. Each is responsible on an individual basis for a marketing programme that generates the bulk of its visitor business. Spread around England, the eight are hardly in direct competition, even for foreign visitors, and they see strong advantages in joint marketing activity, which included, for 1992:

● Advertising themselves in guides and other media, as a group.
● Production of a joint leaflet, incorporating privilege voucher discounts, primarily for distribution overseas, but also available in the UK, with each property acting as a referral system.

- Production of showcards and posters for use in support of the leaflet, and at exhibitions.
- Use of joint stands at major workshops and travel exhibitions.
- Production of a travel trade manual to facilitate the way in which tour operators, coach-tour firms and others in the travel trade can build the properties into their programmes.
- Joint PR, as the opportunity presents or can be created.

The group does not publish its financial arrangements, but it is understood that members contribute on an equal basis so that their group subscriptions probably amount to between 5 and 20 per cent of their individual marketing budgets. For that outlay, they achieve valuable coverage, especially in guides and through distribution of leaflets, which they could not achieve on their own for an equivalent sum. They also generate marginal admission revenue through the working of the privilege voucher scheme included in the group leaflet, which incorporates a competition for visitors who go to any of the houses. The size of the group's activities and of course the intrinsic quality of the product have made it possible to draw in sponsors to supplement the group budget. Lastly, the process of meetings necessary to agree the scope of each year's activities provides lines of management communication between the properties, which are used for exchanging information on market trends and other aspects of mutual interest, thus adding value to the more tangible forms of co-operation noted above.

Case studies supporting this chapter

The appendix of the book contains two cases relevant to marketing managed visitor attractions. The first of these is from the USA where Old Sturbridge Village, a mature attraction, is successfully marketed against extensive competition. The second is from the UK, where the marketing issues surrounding a major exhibition in a national museum are discussed.

Chapter summary

Stressing the important motivating role of attractions as one of the core elements in the overall tourism product for leisure travellers, this chapter identifies the common operating characteristics that determine how managed attractions may be marketed. Ten categories of managed attractions are set out, all of which are controlled and managed, sometimes for their own sake to protect and conserve precious heritage resources, but mostly for the enjoyment, amusement, entertainment and education of visitors. These attractions usually charge admission prices and, increasingly, the larger ones are professionally managed and marketed. The bulk of all attractions, however, are mostly small in visitor numbers and revenue, and are inherently product or resource-orientated. They have low levels of visitor management and marketing skills. The 'corporate culture' and the profile of this latter group, many of which provide their facilities free or at low admission charges, are obviously not conducive to the development and application of the systematic marketing procedures recommended in this book. For reasons discussed, the pressures of competition and the need to generate revenue are forcing changes in professional management throughout the sector.

The definition of *products as experiences*, and research to assess the components of the experience for product formulation, are important to successful marketing. Product formulation has to be based on identified segments, and this also means market research among visitors. Owners of attractions, in common with other producers of travel and tourism services, always have a 'captive audience' on their premises, providing opportunities for cost-effective research which should be exploited as the first step in the marketing process.

The *strategic marketing* tasks for attractions reflect the high fixed costs of operation, the seasonality of visitor flows, and the constant need to motivate first-time visits. Marketing strategy focuses on segmentation, product formulation, and positioning, and the need to ensure that the benefits offered by the attraction are clearly understood by targeted prospective visitors. As a British Tourist Authority report expressed it, reflecting on lessons learned from studying museums in the USA, 'Marketing is a positive analytical matching of a product to its market. For a museum this is the presentation of its collection or theme in a way which best communicates this to its audience or potential visitors' (BTA: 1983, p. 21).

In their essential need for marketing, managed attractions are not different in principle from other travel and tourism producers. Their small scale puts a particular emphasis on linkages for management purposes, however, which most have not yet adopted. Their needs at *tactical level* to achieve extra, marginal admissions, through maximum awareness and distribution of products, are common to all sectors.

22

Marketing transport operations

Transport is one of the five integral elements of the overall tourism product defined in Chapter 8. The forms of transport available at any period of time, and the ways in which they are marketed, have a massive influence on the pattern of tourism flows and on the types of product travellers purchase.

It has to be understood, however, that the development of transport systems by road, rail, inland water, sea, or air, has not usually been associated with travel for leisure purposes. Historically, transport design and development owe their impetus to the need to move goods and mail, the need to administer countries and empires, the need to move armies and military equipment, the development of new weapons of war, and the need to move people more efficiently in the conduct of their day-to-day lives. Most transport systems are still primarily geared to business, administrative and military interests. Increasingly in the latter part of the twentieth century, they are extending their original orientation towards leisure and recreation travel. The reasons for this shift in emphasis reflect the operators' need to develop into new and growing markets for transport products, and to utilize surplus capacity, both overall and especially at times of otherwise slack demand. This means creating new products, especially those that contribute to economies of scale, as part of an integrated portfolio of transport operations.

This chapter traces briefly the historical links between transport supply and tourism demand, and the increasing orientation of transport systems to travel for leisure and recreation purposes. It proceeds by defining the nature of transport systems and products, the constraints on their marketing, both internal and external, and the nature of strategic and tactical marketing tasks for passenger transport.

Historical links between transport supply and tourism demand

Transport represents the physical means of access whereby travellers can reach their chosen destinations. As such, it is not difficult to trace the ways in which the growth of tourism around the world has been geared to developments in transport. In their unpublished work Burkart and Medlik identify three main phases of development. The first covers the pre-industrial period and takes the story to the early nineteenth century. The second spans the next 100 years or so to the Second World War. The third covers the post-war period of large volume tourism since 1945.

Until well into the nineteenth century the bulk of journeys were undertaken for business, vocational, and military purposes, by people travelling mainly in their own countries. The volume of travel was small and confined to only a fraction of the population in any country. From the 1840s onwards, as the Industrial Revolution in Europe and North America gathered pace, the growth of pleasure travel on an increasing scale can be identified with the development of railway systems and early steamships on inland and coastal waterways. For over a century the railway and steamships dominated passenger travel, both facilitating and stimulating travel between countries and continents.

Early in this century both motor transport and air transport were developed, and the basic infrastructure was constructed. But their full impact was not felt until after the Second World War, when, in the 1950s, tourism became increasingly available to a majority of the population in developed countries. By the 1980s access to cars had extended to approaching two-thirds or more of the population in Europe, with higher levels in North America. Aircraft development received a massive impetus through the war, and planes quickly took over from ships as the main means of long-distance transportation. A growing volume of travel became international, and on many routes vacation traffic came to match and often greatly exceed other purposes of travel. Tour operation emerged on a large scale and supported the development of charter airlines, which now carry more traffic than scheduled airlines on many European routes. Since the early 1990s, the distinctions between scheduled and charter airlines are being reduced under more liberal competition policies introduced by EC rules.

While the dates noted above are not precise, the ways in which tourist destinations developed are obviously closely linked to changes in the means of transport. For example, in the nineteenth century, seaside resorts in northern Europe could not have developed as they did without the building of railway links to provide access for the markets emerging in the growing industrial cities and towns. Across the Atlantic, the state of Florida could not have developed as a major vacation destination in the 1970s for domestic and international tourists without its national and international air links and the corresponding development of the state road system for cars and buses. In the South Pacific tourism destinations are almost entirely dependent on the availability and cost of air transport.

The nature of transport systems

Figure 22.1 summarizes the wide range of modern transport systems, the marketing of which affects all tourism destinations to some extent. Most destinations are simultaneously influenced by several of these systems. At first sight it is easy to suppose that each of the forms of transport is so different in kind that comparisons, and the development of common principles for marketing, are impossible. In fact all the systems share some common characteristics, which have important implications for marketing practice. As Burkart and Medlik expressed it: 'A transport system can be analyzed in three parts: the track, the vehicle, and the terminal' (1981, p. 111).

Tracks:	controlled air routes, sea routes, canals, permanent ways (railways), roads, trunk routes and motorways.
Vehicles:	aircraft, ships, trains, buses and coaches, private vehicles.
Terminals:	airports, seaports, stations, garages, and off-street parking.

In considering the external threats and opportunities in the environment influencing marketing managers' product responses in transport, one should note that, railways excepted, the three basic elements outlined above are owned and controlled by different parties. For example, in the case of air transport

Air transport	**Long-haul scheduled airlines** operate networks that carry most long-haul travellers, for all purposes, around the world, and offer an extensive range of promotional fares for economy class leisure travel.
	Medium/short-haul scheduled airlines operate networks serving travellers for all purposes, offering an extensive range of promotional fares.
	Charter airlines – long or short haul operate networks that serve mainly leisure travel of all kinds; are sometimes subsidiary companies of scheduled airlines, or part of tour operator groups; they dominate European short-haul air travel for holiday purposes. The traditional distinction between charter and schedules has become blurred under recent de-regulatory agreements.
Sea transport	**Ferries** operate scheduled networks on short sea routes, serving as extension of road network; carry passengers for all purposes; mainly roll-on, roll-off design to suit cars, coaches and trucks; have increasing links into the inclusive tour business.
	Charter cruise ships serve as floating resorts; important market in USA, but smaller elsewhere.
Rail	**Scheduled rail services** – tourism use is restricted mainly to scheduled inter-city services for all purposes of travel; extensive range of promotional fares for leisure; links with conference and accommodation; important for day excursions.
Bus and coach	**Scheduled bus** tourism use is restricted mainly to inter-city services, serving mainly non-business forms of travel.
	Charter or private hire includes coach tours and long-distance coach transport to resorts, which are a significant element of inclusive tour holidays; coaches are an important form of intra-resort travel for transfers and excursions; coaches service many forms of organized group travel for all purposes of visit.
Private transport	**Private cars and car rental** are the dominant forms of travel in domestic tourism, leisure day visits and recreation, and in international travel in continental Europe; car rental fulfils a substitute private transport role and has close links with other transport operators, tour operators and accommodation providers.

Figure 22.1 *Principal passenger transport systems used in travel and tourism*

the vehicles are owned and operated by airlines, the routes are effectively owned by governments that allocate and control air space, and the terminals are owned for the most part by national, regional or local governments and their appointed agencies. In the UK current government plans to privatize parts of British Rail are expected to lead to separation of vehicles, track and terminals for the first time.

Without permission to fly to a country, or with permission to fly only a specified capacity of certain types of product (such as scheduled rather than charter flights), marketing managers do not enjoy full scope for responding to the market forces they perceive. Similarly, if the external agencies controlling the routes or the terminal facilities cannot cope with the added volume, marketing decisions to develop new routes or products have a very restricted meaning. Marketing constraints are arising in the 1990s through airport congestion in much of Europe, for example, because air-traffic-control systems have not been developed fast enough to cope with increases in demand.

In the case of private transport the vehicles, and to some extent the off-street parking, are owned and controlled by individuals; but routes are typically developed, owned and controlled by government and its agencies. At destinations, the bulk of the terminal or parking facilities available for private transport are often provided, and mostly regulated by local government.

So far as destination interests, such as national or regional tourist offices or attractions are concerned, marketing strategies which not related to the changing capacity, routes and terminals of both public and private transport are very unlikely to be successful. Transport factors are usually a key element also in the external environment for all other operators in the travel and tourism industry.

In summarizing the common characteristics of transport systems influencing marketing decisions, it should be noted that:

- All passenger transport systems work via more or less closely controlled and regulated vehicle movements, along networks which link points of origin and destination.
- The operation of all such systems requires continuous concern with the utilization of available capacity, whether of vehicles, routes or terminals.
- All systems display typical characteristics of peaks and troughs in demand, whether by month, week, day or hour.
- Most systems need massive investment in infrastructure, vehicles, track, and control systems, requiring efficient marketing both to justify and to pay back the expenditure.
- Most systems move freight as well as passengers, and freight requirements may take precedence.
- Most systems are only partly concerned with leisure travel.
- All systems put pressure on the physical environment, especially that of host communities.

Supply increasingly leads demand for transport products

Historically, transport services have generally developed in response to economic and other demands. But it is increasingly difficult to be sure to what extent demand creates supply, or supply generates demand. As Shaw puts it, 'demand analysis in any transport industry poses problems because it cannot be viewed in isolation. Rather, it has inextricable links with supply. When an airline introduces service on a route, notable developments may follow' (1982, p. 13). The ability of supply to generate demand is clearly also true of roads and bridges. The Channel Tunnel between England and France, for example, is expected to be an important generator of new traffic when it is opened in 1994.

The supply effect can be seen in all types of travel, but it appears to be especially true of modern forms of leisure travel, which can be persuaded through effective marketing and promotion to switch its choices to alternative destinations. There is in Britain, for example, a huge potential demand for holidays in the USA. Whenever the dollar/pound exchange rate has been favourable to the British, the traffic has surged. The greatest obstacle to growth is the cost of travel across the Atlantic, despite the range of promotional fares available. If the cost of transport could be significantly reduced through new economies of scale, or through some technological, cost-saving breakthrough, there can be little doubt that demand would be led by the supply of cheaper transport.

The powerful leading effect of supply of transport in tourism markets is especially obvious in the case of islands, such as those in the Pacific area, where the development of new routes acts almost like a tap for new demand. The important point in travel and tourism is that supply and demand are essentially interactive. It is an interaction that can be exploited to good effect by transport marketing managers.

Functional role of transport in the tourist product

Although it is one of the five integral elements of travel and tourism products, modern transport is not normally a part of the motivation or attraction of a destination visit. There are some exceptions to this, such as steam railways, the Orient Express, or cruise ships, although the latter are better viewed as floating hotels or resorts than as forms of transport. The transport element, as Holloway described it (1985, p. 23), is only an 'enabling condition', i.e. a functional element essential to the existence and growth of tourism, but not of itself a sufficient reason for travel.

The role of transport in leisure travel was not always so functional. In the pioneering days of both public and private transport, journeys of all kinds, especially those by air and sea, could be presented as exciting, glamorous, and romantic. In those circumstances the journey was an adventure and an important part of travel motivation. By the 1980s, however, except possibly for children and first-time travellers by air and sea, the journey had lost most if not all of its earlier magic. Experienced travellers, especially those on business trips, increasingly see the journey element as a necessary but often unpleasant part of the trip. Journeys by public transport have to be paid for not only in money terms but also in the stress and strain of heavily congested access routes, queueing in crowded terminals, and increasing risk to personal safety. With private transport, the strain of driving along congested trunk routes and of finding parking space at the destination, has removed most of what was once the glamour of the open road.

This changing attitude towards a key experience within the travel and tourism product is most clearly evident among frequent business travellers. But it has many implications for the marketing of transport and especially for the way in which product 'benefits' for business users are developed and presented to prospective customers. In particular it encourages transport operators in the leisure industry to move closer to destination interests, which provide the principal motivation for journeys. This important point is explored later in the chapter.

The transport product

For charter airlines and long-distance coaches the transport element is no more than one component within the overall tourism product, and the marketing of such products is not normally the responsibility of transport operators. By contrast, although they may also negotiate links with accommodation and destination interests, scheduled transport operators have full responsibility to design and market specific products based on their services and route networks. They compete with these products for shares of passenger markets, and it is in this context that most transport marketing takes place.

As defined in Chapter 8, any specific service product offered to customers represents a combination or 'bundle' of components available at a specified price. The main components in the transport bundle are:

- Service availability and convenience (reflecting routes, schedules and capacity).
- Cost in comparison with competitors.
- The design and performance of the vehicle.
- Comfort, and any services offered in transit.
- Passenger handling at terminals and carparks.
- Convenience of booking and ticketing arrangements.
- Image and positioning of each operator.

Viewed from the customer's standpoint, the basic products offered by operators of the same type of transport, such as airlines or sea ferries, tend to be remarkably undifferentiated in comparison with the products offered in other sectors of the tourism industry. Perceived 'sameness' of product is an obvious problem for marketing managers and it is interesting to note the reasons for it. In what has traditionally been a closely regulated transport environment, formal and informal agreements between governments, other regulatory bodies, and other transport operators, served to produce virtual uniformity in the basic components of *the formal product* (see Chapter 8). In the case of international air transport until the late 1970s almost every aspect of the product, from price down to the smallest detail of in-flight services, was covered by agreements. The products were commonly offered in identical aircraft with the same cabin layouts.

In the more liberated or deregulated climate of the 1990s the use of the same type of equipment, shared terminals, and fierce price competition, still produce virtual uniformity in the formal product. As a result, most airline advertising has tended to focus on corporate images and the quality of service, rather than on promoting specific products. Apart from obvious distinctions between first-class, business-class, and economy-class products, and with limited but important exceptions such as Concorde, the traditional approach to marketing airline products, now appears rather sterile. As Shaw put it, 'the airline product is intangible, amorphous, and difficult to analyse' (1982: p. 114).

A more fertile approach to understanding transport products lies in the analysis of demand. This is a customer segmentation approach working from the profiles, attitudes, and behaviour of the identified groups in the total market with which the transport operator is concerned. Although the main components of supply remain the same, it is in the area of customer-orientated *product augmentation* (Chapter 8) that there is real room for manoeuvre and differentiation in the formulation of transport products. From this standpoint an operator's portfolio of products is best conceptualized as a portfolio of responses to the needs of customer segments. The knowledge an operator has of the profile and needs of its segments is the logical basis for effective marketing strategy and tactics. Such knowledge requires a massive commitment to customer databases and marketing research of the type discussed in Chapter 11. The same research serves also to identify the relevant links with other elements of the tourism product that can be exploited for marketing purposes.

The dominance of the external environment

Part One of the book emphasizes the ways in which the external environment surrounding all kinds of businesses dominates the marketing decisions of producers. In particular the marketing decisions of transport operators are influenced by their response to seven specific external factors, over most of which they have only very limited control. These factors are listed and briefly discussed below:

- Vehicle technology (major innovations).
- Information technology.
- Regulatory framework.
- Price of fuel.
- Economic growth or decline (national and international economy).
- Exchange-rate fluctuations.
- Environmental issues.

Vehicle technology

From private cars through cruise ships to aircraft, competition among manufacturers is constantly developing the capabilities of vehicles in terms of their size, seat capacity, speed, range, fuel efficiency, noise, and passenger comfort. Such changes affect the profitability of operations and can also influence customer choice. Over time, as noted earlier, the changes also determine which destinations can be reached within acceptable time and cost constraints. The development of wide-bodied long-haul jets, for example, made possible the rapid expansion of tourism between continents during the 1980s.

While the implications of developing vehicle technology for tourism markets are most obviously seen in public transport, the extension of car ownership and the increasing comfort, reliability, and efficiency of the vehicles, is equally vital to the market growth of many forms of tourism. Short weekend breaks, self-catering accommodation, and day visits to attractions are all highly dependent on car travel.

Information technology

The development of computers since the 1960s and the widespread application of the technology during the 1980s made it possible for passenger transport operators to deal efficiently with the increasing volume of business. Led by airlines, the process of reservations, can-cellations, ticketing, invoicing, options on routes and fares, is now handled by computers. These processes simultaneously generate a wealth of research data on the characteristics of customers, of great value in the marketing planning process. Information technology (IT) has also transformed the distribution process for travel and tourism generally. Many of the developments have been led by transport operators in search of greater cost-efficiency in the conduct of routine operations and, equally important, in the conduct and control of their marketing operations. New marketing linkages between product elements are greatly facilitated by the creation of interactive, on-line computer networks, bringing together, for example, the reservation systems of airlines, hotels, and car rental organizations. The airline-led international/global CRS systems are discussed in Chapter 18.

Regulatory framework

For most of the twentieth century, the operations of international and national passenger transport systems have been closely controlled and regulated in all countries, both for domestic and international movements. In air transport permissions to fly into airports, between countries, and through national air spaces come from treaty agreements between governments. They cover which airlines will be permitted, over what routes, with what capacity, and with what price ranges and options. The government agencies controlling these decisions, such as the Civil Aviation Authority (CAA) in the UK, are in effect participating directly in crucial areas of marketing decisions and acting in lieu of market forces. Whichever agency controls product capacity (supply of seats), and determines or influences price, obviously has a very powerful influence over demand.

Requiring non-commercial agencies or governments to act in lieu of market forces is increasingly seen as inefficient. Originating with legislation in 1978 covering USA domestic airlines, there has been a widespread international shift towards removing regulatory controls. There are strong arguments that the forces of supply and demand, and relatively unfettered competition between operators, produce a better way to determine air-transport markets than regulation. The same arguments have been applied to other forms of transport. The full, long-term effects of deregulation in the USA are still far from clear at the time of writing, and by 1990, of over 100 new entrants to the airline industry, the majority had failed and the evidence pointed to market dominance by four or five very large corporations.

In the early 1990s the pace of change in air-transport deregulation has been dramatic. 'The airline industry throughout the world is in the process of profound change. Fresh news about deregulation, privatisation, mergers, alliances, foreign ownership and other developments appears in the press almost every week' (Wheatcroft :1992, p. 5). Wheatcroft predicts that around the turn of the century there will be no more than around a dozen very large/global airlines with four based in the USA, four in Europe, and four in the Far East. He notes that at the end of 1990 there were fifteen airlines in which privatization had been completed, seventeen in which partial privatization was in progress, and a further ten in which it was under consideration. This is a major revolution since the early 1980s and a quantum leap in competition. It has profound marketing implications, especially as subsidies are removed from former state-owned airlines.

In Europe, where control of transport policy and competition rules has passed to the EC, a phased process of dismantling key elements of existing airline regulation took place as part of the process of clearing barriers to the Single Market, which came into force in 1993. The scope of these changes is too complex for analysis in this chapter, but they influence the evolving framework within which transport marketing takes place. Free market arguments for transport are not without critics, but the shift to deregulation appears unstoppable in the 1990s in most parts of the world.

Environmental issues

There are five main areas of environmental concern for transport. They are noise, emissions, use of energy, congestion, and waste production and disposal. In the 1980s these issues had only minor implications for the conduct of marketing. But they are all subjects for growing regulatory control in the 1990s, e.g. the EC draft policy statement on transport issued in 1992, and these regulations seem certain to affect future costs and the types of products which can be marketed. Short-haul journeys by air, for example, may be discouraged in favour of rail travel in some countries. Not all these issues are new, however, and airlines in particular have been active for two decades in reducing the noise impact around airports and increasing fuel efficiency.

Aircraft are subject to noise certification standards established by the International Civil Aviation Organization (ICAO). Emissions of carbon dioxide – produced by all forms of transportation using fossil fuels – are also under regulatory influence as carbon dioxide is the principal global warming gas. Aircraft emissions of carbon dioxide are estimated at 1 to 1.5 per cent of global warming, and are small in comparison with those of motor vehicles, although large measured in emissions per passenger carried.

Congestion of transport systems, e.g. at airports and on motorways, is a major contributor to environmental costs, as it leads to delays, extra fuel usage and increased emissions. In Europe air traffic control systems (ATCs) are an important cause of congestion. Europe had thirty-one different ATCs and thirty-three different computer languages to control its air traffic in 1992.

Engineering and maintenance operations for transport systems generate special types of waste, some of them highly toxic, which are subject to increasingly stringent disposal regulations. The Environmental Protection Act of 1990 in the UK means that an operator's responsibility for waste now continues to and beyond its final disposal. CFC gases, which damage the earth's ozone layer, are also under regulatory control.

In the early 1990s leading airlines set up environmental departments and introduced environmental-management programmes. British Airways is a leader in this field and aims to integrate environmental considerations into all the airline's normal business practices. In addition, many airlines now recognize the importance of sustaining the quality of the natural environment of the destinations they fly to, respecting their role as one of the principal determinants of future leisure travel. It is perhaps ironic that, as the traditional regulation of routes, capacity and prices is being lifted from transport operators, new forms of regulation for environmental purposes are being introduced. They appear certain to influence future marketing.

Other external factors

External economic factors generally are discussed in Part One of this book and in Chapter 9 on pricing. Economic growth or recession obviously has a major influence on the market volume carried by transport operators for business and leisure purposes, with the latter especially susceptible to fluctuations in exchange rates. The massive power of economic and political factors over market demand has been highly visible in the economic recession of 1990-2. For 1990, it was estimated by the International Air Transport Association (IATA) that the costs of the world's scheduled airlines exceeded their revenue by $2.7 billion dollars. It was the worst loss suffered at that time since 1945. In 1991, affected by international economic recession and the Gulf War, international airlines lost a further $4 billion, and several went out of business.

The reality of these figures in terms of load factors, revenue yield, and the crucial importance of the margin for marketing purposes, was neatly summarized by Harvey Elliot in the context of American Airlines. 'If one less passenger flew on each of American's flights (in 1991), its annual revenue would fall by $114 million. The calculation is simple. Each passenger carried on the airline's 854,461 departures last year paid, on average, $134 for a ticket. Remove one passenger per flight and, with costs fixed, the missing $114 million carried through directly to the bottom line.' In fact American Airlines, the world's largest carrier, posted a $240 million loss in that year. (*The Times*, : 22 February 92).

Operational constraints on public transport operations

The previous section considered the influence of factors in the external environment on marketing decisions. This section focuses on the internal constraints that arise from the nature of operating a passenger-transport system.

Capital investment and fixed costs

A principal characteristic of any modern transport operation is the high level of capital investment and fixed costs that is required in terms of purchasing and maintaining vehicles and equipment, setting up and maintaining route networks, and employing staff to operate the system. The level of investment is especially high for airlines, with modern long-haul 'jumbo jets' costing up to £100 million each at 1992 prices. But the same characteristic, relative to the size of their revenues, applies equally to shipping lines, railway systems, or to bus and coach operations. In each case expensive new equipment, often associated with increased seating capacity, is usually justified on the grounds that through more efficient operation it will lower the operating cost per passenger seat mile and thus permit potentially lower fares to be charged, or more profit to be made at the existing prices. A vital proviso in this argument is that the potentially lower costs can only produce real savings, *if* enough of the seats on offer are sold.

A second dominant characteristic acting as a constraint on marketing decisions is that the committed costs, or 'fixed' costs, as they are known, of operating any service are high and the variable costs low. Accountants and economists have different conventions for deciding which aspects of costs are fixed and which are variable. Strictly, for airlines, fuel costs and landing charges are variable costs since they are not incurred if a flight does not take place. In practical terms, once the decision is taken to fly a particular route at a particular time, all the main costs become effectively 'fixed', since they have to be paid regardless of the number of seats sold. While full aircraft use more fuel than empty ones, the difference measured on a per seat/mile basis is very small. From a marketing standpoint, it concentrates the mind to recognize that any seat sales achieved after the decision is made to operate a service, which may be weeks before it is performed, represent over 90 per cent revenue gain. This revenue gain goes either to cover committed fixed costs or, once the break-even load factor is reached, it represents gross profit.

Load factor yield, and fleet utilization

Because of the investment and high fixed cost implications of passenger-transport operations, there are three key measures of operational efficiency that are especially relevant to marketing managers. The most critical measure for marketing is seat occupancy, known technically as the *load factor*. The second vital measure is *yield*, a revenue factor defined as load factor × average seat price paid. For example, a load factor of 55 per cent for a flight in which half the passengers were paying business fares, and the others full economy fare, would yield very much more revenue than a load factor of 60 per cent if only a quarter of the passengers were paying business fares and the others were travelling on heavily discounted promotional fares.

The third key measure is *fleet utilization*. As in any form of production based on expensive plant, the more intensively a piece of equipment is used, the better the performance in terms of revenue achieved against the fixed costs incurred. If, for example, an expensive aircraft (on long-haul routes) can be kept in the air and flying with more than a break-even load of passengers, for an average of some 10 hours in every 24 around the year (including allowance for routine inspections and servicing), it can obviously generate more revenue to cover its

fixed costs than the same aircraft flying for an average of only 8 hours a day. Utilization is partly a function of efficient maintenance and scheduling the network to achieve the shortest possible turnround of vehicles; but it is much more a function of generating sufficient demand to justify the flight frequency.

The role of marketing in passenger transport is not confined solely to achieving higher load factors and increased yield and utilization at the margin. Nevertheless, the imperative need to maintain the level of seat occupancy on each service performed, and at the same time support economically high utilization rates throughout the year, underlies all transport marketing thinking. The absolute importance of achieving marginal revenue can be seen in the break-even load factors of scheduled European air transport carriers, which varied in the years between 1978 and 1984 from 50 per cent to 53 per cent. Actual load factors achieved in the same years varied from 50.7 per cent to 55.4 per cent (Wheatcroft and Lipman: 1986, p. 35). Only in two of those years did the load factor exceed the break-even level by more than 2 percentage points; in none of them did the carriers generate sufficient revenue for their investment needs. Airlines gained only brief respite in the late 1980s, before load factors fell again in 1990 and 1991 and losses escalated, leading to the demise of several famous names such as Pan Am.

The nature of the marketing task for passenger transport operators

The marketing process summarized in Figure 2.1 and explained in Parts Two and Three of this book is as applicable to transport operators as to any other producer of consumer products. The marketing tasks in passenger transport derive logically from the characteristics of operations, and the internal and external environment in which they are conducted, as explained in the preceding two sections. The main tasks may now be summarized under the headings of strategic and tactical marketing, which apply to all forms of public transport operators, whether by rail, road, air, or sea.

Strategic marketing

The strategic marketing task has four main elements. The first, through extensive use of marketing-research techniques and continuous passenger monitoring, is to provide forecasts of market potential, on the basis of which future operational networks, schedules, and the associated investment can be planned. Because fleet purchases along with other investment needs are geared to revenue forecasts (volume of customers × the average price they will pay), the ability of marketing managers to provide realistic inputs to demand forecasting is crucial to the profitable development of any transport business. Estimates of traffic flows have to be built up route by route, separately for each main market segment. In practice, while forecasting models are normally the responsibility of transport economists and statisticians, the quality of the marketing-research inputs relating to segments, products, customer satisfaction and market developments, is vital.

At the time of writing, a high profile demonstration of this strategic role is being fought out on a grand scale by passenger transport competitors targeting travel across the channel between England and France. The Channel Tunnel, with its terminals and system of shuttle trains, opens in 1994. It is essentially a privately funded enterprise that has to generate profit and begin to pay back borrowing and capital estimated at £8.4 billion in 1992. The tunnel has to fight for market share with the existing sea ferry operators in addition to its endeavour to make the total market expand. The ferries and the seaports have to fight back, and have invested heavily in facilities, ships and marketing developments with which to do so.

The scene is set for an epic struggle in the mid-1990s. The strategic ability of marketing managers to forecast and capture their targeted segments with competitive products matching customer needs will be vital to the winners (see also Chapter 15).

Inevitably, estimates of traffic flows will always be surrounded by risk because of the unpredictable nature of the business environment. But the better the operator's knowledge of customer behaviour, the better the chance of reducing the risk. Marketing strategy can be seen, in this context, as contributing to the balance every operator seeks to achieve between his portfolio of products and markets.

As part of the process of converting the estimated market potential into real revenue, the second element in marketing strategy lies in the way in which operators match, and seek to lead, their competitors in the continuous struggle for market shares. In an increasingly deregulated market environment, strategy tends to focus on identifying operators' strengths from a customer standpoint. These strengths may be developed into corporate images or 'positions', built into the customer appeal of products and communicated through advertising to targeted segments. At the highly sensitive margin of business either side of the break-even load factor, uncommitted potential customers may have their choice influenced by positive or negative images of different operators. Recognition of the power of such images explains the considerable commitment of operators to both corporate and product advertising.

The third common element in strategic marketing lies in the effort all operators now tend to put into creating and retaining regular, repeat buyers of their services. Mostly business travellers, a small number of frequent users may provide a high proportion of total revenue. For example, 20 per cent of customers could easily generate 50 per cent of all revenue on some routes, because of the fares they pay and the frequency with which they travel. Such customers are worth careful cultivation, and one of the strategies used is to create schemes to reward people who make repeat purchases with the same operator. Traditional season tickets have been available for many years on rail and road commuter routes, but competition between airlines is generating new forms of loyalty schemes, which are likely to develop further in the rest of this century (see also Chapter 16). Identifying the small number of customers who are very important to the business is not restricted to transport operators; it is now also common in accommodation marketing, again mainly for business travellers.

The fourth element in marketing strategy lies in the way in which some transport operators are increasingly shifting their focus outwards, away from the performance of their traditional roles as operators of vehicles, routes and terminals, towards linkages with other elements of the overall travel and tourism product – in other words, the extent to which providers of transport seek strategic marketing links with destination interests and with the distribution network for travel products. The scope for these links is already wide, and ranges from relatively limited links with accommodation providers and attractions all the way up to full integration with marketing organizations such as tour operators or wholesalers. From the earliest days of railways, links with terminal hotels were seen as necessary to the efficient development of transport businesses. A century later some airlines formed similar links with hotel groups for exactly the same reasons. In leisure travel the logical extreme of the linkage strategy is seen most clearly in the charter airlines that are integrated with tour operators in Britain, such as Britannia (Thomson Holidays), and Airtours International (Airtours). In this latter context the charter fleets provide a vital but essentially functional role within a wider product, of which the marketing is undertaken by the principal and not by the transport operator.

Closer linkages between transport and the other elements of the product, especially with destination interests, appear highly probable in the rest of the twentieth century. In the case of the Channel crossing between England and France, most sea ferry companies have already formed functional links with accommodation interests such as holiday cottages in France (Gites) and campsite operators, and most offer short-break packages in which the transport is just a component of the overall product. This appears to be more than product augmentation and a real shift into packaging of the kind discussed in Chapter 24.

The formation of strategic networking alliances between international airlines in the post-regulatory era of market liberalization and growing privatization, has been one of the most striking developments of the last 5 years. It seems to be set to continue. Such alliances are designed to facilitate the airline's 'core business' but, through the medium of CRS, they lend themselves naturally to strategic links with destination interests, too. The alliances make it possible to exploit and facilitate global computerization and reservation-system linkages, and develop dominant marketing positions; they offer ways to achieve the vital marginal increments to seat occupancy and yield; to share marketing costs, and achieve a competitive edge in a fiercely competitive market place. There are also economies of scale in operational costs, e.g. shared engineering services. Recent illustrations, although the pattern changes continually, are British Airways' links with USAir, Qantas and TAT; and Swissair with KLM, SAS and Austrian Airlines. Swissair also has links with Delta (USA) and Singapore Airlines.

Marketing expenditure in transport operations

It is not easy to get a precise understanding of the level of expenditure on marketing by transport operators. The full marketing cost includes not just advertising and sales promotion but the major investment in providing CRS systems, securing distribution channels, and paying commissions. In 1990, for air transport, the average figure for 'ticketing (including commissions) and sales promotion represents almost 18 per cent of total operating costs of scheduled airlines of ICAO member states' (Doganis: 1991, p. 167). Singapore Airline and Qantas were estimated at over 25 per cent, and it seems likely that even these are fairly conservative figures.

If one works on an estimate of an *average* marketing to sales ratio of 20 per cent in the early 1990s, it is interesting to compare it with the net profit generated by international airlines expressed as a percentage of sales revenue. According to Doganis, it has reached 5 per cent only once in the last 25 years (in 1965) and for several years there have been massive losses. The years 1990 to 1992 have been the worst that international airlines have experienced. To continue marketing expenditure at around the 20 per cent level is probably the best proof of its perceived effectiveness that one can muster.

Tactical marketing

Tactical marketing in passenger transport takes many forms, reflecting the wide range of promotional tools discussed in Chapter 16. The tools are used with one principal focus - to secure on a daily basis throughout the operating year the vital marginal increment in customer purchases, which can make such a major difference to profit or loss in the high fixed cost operations of passenger-transport systems. Of course some routes at some times of the year are likely to be fully booked. But for the bulk of any transport operator's planned services, extra demand at the margin makes a great difference to annual profitability. Around the break-even level of seat occupancy, or in achieving additional hours of profitable utilization for expensive vehicles, the contribution of tactical marketing is to mould demand. The object is to manipulate customer behaviour to buy more of the available supply or capacity of products than would occur without such expenditure.

On first consideration, this role for tactical marketing could be confused with a production or sales-orientated business philosophy. On reflection, it should be clear that there is nothing necessarily product-orientated about demand manipulation. The success of promotion is measured in revenue achieved in relation to the size of the marketing budget deployed, and this in turn is directly related to the knowledge marketing managers have built up of the profile, needs and the probable behaviour of the customer segments with which they deal. Chapter 14 stressed that commitment to knowing the customer is a necessary prerequisite for the planning and execution of all forms of effective promotion. The more that promotion is segment- and product-specific, the greater the need for a detailed understanding of target customers.

For transport operators, most tactical marketing will tend to be segment specific. This is true whether the object is to seize and exploit a marketing opportunity resulting from some unexpected event in the external environment, or to defend a position from the threats posed by less favourable circumstances, or by the actions of competitors. For example, railways usually do not need to reduce the fares paid by commuters, because their services are overcrowded at commuter times. Similarly, they do not seek to reduce the fares paid by first-class travellers, because most of them are travelling on business and their demand is known to be relatively inelastic to changes in price. On the other hand, operators have every incentive to use price to promote use of the network outside peak periods. A common response is to devise segment-specific fares with conditions designed to prevent the 'dilution of revenue', as it is known, if passengers switch from higher fares they otherwise would have paid.

The whole concept of segment-specific fares, often accompanied with the presentation of services as special products, is found internationally under a multitude of different names. Advanced Purchase Excursion Fares (APEX), which are widely used in Europe and North America, are examples of the same concept of segment-specific fares and products. They usually depend on minimum lengths of stay at a destination and restricted times of travel, to reduce the possibility of revenue dilution. The object is to generate the marginal revenue on specific operations that would otherwise be performed with many empty seats. Where it is possible to provide group fares for pre-booked parties, operators will invariably allow a very significant price reduction; in this context groups are just another illustration of segment-specific promotional activity.

Reflecting the many unpredictable variations in the external business environment, there is always a strong element of contingency planning in marketing tactics for transport operators. Each year brings its own examples. In the early months of 1986, following record carryings in 1985, transatlantic airlines were confidently planning for a similar volume or some increment on the previous year. They had organized their network planning and capacity on that basis, and most were committed to investment in fleet replacement based on revenue forecasts. Over the period May to July the impact of three events produced a slump in passenger volumes of crisis proportions. The US dollar weakened against European currencies compared with 1985; the American reprisal raid on Libya, following terrorist attacks on European airports, had a considerable psychological effect on prospective US travellers; and the nuclear pollution threat from the leak at Chernobyl power station added to travellers' worries. These events combined to cause an abrupt drop in holiday travel out of the USA to Europe, which is estimated in some places to have fallen in volume by some 40 per cent against forecast. At one point British Airways was estimated to be losing up to $500,000 a day in actual revenue compared with its target.

Crisis conditions of this magnitude required a massive promotional response, far in excess of any planned budget. A series of promotions and competitions, designed to restore confidence and promote American visits to Europe, added to the planned marketing costs by many millions of dollars. But such costs must be compared with the size of the daily losses. By the end of the summer transatlantic traffic was beginning to return to the levels forecast, but it was too late to recover the volume lost over the peak summer period. In marketing terms the tactics employed were clearly the only way to limit the damage, which could not have been foreseen. While this example is an extreme case of responding to crisis, the perishability of service products, and the need to cover the high fixed costs of operation, will always oblige marketing managers to devise contingency plans and be able to implement them at great speed. Only 5 years later, in 1991, British Airways had to respond again to an even bigger crisis (see Part Six).

Case studies supporting this chapter

Part Six of the book contains one case relevant to marketing airlines. It sets out the rationale and operation of British Airway's 'The World's Biggest Offer' promotion, a global campaign mounted in 1991 in response to the dramatic slump in air travel, which occurred during the Gulf War.

Chapter summary

This chapter stresses the functional links between the development and capacity of transport operations and the demand for travel and tourism products. Although transport is only one of the five elements of the overall product, and performs an enabling rather than a motivating role, accessibility is a fundamental condition for the development and growth of any destination. The extent to which transport marketing is constrained by constantly changing factors in the external business environment, and the pressures of operational constraints, are explained. The continuous preoccupation with achieving revenue above the break-even level is emphasized. The contrast between the overall tourism products that ultimately determine travel flows and the specific transport products that are the focus of transport marketing campaigns is discussed. The route to product augmentation through a detailed and carefully researched knowledge of consumer segments is stressed.

Throughout, this chapter seeks to define and illuminate the characteristics of marketing strategy and tactics practised in all forms of transport, rather than focus on the specifics of either airline, rail, or other forms of surface travel. Undoubtedly there are aspects of marketing which are particular to individual forms of transport, but they are derived from the general principles outlined here and they do not alter the conclusions drawn.

The chapter does not deal specifically with charter airlines because these are referred to later in Chapter 24. In practice most charter airlines adopt a form of *industrial marketing* in which they negotiate their routes, products, and capacity, with a relatively small number of major clients. Major charter operators are owned or linked financially with tour-operating companies, and usually they do not market their products directly to individual customers. In these circumstances charter airlines provide a vital operational function for tour operators, but it is the latter who take on the responsibility for marketing to the public.

23

Marketing accommodation

Apart from same-day visits from home, all tourism means staying away for periods of one or more nights and thus requiring overnight accommodation. Accommodation is therefore described as one of the five integral components of the travel and tourism product defined in Chapter 8. The many different forms of accommodation and the ways in which they are marketed have a massive influence on visitor choices, behaviour, and the types of product they buy. In terms of influence over demand there are strong similarities between accommodation and transport marketing, and the two forms of marketing are increasingly being brought together with the interests of destinations, to achieve maximum impact through co-ordinated activities.

As with transport, the early development of accommodation was not concerned with leisure travel. Historically, inns and hotels were developed to meet the needs of those required to travel in the conduct of commerce and industry, and in the administration of countries and empires. Since the eighteenth century, the development of accommodation for travellers has been inextricably bound up with servicing the growing and changing needs of transport systems. Inns and the forerunners of modern hotels were located logically in cities and ports and along the routes that linked them, for much the same reasons that modern hotels are located in areas served by airports and road systems.

Chapter 22 noted that transport systems are still vitally concerned with non-tourism products, such as journeys to work and the carriage of goods. Accommodation services also have important dimensions unconnected with travel and tourism, such as institutional and welfare provision, accommodation and the related provision of catering in sectors as diverse as schools, prisons, hospitals, the armed services, and the care of the elderly. In all these areas of hospitality the influence of marketing is being felt, but this chapter is of course only concerned with tourism products.

Thus, when considering the meaning of marketing for transport and accommodation operations, it must be recognized that tourism contributes only part of the turnover in each sector. Many hotels, depending obviously on their locations, also provide food and drink for residents in their surrounding local communities who are not visitors.

In the latter part of the twentieth century most of the major national and international hotel groups are still very much orientated to the needs of business travellers. The provision of accommodation designed for leisure needs in tourist destinations, however, has become a major area of market-led development. In the sunshine resorts of the USA, Europe, and the Pacific area, thousands of resort hotels have been built specifically to cater for the needs of vacationers. Similar developments in timeshare resorts also owe their origins to leisure travel. In all such cases developments have exploited the market potential made possible by modern transport systems.

This chapter begins by defining the constituent parts of the serviced and non-serviced sectors of accommodation and their role in the tourism product. It considers accommodation products as experiences and discusses business characteristics common to all forms of commercial accommodation operations. The marketing tasks for accommodation suppliers are considered under the headings of strategy and tactics, and the implications of these for the size of marketing budgets in the sector are reviewed.

Defining tourist accommodation

For the purposes of this chapter, tourist accommodation is deemed to include all establishments offering overnight accommodation on a commercial or quasi-commercial basis to all categories of visitor. The marketing of catering is therefore excluded from the discussion. Also excluded are all forms of privately owned accommodation used for holidays, such as second homes, caravans or chalets in private ownership, boats, and wholly-owned apartments in condominiums.

'Quasi-commercial' refers to the many tourist accommodation products outside the commercial sector, for which a charge is made to contribute to costs (even if a subsidy is involved). For example, the British Youth Hostels Association (YHA) is a membership organization that provides a national network of hostels in the UK, mostly for young people willing to use inexpensive dormitory and shared accommodation. YHA is a non-profit-making body but, in the context of its corporate objectives, it operates increasingly on commercial principles to secure the revenue needed for its refurbishment and development programmes. Other forms of quasi-commercial

accommodation products may be found in colleges and universities, many of which have begun in recent years to market their accommodation capacity for conferences and for holidays, at times when students are not in residence. Such operations are increasingly required not only to cover their direct operating costs but also to make a contribution towards the overhead costs of their parent institutions.

An important distinction in accommodation for visitors is the split between serviced and non-serviced types. Serviced means that staff are available on the premises to provide some services such as cleaning, meals and bars, and room service. The availability of such services, even if they are not in fact used, is included in the price charged. Non-serviced means that the sleeping accommodation is provided furnished on a rental basis, normally for a unit comprising several beds, such as an apartment, villa, cottage or caravan. While services for the provision of meals, bars and shops may be available on a separate commercial basis, as in a holiday village, they are not included in the price charged for the accommodation.

The serviced sector ranges from first-class and luxury hotels, which provide full service on a 24 hours a day basis at relatively high cost, all the way down to homely bed and breakfast establishments, which may only operate informally for a few weeks in the year. The non-serviced sector, which is known in Britain under the unattractive label of 'self-catering accommodation', comprises a wide range of different units, including villas, apartments, chalets, cottages and caravans, the bulk of which are rented equipped but with no personal services included in the published price. Some of these units, e.g. in converted historic buildings, are furnished with antiques and may cost more per person night than four-star serviced accommodation. The bulk of self-catering units, however, still cater for a budget-priced market, and the cost per person per night is very much less than could be obtained in the serviced sector.

In the late twentieth century there are so many variations of serviced and non-serviced accommodation products that the distinction is often blurred in practice, although it remains useful for the purposes of analysis and discussion of marketing implications. For example, the accommodation in many holiday villages and timeshare resorts is marketed as 'self-catering' units. But within the village or resort there is often extensive provision of bars, restaurants, coffee shops and a wide range of other services available for purchase, although not paid for in the initial holiday price. In these circumstances the real difference to the operator between serviced and non-serviced accommodation looks increasingly irrelevant. In the customer's perception and from a marketing standpoint, however, there may be all the difference in the world. The endeavour by accommodation interests and tour operators to keep down published holiday prices explains much of the growth in non-serviced tourist accommodation in recent years.

Using the serviced/non-serviced split, discussed above, the types of accommodation referred to in this chapter are summarized in Figure 23.1. The boxes in the diagram divide each of the two accommodation sectors by destination and by route, because this fundamentally influences the nature of the accommodation products that are offered. It further distinguishes segments of users for business and other non-leisure purposes from users for leisure and holidays. Non-leisure purposes include stays away from home on family business such as school visits, funerals, or stays in an area while seeking a new house or apartment, and so on.

Functional role of accommodation in the overall tourism product

When the purpose of a visit to a destination or an overnight stay en route is for business or other non-leisure purposes, it is obvious that

Market segment / Sector	Serviced sector		Non-serviced sector (self-catering)	
	Destination	Routes	Destination	Routes
Business and other non-leisure	City/town hotels (Monday–Friday) Resort hotels for conferences, exhibitions Educational establishments	Motels Inns Airport hotels Budget hotels	Apartments	Not applicable
Leisure and holiday	Resort hotels Guesthouse/pensions Farmhouses City/town hotels (Friday–Sunday) Some educational establishments	Motels Bed and breakfast Inns Budget hotels	Apart hotels Condominia/timeshare Holiday villages Holiday centres/camps Caravan/chalet parks Gîtes Cottages Villas Apartments/flats Some motels	Touring pitches for caravans, tents, recreation vehicles YHA Some motels and budget hotels

Figure 23.1 *Principal serviced and non-serviced types of accommodation used in tourism, by market segment*

accommodation is not normally a part of the trip motivation or any part of the destination's attraction. Rooms, serviced or otherwise, provide a necessary facility that makes it possible, convenient, and comfortable to engage in the primary reason for travel. In marketing terms, factors of locational convenience and high standards of comfort and efficiency are therefore the primary elements to be built into accommodation products. Within their price band the extent to which the primary elements are believed to be delivered is the basis for customer choice and the platform for communicating product benefits through promotional means.

For holiday and leisure purposes, accommodation plays a very different role in the tourism product. While a destination's attractions are likely to remain the dominant motivation for most visitors, customers' destination choices are also influenced by their perceptions and expectations of the accommodation available. Sometimes, as with repeat trips to stay at the same hotel or caravan park, the image and quality of the accommodation may be strong enough to make it a primary rather than a secondary aspect of destination choice. More often, however, the destination's appeal is the more important element in motivation and choice of destination.

Leisure visitors are also likely to spend many hours of a stay in their accommodation, especially if the weather is poor. Serviced or non-serviced, their trip and destination enjoyment will be highly geared to perceived value provided, and satisfaction experienced with the bedrooms, bathrooms, and any other rooms and facilities provided. This holds good for tented pitches in camping sites as well as for bedrooms in five-star resort hotels offering high standards of service.

In other words, for leisure purposes, accommodation is integrally related to the attractions of a destination as well as part of the facilities. While transport in the late twentieth century appears to be losing much of its former

glamour and appeal as part of the attractions of a trip, it appears probable that accommodation is moving in the opposite direction and enhancing its appeal. Current marketing trends to shorter stays suggest that destination and accommodation marketing are likely to come even closer together in a logical partnership of mutual interests.

The accommodation product as an experience

It is worth restating that accommodation products of all types are perceived by customers as experiences. The experience is organized by suppliers to meet the identified needs and benefits sought by customer segments, as described in Chapters 7 and 8, and it comprises a series of service operations. For larger organizations, these operations correspond with operating departments, of which the most important are:

- *Booking services* – handling enquiries and bookings, including telephone, mail and computerized systems.
- *Reception/checkout services* – registering arrivals and departures, checking bookings and allocating rooms, possibly associated with support services, such as baggage handling – includes invoicing and settling accounts.
- *Rooms/site services* – delivering rooms or self-catering units cleaned, checked, ready to occupy.
- *Food and beverage* – (if provided) including restaurants, bars and coffee shops.
- *Other services* – (if provided) including shops, leisure facilities, secretarial services, dry cleaning, and all other services.

Product experiences are complex, and are affected by physical elements (such as food and drink); sensual benefits (experienced through sight, sound, touch, smell, and conveyed by the quality of buildings and their furnishings); and psychological benefits experienced as mental states of well-being, status, comfort and satisfaction (see, for example, Sasser *et al.*: 1978, p. 10). For holiday visitors, the perceived benefits of the accommodation product are likely to be closely associated with the benefits provided by the destination's attractions. In other words, a successful destination may provide a 'halo' effect for its accommodation, and an unattractive destination experience will have the opposite effect.

In Chapter 8 an accommodation example was used to explain recommended product formulation methods for tourism, organized around an analysis of target customer segment's needs and benefits sought. The basic components of *core formal* and *augmented* products were described. and are not repeated here although they are completely relevant to this chapter.

The nature of the accommodation business

This section focuses on five particular characteristics of any accommodation business, serviced or non-serviced, which strongly influence the way in which marketing is conducted at the strategic and tactical level. The commercial accommodation sector displays of course the special characteristics common to service producers, which were defined and discussed in some depth in Chapter 3, and which underlie the management of the marketing functions discussed throughout Part Five of the book. They are generally assumed in this chapter but not repeated in any detail. Of particular relevance here are:

- Choice of location.
- Existence of peaks and troughs in demand.
- Influence of room sales on profits.
- Low variable costs of operation, especially at the margin.
- Focus on 'bookers', not occupancy levels.

Location

Location tends to dominate all accommodation operations. It determines the customer mix the business can achieve, and therefore the direction of marketing strategy and tactics. Location also largely determines the profitability of an operation. Where feasibility studies are undertaken to investigate the value of alternative sites before investment in new facilities, the inherent demand potential for each location under investigation is always the primary consideration. Of course once an accommodation unit is established, location of operations becomes fixed for the lifetime of the asset. Whereas an airline can move its fleet around the world to serve alternative destinations as its markets justify, a hotel is an immovable fixture. It has to use its skills in marketing to overcome any difficulties that may emerge after the initial location is determined.

Many of the difficulties experienced in accommodation marketing are in fact difficulties stemming from external changes affecting the market potential of the locations in which they are established. For example, seaside resort hotels in Britain, which relied on the traditional summer holiday market, were in considerable difficulty in the 1980s because their locations were no longer able to attract the volume of holiday demand for which they were originally built. For very different reasons, associated with over-investment, hotels in Singapore faced very difficult times in the late 1980s because too much capacity was built to accommodate a demand that did not grow at the rate anticipated by such limited feasibility studies as were undertaken. Greater commitment to sales and marketing was the inevitable response of the Singapore hotels in a successful attempt to influence demand. Marketing of course cannot cure all problems. In the not uncommon circumstances faced in Singapore, many hotels are forced to operate at a loss for as long as their resources allow or until the market expands. The only alternative is to sell properties, which in a buyer's market, usually means a massive capital loss. Such forced sales are a common phenomenon in the industry, especially among smaller businesses with limited financial resources.

Less obviously, the type and architectural style of accommodation provision influences many destinations no less than they are influenced by it. In vacation destinations certainly the physical appearance of hotels, apartments and other accommodation buildings becomes part of the image as well as part of the physical environment of a destination. The attractions of the new island destinations on the Great Barrier Reef in Australia are in fact identified with the physical appearance of the accommodation structures built upon them; the image and attractions of Austrian ski resorts are highly dependent on the traditional wooden chalet style of hotel building, which gives them a distinctive appeal and position in prospective customers' minds. In Britain Brighton's image and appeal is strongly associated with the fine Victorian architecture of its promenade hotels, while in Singapore the appeal of Raffles Hotel is an important element in the destination's image. In some Spanish resorts and in Honolulu, for example, there is evidence that the over-dense construction of functional but ugly buildings of no architectural distinction is creating negative images in the minds of some prospective customers.

Business peaks and troughs

By weeks in the year and days in the week, nearly all forms of accommodation are vulnerable to highly variable demand patterns. These reflect the nature of the market demand the location sustains. Thus hotels in many towns and cities in northern Europe can normally expect high occupancy from business travellers from Mondays to Thursdays, and the peak of their occupancy in the autumn and spring; business falls at weekends and in the July–August period. Most self-catering units by the seaside can anticipate full demand in a

period of little over 12 weeks, and many still close completely for around 5 months of the year. Accommodation is not unique in this existence of peaks and troughs, but it is a matter of particular concern with which marketing managers are continuously engaged.

Marketing efforts cannot reverse these natural locational rhythms of demand, but campaigns can be targeted around identified segments to lessen the impact and to generate increased business at the margin.

Profit is linked to room-night sales

Although sales of room-nights, especially in the serviced hotels sector, seldom contribute more than around 50 per cent of total sales revenue, the average contribution of room sales to profitability is very much greater. According to Horwath and Horwath, in London in the 1980s the gross profit on room sales averaged over 75 per cent (defined as room sales less room operating costs), while the gross profit on food and beverage sales was in the region of 20 per cent. The effect of high fixed costs means that the profitability of additional or marginal room sales is often greater than 75 per cent, while the marginal profitability of food and beverage sales tends to remain fairly constant.

Of course the level of room occupany directly affects the sale of food and beverages within a hotel and such other services as a hotel provides. Effective merchandising to customers once they are 'in-house' is a logical marketing approach to increase total turnover. Accordingly, by the nature of the accommodation business, the main focus and effort of marketing has to be on room-night sales. In practice, because nine out of ten people typically make reservations as distinct from impulse purchases by walking in off the street, this means focusing on bookings that are made in advance of the customers' arrival. The only exception to this natural focus on room-nights and bookings occurs, for example, where hotels develop banqueting business, which does not lead to overnight accommodation. The focus on accommodation sales and on advance bookings is even more important for self-catering operators.

Targeting 'bookers', not room or bed occupancy

Following on from the previous section on room night sales, it is important to clarify a common misunderstanding about the nature of the accommodation business – that marketing focuses on room or bed occupancy. The preoccupation with occupancy is certainly understandable for reasons already discussed, but marketing targets cannot sensibly be expressed as occupancy levels. Occupancy levels represent the *results* of marketing effort, and they are a retrospective statistical measure of marketing success or failure. Marketing targets are always *prospective customers* and, to use an unattractive but useful word, not just customers but *bookers*.

A *booker* is a customer, or an agent of the customer, who makes a reservation for one or more persons, for one or more nights, in any form of accommodation. Thus, a person making a family booking for two rooms over 7 nights for four people (14 room-nights and 28 bed-nights), is a proper target for marketing strategy and tactics. A secretary who makes hotel reservations for one or more members of a company may never see a hotel or meet its staff, but he or she is a 'booker'. The secretary of a national association, responsible for organizing an annual conference for members, may be seeking several hundred room-nights in more than one hotel, but is also a booker, and so on. Medlik uses the term 'buying agent' to distinguish those who book on behalf of customers, from the customers themselves (Medlik: 1989, p. 22).

In the holiday parks sector of accommodation, offering caravans and chalets for rent, marketing is traditionally considered in terms of unit sales or 'static' unit rentals. These terms are no more than trade jargon, and logically the marketing task in this sector, as in the others, is to identify, persuade, sell to, and satisfy targeted groups of bookers and buying agents.

High fixed costs of operation

The marketing implications for service businesses operating with high fixed costs and low variable costs are discussed in several parts of this book and require little further comment here. Suffice it to note that, once the fixed costs of operation have been covered at the break-even level of occupancy, the marginal costs of operating an additional, otherwise empty, room are negligible in all sectors of accommodation. Beyond the break-even level the contribution to gross profit of additional room sales is very high, especially for self-catering operations, where the marginal costs are even lower than in the serviced sector.

Because the marginal cost of supplying an additional product is low, accommodation suppliers are often tempted to reduce prices in an attempt to achieve sales, especially last-minute sales before unsold capacity is lost forever. As Kotas put it, 'the higher the proportion of fixed costs to total costs, the wider the range of price discretion' (Kotas: 1975, p. 32).

The nature of the marketing task for accommodation businesses

Although, ironically, his company was taken over a few months after this statement, the former president of Holiday Inns succinctly summarized the marketing task, as follows:

> All segments of our travel and tourism business have become more competitive. A growing number of competitors offer their products to the same customer groups . . . travellers have a wider range of choices than ever before for matching a hotel to their particular travel needs. Those needs change

according to the travel purpose. Unless a company can understand those changing needs and deliver a quality product and services appropriately targeted to specific customers needs, wants, and expectations, that business cannot survive (TTRA: 1986, p. 1).

Strategic marketing tasks

There are four main elements in the strategic marketing response that accommodation suppliers make to their external business environment, and the operational characteristics previously noted. These are:

● Planning the most profitable business mix of segments and products/price ranges, having regard to yield rather than volume.
● Deciding the position or image each accommodation unit (or chain of units) should occupy.
● Encouraging and rewarding frequent users.

● Developing marketing integration between units in common ownership (chains) or units in individual ownership (voluntary co-operatives).

Planning the business mix

In the context of the demand potential inherent in each location the basic strategic decision for accommodation businesses is to determine the optimum, or most profitable mix of segments, for whose needs specific products may be created and promoted. For example, a city centre hotel will obviously target clients travelling for business purposes, a resort will draw different categories of leisure visitors, and so on. Figure 23.2 provides a fairly typical illustration of a customer mix which has important implications for the conduct of marketing. The same figure, with additional calculations (Figure 23.3), is used later in the chapter to illustrate an important point about marketing budgets.

Resort hotel located near to a business centre generating visitors for conferences and general commercial purposes as well as holiday visitors.
120 twin rooms, with 65 per cent annual room occupancy = 28,470 room-nights' capacity over a year (120 × 365 × 65 per cent).
Rack rate £100 (twin/double) per room night, including breakfast; £75 (single occupancy).

Customer mix	% of room sales (per annum)	Volume of rooms sales (per annum)	tariff type
1 Business (individuals)	20	5,695	rack rate
2 Business (corporate clients)	30	8,540	corporate rate
3 Vacation (individuals)	10	2,847	weekly rate
4 Coach tour clients	10	2,848	inclusive group rate
5 Holiday breaks (i)	15	4,270	inclusive price
6 Holiday breaks (ii)	15	4,270	wholesale rate
Totals	100	28,470	

(i)   Marketed directly by the hotel to customers.
(ii) Rooms allocated to tour operators; and packages marketed by the operator.

Figure 23.2   *A typical product/market mix for a resort hotel*

It is based on a coastal resort hotel in the South of England with a location that supports a significant element of business visits within its chosen mix of segments. The hotel has two basic customer types (business and leisure), which permit of six segments, each representing a strategic choice, and requiring separate treatment in marketing campaigns. For convenience of illustration, the business/leisure ratio in figure 23.2 is 50:50, but it could vary from, say, 70:30 to 30:70, according to the strategy of the hotel's owners, reflecting their judgement of marketing potential and what they seek to achieve for the hotel in its location.

The optimum customer mix for most businesses will usually comprise several segments, which combine to maximize achievable revenue yield and minimize the effects of seasonality and other normal business fluctuations.

While hotels and the rest of the serviced sector may appear to have more scope to plan a co-ordinated customer mix, exactly the same principle operates for self-catering operators in the non-serviced sector. For example, holiday-park owners who market units such as caravans and chalets for holiday lets, may plan a segmentation strategy that separately targets adults aged over 50 travelling in pairs, from families with children of school age who are largely tied to school holiday periods. They can differentiate between visitors who purchase traditional 1 or 2 weeks' stays, and others who are interested in weekends and shorter stays.

Devising the optimum mix for any accommodation business usually requires some form of marketing research or at the least an analysis of guest-registration records to analyse the volume and revenue potential of current and prospective customers in each location. Very few operators in the commercial accommodation sector cannot achieve at least a four-way customer split, or business mix, as the basis for a more efficient marketing strategy.

Deciding the position or image

Relevant always to selected target segments, the next, and obviously related strategic consideration for accommodation suppliers is to determine the 'position' each unit or group of units should aim to occupy in the minds of its targeted customers. Increasingly, where competitors offer closely similar products to the same group of customers at very similar prices, it becomes necessary for operators to differentiate and brand their products with particular identities that can be communicated. Identities, known in marketing jargon as 'positions', are perceptions in the minds of customers, which may be based on specific associations with a company name, such as Four Seasons or Dorchester, on the strengths of a building and its location, the specifics of products on offer, the quality of service provided, the design and quality of rooms and furnishings, or any combination of these characteristics.

To illustrate the point, in developed countries all around the world hoteliers have for decades recognized the value of their regular business visitors. Yet the systematic marketing battle for the favourable opinions of these all-important customers in Britain can be dated to around 1984, when a regular, syndicated survey of frequent business travellers was launched by NOP Market Research Ltd. Frequent business travellers, defined by NOP as people who stay at least 21 nights a year in hotels, are estimated (by NOP) to contribute some two-thirds of all nights stayed in British hotels. The survey measures awareness of advertising, ranks preferences for different hotel companies in terms of users and non-users, and quantifies customer perceptions of the wide range of attributes on which such hotels are positioned. The survey provides a sophisticated measuring tool, enabling competing hotels to trace the success or failure of their positioning strategies over time. It puts marketing for the larger hotel groups on much the same footing as the marketing of fast-moving consumer goods, most of which have had the benefit of this type of research monitoring for at least 20 years.

Encouraging and rewarding frequent customers

The third element in strategic marketing responses for accommodation suppliers is to find ways to encourage and reward regular customers. Not surprisingly, for the same strategic reason as airlines, most hotel groups created membership clubs and other schemes during the 1980s, often supplying privileged user cards designed to appeal to their regular customers. Some of these schemes offered credit facilities in addition to the normal range of benefits, such as rapid check in and check out. Some also offered awards through which frequent travellers could earn points for each stay, leading to attractive prizes according to the number of points collected over a given period. In most cases the frequent or 'loyal' customer schemes require the building up of name and address lists into databases suitable for direct-response marketing initiatives, as discussed in Chapter 19.

While the strategic objective of rewarding repeat visitors is clear, not all of the schemes currently in use are immediately or fully successful. In part this is because they are difficult and often expensive to administer, and partly because they may also serve, unintentionally, to reduce the average room rate to some customers who were prepared to pay a higher price. Horwath Consulting estimated the level of repeat customers in larger hotels in Britain in 1985 at between 30 and 40 per cent. Some smaller accommodation businesses, both serviced and non-serviced, may achieve over 60 per cent repeat visits, and a customer loyalty strategy appears generally valid for all suppliers offering visitor accommodation.

Regular customers represent an important strategic marketing asset, not only in terms of their own decisions but because they provide a very cost-effective route through which it is possible to reach their friends and others like them, using carefully designed and targeted direct-response promotions.

Integrating marketing across several units

The fourth strategic consideration reflects a rapidly growing dimension in accommodation marketing, which is relevant to the other three elements and focuses on the level of co-ordination that individual units can achieve in marketing their products. The strategic advantages of *marketing co-ordination* may be summarized as:

Distribution	referrals of business between units central reservations service better access to distribution networks
Promotion	corporate positioning and branding joint advertising opportunities use of professional marketing teams access to group brochures and leaflets group representation at trade fairs and shows
Product and price	harmonization in group quality assurance schemes designed to build up customer satisfaction.

Obviously, co-ordination is most easily secured through ownership and is part of the process whereby large, multi-unit accommodation chains have emerged over the last 20 years and expanded the scale of their operations. Multi-unit chains are now found in all parts of the world; many of the chains are international in their scope, and there is no indication that this level of growth has reached any natural limits in the early 1990s.

The process of growth and the economic and marketing reasons for it are a vast topic, explored for example by Housden (1984), and lead into issues of franchising, leasing, turnkey operations and the separation of management from the ownership of accommodation properties. It helps to explain the reasons for the emergence of voluntary co-operatives of independent hoteliers such as Best Western and Consort in Britain. Most recently, the search for the marketing advantages of co-operation is spreading into the small businesses sector of both serviced and non-serviced units. The marketing of 'gites' in France, and holiday cottages in the UK, are examples.

Tactical marketing

Strategic decisions are expected to generate a profitable mix of bookings and room occupancy through the production and distribution of appropriately priced, distinctive products, which match the needs of identified customer segments. In other words, for accommodation operators in all sectors, three of the four Ps of the marketing mix are strategic decisions, and even the fourth, promotion, is planned within boundaries set by the positioning strategy.

Tactically, as for passenger-transport marketing, the main contribution of marketing is to secure additional marginal sales from targeted buyers at times when rooms are predictably likely to be operating at less than optimum occupancy, usually reflecting normal seasonal variations. Its other contribution is to cope with sudden and often dramatic losses of anticipated business, which happen all too often as a result of unpredictable economic or political events.

Occasionally, in certain destinations at certain times, room occupancies in hotels may exceed 80 per cent on an annual basis, as they did in London in the late 1980s. At this level, most hotels are full for most of the time, and the inevitable result is a rise in prices and profitability. Such circumstances are exceptional and usually are not achieved by marketing alone but by a combination of favourable circumstances in the external environment. It is more common for accommodation businesses to operate somewhere between 55 and 65 per cent of room occupancy over the months in which they are open for business. In extremes, as in 1991 during the Gulf War crisis, they may drop to 40 per cent or less.

As in other sectors of travel and tourism, reflecting the highly perishable nature of the products, marketing managers are required to manage demand by stimulating additional bookings on a daily and weekly basis. The high fixed costs and low variable costs of operating accommodation give extensive scope for providing short term incentives to buyers. Tactical marketing for accommodation businesses requires choosing from the range of sales promotion tools discussed in some detail in Chapter 16. See, for example, Figure 16.2.

Specifically, sales promotion tactics for accommodation businesses include:

- Short-term price discounting, used especially to sell unsold capacity in unanticipated circumstances (see also Chapter 9).
- Sales promotions, adding temporary value to products in order to attract targeted customer segments, and often used to attract business at times of predicted seasonal troughs in demand.
- Sales promotions, often using commission incentives, designed to motivate a retail distribution system (where applicable) and achieve added influence at points of sale, including improved display for brochures.
- Sales promotions, invariably using deep price discounts, designed to motivate and conclude deals with third parties such as tour operators, coach-tour operators and other agents making bulk contracts for the supply of accommodation. (This form of selling capacity may have strategic as well as tactical implications.)
- Use of a sales force (where applicable) to generate additional sales, both from the range of normal buyers and from others targeted for short run sales initiatives.

● Tactical use of advertising, usually in association with items 1, 2, and 3, in order to achieve better communication of promotional offers.

While the use of these tactical techniques is clearly sales-orientated, their efficient use depends on the detailed knowledge marketing managers have of the profile, needs, and probable behaviour of target segments in responding to promotional incentives. Because, like transport companies, the accommodation sector is so often subject to unpredictable external factors, it is always necessary for operators to allocate contingency funds to be held in reserve for use in influencing short-run demand, as the need arises.

The size of accommodation marketing budgets

With an understanding of the size of the task of implementing strategy and tactics in accommodation marketing, it is appropriate to consider the implications for the size of budgets. The cost of achieving marketing objectives is usually a relatively high proportion of sales revenue, and the budget allocation is rightly seen as a high-risk decision. A systematic procedure for allocating money to marketing campaigns in order to achieve planned volume and revenue targets is set out in Chapter 14; the principles in that chapter apply fully to all sectors of commercial accommodation.

This section sets out to challenge what continues to be a widespread belief in the industry in a norm, or rule of thumb, that it is appropriate to spend between 2 and 5 per cent of total sales revenue on marketing. Thus, commenting on the annual surveys of international hotel accounts undertaken by Horwath and Horwath in the 1980s, Medlik notes, 'hotels appear to have spent 2-6 per cent of their total revenue on marketing activities' (Medlik: 1989, p. 118). The Horwath and Horwath percentages have remained fairly

constant over time in many countries and have become part of the received wisdom in the industry. These are average figures, and many hotels clearly spend less than 2 per cent of total revenue.

Of course the percentage depends on the definition of what the marketing budget should include, but this author believes that the real proportion of sales revenue devoted to marketing by most successful organizations in the accommodation business is very much greater than 2–6 per cent. Properly calculated, and based on the view of marketing expressed in this book, the real average proportion of sales revenue devoted to marketing activities by accommodation businesses of all types is probably over 20 per cent in most countries. Many firms spend more to secure their business turnover. This is obviously a highly contentious statement. Supporting calculations for the argument will be found in Figure 23.3 and it is justified as follows:

1 In analysing the accounts of a business providing visitor accommodation, rooms sales revenue should always be calculated in two ways. First, the sum of actual receipts for a year from accommodation sales should be calculated (this figure, divided by the number of room-nights sold, provides the average room rate achieved over a year). Second, room sales revenue should be calculated as the sum of theoretical sales revenue achievable if rooms were sold at the published rack rates (with allowance for *planned* discount rates, as noted in Figure 23.2).

2 Marketing expenditure should then be calculated as the sum of the costs of *all* the decisions marketing managers take to secure the business they actually achieve (not just the expenditure on advertising and sales promotion). The total expenditure should be expressed as a percentage of room-sales revenue and total sales revenue achieved over a campaign period.

Although hotel accounts are not normally drawn up as suggested above, highly valuable marketing insights can be gained if the calculations are undertaken by marketing managers for their own purposes. They will reveal the true marketing costs by targeted segments. Figure 23.3 provides a method.

In an ideal world a hotel with an excellent product range and a good location will set its rack rates, corporate rates, and other group rates for the year ahead and complete the trading period without unpredicted events preventing it from achieving the targeted mix of bookings that best matches its capacity. No one in this ideal position accepts group bookings at a discount if they are confident of filling their rooms with rack-rate business, which raises their yield towards the theoretical maximum. No one offers special rates for leisure-break business if they can fill their rooms at higher rates.

In the real world hoteliers and operators of other forms of accommodation are daily forced to tackle the realities of regular payment of contracted fixed costs out of cash flow, while contemplating unsold rooms and beds and consequent loss of potential revenue. In these circumstances they discount their rack rates in order to manipulate short-run demand. Putting the point bluntly, they reduce prices in order to 'buy' business from whatever sources they can find at whatever price they think is better than the certain alternative of lost sales. The high fixed cost of accommodation operations makes business at almost any price appear worthwhile in the short run. Of course, over time, price discounting may be counter-productive, because it damages regular customers' goodwill, but businesses in serious cash-flow crises may not have a long run, and they will aim to survive by any possible means.

The foregoing explanation is designed to make the point that marketing expenditure should always be calculated as the full cost of all the expenditure managers decide to incur to achieve their actual turnover. Marketing costs therefore include expenditure defined in the 8th edition of the *Uniform System of Accounts for Hotels*, on:

● Advertising, PR, and other media.
● Sales promotion and merchandising print.
● Production and distribution (including direct mail).
● Marketing research.
● Consortia fees (marketing proportion only) or group marketing levy imposed by chains.
● Staff costs, expenses and share of overheads for all undertaking marketing work.

It should also include the full costs incurred in:

● Negotiating with, servicing and paying commission to travel agents, wholesalers and any other distributors who receive comission.
● Negotiating and agreeing discounts for tour operators, coach-tour companies and any other bulk sales.
● Providing discounts for other forms of group business, such as conferences or airlines.
● Share of costs of central reservation systems since this these are vital tools of efficient marketing operations, which must be organized around marketing requirements.

It has to be stressed that several cost elements noted above, which account for the bulk of all the costs of securing business otherwise judged to be at risk or lost (the only valid reason for incurring the costs), are not in practice included as marketing costs in the *Uniform System of Accounts for Hotels*. This is not a criticism of the uniform system, because it was not conceived around marketing principles but in order to make industry comparisons by means of standard definitions. Experience suggests that, *Uniform System* not withstanding, most hotels do not, for example, include the full cost of commissions under a marketing heading and are underestimating the full cost. If an accommodation supplier wishes to understand costs and revenues and make his marketing more efficient, however, he must count all the costs noted above.

Because revenues and the costs of marketing accommodation are related to segments, it is obviously sensible that an accommodation business should budget for marketing, not as a percentage of total sales revenue but separately, according to the costs of securing sales in each segment/product group with which the business is concerned.

Marketing a resort hotel

This section, with its important illustrations in Figure 23.3, provides a model for analysing a hotel's annual room-sales revenue by segments and products. The text explains why the actual revenue achieved is usually less than the theoretical revenue targeted by managers at the start of a budget year. To set the section and the model in a broadly practical context, the example chosen is a medium-sized, four-star hotel, part of a national chain, in a seaside resort in Britain. Its location generates a mix of business, and justifies an average bed and breakfast rack rate per *room night* of £100 (assuming double occupancy). The hotel has 120 twin rooms and is targeted to achieve 65 per cent room occupancy over 12 months.

Originally built for holiday customers 50 years ago, changing markets have caused the hotel to shift its focus and upgrade its facilities

---

Resort hotel located near to a business centre generating visitors for conferences, general commercial purposes as well as holiday visitors.

120 twin rooms, with 65 per cent annual room occupancy = 28,470 room nights capacity over a year ($120 \times 365 \times 65$ per cent).

Rack rate £100 (twin/double) per *room* night including breakfast; £75 (single occupancy)

Customer mix	% of room sales (per annum)	(a) Volume of rooms sales (per annum)	Tariff type	(b) Published room rates (in brochure)	(c)* Actual room rate achieved	(d) Theoretical revenue (a × b)	(e) Actual room revenue achieved (a × c)
1 Business (individuals)	20	5,695	rack rate	£100	£78	£569,500	£444,210
2 Business (corporate clients)	30	8,540	corporate rate	£85†	£66	£725,900	£563,640
3 Vacation (individuals)	10	2,847	weekly rate (per night)	£60	£55	£170,820	£156,585
4 Coach tour clients	10	2,848	inclusive group rate (per night)	£60†	£42	£170,880	£119,616
5 Holiday breaks (i)	15	4,270	inclusive price	£70	£63	£298,900	£269,010
6 Holiday breaks (ii)	15	4,270	wholesale rate	£70	£50	£298,900	£213,500
Totals	100	28,470				£2,234,900	£1,766,561

*Includes allowance for corporate/group rates; single occupancy of rooms; and retailer commissions for segments 4 and 6 of the customer mix

† not published
(i) sold directly by the hotel to customers
(ii) rooms allocated to tour operators; and packaged and marketed by the operator

Figure 23.3 *Calculating the full impact of discounts and sales commission on potential hotel revenue*

to appeal to a business market. The hotel does not have its own conference facilities but it is located near a resort conference centre from which it draws a significant part of its total visitors for business purposes. Short-break holiday business, to fill the weekends when business visits are not available, is now its principal involvement in the leisure market.

The business mix and tariff types

Following normal marketing logic, the total annual business is divided into segments. It is necessary to organize different products, prices, promotion, and distribution for each of these segments. As set out in Figure 23.3, there are two types of customers (business and vacation visitors) but they generate six viable segments. All other types of customer are excluded from the figure to avoid complicating the example. The rationale for the segmentation strategy is simple. The location does not generate its target occupancy at rack rates, and the hotel has to organize marketing initiatives (in this case with its parent company) to secure the targeted level of sales at discounted prices.

Of the six visitor segments shown in Figure 23.3, only the first group pays the full rack rate, comprising only 20 per cent by volume of the hotel's business. The second segment is composed of business visitors paying a corporate rate that is 15 per cent below the rack rate; some of them are conference visitors, who also receive an average discount of 15 per cent off the rack rate.

Of the vacationer groups, it would not be possible to achieve targeted levels of business at the full rack rate, and most hotels offer a special rate for these customers, usually built into a product with a minimum length of stay and perhaps meals and other services to reduce the possibility that such rates will be used by business visitors. If the individual vacation business is projected on the evidence of recent years to leave many rooms unoccupied, the hotelier will normally approach tour operators,

in this case coach operators (segment 4 in Figure 23.3). Such operators will, if the hotel suits their own product range, take allocations of rooms. If they do, it will normally be at a large discount in order to cover their own costs of administration and marketing, including distribution. The discount, which must also cover the tour operator's profit, will be calculated on the hotel's published tariff for that type of business (in this case an average per room night of £60).

The two final vacation segments are short breaks of 2 to 3 nights offered as an inclusive product. For segment 5, the product is sold from a brochure put together by hotel marketing executives at group level and there is no discount from the target tariff of £70 per room night. Because this hotel still has spare capacity at weekends, it also makes an allocation of rooms to another wholesaler or tour operator, which includes the hotel in a brochure comprising a range of products marketed under a brand name. In Britain several such brochures are currently branded and marketed under labels such as *Superbreaks*, and *Rainbow*. As with the coach-tour operators, marketing through a group has to be paid for, and discounts of around 30 per cent are common, to cover wholesaler costs, marketing, and profit margins.

Revenue calculations in Figure 23.3

Column (a) shows the volume of room-night sales per annum for each segment, as targeted at the beginning of the year in the hotel's marketing plan. The total of 28,470 is the sum of 120 rooms × 365 days × 65 per cent occupancy. Column (b) lists the published room rates per night designed to attract each of the segments. Column (c) converts these into actual room rates achieved. The column (c) figures would in practice be calculated by the hotel accountants, and they allow for the fact that some of the rooms are let to only one person at less than double occupancy rate, that group discount must be deducted from some segments, and that travel agency commission is payable on some sales. Where reception staff are instructed to accept last-minute bookings with even bigger discounts, this would also be accounted for in column (c).

Column (d) shows the maximum revenue potentially achievable if all rooms could be sold at target published prices for each segment. The only reason for making this calculation is to demonstrate that there is always a cost, represented as potential revenue foregone, in accepting business at less than the optimum target rate. In fact, not all target prices are published to the public but are commercial negotiating rates established in a marketing plan.

Column (e) shows actual revenue received over the year (a × c). By comparing the actual and theoretical revenue totals, it can be seen that the sum of column (e) is 79 per cent of column (d). By dividing the total revenue (e) by total room sales (28,470), the average room rate achieved can be calculated at £62.05 over the year.

To summarize, almost every accommodation business will operate at average room rates significantly below its theoretical maximum. The difference between actual and potential reflects the composition of its segment/ product mix and the level of discounting and commission required to achieve business in each segment. Measured over periods of time and between different hotels in a group, the size of the gap between theoretical and actual revenue provides a measure of a hotel's marketing efficiency.

Cost of marketing

In Figure 23.3 part of the costs of achieving sales in some segments is reflected in the discounts and commission payable. Additional costs include advertising, sales promotion, print, and any other expenditure on marketing judged necessary to secure the targeted 65 per cent occupancy. In the example discussed part of this marketing expenditure will be paid by the hotel direct, and part through the group to which it belongs, usually through a group marketing

levy amounting to around 3 per cent of the hotel's annual turnover.

Whichever way the marketing budget is calculated, it is obvious that the true cost of marketing reflected in Figure 23.3, will be a very far cry from the comfortable industry 'norm' of 2-5 per cent usually quoted.

Timeshare resorts – marketing holiday exchanges

Not to be confused with the marketing of capital investment in timeshare properties to prospective owners of one or more week's share in a resort, the marketing of holiday exchanges to existing timeshare owners has grown remarkably in the last decade. Its growth has continued right through the international recession of 1990–1993 and the market is projected to double again in the next decade. Timeshare holidays represent a very interesting international example of accommodation marketing which meets all of the strategic and tactical marketing requirements outlined in this chapter. The marketing issues noted below also form a bridge between this chapter on marketing accommodation and the next on tour operation. It appears significant that many of the leading players in the American hospitality industry are engaging in timesharing for its marketing as well as its investment potential.

By 1993 RCI was the largest of the marketing exchange companies in this field with over 2700 timeshare resorts affiliated to it in some 70 countries around the world. RCI is a membership club comprising over 1.6 million households representing some 5 million individuals. The number of owners has doubled since 1988, notwithstanding a world economic recession. In the most recent year RCI handled the holiday arrangements of some 3.5 million customers making it one of the world's largest tour operators.

Initially a marketing response to a crisis in the USA condominium market following the major international energy crisis and its effects in

1972/3, RCI has developed to become a major and growing international player whose exchange products are essential for the successful financing and marketing of resort properties. It is also a global tour operator. Its operations are based on direct-response marketing to a membership club comprised of owners in timeshare resorts. RCI does not own the resorts which affiliate with it but performs a marketing exchange role for the millions of individual timeshare owners.

For the companies that manage the resorts, affiliation with RCI enables them to operate at over 90 per cent occupancy levels around the year; for the individual owners, the opportunity to exchange provides a powerful extra incentive to make their initial capital investment. The principal marketing advantages can be summarized as:

● Marketing to a 'captive' audience of club members; many of whom are virtually 100 per cent loyal/repeat and regular customers. State of the art direct response marketing methods based on highly sophisticated computer technology needed to effect the exchanges and available for use for marketing database purposes (see Chapter 19).
● Full control over the costs and efficiency of promotion and distribution methods.
● Powerful influence, if not control, over the quality standards delivered by the resort operators, achieved by continuous marketing research and especially the evaluation of customer satisfaction scores (see Chapter 24). RCI can dis-affiliate resorts in cases of abuse.
● Purpose-built framework for marketing innovation and testing – both for product design and alternative marketing methods.

Case studies supporting this chapter

Part Six of the book contains one case relevant to marketing accommodation. It sets out the retail distribution strategy employed by Superbreaks Mini Holidays to market short breaks in serviced accommodation in the UK.

Chapter summary

This chapter is concerned with marketing overnight accommodation to visitors by commercial, and what are defined as quasi-commercial, operators. Categorized according to serviced and non-serviced provision, accommodation is one of the five integral elements of the tourism product, with a strong influence on the volume and patterns of tourism flows to destinations. Being fixed in location and part of the destination environment, accommodation is normally strongly associated with the attractions of a destination. For leisure segments, accommodation and destinations are often closely linked in the customer's mind. In many cases accommodation products may be as strong as a destination's attractions, and constitute the principal motivation for a tourist visit.

The chapter seeks to define and illuminate the characteristics of operations and marketing practice that are common to all sectors of serviced and non-serviced accommodation. It is not restricted to a particular sector or only to large operators in the industry. As with transport, some aspects of marketing are peculiar to individual sectors, but the common aspects are more important than the differences. The principles outlined are broadly relevant to all the sectors of accommodation.

As in other chapters dealing with key elements of the tourism product, this chapter stresses the importance of linkages between sectors in the tourism industry for marketing in the future. Other important marketing linkages are currently occurring *within* sectors, such as those found in accommodation consortia formed by serviced and non-serviced operators. Individual producers, especially those owning small units, see consortia as a logical route to achieving economies of scale in marketing. Such economies are vital to successful competition against the growing power of the large organizations, with their multi-site networks of units operating to common standards within corporate identities.

24

Marketing inclusive tours and product packages

This chapter focuses on the mainly commercial operators that assemble the components of tourism products and market them as packages to the final consumer. Defined in the first part of this chapter, a package is essentially a selected combination of individual elements of the travel and tourism product, marketed under a particular product or brand label, and sold at an inclusive price. Most such products are aimed at leisure and holiday markets, although most forms of business incentive travel and many conferences are packaged in similar ways.

National tour operators, such as Thomson Holidays (UK) and Touristic Union International (TUI) in Germany, take millions of customers abroad every year, and are the best known and most obvious illustrations of modern tour operation. But tour operators are by no means the only businesses marketing travel packages.

The history of tour operation goes back to the nineteenth century in Britain, although in its modern form it can be traced to the 1950s. At that time the availability and technology of air transport, and the growing level of affluence of the holiday market in Britain and other countries, coincided with the needs of both customers and component suppliers, and facilitated a large volume market for packages,

or inclusive tours (ITs), as they are known in the trade. This is now a major market for domestic as well as international tourism. It includes surface transport and there appears to be much scope for further growth in the rest of this century.

This chapter begins with a brief historical review of the development of travel organization and tour operation, followed by definitions presenting a broad view of packages. It proceeds to consider the role of tour operators in the overall travel and tourism product, and the nature of the tour-operating business which determines the marketing response. This is followed by an assessment of the marketing task for tour operators, and the implications for strategy and tactics.

Historical development of tour operating

The origins of travel organization and tour operation are usually traced back to 1841. In that year Thomas Cook, founder of the internationally famous company bearing his name, took on the personal responsibility of organizing one of the earliest whole train charters, for a day excursion to a temperance meeting. The excursion was a sell-out, achieving 100 per cent seat load factor! By 1845 Cook was operating longer, overnight tours in Britain on a commercial basis, and in 1871, he organized the first round the world tour (Swinglehurst: 1982, p. 9).

Over the century to the Second World War tour-operating developed internationally through railway companies and ocean liners, and there were well-patronized circuits around Europe, especially to Switzerland and the South of France. Skiing tours owed their origins and early popularity to another Briton, Sir Henry Lunn, in the 1880s. After the First World War pioneer coach-tour operators established themselves, and began to run excursions and longer tours in the 1930s, adding a new dimension to the possibilities for packaging.

Coming up to date, the Second World provided a quantum leap in transport technology, especially for long-distance aircraft originally designed to carry a large payload of bombs. It left a large surplus of transport equipment, especially aircraft, which was put to early tourism uses by the forerunners of modern international tour operators. In fact Thomas Cook claim to have pioneered the first air inclusive charter holiday to the South of France, planned for 1939. But war put back the development of air ITs to 1950, when Vladimir Raitz of Horizon chartered 300 seats in his first year's operation to Corsica. Out of such modest beginnings the modern European tour operating industry developed. The British market for ITs abroad (air and sea), still the largest in Europe, was measured at just over 1 million packages in 1962, when formal measurement began. Sales exceeded 12 million by 1989 before dropping back to just over 11 million in 1992. Over that time, from a tiny minority of the British that had ever travelled abroad, the early 1990s estimates are that over two in three British adults have travelled abroad at some time in their lives, and the proportion is higher among the more affluent socio-economic groups. While Britain's island situation and climate have been particularly conducive to the growth of packages, similar trends may be observed throughout northern Europe.

Although appearing much later than the packages to destinations abroad, the production of domestic holiday packages has also enjoyed remarkable growth over the last decade. Depending on definitions used, for there are no accurate statistics in this sector, the volume of British domestic holiday packages is probably about the same size as the volume of holiday packages abroad, although much smaller in value.

Thus modern, risk-taking tour operators, and others with interests in packaging aspects of transport, accommodation and attractions, have a history of continuous development over the last century.

Role of packaging in the overall tourism product

In Chapter 8, the overall tourism product was introduced as a package and defined in terms of five main components, comprising destination attractions, destination facilities and services, accessibility of the destination, images and perceptions, and price to the customer. Drawing on Burkart and Medlik's succinct view, an inclusive tour operator is 'the manufacturer of a true tourist product; he buys the components of the package, the inclusive tour (transport, accommodation, etc.) from the suppliers of the individual tourist services and packages and brands them into a single entity' (Burkart & Medlik: 1981, p. 216). Although the manufacturer concept most accurately describes independent tour operators, who contract with suppliers for all the components they build into the products offered in their brochures, the same principle holds good for packages put together by owners of one or more of the components, such as an airline, sea ferry company, or a hotel group.

From the customer's viewpoint, packages generally appear similar in kind when presented in brochures, and who owns or contracts for the components is neither evident nor relevant to the buyer. For example, Club Méditerranée owns its villages, which are a combination of destination, attractions, accommodation, and supporting facilities, and it usually also controls access and acts as a tour operator. In the eyes of prospective customers the brochures it puts together and the processes of promotion and distribution are not different from other competing tour operators, except in so far as there are intrinsic or perceived differences in the product offer or quality. Club Med is not normally described as a tour operator, yet the company is most certainly 'manufacturing' products for its target customers. In other words, the packages which operators assemble are drawn from the five basic elements of the overall tourism product, plus whatever added value of their own operations is built in, such as price guarantees, convenience, accessibility to the customer, image, reputation for high standards and sense of security in dealing with a reputable operator.

Defining inclusive tour and product packages

This chapter takes a deliberately broad view of packages and includes two distinctive types of operator. The first type always includes transport in the package – in Europe mostly chartered air transport. These are the traditional tour operators, of whom the biggest in Britain are structurally integrated with charter airlines, from which much of their profit is derived. The second type always includes accommodation in the package, and may or may not include transport; most of these operators primarily deal with accommodation, although some are now independent package operators in their own right.

Thus it makes most sense to define operators of packages according to the products they offer to the public. So many commercial and non-commercial organizations in the travel and tourism industry are now marketing packages of every kind that it is important to be precise. There are three main considerations in a broad definition of packages, reflecting:

● The nature of the product itself, which is always a package.
● The business relation between operator and main product elements.
● The dominant method of distribution to the customer.

The nature of the product

Product packages are:

Standardized, quality-controlled, repeatable offers comprising two or more elements of transport, accommodation, food, destination attractions, other facilities, and services (such as travel insurance). Product packages are marketed to the general public, described in print or other media, and offered for sale to prospective customers at a published, inclusive price, in which the costs of the product components cannot be separately identified.

This definition *includes* a wide range of tour operators and producer organizations marketing standardized packages, such as air-inclusive tours, coach tours, short holiday breaks, weekend breaks, activity packages of all kinds, and sea cruises. Most modes of accommodation and transport are increasingly offering packages. The definition *excludes* special packages put together for a particular purpose or for a closed group of users. For example, many conference products in hotels have standard elements and are often referred to as packages, but they are generally put together to meet the needs of specified members of particular organizations, and are 'one-off' events adapted for each group purchaser. While important, such packages are not marketed according to the principles outlined in this chapter.

The term 'standardization' does not imply mass production of one type of identical product. It means that products offered for sale will be delivered in a reasonably consistent or quality-assured way – as judged by targeted prospective customers. In practice, quality means delivering product consistency to match the needs and expectations of consumer segments; product-quality control is the management process whereby it is achieved (see later in this chapter).

When the EC Package Holiday Directive was drawn up for implementation in all EC countries in 1993, it used a definition similar to that in the first edition of this book:

> Package means the pre-arranged combination of not fewer than two of the following when sold or offered for sale at an inclusive price and when the service covers a period of more than 24 hours or includes overnight accommodation: transport, accommodation, other tourist services not ancillary to transport or accommodation and accounting for a significant proportion of the package (EC Directive).

Referred to later in this section, the decision of the EC to implement a Package Holiday Directive in 1993 is part of a Community approach to securing and enforcing customer protection. At the time of writing the full implications of the regulation were still being debated, but there is little doubt that the Directive will limit the flexibility with which operators can respond to a changing business environment. It will add to the costs of many as they make the requisite financial arrangements to compensate clients in the event of claims.

Business relations between operator and product elements

The second consideration distinguishes between a category of operators that conduct their business as independent contractors, free to purchase whatever components of a package may make best commercial sense, and a second category owned by or closely linked with producers of one of the package components, such as hotels or airlines. The first category includes the major British contracting operators of packages, such as Thomson, Airtours, Owners Abroad, Superbreak, Hoseasons Holidays, and Rainbow. The second category includes producers marketing packages, such as Forte Hotels (Leisure Breaks), British Airways (British Airways Holidays), Wallace Arnold, and Haven Warner. Although no figures are available, it seems probable that the second category of operators generate at least as many packages conforming to this chapter's definition as the better-known first category. The key point to note is that there are strong similarities in the ways in which both categories approach their strategic and tactical marketing. From the customer's viewpoint, the packages produced by each category are essentially in direct competition.

Distribution method

The third consideration relates to the form of marketing used to sell the packages. Organizations marketing packages have a basic choice between a strategy based on direct-response approaches to the customer or marketing through third-party distribution networks (see Chapter 19). Some operators, especially those in the producer rather than the contractor category, have a split strategy of part direct-response marketing and part distribution through retail outlets.

The function of tour operators

As explained earlier, large tour operators are mostly independent contractors which bring together the products of individual suppliers, and market them as packages to the final customer. As such they would not survive unless the services they provided were firmly rooted in the needs of both parties.

It is possible to identify four reasons to explain the development of independent tour operating businesses:

● Overcoming the inherent inefficiencies in the markets for leisure travel and tourism, especially for international travel.
● Facilitating and simplifying the process of choice and booking for customers, and providing both psychological and financial security in a 'single purchase' transaction.
● Ensuring product quality and the delivery of the promise.
● Delivering price advantages that customers are usually unable to achieve for themselves.

First, with a few exceptions at certain periods and in certain locations, the matching of tourism supply with demand is a remarkably inefficient process, especially in leisure markets. On the supply side producers of accommodation and attractions are mostly small businesses operating in a single fixed location, aiming to attract infrequent buyers, many of them buying for the first time and on a once-only basis. Moreover, prospective buyers are usually drawn from a very wide catchment area. For example, over the space of 3 months in the summer, a hotel in Wales may draw its customers from up to six overseas countries and up to half of all the counties in England and Wales. A resort hotel in Cyprus may draw most of its customers from only four or five countries, yet their addresses may be geographically spread across half the land mass of Europe and the Middle East.

Effective marketing on a national and international basis in order to secure exposure and promotion of their product offers to target customers is not an option for independent hoteliers. While advertising in national tourist office guides will be as sensible for the Cyprus hotelier as for the one in Wales, it will hardly be a certain or sufficient process to secure the sale of otherwise unsold capacity on a daily basis.

Both will tend to look to other sources to supply business they are not able to achieve through their own direct marketing efforts. 'Other sources' usually means tour operators looking for room allocations, which explains the prime function of tour operators for suppliers, and why they are able to secure such favourable bulk prices for the product allocations they contract.

The contrast between holiday tourism and the operations of most small service businesses is extreme. For example, a small local grocer will derive most of his sales from a small group of frequent repeat buyers, drawn from a local catchment area within a small radius of his shop's location. Most cafés, pubs, restaurants and fast food outlets will similarly draw on a small catchment area and rely heavily on repeat customers for much of their turnover. Their marketing problems are quite different to those faced in holiday travel and tourism.

Second, from the customer's point of view, purchasing the elements of an overall product separately, especially for the first time in an unknown destination, is often a very hit and miss process. It is fraught with the risk of making an expensive mistake. Where large sums of money are ventured, as well as a personal sense of achievement or failure, as is normally the case with purchasing holidays, the sense of risk may be acute. For travel abroad, with its added complications of language, currency, and distance from home, the problems for inexperienced travellers acting on their own account may be too daunting and too time-consuming, even if the cost is not a problem.

Third, through their contracting procedures, specification of the product in brochures, use of representatives at destinations, and through close monitoring of customer satisfaction, tour operators can sustain and develop product-quality standards. The standards promote confidence in buyers and reassure them at the point of sale. In EC countries since 1993 the legal requirements implicit in meeting the new Package Travel Directive reinforce (though they did not initiate) this role.

Fourth, the prices charged to individuals putting together the components of their chosen packages on an individual basis will be relatively high, because individuals cannot obtain the volume discounts available to any large buyer in competitive conditions. Tour operators, from the time of Thomas Cook onward, have been able to achieve volume discounts large enough to cover all their own costs and still pass on (in almost all cases) a price significantly less than the customer could achieve for himself. In the highly price-elastic leisure market this is often seen to be the tour operator's most important function.

To summarize, the tour operator's essential role is to solve producers' needs to sell their capacity, and customers' needs for convenience and security at advantageous, affordable prices. At a profit to themselves, tour operators solve the natural inefficiency that is inherent in matching demand and supply in most leisure sectors of travel and tourism. That is their role and the reason for their importance in the industry. There appear to be no reasons why these four fundamental marketing contributions will diminish in importance over the next decade.

The process of constructing an inclusive tour programme

All those engaged in marketing packages assemble product elements into what are known as programmes. A programme is normally expressed in a brochure, which usually contains a range of product choices in several destinations. To explain how programmes are constructed, this section focuses on air-inclusive tours as the most developed sector of packaging, but the principles are the same in constructing any programme.

A tour operator offering ITs by air has a choice of using reduced fares (known as ITX) on scheduled airlines or bulk fares available from charter airlines. The cost per seat on charter airlines naturally varies according to volume bought and whether the operator charters the whole flight or only a number of seats. The largest international tour operators have their own subsidiary airlines to transport the bulk of their programmes, and are thus able to secure the lowest possible seat cost available. For example, Britannia Airways, owned by the International Thomson Organization, carried over 5 million passengers in 1990, and is a bigger and more cost-efficient airline than many of the scheduled carriers in Europe.

A large air IT programme out of Britain in the 1990s uses up to twenty airports of departure; up to 100 resorts in a dozen or more countries; and a range of products based on accommodation types from luxury hotels to simple self-catering apartments. Putting a large programme such as this together depends on translating estimates of market demand into production capacity, and matching aircraft seats with beds in batches, adding up to full aeroplanes flying between pairs of airports. The skill lies in matching potential demand with contracted supply, to achieve optimum average load factors for flights and maximum occupancy of available beds. It is an instructive exercise for students to take a current IT brochure and identify the products, destinations and airports of origin.

The process of putting a programme together is shown in Figure 24.1, in a diagram adapted by the author from an original version produced by Roger Heape, when he was Director of Marketing for Thomson Holidays. The diagram reflects the initial planning dialogue, common in all marketing, between marketing research and forecasting, corporate strategy, and marketing implementation. The hardest decision in programme planning is what volume of products will be offered in the year ahead. Planning will start at least 18 months before the first customers travel, and product volume has to be turned into numbers of seats and beds in order to see how flight schedules and bed

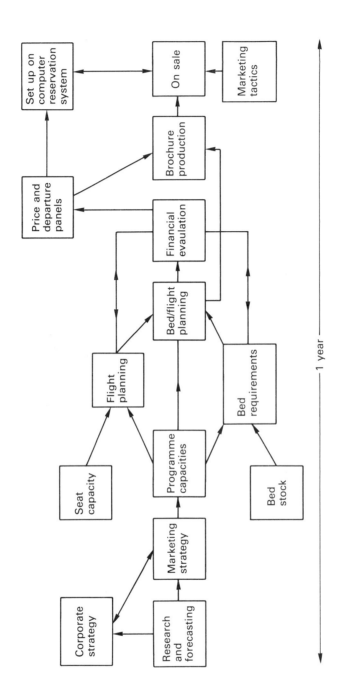

Figure 24.1 *The logical sequence of constructing and marketing an air-inclusive tour programme*

capacity in resorts can best be matched. This process identifies capacity objectives for the staff who negotiate for beds and seats. In the 1990s optimizing flight schedules and blocks of beds to achieve the most cost-efficient utilization of aircraft and hotels is always carried out by computers. It is an interactive process, strongly affected by the hotel prices being contracted.

With a draft programme worked out to meet projected demand, the next stage is to draft the all-important price and departure panels, which will appear in the brochure, stating the price of each product according to the date of departure and number of nights. (See Chapter 9 for a discussion of pricing.) Normally included on each product page of the brochure below the description of the accommodation, price and departure panels are sometimes produced separately in loose-leaf format to facilitate tactical price changes without reprinting the whole brochure. Up to this stage there is ample room for change in all aspects of the programme, and there are numerous feedback loops in the process, although not all are shown in the diagram, to avoid clutter. Product prices and capacity are not in practice finalized until the last possible moment, about 10 weeks before the brochure is distributed and customer purchases begin. Even then, as noted later under tactics, both may have to be changed more than once after publication.

As soon as the programme is on sale, the available capacity is put into a computerized reservation system, as discussed in Chapter 18. In the case of larger tour operators direct on-line access to capacity is provided for distributors through the installation of desk-top terminals in travel retailers' offices. These terminals provide continuous information about products for sale, and their value, both for cost-efficiency in handling bookings and in providing vital information for tactical marketing purposes, is noted later.

In order to put together a credible programme and sell it through the process noted above, it is essential that each product should, so

far as humanly possible, be carefully controlled to deliver consistent quality. Customers who read and select between the various brochures on offer have to make the assumption that the operators can achieve consistency, or they have no effective basis for making their decisions. In this, tour operators are acting exactly as the manufacturers of cars or TV sets do. All manufacturers have quality-control procedures. Modern marketing cannot be undertaken on any other basis.

The nature of the marketing task for tour operators

For tour operators, as for other producers in the travel and tourism industry, it is appropriate to divide the discussion of the marketing task between strategic and tactical considerations. In practice, as any reading of the travel trade press will confirm, the nature of tour operation, with its daily fluctuations and seemingly continuous atmosphere of 'boom and bust', puts great emphasis on short-run tactical considerations. Tactics are required to survive in a fiercely competitive market place. The strategic dimensions are nevertheless very important. They are likely to become more so as markets, which have grown for some 30 years with only a few minor setbacks, reach maturity.

Tour operators are first and foremost marketing organizations with a strong commitment to customers and products. Nevertheless they do have strategic considerations that are wider than marketing. Many are concerned with vertical integration between themselves, transport, and distribution, especially charter airlines and travel retailers. Others may own or have other forms of linkage with supplier organizations in travel and tourism. This chapter is not concerned to analyse these broader elements of corporate strategy, but it is interesting to note a shift in the early 1990s in the strategic alliances operators make to achieve a competitive cost and marketing edge. These alliances, led by tour operators, involve ownership or strategic partnerships between the operators and airlines, retailers, and, significantly, direct-response tour operation companies. There appear to be implications for European countries generally, as demonstrated by the recent expansion of LTU. In the UK, at the beginning of 1993, the three leading players had formed strategic alliances, as noted in Table 24.1.

Table 24.1 *Strategic alliances in travel and tourism*

Operator	Airline	Retail chain	Direct marketing
Thomson	Britannia	Lunn Poly	Portland
Airtours	Airtours International	Pickfords / Going Places	Camping programme
Owners Abroad	Air 2000	Thomas Cook*	Martin Rooks Tjaereborg

*Thomas Cook is owned by LTU, giving direct links with several European countries

Strategic marketing

Five elements are noted in this section:

● Interpreting the strength and direction of change in the external environment.
● Strategic decisions on volume and pricing.
● Choice of product/customer portfolio.
● Positioning and image.
● Choice and maintenance of distribution systems/preferred marketing method.

The external environment

External influences are especially powerful in their implications for tour operation, reflecting both the non-essential character of most leisure products, and the international nature of much of the business. The total British market for inclusive tours demonstrates large annual fluctuations triggered by economic events

affecting employment, levels of wages and real income, and the impact of international exchange-rate movements on prices. Tour operators have influenced and in turn been very much influenced by the rapid introduction of new information technology for reservations and bookings. Without it, the growth of multiple chains now dominating travel retailing in Britain could not have occurred. Above all, the operator's external environment reflects the actions of competitors whose intense rivalry dominates the responses of all operators in the market. The susceptibility of operators to changes in the external environment is of course heightened by the relatively long lead times in putting a programme together. It takes about 18 months from the start of the assembly process to delivery of products to the first customers.

A significant new factor emerging in the 1990s is the effect on tour operators of consumer attitudes to growing awareness of global environment problems. The Brundtland Report of 1987 and the Earth Summit of 1992 at Rio de Janeiro received massive media coverage internationally. In Europe an attitude shift appears to be changing the perceived attractiveness of the 'packaged' Mediterranean coastal resorts, developed with so little concern for the quality of the environment in the 1960s and 1970s. Less than a decade ago tour operators encouraged developers to believe that customers would buy 'any beach as long as it's hot, sunny and cheap' (with apologies to Henry Ford). This appears to be changing.

Overbuilt, ugly superstructure and congested roads and airports have created a reaction. Out of the UK, Spain attracted 4.5 million package tours in 1988. This had fallen to 2.6 million in 1991. Much of this fall is explained by economic recession, but changing attitudes toward the destination environment have played a part. The International Federation of Tour Operators (IFTO), with members in seventeen countries, clearly thinks so, and it should know. It is no coincidence that IFTO achieved a large grant from the EC, the Spanish Government, and

Balearic Island authorities in 1992 for a major research project designed to show how the destination environment can be protected, managed and developed in sustainable ways. This would not have occurred in the 1980s. It is indicative of future pressures on tour operators in other parts of the world.

Strategic decisions on volume and pricing

For hotels, visitor attractions and transport operators, annual decisions on capacity and average price levels are essentially tactical decisions in the light of previous strategic judgements and investment in buildings and equipment. Not so for tour operators. A combination of long lead times, the dominance of an unpredictable external business environment, and the ability to contract additional capacity, means that annual decisions on volume and average price levels are strategic rather than tactical issues. The two decisions are of course closely related because of the influences on pricing policy of what the market will bear at any point in time.

If the initial guesstimates of capacity and pricing are proved wrong by events, the whole of marketing tactics revolve around attempts to retrieve the situation in the face of fierce competition for share of market. These decisions need strong entrepreneurial flair and very strong nerves to hold to decisions or change them boldly as events occur. Figure 14.1 provides ample evidence of the narrowness of the margins at stake in the crucial volume and price decisions.

Product/market portfolios

The third, and related, strategic consideration for operators is concerned with the content and balance of the product portfolio, as represented in their programmes. The volume and price aspects noted earlier are not independent variables but functions of specific product types. A product portfolio is a mix of destinations, accommodation types, and range of elements to be included in the product, such as excursions. To give two examples, there was a massive switch to self-catering apartments and villas abroad offered to the British holiday market in the 1980s, reflecting a strategic portfolio change. From a small base, the demand for self-catering holidays trebled between 1981 and 1985, while the demand for tours based on hotel accommodation increased by less than a half. In terms of markets inclusive tours to Italy from Britain fell by 25 per cent between 1988 and 1991, while ITs to France grew by 33 per cent over the same period. The inclusive tour market from the UK to the USA grew by 258 per cent between 1987 and 1991, but from the USA to the UK it fell by nearly 50 per cent in the same period. Where profit or loss is balanced on just a few marginal percentage points above break-even load factors, it becomes vital to offer the range of products most in demand.

While segmentation of tour-operator products is still developing in the 1990s, it is already reflected in the way in which brochures, the main marketing tool for operators, are put together. There is a strategic balance to be struck between the need for separate brochures to appeal to different market segments, and the even more powerful current need to reduce the number of brochures because of the limitations of rack space in retail outlets. There is an uneasy balance at present in which segmentation often occurs within the brochure, but this is not necessarily a cost-effective or consumer-appealing procedure, and strategic changes may be expected in the next few years.

Positioning and image

Competition between tour operators has tended in the last decade to focus primarily on price and on product portfolios. Image and positioning, although not ignored, have very clearly taken second place to price competition. This probably reflects the strong growth trends that low prices stimulated in a highly price-elastic market. As the market reaches maturity, however, competition seems certain to switch from price to branding and images. Hotels in developed countries already operate in mature markets in the 1990s, and it is interesting to observe the extent to which positioning has become a major element in their marketing strategies. The Thomson case in Part Six of the book reveals interesting evidence of positioning on quality.

Distribution

The fifth strategic issue to be noted in this section is that of distribution or providing access for customers. For all tour operators the cost of distribution is normally the largest item of their total marketing expenditure. Apart from the basic variable costs of commission paid on sales, there are heavy, essentially fixed costs incurred in distribution, including the printing and distribution of brochures, installing and maintaining computer links with retail outlets, regular sales promotion and merchandising efforts to maintain display space, and educationals. A sales force may also be required in the continuous process of motivating distributors in competitive conditions.

For all operators there is a strategic choice to be made between marketing direct to customers or achieving sales through travel retailers. In 1993 most operators of ITs in Britain were members of the same trade association as the retail agents, the Association of British Travel Agents (ABTA). The USA equivalent is the American Society of Travel Agents (ASTA), although tour operators are far less important in the American market than in the British. Some tour operators, such as Portland Holidays, Martin Rooks and Tjaereborg, have chosen to pursue a straight direct-response marketing policy, with no retail agency involvement. The major operators in Britain are Thomson Holidays, Airtours and Owners Abroad (1993), and they sell almost exclusively through retailers. In the early 1990s it seems probable

than some 80 per cent of all ITs to destinations abroad are sold through agency outlets.

Apart from the basic choice, direct or retail sales, many nuances are also strategic matters. For example, should particular retailers get extra support? Should extra commission be paid in some circumstances but not in others? Is there scope for some retailers to put their own labels on to some tours? Above all, because general travel retailing of holidays is not a very skilled business, given modern technology, and carries few risks or capital start-up costs, is there scope for creating completely new retail travel outlets by exploiting the earning capacity of space in high-street outlets such as national banks, post offices, and supermarkets, which may be currently under-utilized?

In the early 1990s these important issues were seldom addressed openly, since they called into question the whole business relationship between retailers and operators, as well as their 'political' relationship within ABTA. Strategically, because operators carry the main risk and control prices, operators are in a stronger position in distribution channels than manufacturers of consumer goods dealing, for example, with supermarkets, which do take risks. At the time of writing there is an uneasy *status quo* between operator and retailer, in which both are more or less satisfied. Again, as markets mature, these issues seem certain to emerge and will require careful strategic response. The change in status of ABTA following the implementation of the EC Package Holiday Directive in 1993 appears likely to provoke changes in the next 5 years. UK tour operators are expected to form their own separate association in 1994.

Tactical marketing

As noted in the previous section, strategic decisions will determine the product/market portfolio, the product images and positioning, the capacity of the programme to be offered, the price range in the brochures, and the structure of the distribution system to be used. In other words, all the four Ps are essentially strategic decisions, and the principal role for marketing tactics is to secure a continuous flow of bookings for the programme from the day it is offered for sale. The flow of bookings is of course related to the target load factors for seats and beds, on which the profitability of the operator depends. The rate at which bookings and deposits are achieved also determines the weekly cash flow of both operators and retailers, and is required to meet regular commitments to fixed costs and contractual obligations, especially deposits to air-charter operators.

Because of the long lead times in getting a programme from initial planning to the point of sale, and especially because competitors' prices and the capacity of their programmes cannot be known in advance, it is almost inevitable that every year operators will find themselves with too much or too little capacity in relation to the available demand. This is not incompetence, it is the nature of the business described earlier in the chapter. In this tactical context it is easy to support the view of Alan Sugar (entrepreneurial boss of the Amstrad corporation), who informed an astonished audience at the City University Business School of London in 1987 that 'in a way, marketing is just like a stall in Petticoat Lane . . . Frankly it is no different'. Tour operators have products as perishable as any on a market stall and they have a fixed amount of product they have to sell in the time available to them. If sales are slow (see below) customers will have to be stimulated through the range of available tactical methods. In the short run, a sales focus will be an inevitable response.

Figures 24.2 and 24.3 illustrate the key point that tactical responses are a function of the rate at which bookings are achieved over the selling period for each programme. Any programme that has been on the market for a year or more will have established a sales pattern, which can be represented as a graph with percentage load factor on the vertical axis, and weeks during

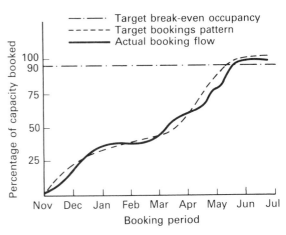

Figure 24.2 *Targeted and actual bookings achieved – normal year*

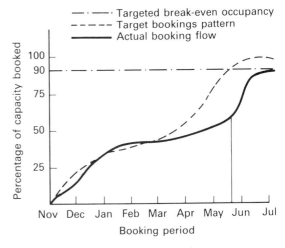

Figure 24.3 *Targeted and actual bookings achieved – problem year*

which the product is on sale on the horizontal axis. For new products, the pattern will have to be estimated from any previous experience with comparable products. With modern computer technology linked to reservation systems, it is easy to plot actual bookings against target on a daily and weekly basis.

If bookings follow the predicted path, the operators' strategy is working, and tactical promotional intervention will be minimal, with no need to commit contingency funds. Some last-minute intervention may still be necessary in the 4 weeks before departure, but otherwise Figure 24.2 represents the implementation of a successful strategy. If bookings move significantly ahead of prediction and are sustained at high level over some weeks, provided that the market indications remain favourable, the tactical response will be to look for additional product capacity and to reduce promotional spending. If, on the other hand, bookings fall below the targeted level, as they do over the months of April and May in Figure 24.3, decisive, aggressive tactical action becomes essential to reach the targeted break-even occupancy level represented in the figure at around the 90 per cent load factor level. For every booking below the 90 per cent level, the operator loses money; for every booking above it up to maximum occupancy, he generates a significant addition to profit. The incentive to engage in active tactical promotion will be obvious.

It is of course very much a matter of judgement as to when any additional promotion starts, and to what extent it occurs. Assuming that operators' prices and products are broadly competitive, if one operator sees the trend noted in Figure 24.3, it is probable that all operators in the same product field will experience similar weakness in their rate of bookings about the same time. They will all have to react, but how quickly and by how much will be closely guarded commercial secrets, reflecting their view of the influences at work in the external environment.

For tour operators, the choices for tactical promotion are:

- Increased advertising weight.
- Sales promotions aimed at consumers, such as competitions, free childrens' places (assuming these are not part of the original product), special discounts for bookings received by a certain date.

- Sales promotion aimed at retailers.
- Price-cutting to stimulate sales for targeted weeks.

In Figure 24.3 the tactical action taken in mid-April is shown to push the rate of bookings back up towards target, although only to the break-even level. If such tactical effort did not succeed, the operator would have no choice but to consolidate his programme in order to avoid a heavy loss. Consolidation is the technical term used in charter airlines to denote the cancellation of specified flights that would be uneconomic to operate at the load factors available. Passengers would be offered other flights in the expectation that, say, two flights could operate profitably where three might all operate at a loss.

Consolidated flights lead to cancelled accommodation allocations, and are understandably unpopular among customers as well as hoteliers. Since tour operators depend heavily on the goodwill of clients and suppliers, there is every reason to stimulate demand before taking the superficially less costly option of consolidation. The powerful interest of the mass media in stories about badly treated holiday-makers is an ever-present concern for operators, as are investigations by consumer associations seeking to expose unreasonable business practices. With the operation of the EC Package Holiday Directive since 1993, traditional last-minute consolidations are in any case no longer an option.

The operators' links with retailers, especially where on-line computers can be used to communicate the late availability of products and handle bookings, are enormously helpful in the tactical process of notifying and selling last-minute discounted offers. The merchandising power of a national retailer distribution system to secure last-minute sales, often just days before departure, is perhaps the retailers' most powerful advantage to operators. No other form of marketing in the industry works as fast and cost-effectively as the combined operator and retailer promotion focused on price. It is widely recognized in the industry that the first 60 per cent of bookings are easy to achieve on a well-designed programme. The next 30 per cent, and especially the last 10 per cent, on which so much of the profit depends, are very much more difficult; these sales at the margin are the main target of tactical marketing.

Case studies supporting this chapter

Part Six of the book contains one case relevant to marketing for tour operators. It sets out the strategy employed by Thomson, the UK's leading tour operator, to develop and promote enhanced quality products in its main summer holidays programme from the UK to Mediterranean destinations.

Chapter summary

This chapter sets out a deliberately broad view of marketing inclusive tours and product packages, intended to stress the similarities existing between the major contracting firms and producer organizations increasingly interested in marketing their own packages. As product suppliers, such as accommodation interests, surface transport companies, and the larger managed attractions grow in size and are large enough to justify their own central marketing departments, they are increasingly likely to assemble and market their own packages to improve utilization of their high fixed cost assets. The bigger independent contractors take far greater risks of course, especially in contracting air-transport charters, for which there are significant penalties if the contracts cannot be met because of inadequate demand.

All packages are intended to solve the natural inefficiencies inherent in matching demand and supply, especially in the leisure sector. All are intended to optimize utilization rates for available capacity that would not otherwise be sold.

The pressure on marketing managers to sell their programmes is enormous and puts great emphasis on the day-to-day tactical sales management of demand. On the other hand, the chapter stresses the strategic advantages of marketing packages. These are likely to become more significant over the next decade, especially if the rapid market growth of the 1980s slows, and the emphasis of competition shifts from price to other aspects of the marketing mix. As this author put it in 1991, 'There are sound reasons for believing that the concept of packaging, more effectively presented, will become more not less attractive to customers in the 1990s . . . The share of market taken by truly independent travel, organized and paid for individually at published tariffs, is likely to decline'.

Finally, it is interesting to consider that a tour operator's brochure demonstrates all an operator knows about the aspirations and needs of his targeted customers. What appears in print therefore represents the state of the marketing art as it is understood by operators of packages at any point in time. As discussed in Chapter 17, the brochure is the tangible representation of the product portfolio and prices; it is a principal form of promotion, and the way it is distributed to customers represents a most important strategic marketing choice. Few other 'manufacturers' have to wear their marketing knowledge 'on their sleeve', as tour operators must. Content analysis of brochures is a good exercise for students and competitors.

Part Six

Case Histories of Marketing Practice in Travel and Tourism

1

Marketing Canada – to the US market

This case sets out the market-led evolution and development of *Tourism Canada*'s marketing goals and strategy aimed at targeted market segments in the USA. The case focuses mainly on the advertising element of the total campaign, which used a carefully researched strapline, 'Canada, The World Next Door'. The campaign started in 1986, and, with a process of continuing development and adjustment described here, was still running in 1992, when the case was written. As the results show, the campaign was instrumental in shifting attitudes and awareness among target groups in the USA. It is also judged to have had a major influence in halting a 10-year slide in the number of American visits to Canada and helped to achieve growth of some 750,000 visits a year between 1985 and 1990 (see the Table A1.1).

Table A1.1 *United States visits to Canada, 1974 to 1990*

Spending one or more nights	
Year	Number (millions)
1974	12.8
1976	11.7
1978	11.3
1980	11.0
1982	10.5
1984	11.3
1986	13.6
1988	12.8
1990	12.3

Source: Statistics Canada

The case explains why a new marketing campaign was needed and places particular emphasis on the strategic role of market research surveys. Research not only determined which segments to target but also provided the basis for all stages of the campaign strategy and guided the development of advertising materials. Research was also used to monitor and evaluate the results achieved.

Readers may find it interesting to contrast the sophisticated approach to developing a campaign adopted by a large national tourist office of a developed country to influence its major international market, with the totally different approach to marketing adopted by developing island nations in the South Pacific to influence their long-haul target markets in Europe. *Tourism Canada* could afford to approach its target markets directly through advertising as well as facilitating and supporting the work of its provincial partners and travel trade. The South Pacific islands had to seek an indirect route through tour operators. Both approaches are valid and are justified in the context of the cases.

1 Background

Tourism Canada, the national tourist office for Canada, is a branch of the federal government. At the time this strategy started in 1986 it was part of the Department of Regional Industrial

Expansion. It is now located (1992) within the Department of Industry, Science and Technology. Canada's tourism interests in foreign countries are represented by the Department of External Affairs. *Tourism Canada* is managed by an Assistant Deputy Minister and in the late 1980s was divided into three divisions: marketing, development, and policy-research. There have been minor changes in organizational structure since 1985 but the main responsibilities have remained. In the marketing area its concern is with foreign visitors to Canada. Each of the Canadian provinces and territories has a government department or agency responsible for tourism marketing and development. As a result, there is a clear requirement for close co-operation between federal and provincial authorities, on the one hand, and the tourism industry, on the other.

In the period 1973 to 1982 the number of American tourists arriving in Canada decreased from 13.5 million to 10.5 million – a loss of 3 million tourists in a 10-year period. This loss of more than 20 per cent was in sharp contrast to worldwide tourism growth. It also occurred in a period when foreign travel by Americans was growing. A complete review of Tourism Canada's activities took place in 1984 and resulted in the publication of a landmark document, *Tourism Tomorrow – Towards a Canadian Tourism Strategy*. The release of this report was followed by a 4-month period of consultation with industry in all parts of the country. This consultation was completed by a 3-day conference in Ottawa in October 1985. This process led to the development and adoption of a new marketing strategy for the US market.

In order to develop a better understanding of the American market and to provide the information necessary for a marketing strategy geared to the mid-1980s, a massive market research project was commissioned in June 1985. Early results were available for the October 1985 conference and final results by January 1986.

The study was based on 9,000 in-home personal interviews that averaged 50 minutes to administer. In order for the results to be usable and valid both nationally and regionally, the sample was designed to provide 1,000 interviews in each of the nine census divisions of the United States. The study identified eight pleasure-trip types in the American market and indicated that Canada had good market opportunities in three of them, *touring, outdoor* and *city*. The study also brought out Canada's strengths and weaknesses for each of these types of tourism. The new marketing campaign was designed to target the three key trip-type segments, and to overcome the negative images of Canada while reinforcing the positive elements.

2   Analytical and strategic issues

The research and analysis process identified three major segments that had a high potential for visits to Canada. It illustrated quite clearly the strengths upon which Canada could build and the real or perceived weaknesses in Canadian tourism products, related to these segments, that needed to be overcome. The three segments were:

1 *Touring*. The one key benefit that differentiated Canada from the United States was the fact that Canada was a foreign country, perceived as offering a different set of cultural experiences and way of life. This segment is one that values the cultural factor, lives in major urban centres and is likely to be 'upscale' in socio-economic terms. Major weaknesses were reported in the infrastructure in Canada – hotels, restaurants, landmarks and things to see and do.
2 *Outdoor*. Canada's historic image in the United States is that of the great outdoors. The research indicated, however, that

Americans were equally positive about their own areas, which were much closer to home. Canada's outdoors were seen as more natural and untouched than those in the USA, and Canada was seen as offering a different life style. Weaknesses focused around Canada being less well known; having a poor climate, which made the country less suitable for a wide variety of water sports; being too far away; having fewer things to see and do, and being a bit too wild. The research showed that the best outdoor appeal to the market would be in the form of specific niches – fishing, hunting and exploring wilderness areas that provided a sense of adventure.

3 *City.* While Americans had a positive image of Canadian cities, they had an even better one of their own cities. Strengths for Canadian cities included such items as inexpensive, clean, uncrowded, safe, beautiful, offering different cultures and way of life. Weaknesses were reported in such things as popularity, accommodation, food, excitement, and things to see and do. A major gap appeared in the perception of Canadian cities and what they really had to offer.

The strategic issue emerged as one of convincing the three segments that Canada could offer what they were looking for, and that in many cases the reality of the product delivery was far better than their perception.

3 Marketing objectives and strategy

1 *Goal.* Contribute to an increase in Canada's tourism export revenue.
2 *Means.*
  (a) Raise awareness of Canada as an international travel destination.
  (b) Strengthen Canada's image as a major international travel destination with a distinct identity.
  (c) Assist selected operators in the Canadian and foreign tourism industries through a

variety of trade development programmes and the dissemination of market and product information.
3 *Guiding principles.* Tourism Canada will:
  (a) Develop federal efforts in consultation with public and private sector partners.
  (b) Execute market-development activities in partnership with the public and private sectors wherever possible.

4 Segments targeted

Three markets in the United States were targeted:

1 *Touring.* Touring visitors take trips that have no single focus, consisting of a mix of individual products and an average duration of about 8 days. The automobile is the primary mode of transportation, but just over half the trips are by planes, bus, or rental cars. Nearly half the trips used motels for accommodation and over a third used hotels.
2 *Outdoors.* Outdoor visitors usually comprise younger American families with children. Travel is by car, truck or recreational vehicle to natural areas. Visitors undertake a minimum amount of planning, and visits last for 3 to 4 days.
3 *City.* City trips are typically taken by Americans who are married, middle-aged, and above average in income and educational levels. The city selected is likely to be famous, beautiful, popular with travellers, and have a variety of services and amenities. The trip is in many ways an extended weekend with an average duration of 3 days.

5 Products involved

From the wide array of product components available in Canada, it was necessary to bring together or coalesce these elements into 'bundles' that would meet the needs of the targeted segments, build upon the strengths of Canada and start to overcome the negative images. The touring product was designed around a selection of images used for both television and print that stressed the heritage and the 'foreign' feel of the country. The outdoor product positioned Canada's wilderness as a natural yet warmly hospitable playground open to everybody. The city product was built around fun and games and nightlife in Canadian cities. In all three products stress was placed upon the quality and choice of the tourism 'infrastructure', such as accommodation, restaurants and other visitor facilities.

6 Marketing campaign details – advertising

The promotional campaign developed around four main types of media: TV advertising, print advertising, co-operative advertising, and promotional materials. This case study deals primarily with the television-advertising aspect of the campaign. All media messages were based around three themes that related closely to the targeted segments. The touring segment was developed around a theme or concept labelled *Old World*, the outdoors segments into one called *Wild World*, and the city into *New World*.

The new campaign was put through an extensive testing programme. The first 'concept boards' (sketches of the way the advertisements would appear) for the three themes were exposed to focused group discussion sessions in Atlanta, Boston, Chicago, New York and San Francisco. These tests indicated that *Wild World* and *New World* required further development. *Wild World* still left doubts about access, family activities and amenities, while *New World* persuaded the market that Canada did have modern cities but left doubts about the possibilities of having fun. Further work on both the television and print advertising

culminated in a further round of focused group discussions and evaluation.

At the same time, testing was carried out for a winning campaign slogan. The importance of the foreign atmosphere and of being able to experience cultural differences relatively close at hand lead to the slogan *The World Next Door* being adopted.

By the end of 1985 the new campaign was ready to launch in the spring/summer campaign of 1986. Television was to be used dramatically to enlarge and enrich the image; print to highlight particular points of entry, touring details, and provincial and territorial phone numbers to call for more information.

A very large proportion of Tourism Canada's promotional budget in the United States has been devoted to the consumer spring/summer campaign over time (see Table A1.2). *The World Next Door* campaign did not change the seasonal weighting pattern.

The lower share for the spring/summer campaign in the first 3 years of the *New World Next Door* campaign is accounted for by expenditures on fall and winter campaigns. Such campaigns had not been part of the programme in fiscal years 1984-5 and 1985-6.

Concurrent with the introduction of the new marketing campaign came the launch of performance monitoring and evaluation activity that had as its objective 'to determine the effectiveness of Tourism Canada's spring/summer advertising campaign in the

Table A1.2 *Tourism Canada's promotional spending*

Fiscal Year	Budget in 000s – Canadian dollars	
	Spring/Summer	Total for the year
1984-85	13,030.0	16.460.0
1986-87*	13,091.0	18.043.3
1987-88	17,500.0	23.485.0
1988-89	15,709.5	21.419.0
1989-90	16,033.0	19.871.8

*Start of *World Next Door* Campaign
Source: Tourism Canada

United States'. The evaluation was based on two waves of telephone interviews with samples of respondents in Boston, Chicago, New York and San Francisco, drawn to represent the target markets. One wave of interviewing was done before the start of the campaign, the other immediately after the end of it. The evaluation research has been conducted annually since 1986.

7 Results achieved and case summary

The goal of the campaign was to increase Canada's tourism export revenues from the United States. To measure the results against this goal, changes in the number of overnight visits from the United States to Canada are used. The actual dollar value of tourism expenditure in Canada could have been the unit of measure, but visitor numbers are a suitable surrogate, as the impact of monetary inflation does not have to be discounted. In using either measure it must be remembered that two major events, Expo 86 in Vancouver, BC, and the Winter Olympics in 1988 in Calgary, Alberta, generated large numbers of visitors and worked to increase the awareness of Canada in the American market. A major increase in American visitors was recorded in 1986, when 2 million more of them came to Canada than in 1985, an increase of just under 18 per cent. In order to take a longer term view of the case, there was a growth of over 750,000 visitors, or 6.6 per cent, between 1985 and 1990, with the 1990 total exceeding 12.3 million. Thus there was an increase since the start of the campaign in 1986 and the visitor results show that the erosion which had been characteristic of the market between 1972 and 1983 had been reversed. The campaign had met its overall goal of increasing tourism export revenues.

Two of the objectives set for the campaign were to raise awareness of Canada as an international travel destination and to strengthen Canada's image as a travel destination. The advertising evaluation research results (Tables A1.3 and A1.4) have provided measures of how well these objectives were met. Spontaneous awareness of Canada by trip type has shown differing trends over the period 1986 to 1990. The 1986 campaign significantly increased awareness of Canada, particularly for touring and outdoor trips. Awareness of Canada for city trips reached a high point in 1988. There was a lowering of awareness levels over time since the high point for touring and outdoors in 1986, and for cities in 1988.

There was a significant improvement in Canada's image as a vacation destination since the research started in 1986. All of the image

Table A1.3 *Post-campaign indicators*

Percentage of respondents answering positively

Year	Awareness of Canada	Awareness of ads	Recall of slogan
1986	38	60	45
1987	37	59	50
1988	38	60	60
1989	31	59	72
1990	28	58	59

Source: Angus-Reid, 1990 USA Ad Tracking Study, Final Report, October 1990

Table A1.4 *Image of Canada on specific attributes*

Percentage of respondents answering positively

Year	Cultural Diversity	Touring Vacation	Foreign Flavour	Exciting	Nightlife
Pre 1986	69	69	47	49	23
Post 1988	73	73	56	62	37
Post 1989	72	69	53	58	36
Post 1990	75	74	57	58	39

Source: Angus-Reid, 1990 USA Ad Tracking Study, Final Report, October 1990

attributes measured registered an increase at some time during the 5-year period. Three attributes, *foreign flavour, nightlife* and *exciting* showed the most long term growth. Two others, *cultural diversity* and a *place for a touring vacation,* were key strengths at the start and their strong position was reinforced. Spontaneous and aided recall of the campaign slogan was also tracked. This measure showed consistent growth from 1986 to 1989 but registered a decrease in 1990.

It may be concluded that the campaign had mostly positive results in raising Americans' awareness and image of Canada.

The results of the campaign were continually monitored and necessary adjustments were made to the strategy over time. A history of the television commercials between 1986 and 1990 illustrates the nature of the creative changes that were made. The original three, *Old World, Wild World* and *New World,* were used in 60-second versions in the spring, summer and fall campaigns of 1986 and the spring and summer ones of 1987.

The evaluation research indicated at the end of the 1987 campaign that even greater play could be given to Canada's foreign flavour. Two new television commercials were developed as a result of the research and pre-production consumer reaction testing. These commercials, *Trapeze* and *Rodeo,* were montages that blended the three trip types into specific executions. They were produced in 30-second versions and were the basis of the 1988 and 1989 spring and summer campaigns. In 1988 they were joined by *Pioneer,* a 30-second commercial designed specifically to feature autumn in Canada and to appeal to an off-season market.

The evaluation research at the end of the 1989 campaign indicated that *Trapeze* and *Rodeo* were showing signs of wear, and that a good deal of the positive response to the campaign was the result of the execution of the ads themselves rather than to Canada as a travel destination. In 1989 Tourism Canada updated the market knowledge gained through the 1985 study by participating in new research known as

'Longwoods Travel - USA'. The results of the new study confirmed many aspects of the earlier one and permitted a measurement of how Canada had fared in the market since 1986. The market and evaluation research lead to a revision of the TV advertising after completion of the 1989 campaign.

Four new commercials were developed to pursue the advantages that Canada has in the American market and to differentiate the Canadian message from the clutter of a good deal of television advertising in the United States that had adapted the montage approach. These new commercials expressed Canada's distinctiveness in terms of culture, foreign flavour, urban appeal and outdoor appeal. They were subjected to the usual pre-testing before final approval and production. The four, *Deux Cafés, The Raven, My Dream,* and *Out and About,* were 30-second versions and provided the backbone of the TV advertising campaign in 1990 and 1991.

8 Case summary

The 'World Next Door' campaign illustrates several key elements that are vital to success in marketing for national tourist offices in developed countries:

1 A detailed in-depth knowledge of the market obtained from well-designed and well-executed research. The research must be carefully analysed and the implications for marketing clearly defined and justified.
2 The research results must be integral to the objectives and to the creative strategy developed.
3 Market testing of all creative concepts and of finished material must be standard aspects of advertising development.
4 A well-designed, well-executed and consistent monitoring and evaluation research procedure must be set up and maintained.

5 Adjustments to the campaign must be made, in accordance with the findings of the evaluation research.

6 Market knowledge can get out of date very quickly, hence follow-up research must be carried out at regular intervals. The follow-up research must be consistent with the prior study.

All these steps provide a basis for the successful execution of creativity and contribute in a major way to the fulfilment and attainment of the objectives.

The 'World Next Door' campaign had been in existence for 6 years when this case was written in early 1992. It was expected that there would be a reassessment of the advertising that has been used for the past 2 years, and any necessary changes would be instituted when the results of the 1991 evaluation research were available.

Case contributed by Gordon D Taylor, former Manager, Research and Analysis for Tourism Canada (now a consultant).

2

Marketing South Pacific islands – to European countries

Twelve South Pacific island nations are the subject of this case. They are mostly very small, their national tourist offices usually have fewer than six executive staff; and their budgets and expertise are too limited to make any impact on long-haul markets such as the USA, and Europe.

In common with many other developing countries, the islands face major constraints in tourism marketing. They need more tourism in order to grow economically and to be able to sustain their cultural and physical environments. But they already have a high proportion of Australians and New Zealanders from their own region, and these are mainly price-conscious mature markets, unlikely to provide the level of growth the islands need to support their populations. They need therefore to attract high-spending long-haul markets, but they are too small individually to undertake professional marketing campaigns.

Their response, stimulated and undertaken through an EC-funded project over recent years, has been to form a co-operative organization known as the Tourism Council of the South Pacific (TCSP). The Council was formed for marketing, development and other purposes. This case explains how the TCSP, using the techniques explained in Chapter 20 of this book, developed a marketing strategy to tackle long-haul-markets in Europe. Their chosen strategy

was to concentrate on marketing indirectly through tour operators as their principal target 'customers', providing the maximum level of *facilitation* in the target markets of origin that their budgets would allow. The promotion and distribution strategy is described in the context of products available in the islands, and the main results of the campaign are presented.

The case stresses that facilitation was also needed to stimulate and help co-ordinate the suppliers of tourism products in the islands, and this was one of the benefits of a market-led strategy. The exposure of local operators to visits by tourism professionals from countries of origin is an important and more effective way to communicate the need for high standards than any amount of NTO seminars and advisory publications.

1 Background

The twelve member countries of the Tourism Council of the South Pacific (TCSP) listed in Table A2.1 received 650,000 foreign tourist arrivals and earned US$483 million in tourist receipts in 1990. Although this is less than 1 per cent of world totals, tourism makes a significant contribution to the economies of these generally small island nations, in terms of foreign

Table A2.1 *South Pacific tourism sector statistical profile*

Total number of hotel rooms in 1991	:	13,480
Number of tourist arrivals in 1990	:	650,759
Total tourist receipts in 1990	:	US$483 million

Key tourism indicators in 1990

Country	Population (000s)	Int'l tourist arrivals	% share	Int'l tourist receipts (US$ m)	% Share	Number of hotel rooms	% share
Am. Samoa	39	47,337	7.3	10	2.1	230	1.7
Cook Islands	18	33,882	5.2	16	3.3	700	5.2
Fiji	736	278,996	42.9	227	47.0	5,050	37.5
Tahiti	195	132,361	20.3	142	29.4	2,820	20.9
Kiribati	72	3,332	0.5	2	0.4	80	0.6
Niue	2	640	0.1	†	–	30	0.2
PNG	3,670	40,742	6.3	28	5.8	2,650	19.6
Solomon Is.	310	9,195	1.4	4	0.8	270	2.0
Tonga	96	20,919	3.2	9	1.8	550	4.1
Tuvalu	8	671	0.1	†	–	30	0.2
Vanuatu	143	35,042	5.4	25	5.2	630	4.7
W. Samoa	164	47,642	7.3	20	4.2	440	3.3
TOTAL	5,453	650,759	100.0	483	100.0	13,480	100.0

† *less than one million US dollars*
Sources: TCSP Visitor Surveys, Balance of Payments data, National Statistics Offices

Tourist arrivals to TCSP countries by main market area, 1987 and 1990 (000s)

Market	1987	% share	1990	% share	Growth rate 1987–90 (%)
Australia	116.3	21.6	167.9	25.8	44.4
New Zealand	61.6	11.5	72.8	11.2	18.2
USA	144.3	26.9	108.9	16.7	–24.5
Canada	24.6	4.6	27.2	4.2	10.6
Europe	83.0	15.4	117.5	18.0	41.6
Japan	13.1	2.4	40.3	6.2	207.6
Pacific Is.	73.0	13.6	88.0	13.5	19.6
Other Asia	5.5	1.0	14.7	2.3	167.3
Others	16.0	3.0	13.6	2.1	–15.0
TOTAL	537.4	100.0	650.9	100.0	21.1

Sources: TCSP and National Statistics Offices

* Statistical data cover the following twelve TCSP member countries: American Samoa, Cook Islands, Fiji, French Polynesia (Tahiti), Kiribati, Niue, Papua New Guinea, Solomon Islands, Tonga, Tuvalu, Vanuatu and Western Samoa. Data on two other recent members of the TCSP – Federated States of Micronesia and Marshall Islands – are not available.

exchange earnings, income and job creation. See Table A2.1 for a list of the TCSP countries and a summary statistical profile of the tourism sector.

Traditionally, Australia and New Zealand have been the main visitor-source countries for most South Pacific Islands. However, it has been generally recognized that these two relatively mature markets cannot provide a sufficiently large volume of potential tourism to ensure future growth in the region. Other potential markets have to be developed, and the long-haul markets of North America, Europe and Japan have been analysed and targeted for development.

Individually the national tourism organizations (NTOs) of these island countries are small and seriously under-resourced in terms of marketing budgets and manpower. With the exceptions of Fiji, Papua New Guinea (PNG), Solomon Islands and Tahiti, Table A2.1 shows that eight of the twelve member countries have resident populations of under 200,000 people. In at least eight of the countries the NTO comprises five or less executive officers.

Size alone therefore implies a massive constraint on what each country can achieve on its own account. They lack both staff and budgets to engage effectively in international long-haul marketing, and, in particular, to cultivate the growth potential of niche markets in European countries of origin.

Over the last 20 years the South Pacific island region has been the focus for development aid by Australia, Japan and increasingly, the European Community. The advent of TSCP itself is closely related to this regional aid and the recognition of tourism as one of the sectors of the island economies that holds substantial potential, and therefore merits appropriate assistance.

Founded in the early 1980s as an informal association of NTOs in the region, the TCSP became a regional intergovernmental organization, with a permanent secretariat based in Suva, Fiji, in 1988. Its fundamental objective is to foster regional co-operation in the development and promotion of tourism in the island nations of the South Pacific. It therefore aims to achieve benefits for its members through the pooling of resources and other advantages of collective action within a regional approach.

Since 1986 the TCSP has been assisted by the European Community through the Pacific Regional Tourism Development Programme, a technical and development assistance project financed from the European Development Fund within the framework of the Lomé Convention. In recent years the TCSP annual budget, which covers a work programme of marketing, planning and development, research and statistics, and education and training activities, has been approximately £1.25 million. It has an executive staff of five officers supported by technical assistants.

2   Analysis and strategic issues

As a matter of priority, systematic strategic marketing planning was undertaken in 1987, with guidance and expertise provided through the EC-funded project. Extensive research in key European tourist generating countries provided the basis for the selection of products and markets and the formulation of strategy.

The South Pacific islands possess significant natural and cultural attractions and an outstanding marine environment, as well as their sun-drenched tropical ambience and exotic image. These attractions provide a strong base for a wide range of tourist activities and interests, especially holidays. However, in relation to potential long-haul markets in Europe there are a number of constraints that directly influence marketing strategy. These key strategic issues relate to:

● Lack of market awareness of the region throughout Europe as a potential tourist destination on the part of both the travel trade and the consumers.

- Relatively difficult and costly access (over 20 hours' flying time), reflecting distance from European markets, inadequate air services, insufficient interline airfares and the high cost of intra-regional fares.
- Qualitatively inadequate accommodation facilities in certain islands, which precludes penetration of some up-market segments.
- Insufficiently developed attractions to meet the modern demands of travellers already used to international standards.
- Environmental constraints designed to protect the unique, yet fragile, natural and cultural environment of the islands, on which tourism is founded and on which its long-term future depends.

These constraints were compounded in 1989 by:

- Lack of any form of field marketing organization to represent the region in key long-haul markets.
- Insufficient budgetary resources to enable any form of large-scale consumer and sales promotion, especially advertising.
- Generally weak NTOs, owing to small size, lack of training and political influence.
- Relatively weak trading partners in the islands (accommodation, attractions, tour operators), again due to small size and lack of training and experience.

Finally, while Fiji and Tahiti's dominance of current tourism markets provides opportunities and a springboard for promoting the region, it is necessary for TCSP to focus attention on the strategic need for achieving a wider regional spread of tourist traffic, naturally within the limits of available capacity and environmental constraints.

3 Marketing objectives and strategy

The Council's marketing objective is to promote market-led growth for sustainable development of the tourism sector of the region by stimulating market awareness and demand, acting as a catalyst, and co-ordinating and facilitating all other partners (NTOs, commercial sector, airlines) in regional co-operative marketing activities. Market growth will in turn stimulate product development and help secure the enhancement of product quality.

TCSP adopted a key strategy of travel-trade orientation to respond to existing visitor behaviour and travel patterns in the target markets, to expand destination product availability, and to increase awareness and familiarity with the product in the available distribution channels. While a direct marketing approach to potential markets has merits in some cases, it was not perceived as an option for the regional objectives of the TCSP.

In practice this strategy implies focusing promotional activity on the travel trade primarily to:

- Achieve greater availability and exposure of destination products in the market place through tour operators' (wholesalers) brochures.
- Diversify the destination product offers available by also featuring lesser known TCSP countries and special-interest products in tour operator's brochures.
- Maximize the market reach and effectiveness of the region's promotion resources through co-operation with tour operators.
- Educate, facilitate and incentivize the travel trade to carry out more effective consumer counselling and increase sales of tours to the South Pacific.

It will be appreciated that if TCSP achieves success with targeted tour operators, support from retail travel agents will follow from the normal marketing strategies of those operators – brochure distribution, etc.

4 Market segments targeted

Although Australia and New Zealand have been the traditional major source markets, TCSP has placed more emphasis on long-haul market development in the 1990s, than on promotion in the two traditional short-haul markets. The main reasons for this strategic position are the following:

● Several TCSP countries are already well represented individually in both markets and are relatively familiar to the travel trade.
● Fairly adequate air access renders the packaging and promotion of tours to the islands possible without special support.
● In both markets several tour operators are already dealing with the South Pacific.
● Most Australians and New Zealanders visit one resort in one country only. Because of the essentially single-destination nature of these segments, individual TCSP countries ultimately compete with each other and, therefore, engage in individual destination promotion.
● TCSP countries are more knowledgeable about the Australian and New Zealand markets than the long-haul ones, and can therefore increasingly undertake destination promotion without the need of outside assistance.

Focusing on the leisure-recreation travel market in Europe, the following general and special-interest travel markets have been targeted. The ranking order below represents the perceived importance of the segments.

General interest	Special interest
Stop-over market	Cultural tours market
Touring and sightseeing market	Nature tours market
Inter-island pleasure cruise market	Expedition cruise market
Honeymoon travel market (including weddings market)	Adventure tours market
	Dive travel market

5 Regional product strategy

It would not have been practical for TCSP to attempt to market the whole range of products available across the region. It has therefore focused its resources on a limited range of selected products. (Concentration on a limited regional product mix has not of course precluded individual TCSP countries from promoting their own full range of tourism products.) Thus the regional tourism product mix adopted by the Council is the following:

● Touring and sightseeing travel.
● Beach-based holidays/vacation, including inter-island pleasure cruises/sailing, honeymoon trips and weddings.
● Cultural tours, including expedition/exploration cruises.
● Nature tours (bird-watching, butterfly-viewing and collecting trips, orchid-viewing tours etc).
● Adventure tours (bushwalks, treks, white-water rafting, etc).
● Diving trips.

These products can be provided from the region's resource base in an environmentally sustainable manner, and it is recognized that capacity must be controlled. They account for the bulk of the existing leisure travel to the region and form the mainstay of the industry in many of the TCSP countries. The products in question correspond to markets with considerable growth potential.

It should be appreciated that all these products are relevant to other long-haul markets in Japan and North America as well as in Europe, so that there is also a long-haul marketing synergy to exploit.

6 Marketing campaign – promotion and distribution

The specific focus of this case history is the European market, for which European Community assistance has enabled TCSP to undertake a systematic, though modest, campaign. TCSP European campaign budgets were approximately £60,000 in 1989 and £225,000 in 1990 and 1991. This excludes the cost of participating at ITB Berlin and WTM London, both of which are co-ordinated by TCSP, but for which individual participating countries received separate subsidies from the European Community.

TCSP's European marketing campaign comprised the following main promotional activities:

● Appointment of two market representatives, one in the UK (also covering France, the Benelux countries and Scandinavia) and the other in Germany (also covering Italy, Switzerland and Austria). Their role is to provide a central reference source and distribution point for information on the region, service the travel trade and media, and generally to facilitate TCSP's key marketing partners in the region. Market representatives are paid a fee and agree their objectives and action programmes annually with TCSP. Action programmes are designed in a way that assists evaluation of success as noted later on.

● Selective but systematic distribution of 10,000 copies of the Council's yearly publication, *South Pacific Islands Travel Manual*, to travel agents and tour operators selected and monitored by the market representatives.

● Distribution of a series of promotional brochures on diving, sport fishing, adventure and nature tours printed in English, German and French, in addition to posters and other promotional material. This material is distributed mostly to tour operators and travel agents selected and monitored by the market representatives, and through them to potential clients.

● Co-operation with and assistance to tour operators with a view to increasing the number and scope of tour brochures featuring the South Pacific. This form of 'facilitation' includes provision of product information, contacts with the local commercial sector in the islands, familiarization tours and joint promotional activities. Initially no financial support was made available to assist the production of tour-operators' brochures, largely due to budgetary constraints.

● Participation at major travel trade fairs such as ITB Berlin and WTM London, with a combined regional stand – the South Pacific Village – as well as at other trade and consumer fairs, such as BIT Milan, TUR Gothenburg, Top Resa Dauville, etc.

● Education and facilitation of the European travel trade through an agreed programme of seminars, workshops, sales calls, newsletters and familiarization tours.

● Media relations designed to generate editorial coverage in both trade and consumer media, through releases, supply of editorial material and familiarization trips to the region.

● Encouragement and assistance to local operators providing accommodation, attractions, tour operations and other tourist facilities in the islands in order to focus greater attention on the European market and facilitate participation in regional promotional activities.

Much of this work was being undertaken in Europe for the South Pacific for the first time and was seen by TCSP as initially laying the necessary foundations for more intensive and product specific promotion in the future. While this campaign was being carried out (1989–91), a market research study of travel-trade perceptions of the South Pacific in the UK, Germany and France was undertaken in 1991. This was the first tourism research exercise specifically focused on the South Pacific ever undertaken in Europe. Its immediate objectives were not only to measure the impact of TCSP's initial marketing efforts, but also to provide useful input to future marketing planning.

7 Results achieved

The South Pacific region's initial campaign in Europe, which was planned and co-ordinated by the TCSP, has yielded positive results. Recognizing the considerable benefits of regional co-operative marketing initiatives, member NTOs and private sector concerns have taken full advantage of the new marketing opportunities offered by TCSP. For example, while only one country took part in the 1987 WTM London, no less than nine South Pacific island nations and fifty-five representatives participated in the 1991 fair within the framework of the 'South Pacific Village', which won the 'Most Effective Corporate Image' award. Between them these islands made thousands of contacts, supplied product information and laid the foundation for trade partnerships. It would not have happened without the regional marketing network established by TCSP.

The main results of the campaign, ascertained by either research or analysis of records have been:

- A steady increase in trade and consumer enquiries serviced by the two European market representatives (reviewed annually and assessed).
- A perceptible increase in market awareness of both the region and the TCSP, although still comparatively low and somewhat tenuous as measured by market research conducted in 1991.
- A sizeable increase in the number of tour operators that have included for the first time, or expanded their existing, South Pacific tour package programmes within their product portfolios.
- A very positive response to TCSP's trade promotional activities, such as seminars and workshops, on the part of tour operators and retail travel agents, as measured by attendance levels and feedback recorded by the organizers.

- A 42 per cent increase in European tourist arrivals in the South Pacific between 1987 and 1990. Although no direct causal relationship between TCSP marketing and arrivals can be proved, it is significant to note that throughout this period TCSP was the only major marketing agent active in the European market.

The experience gained from TCSP's initial campaign in Europe, largely supported by the market research findings, indicates the strategy of travel-trade orientation remains fundamentally valid. Certain adjustments or refinements need to be made in the medium term, however, to give the strategy a sharper focus and a harder selling edge.

Within the framework of TCSP's 1992–4 regional marketing plan, the following main adjustments are planned:

- TCSP's promotional brochures are to be revised and developed as more product-specific sales tools, to enhance their existing prime role as generic destination promotion pieces.
- The *South Pacific Islands Travel Manual*, a trade publication, will continue to be refined as a tour planner and sales tool and distributed more widely within the travel trade.

Undoubtedly, the most important adjustment to the regional marketing effort concerns the future distribution strategy. Although considerable progress has been made in introducing South Pacific packages in tour-operators' product portfolios in Europe, these efforts have been adversely affected by the following constraints.

First, the relatively small volume of demand for South Pacific holiday travel results in limited space for the region in tour operators' brochures, which mostly feature the two regional gateways and market leaders, Fiji and Tahiti. Second, because of the small market share generated by these limited South Pacific tour packages, tour operators are not willing to promote them heavily, since the investment required would not be justified by the projected revenue and profit. Third, special-interest tour packages of South Pacific islands, which could often be sold by smaller specialist wholesalers, are rarely available in the market place, again because of perceived adverse business economics.

To overcome these constraints, an enhanced tour operator support scheme will become the central feature of TCSP's European market development strategy. The scheme envisages the use of 'seed money' to incentivize and support operators who will develop substantial tour programmes, to include also the lesser known island countries, and to launch new special interest products. These will be backed by comprehensive and integrated promotion campaigns.

Although each scheme will by definition be a co-operative and jointly financed venture between the TCSP, local South Pacific tourism businesses, airlines and the tour operator concerned, it is the latter who will play the leading role in planning and implementing the promotion campaign. This is because of the operator's better local market knowledge and the fact that selling the tour programme is ultimately his responsibility.

Case contributed by John Yacoumis, Project Manager for The Pacific Regional Tourism Development Programme until 1992.

3

Marketing visitor attractions – Old Sturbridge Village, USA

This case provides a comprehensive example of the modern marketing approach for a large independent heritage attraction (a living history museum) dependent for its survival on generating revenue from the visiting public. Opened in 1946 and reaching its peak visitor numbers in 1972, Old Sturbridge Village (OSV) is an excellent example of a mature product operating in a mature market in New England, USA. It is a complex product that has to balance its multiple objectives as a museum , an educational facility, a speciality retail outlet, and a day out entertainment for a wide range of segments. In addition to providing an interesting early example of a fully designed and 'manufactured' attraction (the village was entirely created in its current fully enclosed location, using original structures brought on to the site), it has also become a resort in its own right, with accommodation available adjacent to the historic village.

Around the world most heritage attractions are facing up to the challenge of enhancing their products, containing costs and having to generate increased revenue 'in face of lower-than-anticipated revenue from the gate'. The case illustrates most of the principles of marketing noted in Chapter 21. In particular, it explains the importance of appreciating the external environment and developing a strategic

response. It describes an approach to segmentation and product formulation, the use of market research, and a proactive approach to targeted and measured marketing campaigns, with specific focus on creative promotion and distribution.

1 Background

Old Sturbridge Village (OSV) is a living history museum located in Massachusetts, which depicts life in a small rural New England community of the 1830s. Approximately 500,000 people from all over the world visit the 240-acre site annually, explore more than forty exhibit buildings, and talk with knowledgeable, costumed interpreters about life and work in the early nineteenth century as it might have existed in a typical farming village of that period. Antique buildings, moved to a new site from various New England locations, comprise a working community of farms, shops, mills and homes, interwoven with fields, gardens, orchards, woods, streams and unpaved roads.

Opened to the public in 1946, the Village, a non-profit charitable institution, now operates with a budget of over $8,000,000 and staff of 376, 145 of whom are full-time. The museum earns about 90 per cent of its budget through admissions, gift-shop sales, royalties, etc., and solicits gifts and grants from individuals, corporations, foundations and government agencies for the balance. Its endowment is valued at slightly more than $4,000,000.

In recent years the economic climate has challenged the museum's management to focus on new marketing strategies and more cost-effective operational structures and procedures to offset the impact of increased costs and lower-than-anticipated revenue from the gate. We have identified a number of factors that must be considered in making our plan.

Key assumptions

- The United States in the 1990s will be in a period of adjustment (slowing of population growth, higher inflation, rapid rise in labour force, participation by women, immigration the dominant source of population growth, rise in energy costs, central city population decline, heavy regulation of environment and growth in information technology) that will impact on all aspects of Old Sturbridge Village's operation.
- Changes in population characteristics alter the market: increasing number of people between 35 and 54, increasing single-parent households, increase in two working member households, decline in the birth rate, growth in upscale, well-educated, population in New England.
- Changing patterns in leisure time, and increasingly more intense competition within the leisure-time industry, demand new approaches to competitive strategy for OSV.
- OSV needs to broaden its national presence, build a broader audience base, further diversify and increase revenue streams, strengthen its financial position and achieve a financial balance through responsible cost control.
- Quality, accuracy, liveliness, convenience, comfort, a credible experience and competent staff are critical success factors, and important in designing our competitive strategy.

- The mission of Old Sturbridge Village will continue to include the lively presentations of history within the framework of a living history museum, the preservation of collections, and access to collections through formal exhibitions.

2 Strategic issues

OSV, like all attractions, is affected by changing economic and social conditions. The present is a time of challenge for the museum as we direct attention to strengthening opportunities for visitors, building market share, increasing access to our collections, and enhancing the museum's financial position. Today the museum is in a stable but tenuous financial condition. Earned income, which accounts for approximately 90 per cent of total revenue, is heavily dependent on attendance and to fluctuations in a difficult economic environment, unseasonable weather, consumer confidence, and the external business world.

The Village is located in a geographic area where population growth is projected at nearly 20 per cent over the next 20 years. The region is expanding and diversifying economically. Following the regional patterns of tourism, 85 per cent of the museum's attendance occurs during the months of May through October (though the museum is open all year round). Attendance peaked at 667,961 in 1972, when the tourism industry was less fragmented, and has averaged somewhat over 500,000 per annum for the past 10 years. The growth curve has been relatively flat in spite of increased efforts in marketing and programming.

3 Strategic objectives and programmes

The primary objective of this case is to illustrate OSV's marketing strategy as it relates to the total strategic plan for the museum. The main goal of the Village's marketing initiative is to maximize

Table A3.1 *OSV's marketing strategy*

Objective	Strategies	Action Plan
Increase paid-for attendance to the visitor centre to 600,000 by 1995	Broaden regional, national, international awareness of OSV. Expand local audience base. Improve utilization of networking institutions.	(a) Develop and implement a marketing plan that focuses on generating new and repeat visitors from northeast region. (b) Develop mechanisms for for tracking results. (c) Increase exposure through retail-product development and marketing. (d) Participate in national and international marketing of New England, Massachusetts, and Sturbridge.
	Increase attendance from special audiences – international, disabled multi-cultural and seniors.	(a) Create new information-dissemination channels. (b) Publicize programs to targeted audiences.
	Strengthen communication with local constituencies.	(a) Take an active local-tourism promotion role in association with others. (b) Participate in local events and community programmes.

awareness of OSV as a museum and visitor attraction. An equally critical goal is to build a broader and more diverse audience. See Table A3.1.

4   Target segments for OSV

Through careful observation and analysis, coupled with extensive marketing research conducted by outside agencies, OSV is able to identify target audiences.

Practical segmentation of our visitors is as follows:

- Residents living within one hour's drive; primarily supporting members.
- Regional visitors making day/weekend visits away from home.
- Visitors staying with friends/relatives within 1 hour's drive of Old Sturbridge Village.
- Visitors on vacation staying in lodging facilities and recreation vehicle parks within 1 hour's drive.
- International visitors coming to New England on holiday.

- Group visits arranged by wholesale motor-coach companies, receptive tour operations, and charter groups by associations.
- School groups and other educational visits.

Segmentation by economic, demographic, and geographic characteristics include:

- Over 75 per cent of our audience is over 35 years of age.
  Approximately 70 per cent of our visitors earn over $35,000 in household income.
- Our served market is predominantly Caucasian.
  More than 50 per cent of our audience has completed at least 4 years of college.
- 70 per cent reside in the northeast (USA) and are employed primarily in professional occupations; 30 per cent are from Massachusetts.
- Primary audience has two or fewer children at home.

As for *psychographic segmentation:*

- Visitors to the Village tend to seek a family experience; 53 per cent are adults with children and extended families.
- 60 per cent are first-time visitors who have learned of the attraction from family and friends.
  Mature audiences (50+ years) prefer to travel to New England in spring/fall and seek convenience, comfort and quality in their travels.
  Visitor expectations are to learn something, to have fun, to relax and escape the pressures of day-to-day life, to be mentally challenged, to do something different and to share an experience with family and friends.
- There are significant attributes underlying adult choices regarding leisure time:

  - Being with people, or social interaction.
  - Doing something worthwhile.
  - Feeling comfortable and at ease in one's surroundings.
  - Having a challenge of new experiences.
  - Having an opportunity to learn.
  - Active participation.

5 The Old Sturbridge Village product and pricing

As outlined in Chapter 8 of this book, the components of the overall tourism product are multi-faceted. The five main components of the overall product – destination attraction, destination facilities and services, accessibility of the destination, image of the destination, and price to the consumer – coincide exactly with the OSV product.

The Village is best categorized as a cultural attraction. However, it boasts the characteristics of a natural attraction in its aesthetic and seasonal beauty, a built attraction with its historic architecture and manicured gardens, and a social attraction by relating the life-style of New England in the 1830s with modern America.

At OSV the distinction between attraction and facilities is somewhat blurred. Because we are a village within a community, we are often viewed as being the community. There is an existing infrastructure of visitor facilities which supplements the Village offering: a food and beverage outlet (Tavern), an accommodation outlet (OSV lodges), and a retail facility (Museum Shop). Each of these shares the primary function of providing facilities and services to our visitors.

As for accessibility, OSV is supported by an infrastructure of travel opportunities. Most visitors to the Village come by automobile; however, our location off the major turnpike in Massachusetts enables easy access from metropolitan areas serviced by plane, train and bus routes. We capitalize on our proximity to major population centres in the northeast and encourage travellers heading to northern New England from the south (and vice versa) to stop and experience Old Sturbridge Village. Most recently the Village has incorporated the concept of location into an advertising slogan, 'Long ago, but not far away', which lends itself to reinforcing the notion that the Village is near primary markets.

Most important to OSV are the images and perceptions of our destination. Given that these consumer attitudes strongly influence buying decisions, the Village takes pride in understanding visitor needs and delivering the Village as an experience. It is viewed by many as an attraction, but also as a museum and an educational institution. The balance between learning, active participation and enjoyment is key to offering a quality product to the visitor. In visitor-experience surveys (conducted by OSV staff during peak seasons) it has been determined that the actual experience consistently exceeds visitor expectations.

OSV's strategic approach focuses on recognition and product differentiation. We compete with other leisure-time activities by presenting a unique and engaging experience. According to survey data, the OSV approach to our target market directly relates to the decision to visit, including:

● Location, authenticity and cleanliness.
● The period of history represented.
● Specific features/topics addressed.
● Lively and engaging programmes.
● Craft demonstrations.
● General atmosphere/ambience.

A continual goal is product enhancement while increasing the visitor's perceived value in comparison to the required expenditure to visit. Pricing is evaluated on an annual basis by the management and Board of Trustees of Old Sturbridge Village. Although pricing of our lodging facility varies seasonally, the admission fee to the Village is constant. Pricing structure is presently based on an adult fee (over 16 years) and young person fee (6–15 years), with children under 6 admitted free of charge. Pricing also offers a 2-day visit option on a consecutive, open day. Group rates are available for parties of twenty or more. Senior citizen discounts are not

offered by the Village. Adding to the options, however, are special incentives for members and their guests. According to recent research, most visitors do not know the cost of admission before visiting OSV. In the past, because of perceived value, consumer demand was not sensitive to pricing at the Village. More recently however, during an economic downturn in the northeast, consumers are seeking more for their money. Recognizing this, OSV has tested pricing promotions as well as aggressively communicated 'value added' in its marketing strategies (see Section 4).

We believe that OSV is held in high esteem by colleagues in the field, and visitors alike. Our product is attractive to varying age groups and has a comfortable and appealing atmosphere that provides a unique experience and opportunity for discovery. The potential for growth, through product development, market expansion and technological advances, is strong.

6 Promotion and distribution

The marketing budget for OSV is approximately $600,000 (7.5 per cent of total operating budget); 62 per cent of this is dedicated specifically to advertising. After many years of utilizing internal talents for advertising, OSV has retained advertising agencies in recent years to assist with the development and placement of advertising. The remaining components of the promotional mix, however, are still co–ordinated by internal staff. The mix has been relatively consistent over the last 10 years; modifications have been to adapt to the changing environment as well as to achieve goals set forth by the administration.

To summarize:

● *Advertising* has gone from a national campaign utilizing print media, to a regional (New England) approach including print (primarily newspaper), radio and outdoor media. Given the need to build audience throughout the northeast, another modification may include further expansion in print and radio. The need to create an urgency to visit rather than image enhancement and increased awareness may result in the elimination of billboard advertising, which has been a 'luxury' medium for OSV for 2 years in two primary local markets.

- Aggressive *public* and *media relations* have been a long time strength of OSV. Full-time, professional staff have been committed to increasing initiatives that result in national and international media coverage and attention. Features included in *National Geographic, Yankee Magazine,* and other major publications, as well as national television, generate more enquiries and visits to OSV than the majority of paid advertising space. Needless to say, the two must continue to appear simultaneously in order to secure 'top of mind' awareness.

- *Direct Sales* is spearheaded by a group sales and international representative staff position within Old Sturbridge Village's Marketing Department. This recent position, in its first 3 years, generated nearly 10 per cent of our visitor attendance.

- *Group* and *international* travel represents high growth for OSV as well as other tourism destinations within New England, yet it takes many years to cultivate the business. Fortunately, OSV had the foresight to maintain initiatives and invest significant dollars in the development of a solid strategy for capturing these lucrative markets.

- *Brochure production and distribution* are a primary means for communicating the OSV message to the broadest of audiences. An attractive, four-colour promotional brochure is supplemented by several specialized collateral pieces, including calendars of events, winter offerings, lodging brochures, group-travel brochures and targeted programme handouts. Distribution, which was once co-ordinated internally, is now

handled by one, and sometimes more, professional distribution services. Direct mail, and distribution through channels such as hotels and visitor information centres, major transportation facilities, and corporate activity offices of major companies in Massachusetts and New York City, spark interest throughout the United States, Canada and overseas markets.

- *Special promotions* are playing a major role in OSV's marketing strategies of the 1990s. Because the Village must utilize creative, more cost-effective means to promote itself, we are initiating more cooperative ventures than ever before. Success has been generated by the following special promotions:

  – Co-operative promotion with a local supermarket chain boasting thirty retail locations within our market area. At no cost to the Village, we communicated with their 600,000 households via the store's weekly mailer to offer youth admission free with paying adult during winter weekends at OSV. Results to date: 110 visitors redeeming offer; intangible added-awareness factor in key market segments.

  – Co-operative promotion with local, recreational mountain (ski trail) targeting families during off season. OSV participated in a 'Kids Fest' at minimal cost during shoulder season. A booth featuring Old Sturbridge Village programmes and family activities showcased our year-round offerings. By utilizing a raffle/survey, we were able to capture names and addresses, as well as limited consumer research, for nearly 1,000 individuals. This was later transferred into our database and used for a mailing that targeted family programmes. Unlimited exposure and awareness, and reinforcement for first-time and repeat visitation by local residents may result.

- A special promotion co-ordinated and paid for by an up-market shopping mall located 1 hour from Old Sturbridge Village, in a key demographic area, lent itself to increasing exposure in a high-growth market. By co-ordinating marketing and membership components of the Village, OSV is well suited to capitalize on an audience that is not only visitor potential but member/donor as well. Timing the promotion so that it coincided with a major portrait exhibition at Old Sturbridge Village, we were able to position ourselves not only as an educational institution, but a cultural site as well.
- By co-ordinating activities with the local tourism promotional agency, OSV is able to extend its marketing arm beyond our direct resources. Encouraging the local agency to utilize the strength of the Village in its marketing strategies, we lend credibility to their efforts while at the same time reaching additional audiences and supplementing our institutional efforts. Not only will this generally increase visitation, it will enhance goodwill between the Village and the community that supports the attraction with additional destination facilities and services.

● *Cooperative marketing networks* are critical to the continued success of Old Sturbridge Village. By working closely with local, regional, state and New England promotional agencies to promote New England, Massachusetts and Sturbridge, OSV maximizes the tourism potential as a whole. By participating in existing networks and dovetailing with their promotional strategies, OSV is assisting with the increase of visitation to New England, which ultimately translates into more visitors and revenue to OSV.

7 Results

OSV is continually seeking new ways to measure results. The bottom line, however, is the number of visitors who pass through our front gate. Increased awareness and inquiries are signs of growth, but the numbers and revenue generated by first-time and repeat visitors is critical to our success.

By utilizing advanced technologies, Old Sturbridge Village has recently been able to measure results not only generally by counting visits but, more importantly, by categorizing visits by geographic breakdowns. At the ticket booth, every visitor's zip code/country code is captured. Then regular reports analysing the data are generated and the findings used to revise media plans based on geographic targets.

Similarly, this extensive visitor-tracking can provide OSV with information regarding numbers of visitors who are members of the institution and those that come to redeem a special offer. This information validates many decisions made by the administration, and in some cases points us in new directions, i.e. increasing the number of Canadian visitors through participating in Canadian marketing efforts with New England and Massachusetts co-operative agencies.

Without such data, Old Sturbridge Village would be less able to adapt its marketing strategies to meet the changing demands of its visitors. Measuring results is a priority for us, so we can continually analyse strengths and weaknesses, eliminating what doesn't work and capitalizing on the things we do best.

Case contributed by Crawford Lincoln, President of OSV, and Michelle Hatem Meehan, Director of Marketing and Communications.

4

Marketing visitor attractions – 'Visions of Japan'

(a special exhibition mounted at the Victoria and Albert Museum, London)

Many large museums stage temporary exhibitions to support and enhance the work of the museum, and to encourage new audiences. They also stage such exhibitions for revenue related reasons. This case shows how the V&A (The British National Museum of Art and Design) effectively used its marketing skills in conjunction with a fully sponsored exhibition:

● To develop awareness of the museum through extensive 'free' publicity.
● To promote 'trial' by new/first-time visitors.
● To stimulate repeat visits.
● To generate revenue to support its other museum activities.
● To develop the museum's marketing expertise for future major exhibitions.

Because the investment costs in the permanent displays of national galleries are high, they must have a life of many years. By contrast, temporary exhibitions provide a vital opportunity to create and communicate a sense of interest, change and activity in a living institution; they bring in new audiences and enhance and illustrate aspects of the permanent collections. In this case the exhibition also introduced, on a temporary basis, formalized admission charges into a museum that actively promotes donations at the entrance but does not apply compulsory admission prices.

Visions of Japan in 1991 was the first major temporary exhibition at the V&A to use gallery space refurbished and planned especially for large exhibitions. The case illustrates many of the principles of marketing noted in Chapter 21. In particular it traces the opportunistic use of publicity to support a temporary exhibition, utilizing market research and a planned and measured marketing campaign aimed at targeted segments. The nature of the experience or 'product' offered by museums creates major opportunities for PR and publicity, which were systematically exploited in this case.

1 Background

The Victoria and Albert Museum (known generally as the V&A) is the National Museum of Art and Design. It was founded in 1852 by Prince Albert, husband of Queen Victoria.

Located next to the Science and Natural History Museums in London's South Kensington, the V&A has a massive and priceless collection of decorative arts from Europe and the Far and Middle East, including the national collections of sculpture, dress, ceramics and glass, furniture, metalwork, silver and jewellery.

The V&A was attracting about 1 million visitors a year in the early 1990s. In common with other leading national museums, it had been given trust status in the 1980s. For the last century, the principal income for the museum has come from government, most recently via the Museums and Galleries Commission in the form of an annual grant (85 per cent of total income in 1992). It was made clear when the trust was established, however, that the museum is expected to generate a growing proportion of its own income through revenue-generating activities. In 1991 the V&A did not apply a compulsory charge for admission, but since 1986 had adopted a system of voluntary charges in which visitors passed through turnstiles manned by museum staff to receive donations. Recommended donations were clearly displayed and most visitors responded.

As part of its corporate plan to generate revenue and at the same time meeting the primary requirements of its educational mission, the V&A restructured and developed its approach to marketing, appointing its first head of marketing and PR in 1991. The museum also organized the renovation of three large, linked galleries on the ground floor specifically for the purpose of staging major temporary exhibitions. There had not been a major exhibition at the museum in the previous decade. Completed in May 1991, the galleries are accessed through the principal visitor entrance to the museum, where it is possible to impose and control compulsory ticketing for exhibitions. *Visions of Japan* (VOJ)

was the first such major exhibition to be held in the refurbished space. It was the first of a series of exhibitions to be mounted in the 1990s.

Visions of Japan was the centrepiece of the Japan Festival held in the UK, from September 1991 to the end of that year. This festival started modestly as a celebration of the centenary of the UK Anglo-Japan Society and grew to a programme of 200 or so events almost entirely sponsored by Japanese companies. Events were staged all round Britain, and brought many artists and cultural activities into the UK for the first time - a Sumo tournament, Kabuki Theatre, traditional musicians, and a weekend Matsuri (open-air festival) in Hyde Park. A Japan Festival office was established to oversee the staging of the festival, to liaise with the Japanese sponsors and embassy on behalf of the many host venues, and to develop Festival awareness through PR and marketing.

Visions of Japan was designed using all Japanese materials. The exhibition contents, which were not finalized until 3 months before opening, were shipped to the V&A in consignments over those 3 months for the opening in September 1991, and a joint UK and Japanese team oversaw the installation. The guide to the exhibition was also prepared in Japan and shipped in only 2 weeks before the opening, sight unseen. All these factors constrained marketing and, *particularly*, public relations activity.

The exhibition was open to the public for 16 weeks, from 17 September 1991 to 5 January 1992.

2 Analysis of strategic marketing issues in presenting VOJ

General Issues

In this section it is interesting to note the considerable overlap between marketing (especially the 'promise', the promotion and motivation of visitors) and the operations of a major museum. Successful modern exhibitions need to be visitor-orientated and influenced by marketing knowledge and broad educational goals. But the delivery of the experience achieved by visitors and the satisfaction derived within the museum are very much operational matters. The two aspects have to be co-ordinated. From a marketing/revenue perspective, the main strategic issues for the museum in mounting the VOJ exhibition in 1991 were:

- Testing the revenue earning potential of large temporary exhibitions in the newly refurbished galleries.
- Developing marketing methods appropriate to such exhibitions, in particular establishing visitor profiles and segmentation methods for development in future exhibitions. All aspects of product formulation, pricing, promotion and distribution come into the successful staging of large exhibitions.
- Establishing the impact of the exhibition on the museum's regular visitors, and in particular gauging the public reaction to ticket pricing at commercial levels. In addition, investigating to what extent exhibitions stimulate visits to and illustrate aspects of the permanent displays – by creating a sense of curiosity, and desire to learn more among the visiting public.
- Testing the museum's visitor management or operational ability to cope with relatively large additional flows of people at peak hours daily. Obviously, if the visitor-management operations failed to live up to the marketing promise, there could be serious difficulties for future exhibitions.
- The V&A, as the National Museum of Art and Design for the UK, attracts an important, knowledgeable and vocal group of friends and other regular visitors who are important to the museum's future. There was a need to explain and justify to them, especially to

influential art critics, how a large hi-tech social and cultural exhibition (including Godzilla and part of the filmset complete with sound effects) 'fitted in' with the V&A's curatorial mission statement.

Specific issues – implications for marketing and visitor management at major exhibitions

- A 10-40 per cent increase in visitors a day to a museum, depending on day of the week, holidays, advertising etc., puts a strain on catering, toilets and other services, and also on security.
- VOJ was the first exhibition to be held in the new 1,800 sq. feet exhibition space at the V&A (accessed by walking through the museum's permanent galleries). This necessitated new routing, sighting and security arrangements, plus recruitment and training of staff and helpers within the exhibition.
- The absence of a booking office at the V&A made it necessary to appoint an advance ticketing agency to help even out visitor flow (critical for the first few weeks after opening). The same agency was required also to respond to group bookings, which are important for exhibitions.
- This was a priced exhibition, whereas normal entry to the V&A is by a voluntary donation, and necessitated a crowd-queuing system, new tills, new banking and accounting arrangements and extra staffing (and all in a restricted lobby area, which also provides public access to V&A shops).
- The relatively high ticket prices, particularly compared to the normal donation system, had to be explained, particularly in relation to the British public's perception of what it should pay for in the 'arts'.
- A large number of interactive exhibits necessitated employing extra staff as 'helpers' within the exhibition, as well as to ensure a smooth visitor flow.
- These interactive exhibits included a lot of audio-visual support, unusual in the V&A.

They had to be presented to the public without undermining or reducing the impact of the permanent gallery displays of the core collections.

3   The nature of the product and pricing

As with any other form of visitor attraction, the 'product' provided by VOJ was an experience. This section describes the characteristics of the exhibition on which the experience was based.

Visions of Japan was an exhibition in three galleries portraying the personal 'Visions of Japan' of four internationally known Japanese architects/designers. Containing artifacts and materials shipped in from Japan, and costing £4 million to stage, the halls corresponded loosely to visions of Japan 'past', 'present' and 'future'.

Hall I, entitled 'Cosmos', explored the role of Japan's heritage on its national culture. It contained a revolving twelfth-century Shinto temple pillar, a seventeenth-century teahouse with walls that opened and closed to show the interior; and a traditional hearse 'crashing' through the wall (symbolizing the afterlife), accompanied by ethereal music.

Hall II, entitled 'Chaos', plunged the visitor into the 'anarchy' of life in a modern Japanese city. It contained, among other things, part of the original Godzilla filmset, with Godzilla itself, vending machines, a karaoke bar, massage chairs, electronic fortune tellers, video games, a shrine, and TV monitors showing scenes of everyday city life, accompanied by city sounds and smells of incense.

Hall III, entitled 'Dreams', portrayed a technological future, using a massive video wall and floor crowded with Japanese scenes and flashing images, predicting a future where information overload leads to social alienation.

Product benefits were defined as:

- Entertaining and educational view of Japanese culture.

- An unusual 'sensory' experience of sight, sound, smell and touch.
- Innovative, challenging experience.
- A 'once in a lifetime' experience, not to be seen anywhere else.
- The first time that many of the exhibits had ever been seen outside Japan, particularly the hi-tech elements.
- Accessibility, in a central London location at a museum that already has considerable attraction to visitors.

Pricing

As noted earlier, it was intended to use VOJ to test public relations to 'commercial' pricing. It was also a strategic objective to generate revenue. Accordingly, ticket prices were set at £5 per adult, £3.50 concessions, £12 family ticket (up to two adults and four children), £3 per head group rate (group of ten or more), and £1 per head for a group in full-time education. Tickets could be purchased in three ways, (i) via an appointed ticketing agency, (ii) at the museum, and (iii) for educational groups, booking direct with the V&A Education Department.

4   Objectives and marketing strategy for VOJ

The objectives stated in the marketing plan for VOJ were:

- To attract a minimum of 150,000 paid entrance visitors to the V&A's first 'blockbuster exhibition' in 10 years, thereby generating significant net revenue for the museum.
- To encourage a large new market to visit VOJ and to generate 'spillover' interest in the rest of the museum.
- To try a number of new (for the V&A) marketing promotions, with measurement mechanisms, which could be used for future

exhibitions and gallery developments in the V&A.

● To attract a younger new market in the 20-45 age range (the current V&A profile attracts two main groupings: large numbers of young people and students below 20 and people over 55).

It should be noted that the costs of creating and constructing *Visions of Japan* in the V&A were covered by the sponsorship of Japanese companies as part of the Japan Festival. The V&A had its own operating costs to cover, but was not producing revenue for sponsors.

The marketing strategy was stated as:

● To develop a flexible marketing mix of promotions, advertising, publicity and PR that would maximize the limited budget and limited staff resources.
● To ensure that all marketing was measurable as far as possible.
● To develop a mix of target segments across all ticket price levels that would allow the museum to maximize high revenue ticket sales, at minimum marketing costs per head, while ensuring highest possible access of all socio-demographic groups, particularly groups in full-time education.

5 Segmentation

Segmentation is relevant at the V&A for media and other promotional targeting but is less important for exhibitions than for many other forms of tourism marketing. The exhibition had to aim to generate as many visitors as possible and to appeal broadly across all segments.

Market research was undertaken in the spring of 1991 to ascertain the profiles of key segments that could most cost-effectively be targeted to achieve the above marketing objectives and strategy. Because the exact 'product', i.e. the

content of the exhibition, was not defined until 3 months before opening, the market research was obviously hampered to a degree compared with the normal circumstances applying to the promotion of a major attraction.

The targets were defined broadly to be:

● Culturally active 15-45-year-old people living in London.
● Families and children living in London and South East England.
● Tourists (domestic and international) visiting London, especially those in commercial accommodation in London.

6 Marketing programme

Marketing staff and budget

A flexible and resource-effective campaign was put together. Resources were two staff (one marketing person and one press officer), the help of an external PR agency, and a total marketing budget of £130,000. Some design and print costs were met internally via the in-house departments. The budget was split £75,000 for 'above-the-line' advertising, and £55,000 to cover 'below-the-line' publicity and promotion, plus bannering and signing, press, hospitality and ticketing expenses.

Press campaign

The key element of the marketing campaign was a co-ordinated and targeted media campaign. The main campaign started 6 months before opening, gradually building up in the weeks to 17 September, and consisted of strategically planned feature and news coverage across all media and opportunistic news coverage throughout the course of the exhibition. The V&A set out to exploit the considerable general public interest in Japan and its culture.

Advertising

Advertising expenditure of £75,000 was divided between a poster campaign on London Underground, executed by the V&A advertising agency Saatchi and Saatchi, and a radio campaign to support the opening of the exhibition on London-wide Capital Radio.

● *Underground:* 'cross track' posters (visible to the public awaiting trains) in September to reach a domestic/commuter and tourist audience; it was decided to add additional posters for November and December, reaching a domestic/commuter and tourist audience. Results: research showed that 20 per cent of visitors were aware of the poster campaign.

● *Capital Radio:* in order to maximize a small budget a deal was reached whereby the advertising for the exhibition (launch week) would be supplemented by an on-air competition (also over the launch week).

Capital has a weekly audience of approximately 4.2 million residents in London. Response to the advertisement/competition is hard to measure, since market research was not conducted during that period. However, the radio advertising/competition, in conjunction with the media campaign, achieved a high level of awareness at the time of opening.

Publicity leaflets

200,000 leaflets were produced and available 2 weeks prior to the opening. Distribution took place within the Museum; at other art and cultural institutions with whom the V&A had a free leafleting arrangement; at other Japan Festival venues; via the ticketing agency to its main public ticketing points, including Victoria Tourist Information Centre, Harrods and Madame Tussauds; and at local hotels and schools and colleges selected by the V&A Education Department.

An agreement was also reached with British Airways to distribute leaflets at its Welcome Desks at Heathrow and Gatwick and at Central London hotels.

Special promotions

● *Capital Radio:* as part of the advertising agreement referred to above, Capital Radio ran a visit to Japan prize competition for the week of the opening, based on guessing the identity of sounds from the exhibition. The competition ran three times daily during prime drive-time and was mentioned by disc jockeys during other shows. British Airways donated a free economy-class return ticket to Tokyo. The V&A paid for a week's hotel accommodation plus £500 spending money. Total cost to V&A of £1380.

The prize competition generated a great deal of interest and awareness of the opening of Visions to Japan, although this was not quantifiable.

● *British Airways Holidays:* as a way of targeting in-bound tourists, an agreement was reached with British Airways Holidays that a two-for-one offer (in leaflet form) could be put into the welcome packs of all arriving holiday passengers from 17 September to 5 December; offer restricted to weekday mornings in order to boost visits at non-peak hours. Potential reach of 32,000 in-bound passengers, plus all visitors to the BA Welcome Desks at Heathrow and Gatwick and central London hotels (13,000 additional leaflets).

No cost to V&A except transit of leaflets. Take up during the designated off peak time was low but research showed awareness among all BA holiday passengers visiting the Museum at all times to be very high - 52 per cent said they had read the leaflet and this persuaded them to visit.

● *British Rail Season Ticket Holder Offer:* to reach Londoners and/or commuters, an offer of concessionary rate entrance was made via a mailing to 350,000 British Rail Season Ticket Holders. No costs to V&A. Take up was 1,000 or 0.3 per cent (much lower than British Rail estimate of 2 per cent).

● *Time Out offer:* to reach young, culturally active Londoners an offer of concessionary rate entrance was made to *Time Out* readers in two subsequent editions. Readership 490,000 weekly. Offer valid for 6 weeks. No cost to V&A. Take up low.

● *Times Educational Supplement Advertorial Teachers Evening:* to target teachers and stimulate educational visits, a preview evening of the exhibition was run with small charge to teachers to cover V&A costs. Circulation of *Times Educational Supplement* 82,636. 500 teachers attended (maximum capacity) with subsequent response in educational visits.

● A variety of other smaller ticker offers were developed as ways of reaching new audiences or supplementing press coverage.

7 Results achieved and case summary

As an exhibition, *Visions of Japan* achieved the strategic objectives set for it.

● 180,000 visits were made, and a high percentage of these paid the full adult admission price.

● VOJ met the strategic criteria established by the museum and set out in Section 2 of this case. The success helped to vindicate the decision to restore the three galleries for use as temporary major exhibition space. It also justified the view that mounting a social and cultural exhibition with many modern elements would enhance rather than detract from the main curatorial mission of the V&A,

and help to promote interest in the displays of its permanent collections.

● VOJ opened at the end of a poor season for domestic and overseas visitors to London, reflecting the impact of economic recession and the Gulf War, and served to boost museum revenue and public profile at a critical time.

In terms of the marketing campaign for VOJ the results were judged to be very successful. Market research carried out at the museum showed that 42 per cent of all visitors had read about or heard about *Visions of Japan* in the media. Publicity in the media was independently valued at the equivalent of at least £250,000 in advertising space (nearly four times the amount actually spent on advertising).

VOJ was, as noted, part of the UK-wide Japan Festival. It was able to benefit from and exploit for its own objectives the marketing and publicity generated by the Festival office and the general awareness and interest in many aspects of Japan. VOJ was, however, also competing directly for visitors with many other Festival events happening in and around London, and its marketing initiatives were essential to exploit the overall awareness.

The exhibition attracted a new audience to the V&A

● One-third of the visitors to VOJ were first-time visitors. Of those who had visited before, nearly half had not been for a year or more.

● 70 per cent of all visitors went on to see other parts of the V&A.

● 90 per cent of all visitors intended to visit the museum again.

The exhibition attracted the targeted segments

● 67 per cent of visitors were non-residents of London.

● 43 per cent of visitors were under 35.

● 26 per cent were between 35 and 45, which served to even out the normal visitor profile (which peaks at younger and older visitors).

● 10 per cent of visitors came in a family group, approximately double the normal family profile for the Museum.

● 13,000 schoolchildren came to the exhibition in school groups.

Visions of Japan also created a high profile for the V&A

● A new audience was attracted.

● A new broader constituency of media was reached, with radio and tabloid press coverage.

● The exhibition became a talking point for much of the autumn in London, being mentioned on radio and TV and within the press quite regularly.

● The Museum succeeded in standing out from the other Festival events: 73 per cent of visitors had not been to another event.

Case contributed by Robyn Griffith-Jones, Head of Marketing and PR at the Victoria and Albert Museum.

5

Marketing airlines – British Airways 'The World's Biggest Offer'

Over the last two decades the airline sector has been no stranger to coping with totally unforeseen political and economic events over which it has no control. The results of these events on load factors and revenue yield have been catastrophic for some. TWA, PAN AM, AIR EUROPE and DAN AIR are just some of the recent casualties.

This case is set in the year of the Gulf War of 1991, when the world held its breath against the possibility of a major war in the Middle East. It was a crisis year for Europe, North America and Japan especially, in which an airplane, its crew and passengers, were embroiled at the outset; a crisis in which there was unprecedented media coverage and a year in which international airlines were already suffering from economic downturn on top of estimated losses of over $2 billion in 1990. At the worst point in the war in 1991 financial losses in the international airline industry were estimated at $30 million a day. Revenues plunged below costs and price competition was unavoidable in a period of massive excess capacity on networks, further eroding revenue yield.

'The World's Biggest Offer' was British Airways' response to the disastrous situation. It was said to be the largest such promotional campaign thus far mounted. With its representation in sixty-seven countries around the world, BA had to mount the campaign

globally in order to influence not only its own customers but international attitudes towards flying, and the desire for travel. Moreover, it had to plan it in the closest secrecy to avoid pre-emptive action by competitors, working against the clock, and within existing budgets.

Above all, the case indicates what can be done with the power of a modern global marketing organization. Although the principal thrust was PR and publicity-orientated, most of the other issues of marketing campaigns are reflected in the decisions that were made. The case is also a classic illustration of the problems that all transnational corporations in travel and tourism now face - how to stimulate demand when it falls well below the planned level in all or most markets, and there is no possibility of storing service products for future consumption

1 Background

On 2 August 1990 flight BA 149 bound for Kuwait, Madras and Kuala Lumpur flew into the eye of a storm that was to bring unprecedented turbulence to an unsuspecting world for the following 8 months. During its scheduled stop in the Gulf, flight 149, its passengers, crew and ground staff became caught up in the Iraqi invasion of Kuwait. It was to be 5 months before all the British Airways hostages, along with other trapped Westerners, were to be returned home. The Boeing 747 which operated flight 149 never came back – it was wrecked in crossfire as the Coalition forces drove Iraq from Kuwait in the final days of the Gulf War. The aircraft served as a sad monument to the effect of the war on commerce in general and travel and tourism in particular.

Conspiring with the political situation in the Gulf towards the end of 1990 was a deepening recession, which began to take its toll on air travel. As events in the Middle East moved inevitably towards war, so the recession accelerated. Uncertainty combined with threats of terrorism and economic cutback in the factory and the home, to produce a deadly mix for the air transport and travel industries. The invasion of Kuwait caused an upheaval in the oil market (the price of aviation fuel doubled in a week) and caused major re-routing of a large number of BA flights (adding even more to fuel costs).

People stopped flying. They stopped flying in their millions around the world. British Airways' load factors plunged by over 40 per cent in 7 months. The industry's collective revenue loss was running at £16 million *a day*. During the first 3 months of 1991 airlines were forced to cancel no less than 30,000 flights. Day-to-day crisis management held sway.

There is always the temptation in deep recession for businesses and staff to suffer from 'recession psychology' – a form of mental paralysis that lasts until the freeze begins to thaw. As an independent airline with no expectation of massive subsidies to cover losses, BA just couldn't afford to wait. It particularly wanted to bounce out of the recession faster and higher than its competitors.

2   Analysis and strategic issues

The analysis in this case was starkly obvious. All airlines were facing a major crisis, their markets around the world being in severe decline.

Unusually in marketing the situation demanded an urgent response involving almost simultaneous aspects of marketing strategy and tactics. BA needed to kick-start its own business and, with global presence, this meant getting the world to fly again.

The main issues can be summarized as:

● The need for marketing action to make a massive impact, which would be global in scope and literally 'wake up' the market places to get people back on the move. BA operates in some sixty-seven countries worldwide and the impact had to extend beyond BA and its routes. Because the scale of the downturn was unprecedented, so the recovery plan had to be conceived on an unprecedented scale.

● Avoiding the danger that long-term consumer lethargy and loss of interest in travel and tourism could set in. Half-empty planes, deserted hotels with closed floors and empty conference venues, darkened theatres and gloomy restaurants could be taken disastrously for granted and create a vicious cycle of decline.

● The need to rebuild staff morale, which was obviously taking a battering in the circumstances, with the obvious threat to jobs and the depression that surrounds a continuing crisis.

● The need to re-establish BA's leadership worldwide as the first choice for business passengers – to get them back in the air and forward in the aircraft – and as the first choice for leisure travel. It was important to make up any lost ground in the interruption of the 'Leisure Traveller Launch'. This was a newly developed range of products aimed at non-business visitors scheduled for launch and major expansion in 1990-1.

● The need, in a time of acute financial pressure, to achieve results within existing budgets.

● The need to achieve the necessary impact against the clock and in total secrecy. A small team of executives, including an essential public-affairs executive, was closeted and charged with creating the vital recovery campaign. It would not be possible for BA to maximize the impact of its campaign if word got out for competitors to develop their own spoiling tactics, especially, as in this case, if the concept could be copied by others. Both colleagues of team members and their senior management were kept uninformed in the campaign preparation period. None of the publications used for the campaign knew what copy they were to take until the last possible minute.

3 Marketing objectives

The objectives followed logically from the strategic analysis. Specifically the aims were:

- To achieve the essential major global impact on airline customers, essential for business recovery.
- To achieve massive media coverage – using the oxygen of free publicity from a newsworthy idea to achieve budget objectives.
- To use a core concept and theme which could be communicated worldwide, thus achieving economies of time, resources and scale – and of course added impact and synergy with the 'World's Favourite Airline'.
- To create a launch pad for specific business and leisure programmes intended to sustain and build the habit of flying among key customer groups.

4 Segments to be targeted

For this campaign the normal concepts of marketing segmentation did not apply. The campaign had to appeal to the whole range of customers who fly. It also had to have an impact on other publics involved with airlines, especially the media and other opinion-formers, and the airline's staff. This range of segments included:

- All business travellers – especially those who fly frequently overseas.
- Targeted leisure travellers.
- Purchasers of corporate travel (businesses, business travel offices, and executive secretaries).
- Travel trade management staff.
- Opinion formers in the media, politics and non-governmental institutions.
- BA shareholders
- BA staff.

5 The creative solution

The team developed the campaign known as 'The World's Biggest Offer' (WBO). This had one big, simple idea, which answered the urgent business needs and could be implemented boldly on a global scale. It was also in keeping with the airline's core values as the 'World's Favourite Airline'. The expression of the idea was a central theme, encapsulated in four words and completely integrated in the banner headline used to communicate it through all forms of media. This integration was vital to maximize value for money from the campaign.

WBO had two sections. The first section was the 'Fly Free Day' – a day when every one of BA's 50,000 international seats, on every plane, everywhere in the world would be made available free. Prospective travellers would apply for the free seats and the winners would be drawn in a series of simultaneous draws and lotteries in every market on BA's worldwide network.

The 'Fly Free' day (also known as 'Up and Away Day') and its attendant publicity would serve to spearhead the second section of the

WBO campaign. This would be a 6-month long promotion programme, presenting a series of follow-up special offers and travel promotions throughout the world under the same WBO banner headline. It would optimize resources and impact by trading off the original newsworthiness of WBO to achieve a maximum and prolonged effect on business recovery within planned budgets.

6   The campaign summarized

With budgets tight, the method of launching and sustaining the campaign was to use the power of public relations. The carefully crafted plan was to maintain secrecy at all costs (a leak in an industry vulnerable to information seepage would have wrecked the scheme) and prepare a launch programme based on a burst of sixty-seven separate, simultaneous news conferences at key locations around the world. Timings, to maintain news value at every location and contend with media deadline requirements, needed to be exact. Once announced, PR would sustain momentum with stories and pictures of the WBO entries, leading to the staged lottery selections and prize draws. This would lead into the fourth phase of the PR campaign, featuring stories of the prizewinners; and ultimately to the free travel day – 'Up and Away Day' – itself, when opportunity for the world's press and broadcasting outlets to be at the airports and travel on the flights with the WBO winners would be maximized in a complex programme of PR logistics.

Timing was initially geared to indications that the Gulf War would continue for several months. It was planned that the global launch would take place in April, the prize draws a week later and the 'Up and Away Day' in May. The unexpected, early conclusion of the war meant that arrangements had to be drastically brought forward. The launch actually took place on 21 March 1991, the draws for prizewinners

on 30 March and Up and Away Day on 23 April, St George's Day. A range of special projects was put in place, such as a Downing Street photocall with the Prime Minister and Transport Minister, a special show with the NBC Today programme in the USA; and a documentary made by Channel 4 (broadcast in September 1991).

All the worldwide news release and background material was, for the aforementioned secrecy reasons, produced in-house in London. Although confidential pre-briefings took place with the British Airways' international network of five in-house PR managers and forty-two consultancies, the presentational News Release and background material, giving full details of the story, was not distributed until three days before the 21 March launch day. This material had then to be localized, translated and produced.

The programme went ahead exactly to plan and to schedule. On 21 March, in every country around the world served by British Airways, senior executives were preparing for breakfast-time press conferences. Each of the sixty-seven news conferences took place in a range of cities from Johannesburg to Jeddah, Sydney to San Francisco, Tokyo to Toronto, Rome to Rio, Hong Kong to Helsinki, and on across the British Airways' network. Similarly, seven days later, the prize draws were staged as news opportunities in the same range of cities. The PR momentum in every market was maintained up to the climax of 'Up and Away Day', on which news and feature opportunities were created at sixty-two airports, and more than 435 reporters, photographers and broadcast crews from sixty countries were carried on eighty-seven separate flights.

As noted, the principal thrust of this campaign was on PR and publicity. Advertising nevertheless played a very important supporting role in achieving applications for the free seats. The first of a range of supporting advertisements appeared on the afternoon of 21 March in the *Evening Standard* (the major London evening newspaper). On the following day the same ad, adapted for each country was running in twenty-seven languages in sixty-nine markets in 290 separate publications. An estimated 1 billion people worldwide saw these advertisements.

Thus the launch was executed as a multi-media event, following the same singleminded theme. Integration was achieved through national and regional press, trade press, radio, point of sale and merchandising by staff – even using the ultimate in flying posters, BA aircraft. The flexibility, central theme and newsworthiness of the creative concept made it possible to use the less expensive media to generate vital publicity, without the necessity for very costly, heavyweight TV campaigns.

BA's leisure travellers are people who fly because they are motivated to visit attractive places. An important part of the follow-up activity to WBO, co-ordinated with the British Tourist Authority, was a programme of product offers targeted at the inbound market to the UK. Known as the 'Key to Britain', this BA programme was particularly successful and helped resuscitate Britain's flagging tourist industry, which had been badly damaged by the events of 1991, especially in long-haul markets. Among the offers was a voyage one way across the Atlantic on the QE2 and back on Concorde, free vouchers for shopping at Harrods, and so on. To help promote this programme and give it maximum exposure in markets of origin, over 1,000 travel agents and their wives from all over the world were invited to London and entertained in the City at the Guildhall, and at Hampton Court.

Apart from some additional outside agency assistance in the staging of the core news conference with the then British Airways Chairman, Lord King, in London, and with the launch by Chief Executive, Sir Colin Marshall, in New York, the entire PR campaign was created, produced and implemented by the airline's existing PR resource in the UK and around the world. The pure PR cost (excluding the value of air travel provided for the media) was a little

more than £100,000. The overall campaign cost £6 million in above and below-the-line activity (funded within existing budgets), plus £10 million for the cost of revenue bookings displaced on 'Up and Away Day'.

7 Results achieved

The 'World's Biggest Offer' is believed to be the most comprehensive global PR campaign ever staged. It resulted in an unprecedented amount of press, TV and radio coverage throughout the world. Independently, the coverage was valued at more than £60 million against commensurate amounts of advertising time and space.

Most importantly, the campaign measurably served to stimulate every major travel market in the world and worked as much for the travel and tourism industry in general, as it did for British Airways. It brought talk of and plans for travel back to the media and the public. During its month of high activity the British Airways World's Biggest Offer was a main topic of public interest and conversation.

More specifically, over 5 million applications were received for the 'Fly Free' day – so at least that many people seriously thought about flying again at a vital time. There were over a million applications in the UK in the first 10 days alone, and it was not just quantity but quality. The highest percentage response came from the 'quality press' and the airline achieved a major marketing boost for its customer databases for future marketing, many of the applications coming from the all-important frequent-flyer group. Marketing offers were subsequently made direct to those who were not successful in the free-flight draw.

A key objective for the campaign was obviously to achieve enhanced awareness of BA. Although the above-the-line media spend was lower for 1991 than in the previous year, the added publicity exposure served to hold up customer awareness for BA brands. In independent tracking studies, awareness of BA almost doubled compared with the previous year.

Confidentiality for the campaign was achieved as planned. *Campaign*, the leading trade paper for marketing and advertising in the UK, noted: 'The most amazing thing about the whole operation is that it didn't leak out anywhere. In 60 countries . . . silence'. BA was able to lead its competitors and push some into 'me too' responses but without the impact of novelty and scale.

In March, before its launch, the international air-travel market was down by an average of 28 per cent, much deeper in some areas than others. By April the downturn had been improved to around 14 per cent, and by May to 5 per cent. Recovery to the traffic volume levels enjoyed before the beginning of the recession was achieved by the end of 1992, though in a weak market still recovering from recession. BA achieved profits in 1991-2, in contrast with most other international airlines.

Case contributed by kind permission of British Airways, London.

6

Marketing short-break products for UK hotels – Superbreak Mini Holidays

This case deals with a very important aspect of marketing for hotels in many developed countries – the marketing of short-stay breaks through contracting with independent tour operators. Commencing as marginal business with 'weekend leisure breaks' in the 1960s and 1970s, packaged short breaks clearly respond to a major market need in the 1990s and have become core business for many hotels. Short breaks now extend year round, cover any length of stay from 1 night upwards, and occur (according to capacity) throughout the week. They are no longer restricted to their original focus on pleasure travel.

Marketing such products is undertaken by hotels and hotel groups, either direct or through travel agents. It is also undertaken for them on a contractual basis by independent tour operators. Many hotels with spare capacity will market themselves, using several methods at the same time in order to maximize their sales potential. There is fierce competition between the independent contractors for this business.

This case deals in particular with how the leading tour-operator brand in the UK domestic market developed a strategy to enhance its existing market leadership in retail travel agency distribution channels, at the same time securing

a competitive edge through carefully targeted strategic differentiation yielding both short-term and longer-run advantages. The case shows the importance of distribution choices and what has to be done to sustain sales successfully in retail channels. *Superbreak* has established a good record for entrepreneurial initiative, which has been recognized in many awards for excellence. It has also exploited marketing opportunities to develop its strengths ahead of its competitors. Significantly, Superbreak identifies its primary customers as travel agents, and its primary products as the range of services and support systems provided for retailers.

Impressive results are revealed in this case. In particular, in the difficult trading conditions reflecting severe economic recession in 1992 *Superbreak* and *Goldenrail* programmes were able to target increased volume, in marked contrast with the overall trends in the UK markets for hotels.

1 Background

Superbreak Mini-Holidays (referred to generally as Superbreak) was formerly the marketing arm for British Transport Hotels, which were owned until 1983 by British Rail. When the hotels were sold, the Superbreak operation and brand name were bought out by its management, established as a separate entity, and became an independent tour operator focusing on the UK domestic market for short breaks in hotels.

Superbreak operates by contracting with UK hotels in the three to five-star categories (Automobile Association rating) and packaging products that are available for 1 night or more, any night of the week, up to any length of stay chosen by customers. Superbreak has stretched and broadened the appeal of the traditional weekend break in hotels for leisure purposes.

In common with other independent tour operators, Superbreak does not own the hotels included in its programmes. It operates by contracting bulk prices in exchange for marketing agreed amounts of bed capacity through programmes of product offers, set out in a brochure, based on prices per person. Some products also offer transport by rail or air at advantageous prices, and other facilities, such as theatre tickets. The price the customer pays is significantly less than the rack rate for the hotel, and it covers all the costs of marketing as well as the margins earned by the tour operator and retailer.

Superbreaks' main competitors in the UK domestic short-break market are other tour operators such as *Rainbow* and the six or so leading hotel groups and consortia that market equivalent products in their own hotels. It is normal practice in the UK for hotel groups to market part of their capacity through their own marketing initiatives and part through the programmes of tour operators.

In its first year of independent operation in 1983 Superbreak featured eighty-three hotels in sixty-eight UK locations in its brochure. By 1986 this had risen to over 200 hotels in 150 locations, of which thirty-eight were in London. For the 1993–4 programme the Superbreak brand featured some 558 hotels in over 300 UK locations, with eighty-eight hotels in Central London. From the start in 1983, recognizing that

it did not own hotels through which to distribute brochures and market direct to known customers, Superbreak adopted a core strategy of distributing its products through retail travel agents. Enhancing that strategy for the 1990s is the focus of this case.

By 1988, reflecting 5 years of significant growth, the management team felt that Superbreak had established itself as brand leader in the UK short-break market, especially with the demise of two of its former competitors, the *Stardust* and *Camelot* brands. This leadership role was confirmed by winning the Silver Globe Award for the best UK holiday operator and the Gold Award for the best short-break operator for both UK domestic and overseas packages. These awards are voted for by travel agents, and reflect the volume of sales achieved as well as excellence in operational procedures with agents.

In April 1989 Superbreak was able to buy from British Rail another tour operation brand based on UK hotels, and known as Gold Star (formerly known as *Golden Rail Holidays*). By receiving a significant price advantage on rail travel, and placing what Superbreak management considered unrealistically small margins on the hotel products, Golden Rail Holidays had developed a substantial volume of sales for their programme and acquired a 'budget' or 'low cost' position in the market. More importantly, although the programme was available in retail distribution, the brand was only sold by travel agents when customers demanded it; there was no recommendation or promotion. Clearly operational standards needed to be introduced to match those of the brand leader (Superbreak) and a realistic pricing policy was implemented. Finally, in 1990, the Gold Star name, which the new management felt was a disastrous change, was dropped and reverted to Goldenrail to benefit from the strong customer affinity for the products, especially in the North of England.

By the calendar year 1991 Superbreak products were bought by some 350,000 customers and Goldenrail achieved sales of just over 100,000. Superbreak was the top-selling UK hotels short-breaks brand with every major multiple retail travel agency in the UK, and outperformed its closest competitor by a factor of at least two. Goldenrail is now established as a major player within the market and provides profitable marketing synergy with its partner brand.

2 Strategic issues

There is currently extensive overlap in the hotels included in the programmes published by Superbreak, Goldenrail, and their main competitor brands. Inevitably this means that the products offered are broadly similar between competitors. Prices charged are virtually the same, and there is therefore little scope to differentiate one product from another on the grounds of price, product design, or quality of product delivery at the hotels.

There is also extensive competition for the available market, and, as the principal growth area in UK domestic tourism, short breaks generally have been subject to considerable marketing investment and initiative. It is necessary to find a sustainable basis for differentiation between brands.

Differentiation through a retail distribution strategy, and, in particular, continual striving to improve the quality of services provided to travel agents, was the strategy that kept Superbreak as the leading brand and enabled Goldenrail to develop as a major contributor to net profitability. Importantly the strength of the position achieved by the company collectively with its brands could not have been achieved individually or as groups by the hotels participating in the two programmes because their volume is too small.

Any successful short-break programme relies on being able to offer its customers a wide range of destination choice and a wide selection of hotels in destinations customers demand. An illustration of this can be derived from choice available at Blackpool during its popular annual Autumn Illuminations period (an annual pageant of lights and entertainment which has been established for over a century in this seaside resort on the Lancashire coast). UK hotel companies may have just one hotel in Blackpool and the rooms may be sold months in advance to a business conference paying premium rates. Superbreak / Goldenrail, however, between them feature five hotels in Blackpool and, as tour operators, are able to contract more bedspace to meet demand. They can also 'switch sell' (promote alternative hotels that have space) to other accommodation in the vicinity of Blackpool. The same principle applies to all leading destinations, especially London. Only large tour operators are able to offer the necessary choice and volume of capacity that justify their use of racking space in retail travel agents and achieve acceptable earnings per space allocated in competition with other brands.

Another strategic issue of relevance here is the relatively low price and therefore small size of the commission earned on most UK short breaks in comparison with the relatively high cost of handling bookings. The average UK short-break purchase in the early 1990s cost under £200, on which the typical retail agent earned just £20. To make this a worthwhile proposition it is essential that bookings can be made quickly, with the lowest possible administrative work. Until 1990 Superbreak (and all its rivals) achieved this by manual telephone reservation systems, and competed successfully on the speed of its response. Even so, however quick the telephone procedures, some retailers will not be convinced that a 1-night booking for an airport hotel – say £60 – is worth transacting. Freephone (0800) lines are used by some hotel companies but not by tour operators, having regard to their nation-wide operation and the narrow margins on which they work. Even freephones can be a lengthy process for a busy agent making a low cost booking.

Finally, Superbreak, through its regular contacts with travel agents throughout the UK, was very well aware of the rapid development of computerized reservations in retail travel agents in the 1980s, using viewdata systems and CRS technology linked to PCs (see Chapter 18). In the context of sustaining and enhancing brand leadership, achieving differentiation and exploiting an established lead in retail distribution among UK domestic operators, the strategy for the 1990s became clear.

3   Product issues and target market

The 'product' in this case is not just what the individual customer buys from the brochures, but the bundle of services offered by a tour-operator company to its retailers. As noted under Section 2, 'Strategic issues', the chosen Superbreak route to differentiation lies in its approach to retailers. They are the target customers.

Of course, if the consumer products are not competitive in design and price, retailers will not sell them. But in travel and tourism a good product available nationally, and distributed with maximum efficiency, will invariably outsell the best of products with weak or inefficient distribution. Superbreak knows its products are highly competitive on quality and price because of the standards applied for inclusion in the programmes and close monitoring of bookings per hotel. In addition, from continuous contacts with retailers as well as by numerous travel trade awards, it believes its close attention to distribution is fully justified.

The 'product' offered to retailers reflects, first, the level of continuous systematic sales support or servicing provided to all who rack Superbreak/Goldenrail brochures. This is based on the company's own sales operation, designed to achieve retailer support by ensuring that they have the necessary awareness of Superbreak products and stocks of brochures on display. The

second aspect of the 'product' is the quality of the response procedures developed to deal with requests, bookings, and confirmation of purchases. These are the vital head-office operations, on whose speed and efficiency brand leadership depends.

Current sales support for retailers

Key parts of the Superbreak/Goldenrail servicing policies are:

- *Brochures.* In excess of 3 million brochures for each brand produced annually and distributed exclusively through travel agents.
- *Sales force.* A team of eight dedicated sales representatives to service travel agents and ensure that the brochures actually receive their agreed shelf space and appropriate display.
- *Sales managers.* A team of three senior managers continually visiting key accounts (multiple travel agencies) to ensure the closest working relationships.
- *Sales information.* Provided on a monthly basis for each sales representative. Multiple travel agents receive national and regional sales statistics by branch.

This level of support currently generates some 600 agency calls every week. It ensures that exposure or racking for Superbreak/Goldenrail brochures among the 5,500 outlets targeted for distribution is at least 85 per cent at the time of a visit by the sales force and over 90 per cent following visits. Comprehensive support at this level is judged to be the only way to gain and keep effective travel-agency distribution for UK short-break products.

Current head office response procedures (1990–1)

Ease of booking, and a one-call transaction as well as access to high levels of product availability, ensure that the quality of Superbreak operational standards matches those of the sales-support standards for retailers.

Through constant interaction with the trade, the operator is already listening carefully to its primary 'customers'. The criteria below reflect their needs:

- A 50 per cent conversion of all incoming calls into satisfied sales.
- Phones answered within four rings.
- Full service telephone operations analysed by computerized monitoring system.
- High level of accuracy in recording booking details.
- Full internal audit trial balance each day.
- Next day ticket/invoice despatch and use of special delivery express mail service.

The combination of a good reputation and frequent calls by sales representatives ensures that Superbreak continually monitors its progress in the constant search to improve its operational responses.

4   Distribution objectives and strategy for the 1990s

By January 1990 the position of brand leadership had been achieved and sustained with high operational standards. A decision had to be made about what to do next to retain and if possible increase this market lead, limiting the ability of competitors to capture market share.

It was decided to aim for brand differentiation and gain a competitive lead by investing in a viewdata booking system for travel agents, to be launched in the Autumn of 1991. Specific objectives were to have over 5,000 agents registered on the system within 6 months of launch and achieve 40 per cent of all sales transactions through the system within 12 months of its introduction. The system had to be available exclusively to travel agents, and be compatible with systems already in use in retail agencies for booking airlines and overseas tour

operators' products. An important criterion was that Superbreak should also be able to respond rapidly and at minimum cost to the last-minute needs of their participating hotels.

Since the 1980s, overseas tour operators in the UK have encouraged UK retail travel agents to have direct on-line access to their computerized inventories, using viewdata systems available on terminals installed in agency outlets. Access for retailers' terminals is either by ordinary telephone lines or so-called 'hard wiring' to the two primary gateway systems, known as *Istel* and *Fastrak*. Such systems allow retailers to check operators' product availability, make bookings, establish exact costs and generate the documentation for proof of purchase automatically for issue to clients. A key objective for Superbreak/Goldenrail was to be the first UK hotels short-break operator to develop a user-friendly, industry standardized system that retailers would immediately recognize and use to best advantage in gaining access the inventory.

5   Costs of the strategy

Working to a tight budget when pioneering national computer applications on which a company's reputation will depend is never easy. Yet the investment described in this case had to be kept within a budget of £250,000. Superbreak estimates that installing a new operation of this sort without the existing hardware would have needed a budget of around £750,000 at 1992 prices. As part of the initial package, Superbreak also has a system up-grade path necessary to cope with anticipated expansion.

There was a calculated risk in the investment but Superbreak had a major cost advantage to exploit, not foreseen in 1989, in that the Goldenrail purchase included computer hardware equipment capable of handling the product inventory of both brands and providing viewdata access to travel agents nationally. It was necessary to invest in setting up the programme inventory on videotext accessible through viewdata systems, but not in purchasing a complete new system. Superbreak was also able to negotiate discounts with equipment suppliers because it was at the leading edge of a development likely to expand in the future.

Obviously the investment cost of achieving national viewdata system access and ironing out operational problems had to be recovered through additional revenue achievable and through cost savings on the former manual telephone-operated systems already described.

6 Marketing and operational advantages of the viewdata system

The viewdata commitment represents the clearest demonstration of Superbreak's good faith in retail distribution. Many travel agents in Britain are concerned that too many domestic operators attempt to use their high-street offices to display and distribute brochures while retaining and sometimes promoting the option to book direct, avoiding payment of commission. With some 94 per cent of all bookings via retailers, this is not the case with Superbreak. The retailer viewdata systems are not of course accessible by the public direct.

The viewdata system is also an operation in which the unit costs of access are only viable if the volume of transactions is large enough. In other words, the system is only affordable by the largest operators in the UK market, and the economies of scale obtained fit very well with Superbreak's market leadership. Also important is the improved ability of viewdata systems to deal efficiently with the flow of last-minute bookings for short-break products in the UK, in which the 48 hours before departure provide vital marginal earnings for operator and hotels.

Other specific advantages achievable in the first 3 years are:

- Hotels participating in the programmes can see a major tangible advantage in contracting with Superbreak/Goldenrail.
- Retailers gain access and reservation technology that saves them time and money and contributes to their bottom line.
- Retailers pay for viewdata access at costs per minute of local telephone calls only – the tour operator paying the difference.
- The information in the system can be made totally accurate – names, dates of travel, etc. – and confirmation is virtually instant. The danger of misunderstandings through telephone calls is avoided.
- 'Switch selling' to suggest options if a first choice is booked is programmed by the operator.
- Products that become available to the operator after a brochure is printed can be featured and sold.
- Any special promotions can be given immediate exposure at the point of sale.
- Brochure errata or hotel changes can be notified with accuracy.
- Any price changes can be made immediately effective.
- Agents are able to book hotels/products offered in the programmes of Superbreak's competitors (provided they are also in Superbreak programmes), using Superbreak's technology.
- Superbreak/Goldenrail receives a daily or even hourly flow of information through the system that enables them to monitor the performance of every aspect of their programmes accurately and identify strengths and weaknesses for management attention. This level of performance monitoring is not practical with manual systems, and provides another aspect of the competitive edge.

Medium-term strategic benefits include:

- Pressure put on competitors to divert energies and funds in a 'me too' response – as followers rather than leaders. Their costs of entry are likely to be higher than that of Superbreak, with consequent pressure on their margins.
- Although Superbreak/Goldenrail continue to operate manual telephone bookings in the early 1990s, there are savings to be made on staff costs. The savings are particularly important at weekends and other 'non-social' hours in which the systems must be operated.
- The viewdata system provides a morale boost for sales representatives, and provides them with a platform to forge closer retailer relationships.
- By achieving success in an area fraught with expensive difficulties if it fails to operate as planned, Superbreak has created a sense of confidence and trust in its market judgement, which is a valuable business asset.
- An advantage is gained in the annual negotiation of commission rates to be paid to retailers. Recognition of the tour operator's investment and the cost-saving available to agents are part of the discussion process.

Over the longer run of 5 years, other marketing advantages are expected to be:

- Facilitation of brand-positioning and market-segmentation for Superbreak and Goldenrail programmes, which can be communicated more easily to retailers.
- Facilitation of product development and enhancement, such as the provision of motoring directions to hotels. Such enhancements provide fresh messages for sales representatives to communicate.
- Facilitation of the extension of Superbreak programmes for sales in overseas markets (inbound to UK), especially in partnership with multiple retail agents, e.g. Thomas Cook selling parts of the programme in the USA.

This is an area for future development and it allows Superbreak to attack new markets. (Already it is seeing considerable interest from travel agents in the Republic of Ireland and in Northern Ireland.)

- The possibility to reduce the cost of providing millions of brochures in the coming years through the wider use of viewdata as a selling tool.
- Superbreak/Goldenrail in the early 1990s have delivered everything their retail partners can expect in the way of servicing. Their commitment to retail sales is not in doubt. This now allows them to explore the flexibility in travel and tourism of additional distribution channels with a clear conscience. There are opportunities for direct marketing and selling through outlets other than travel agents to be explored.

7 Key results

In addition to the advantages noted above covering a range of operational and strategic benefits, key results achieved from the initiative were:

1 Providing viewdata access to Superbreak/Goldenrail products for 5,000 out of approximately 7,000 UK retail travel outlets within 6 months of the launch.
2 The initial target was for 40 per cent of total revenue to be processed through viewdata in the first 12 months following implementation. In the event, after just 8 weeks, over 35 per cent of total revenue was flowing through the system and year one targets were raised. For some multiples, a figure in excess of 50 per cent was achieved in the first 3 months.
3 A significant gain in relatively low value transactions was noted, such as 1-night bookings for airport hotels.
4 Feedback from travel agents regarding the system has been highly encouraging. The

company scored consistently high ratings on all its support and response mechanisms covered in an independent survey of travel agents carried out within 6 months of the launch of the viewdata system.

For these reasons, and having regard to the strategic marketing advantages already discussed, Superbreak considers the investment decision to have been a major success for the company both in the immediate term of 1 to 3 years and for the longer run. The management team was pleased to be coping with difficult trading conditions with a fully operational and widely praised viewdata system on its side, ahead of the competition. By focusing on the quality of its services, Superbreak recognized that this is the core of its differentiation strategy, and also the hardest area for rivals to imitate.

Case contributed by Nick Cust, Joint Managing Director of Superbreak Mini-Holidays, London.

7

Marketing IT products – Thomson Sun Hotels

The Thomson Organization, known as 'Big T' to its friends and rivals in the UK, has been the largest operator in the UK package tour market to destinations abroad for many years. With total tour sales in excess of 3 million in 1990, it has achieved and maintained a market share of around 30 per cent of the total summer market. Until it collapsed at the time of the Gulf War in 1991, International Leisure Group (ILG) was its nearest competitor. The competition between these two was intense and affected the whole market, especially the prices at which the bulk of the programmes could be sold in a notoriously price-sensitive field. This case stems from the fierce price wars of 1986-8 (there have been others since, but the quality/price issue remains at the heart of successful tour operating).

From 1988, in pursuit of what might be dubbed the holy grail of inclusive tour marketing, Thomson set out to develop a 'flagship' product within the main summer holiday programme that would 'differentiate Thomson, thus increasing brand loyalty, moving the purchase decision from price to value and quality, and subsequently increasing profitability through higher margins'. With its widely acknowledged marketing professionalism, Thomson was better positioned to achieve these goals than any of its competitors.

The case illustrates the marketing thought process behind a strategic shift in Thomson's approach to product quality that would commit the organization for years ahead; it required detailed feasibility evaluation and a pilot marketing programme, launched in 1990. All aspects of a professional marketing approach are illustrated here. Market research and detailed product specification, organization issues (a dedicated full-time marketing team was seconded to develop the programme), and precise targeting based on a careful analysis of performance monitoring through consumer-satisfaction questionnaires. Although environmental issues and sustainability were only a minor part of the pilot programme planned in 1988-9, the methodology for tackling consumer response to such issues would be very similar to that outlined here.

1 Background

During the mid to late 1980s there was intense rivalry in the package holiday market. ILG reached a point in 1985 when it seriously threatened Thomson's market leadership. Thomson responded by cutting margins dramatically for its 1986 programmes. The price wars continued between 1986 and 1989, with Thomson establishing a market-share lead of some 10 percentage points by 1988. In 1988 Thomson bought the number 3 tour operator,

Horizon, further increasing the share gap. Thomson's leadership position was no longer threatened, but industry profitability in 1988 and 1989 was virtually zero. The prolonged price wars also resulted in holiday-makers seeing little differentiation between holiday companies, perceiving quality as somewhat lacking and package holidays becoming a commodity. As the project leader for Sun Hotels said in March 1989, 'We want to get back to selling holidays, not prices'.

Thomson, having conducted a major strategic review during 1989, initiated a new project, 'Project S', which was to research, develop, implement and deliver a new, highly specified type of middle-range Mediterranean accommodation. The objective was to deliver a product that would differentiate Thomson, so increasing brand loyalty, moving the purchase decision price to value and quality and subsequently increasing profitability through higher margins. The intention was to specify the product in great detail so that it would consistently meet and exceed customer expectations, and do so in a way that would be difficult for our competitors to follow.

Tour operators have had a history of difficulty in achieving differentiation, principally as a result of sharing hotels, airlines and resorts, so making it hard for holiday-makers to choose on anything other than price. Consumer research suggested that the accommodation element has the most significant impact on the holiday-maker's experience, though in the 1980s few tour operators had made any attempt to exert real control over the attributes and specification of the accommodation they used.

2   Analysis and strategic issues

The approval of 'Project S' by the Thomson Board in December 1988 marked a significant strategic step for Thomson. The strategic review

during 1988 had focused on what direction Thomson should follow in the future. Options ranged from lowest cost, lowest price operator, through to value-added differentiated quality deliverer of overseas holidays and travel experiences. 'Project S' would deliver on the route Thomson believed in, which would build on historic strengths and brand values.

The *Sun Hotels and Apartments* project and programme (as 'Project S' became) confirmed Thomson's refocused strategic direction, and effectively committed Thomson to this route for the foreseeable future. The project was far too expensive to adopt a 'try it and see' approach, and consequently Thomson needed to be certain from the outset that it was in line with ongoing and sustainable strategy. The approach adopted was as follows:

● Conduct research to establish customer needs and priorities.
● Produce detailed accommodation specification to meet those needs.
● Select shortlist of potential accommodation.
● Sell the concept to shortlisted hoteliers, gain commitment to specification and reach final accommodation selection.
● Present new product in *Summer Sun 90* brochure.
● Implement changes necessary to each hotel selected.
● Deliver holidays.
● Monitor, research, feedback for further development.

A project team was created for the project, based in London and made up of full-time staff seconded from the Marketing and Overseas divisions, plus a growing team of external consultants, reporting to a steering committee of the Marketing Director and Overseas Director. This allowed a dedicated, focused and full-time team, totally committed to achieve the project's objectives. It did, however, cut across Thomson's main organizational structure, and consequently much effort was required in internal communication, particularly with the relevant marketing product groups, and the relevant overseas managers.

3 Objectives for the 'Project S' development

The main objective was to develop a new, tightly specified accommodation product in popular Mediterranean destinations for the summer 1990 season and beyond, which would:

● Differentiate Thomson in a sustainable way from other tour operators.
● Provide a holiday experience that consistently met or exceeded customer expectations.
● Reduce the importance of price in the holiday-purchase decision process, and increase the importance of value, quality and holiday content.
● Increase brand loyalty.
● Increase profitability.

The benefits to Thomson would be product leadership, innovation, increased loyalty and profits. The benefits to the holiday-maker would be consistent and assured quality and service, higher product standards and better value for money. The benefits to the participating hoteliers would be happier customers, higher sales and therefore hotel occupancy, higher customer spend within the accommodation, greater cost-efficiency, access to Thomson research, support and training, and consequently a more profitable business.

The specific targets for the project team were:

– To research, develop and introduce the new product into 10-15 units for the Summer Sun 90 programme.
– To gain the commitment and co-operation of Thomson Marketing and Overseas management, of the participating hoteliers and of their senior staff.
– To improve the customer satisfaction levels in the Sun Hotels by agreed amounts.

– To achieve the accommodation-occupancy targets agreed.
– To gain customer feedback during the summer of 1990 to fine-tune the specification and expand the programme for the summer 1991 season.

4 Market segments targeted

The *Sun Hotels and Apartments* product was targeted to meet the needs of the middle-market, relatively conservative, overseas holiday-taker, both families and couples, i.e. core-market Mediterranean Summer Sun holidays. *Sun Hotels and Apartments* was not targeted to meet the needs of leading-edge adventure-seeking holiday-takers, nor was it to be an upmarket *a la carte* holiday product. Thomson had other products and other developments to address these market segments. Neither would Thomson *Sun Hotels and Apartments* be totally standardized, e.g. McDonald's; rather each hotel, or apartment, would offer fixtures and fittings, food, service levels and entertainment to an agreed specification, with a consistent approach in all units. Each hotel or apartment would retain its own individual style and character – some are traditional, others brand new; some offering a relaxing holiday, others more lively.

5 The Thomson Sun Flagship Product

The newly created product referred to here as the 'Sun Flagship product', included in 1991 both hotels and apartments in traditional 3T and 4T accommodation in the Mediterranean which was specially upgraded, according to Thomson specifications developed through extensive customer research. Thomson uses its own rating system for accommodation, the T rating which aims to be consistent across all destinations. The product guaranteed consistent standards and added value for money, and was available in parts of Spain and Greece. No other British tour operator offered holidays to the same hotels or apartments, so giving Thomson exclusivity in the Sun Flagship product.

The Thomson Flagship product was not significantly more expensive than holidays in other 3T and 4T accommodation at the same destinations, but did offer increased value for money. Different accommodation was targeted towards families or couples, with some hotels being suitable for all.

The key Flagship Product differentiators were found in the main accommodation elements of fixtures and fittings, food, service and entertainment, all of which were tightly specified by Thomson. The 300-point specification was drawn up from specially commissioned research, largely among holiday-makers, but also tapping into the experience of Thomson representatives and managers, and of hoteliers themselves. In addition, a number of consultants contributed significantly to this process.

This original research aimed to identify which factors of product and service within the accommodation were most important to clients, to establish desired levels of service or standard of product, to establish the importance of these factors relative to one another, and to identify levels of product/service standards required to achieve the optimum combination and to build brand loyalty. The research findings provided a wealth of action and priorities, which were reflected in the specification, which, in the four key accommodation attributes, covered items such as:

Fixtures and fittings
● Quality, standard and design of fixtures and fittings.
● Appearance (colour of wood, paint, curtains, etc.).
● Non-essential additions (fridges, hairdryers etc.).
● Attention to detail, e.g. power-point near mirrors in bedroom, bedside lamps with

bright enough bulbs to read in bed, plenty of storage space, towels of at least a certain size, etc.

Food
● Menus and choice.
● Method of cooking.
● Temperature of food on serving.
● Presentation.

Service
● Level of English spoken.
● Service standards.
● Staff/client ratio.
● Efficiency.

Entertainment
● Variety.
● Frequency.
● Professionalism.

The specification is highly detailed and each hotelier commits to delivering it. There are quality control procedures within the specification to ensure this happens in practice.

The Flagship Product can best be appreciated by experiencing it, but the following extract from the Thomson Summer Sun brochure sums up the product proposition:

Thomson Sun Hotels and Apartments, successfully launched in Summer 1990, is proof of our determination to give you exactly the holiday you want. We used our extensive knowledge, supported by special research amongst our holidaymakers, to write a 300-point specification to ensure a consistent standard of accommodation and facilities, quality of food, levels of service and entertainments.

We then got together with selected leading hoteliers and have been working closely with them to implement these strict standards. Thus, whichever of our flagship Thomson Sun Hotels or Apartments you choose, whether it is in Spain or Greece, whether it is for families or couples, you can rest assured that they all share the same consistently high standards, commitment to excellence and eye for detail that sets them apart. You may expect to pay a lot for such peace of mind, so you should be pleasantly surprised when you compare our prices. With a new dimension to your holiday, they're hard to beat for added value!

At every Thomson Sun Hotel or Apartment, you can always be sure of the following:

● Accommodation that's well maintained with very high standards of cleanliness
● More thoughtfully designed rooms
● Welcome information pack, including map and hotel guide
● Personal pool towels for use throughout your stay
● Menus offering British style of cooking, plus some local specialities
● Choice of full British or Continental breakfast
● Friendly and welcoming staff
● A whole team of Thomson representatives, plus a 24-hour emergency contact service
● A full evening entertainments programme, including shows by professional British acts once a week, quizzes, dancing, games nights and reps' cabaret
● A range of daytime activities, from 'Aquarobics' to waterpolo, or French boules
● Thomson Sun Entertainment Representatives to coordinate the entertainments programme
● All in all, a holiday atmosphere that's hard to beat.

Product selection was rigorous. The project team shortlisted existing accommodation within the Thomson programme that met specific criteria, which included:
– Thomson exclusivity.
– Thomson CSQ (Holiday Survey) performance.
– Attitude of owner and/or manager.
– Location and environment.
– Number of bedrooms.
– Amount of internal public space (lounges, bars etc.).
– Amount of external space and facilities.

Thomson shortlisted fifty to sixty hotels and apartments, and forty of them were visited for detailed reports. The list was narrowed down to twenty or so, out of which ten to fifteen were selected for the Summer 90 *Sun Hotel and Apartment Product*.

6   Marketing campaign details

The project team planned and developed the marketing campaign in parallel with the product development. The marketing activity fell into several areas:

● Name and logo.
● Brochure design and layout.
● Brochure copy and photography.
● Pricing policy.
● Promotional activity – advertising, PR, agent communication, etc.
● Market research.

These marketing activities cover three of the 'four Ps' of Product, Price, Promotion and Place. The product element has been discussed in the previous section of the case.

Given the decision to launch the product for the Summer 90 season, there were major time constraints. The research and product development took place between January and June 1989; Summer 90 brochures were to be launched in early September 1989, with brochure production schedules starting in May or June 1989.

Taking each marketing element in turn.

Name and logo

A variety of internal and external thinking, research and development took place to select a name that would create the right impact as a flagship product within the main Thomson Summer Sun programme, rather than as a brand in its own right. The name and style of logo within the Thomson brochure needed to convey enjoyable, quality and reliable holidays. A number of more specific names were considered, but 'Thomson Sun' was chosen as being the simplest.

Brochure design and layout

A number of challenges were faced, primarily to determine how different the presentation of the *Sun Hotels and Apartments* should be from the rest of Thomson's Summer Sun brochure. On the one hand, this new exciting product needed to stand apart, but, on the other, it was very much 'flagship within' rather than a separate brand. The use of colour and design, the amount of space, the style of the text, all allowed differentiation without alienation. Excellent and continuous communication and liaison between the project's marketing person and the Thomson Summer Sun marketing team was required.

Brochure copy and photography

New copy was briefed and written, and photography commissioned to allow the brochure to present the accommodation-attributes key to the holiday choice, as highlighted by the customer research and reflected in the product specification. Copy therefore covered the main elements of the accommodation, its food, service and entertainment, and photography created an atmosphere of holiday enjoyment while showing practical examples of these attributes.

There were constraints. Given the long lead times of tour-operators' planning, the brochures had to be prepared before the hoteliers had started their refurbishment programmes, and in some cases before they had formally 'signed up' to meet the specification. Consequently it was not always possible to list all of facilities, amenities, etc. in the Summer 90 brochure. There was also a marketing constraint – Thomson *Sun Hotels and Apartments* was a brand new concept and product, and it was important not to promise too much to potential customers.

Pricing policy

Much effort went into the pricing policy. One of the main objectives of the entire project was to increase profitability.

There were three main pricing issues. What premium, if any, could be charged in the first year or two of operation? What approach should be taken to the new costs, both one-off and ongoing? What relation should *Sun Hotels and Apartments* prices have to the rest of the Summer Sun programme? If prices were set too high, sales would be weak and the project's performance would be damaged. If prices were set too low, the new product would be subsidized instead of generating targeted yield.

After much analysis and debate, it was concluded that, for year one at least, prices for the 'Sun' product should be set in relation to other accommodation within the same T rating category in the same resorts. This did preclude a premium in year one. There was also much effort to split costs, both Thomson's and the hoteliers', between one-off development and set up costs, and ongoing costs, to ensure that the 'Sun' product would not reflect premium cost as well as potentially premium margin. This analysis also helped to determine which possible new-product ingredients would cost more than the value attached to them by holiday-takers.

Promotional activity

The approach to brochures has already been covered; other promotional activities included advertising, PR, travel-agent communication, etc. It was decided early on to avoid above-the-line advertising, if possible, for year one. The belief was that 'seeing (or rather experiencing) is believing' and that experience, word of mouth and PR would be far more effective than trying to advertise a new, relatively intangible concept.

Much effort went into PR - time spent with individuals from the various media to explain the project and its objectives, time spent taking journalists to see the 'before and after' during the implementation phase, and to see the operation for real in May 1990 and beyond. Similar effort was devoted to travel agent communication, with presentations to key agencies, vast quantities of promotional material and point of sale, 'before and after' educational visits, and an ongoing programme of visits.

Promotional activity began before the September 1989 launch of the programme and continued right the way through the Summer 90 season itself. A key objective was to gain support from travel agents, travel media, and indeed our own staff, for the new product.

Continuous market research

Market research on the Thomson *Sun Hotels and Apartments* programme was expected to continue, well beyond the initial product specification. The intention was to set up an iterative research programme of *asking* 'Sun' customers for feedback, *listening* to their comments, and *actioning* relevant changes. This has proved to be a vital ingredient of the success of the new product.

7 Results achieved

The results proved extremely satisfactory, with all the main objectives having been met or exceeded, and some additional benefits not envisaged at the outset. Taking each objective in turn.

Differentiation

There is no doubt that the Thomson *Sun Hotels and Apartments* was unique and unmatched by any competitive product.

Provide a holiday experience that consistently meets or exceeds expectations.

This has been the most successful aspect of the whole 'Sun' activity, and success here has undoubtedly been the most important factor in the overall achievement of the project.

Thomson has always recorded customer satisfaction levels in detail by means of consumer-satisfaction questionnaires (CSQ) completed by holiday-makers on their return flight. CSQ results in Summer 90 for the *Sun Hotels and Apartments* exceeded all targets, with major improvements over the same product in Summer 89, and showing major differential against other non-Sun products in Summer 90. These levels were sustained in Summer 91.

Additional research conducted in Summer 90 and Summer 91, also demonstrated that the specification was both valid and being implemented well.

Reduce the importance of price in the holiday-purchase decision

Sun Hotels and Apartments has been the single most important factor in the gradual shift from price to value in the holiday market, partly because of the experience and recommendation of those who have taken the holidays, but very significantly because of the tremendous and continuing level of media coverage dedicated to 'Sun' and the principles behind it.

Increase brand loyalty

Research shows that 'Sun' customers are more loyal, both to 'Sun' and to Thomson overall.

8 Summary

Commercial constraints prevent too much detail, but Thomson was satisfied with the financial performance of the *Sun Hotels and Apartments* project. Apart from reaching its objectives, the Thomson Sun programme has also achieved or exceeded its sales targets, has achieved an unprecedented and sustained level of media support and has allowed a vast array of spin off benefits across the whole of the Thomson programme. Thomson has gained valuable experience from both an operational and a marketing perspective, which is assisting further developments in many areas of the business.

Internal evaluation suggests that the project and the ongoing Thomson Sun programme of hotels and apartments in the Mediterranean has been a very successful new venture.

Case contributed by Rosemary Astles, Marketing Director of Thomson Tour Operations.

Epilogue

Prospects for travel and tourism marketing

This book contains many indications of the directions that marketing in travel and tourism may take over the next decade. The purpose of this concluding chapter is to draw the key implications together and set them within a framework of perceived change. It is also an opportunity for the author to indulge his taste for speculation and prediction, and perhaps to stimulate discussion. With the benefit of hindsight it seems fair to claim that most of the trends identified in the first edition of this book have developed broadly along the lines indicated. A major change not predicted has been the very rapid growth of awareness of global environmental issues, which, although referred to, were not given prominence in the first edition. That has now been rectified.

Many of the trends discussed in this chapter are already changing approaches to marketing in leading organizations around the world in the early 1990s. They will work their way through over the next decade. It is the speed of change and the international interaction between the trends that cannot be predicted with precision. For example, there is growing global awareness that the per capita consumption of scarce resources in developed countries, and the associated production of pollution and waste, greatly exceed that of the populations of developing countries. International long-haul tourism for leisure purposes is just one example of such high consumption, which may be targeted for some restriction in the next decade.

Looking ahead, the global problem is that growth in the current consumption patterns of Earth's scarce resources cannot simply be continued without grave risk to the world's environment. Beyond the next decade the application of new science and technological break-throughs are likely to produce some quite new trends and alter our understanding of the sustainability of resources. But in 1993 it seems likely to be a race against time, with growing constraints imposed upon high-consumption activities judged to be non-essential. The full implications of this for marketing leisure forms of tourism are not yet apparent, but they are likely to become more significant over the next decade.

It is also possible that mould-breaking entrepreneurs of the stature of Walt Disney, Billy Butlin (the holiday centre pioneer in the UK), Ray Croc (McDonald's) and Gilbert Trigano (Club Méditerranée) will emerge with revolutionary concepts that change our understanding of tourism products. In the 1990s such individuals are likely to emerge in niche markets for new products. They will find it much more difficult to break into the major mature markets, now dominated by highly competitive global corporations, than their predecessors did in the growth markets of the 1960s and 1970s. We are already witnessing fierce commercial stuggles for competitive advantage and for global market share among international airlines, hotels and tour operators;

such battles of the giants appear likely to increase.

The ten prospects identified in this chapter are of course based on an assumption that no major economic, ecological or political catastrophe will occur to force a quantum shift in the whole structure of the world order.

1 Limits to growth imposed by market maturity

Depending on the assumptions built into calculations, domestic and international travel and tourism is already the world's largest sector of economic activity. The 'industry' has the potential to double in size by 2005 (WTTC:1992). In the early 1990s such growth forecasts are widely shared and part of conventional wisdom. But it is risky to assume from past growth of *international* tourism that the *total markets* for travel in developed countries will continue to expand at the pace of previous decades. The best articulated forecasts derive from the air-transport industry and, while most aircraft manufacturers and airlines still appear to operate on very bullish expectations for the 1990s, they are not impartial forecasters but bodies with vested interests in growth. They have to project growth to satisfy their own stakeholders and to influence governments to provide the necessary infrastructure. But air transport serves only a part of the world's total international travel and tourism, and is much less important in domestic tourism. The predictions of its operators do not apply to the total market.

On World Tourism Organization evidence (WTO:1992), international tourism for all purposes grew at an average annual rate of 8.8 per cent between 1960 and 1970, 6.0 per cent, 1970 and 1980, and 4.9 per cent between 1980 and 1990. So the rate of growth has been slowing now for over a quarter of a century. On current (1992) forecasts, international tourism is predicted to grow by between 3.7 and 4.2 per cent per annum in the decade to 2005, producing a volume of some 650 million international arrivals by the year 2000. However, the statistics for such estimates are of dubious accuracy, and there are no global estimates for domestic tourism. Where reliable data are available for domestic tourism, as in North America and some European countries, there is as much evidence of market decline as there is of growth over the last decade.

Interestingly, in a recent analysis for the Economist Intelligence Unit, Edwards addresses the phenomenon of 'ceilings' to growth for international tourism from major markets. A ceiling denotes a level of activity representing market saturation at a point in time, which he predicts will be reached in several developed countries in the 1990s. 'By 2005, travel from seven of the fifteen largest origin countries ... is likely to be significantly affected by ceiling effects' (Edwards: 1992, p. 12). Limited evidence available about the high proportion of populations in developed countries that have already experienced frequent annual travel abroad as well as in their own countries supports this concept of ceilings or market maturity. China and its rapidly developing neighbouring countries in the Far East, Central and South American countries, India and Eastern Europe are potentially capable of expanding much faster than the existing main sources of tourism demand. But in these areas predictions depend as much or more on political events than on economic changes.

Having regard to the trends discussed in this chapter, it is difficult to avoid the conclusion that the scope for expansion in existing major markets for travel and tourism in the 1990s is actually limited. Global forecasts now being projected for growth of around 4 per cent per annum to 2005 appear over-optimistic for international tourism, and are not applicable to domestic tourism (all purposes) in developed countries. It is probable that price increases, necessitated by delivering improved product quality in holiday markets and complying with international regulations designed to protect the environment, may drive some of the existing volume out of highly price-sensitive international markets.

The implications of market maturity, for business travel as well as for leisure and holidays, are that there will be even fiercer competition between large organizations seeking to grow and gain market share. If organizations cannot grow in their own markets, they are likely to look for growth through acquisition, mergers and strategic alliances. Large size and international operations help to spread risk and reduce corporate costs in normal times and global status confers powerful marketing advantages through global branding and international distribution. But large size also inevitably increases the level of risk and increases competition if most of the main markets are in extended recession at the same time. Interestingly, the larger and more efficient that airlines and other tourism operators become, the narrower the margins of daily occupancy and revenue yield on which they operate. Plus or minus a half of one percentage point in the average capacity utilized over as short a period as 4 weeks can have an immense impact on the annual 'bottom-line' profit contribution, as Part Five of this book illustrates.

The effects of major international economic recession, such as that of 1990-3, can be traced in business failures and the billions of dollars lost by international airlines and hotel groups. With extended international economic crises occurring every decade since the end of the 1960s, and growing integration between world economies, economic downturns may be exaggerated rather than reduced by global linkages. It must be prudent to anticipate another recession before 2005.

2 Limits to growth imposed by inadequate knowledge of tourism markets

For decades the publicly available statistics of tourism have been collected by surveys sponsored by government departments or by tourist boards, mostly at national level. Some such surveys are financed partly by users, but this appears to be the exception rather than the rule. For the most part surveys have not been co-ordinated between countries, notwithstanding a series of WTO and OECD recommendations over recent years. A European-wide inititative by governments to harmonize and co-ordinate tourism statistics was conducted under the auspices of the EC with EFTA in 1991–2, and this is expected to lead to improvements in the 1990s. All who attempt to understand international tourism markets or to compare adjacent domestic markets using published statistics of tourism, run immediately into difficulties of measurement. Some countries, such as Australia, Canada, the UK and the Netherlands, have better information than others. But there are major problems inherent in any attempt to interpret market trends globally, in a world region such as Europe, or in most developing countries. Even where tourism is measured with any accuracy, the definitions of purpose of visit between countries, or even between regions within countries, may be incompatible. Estimates of total visits for all purposes, the basis on which global forecasts are currently made, have little practical value to tourist boards or commercial users for marketing purposes.

Reflecting these well-known difficulties, research issues were addressed comprehensively in Ottawa in 1991 in a major international conference on tourism statistics. Out of that conference, and a subsequent series of consultative meetings held by WTO around the world, came resolutions for the improvement of measurement. These were put to the United

Nations Statistical Commission for ratification in 1993.

In the early 1990s there is growing concern for long overdue improvements in the collection of data for use in tourism marketing and planning. Mature markets and more sophisticated marketing require better statistical information. National tourism surveys undertaken by government statistical departments or by tourist boards potentially provide essential research information for the marketing purposes of large companies. But most such surveys are sterile commercially, and it appears that real improvements in tourism data will have to be marketing-led and partly financed by commercial users.

The inability to measure and forecast travel and tourism adequately in the 1990s is becoming in itself an obstacle to growth and a major barrier to better recognition of the size and importance of the industry. It is possible that the concentration of travel and tourism marketing into a smaller number of larger, more influential companies over the next decade will provide the necessary impetus to involve users more closely in the process of improving research. Another impetus may come from governments seeking to hive off traditional NTO activities to the commercial sector. Either way, improvements are only likely to result from a greater financial contribution to surveys.

3 Limits to growth imposed by environmental concerns

Throughout the 1960s, 1970s, and much of the 1980s, the great majority of travel and tourism businesses expanded their operations and utilized the environment generally as a free resource. For leisure tourism, the environment was exploited for profit in many countries, with little awareness or concern for the impact on destination environments. Broadly defined, 'environment' means the physical, cultural and social structure of places in which businesses operate, especially visitor destinations. The transport sector was the exception to this *laissez-faire* rule, because national and international regulations have influenced operational practice for several decades, especially for air transport. For example, there are controls over the construction, size and density of use of airports, and for noise and emissions produced by aircraft. But, until as recently as 1990, hotels, visitor attractions and tour operators have been only minimally constrained in most parts of the world as to where they could operate and build, at what density of construction, and with what consequences for the environment of their operations.

In the early 1990s, following the Brundtland Report of 1987 (World Commission on Environment and Development) and the Rio Earth Summit of 1992, environmental issues generally were shifted significantly up the international political agenda. Reflecting emerging evidence in recent years of global warming, ozone-layer depletion, extensive pollution of the seas, and the implications of loss of biodiversity and related issues, the concerns expressed at Rio will work through in the 1990s. Driven by a combination of legislative requirements and media interest focused by influential pressure groups, manufacturing industries such as steel and chemicals, soaps and detergents, energy production and automotive, have already invested heavily in more environmentally responsible programmes. The soft-drinks industry and fast-food sector are moving in the same direction, especially sensitive to issues of conspicuous waste. But as the Economist Intelligence Unit put it in a recent international survey, 'so far the travel and tourism industry has taken little active part in framing the environmental policies so vital to its own interests' (EIU: 1992).

Because tourism is not a traditional smokestack industry with the obvious pollution potential of much of manufacturing and extractive industries, or the destructive potential of industrialized agriculture, it has not so far been closely examined as to its full environmental impact. Tourism has not produced disasters with the international impact of Exxon Valdez, Chernobyl or Bhopal. But the results of lack of environmental concern in the last quarter of a century can be seen in many areas of cumulative environmental degradation in which development for tourism played an important, sometimes a leading part. Examples can be found in the Alpine region of Europe, as a result of over-intensive skiing; along the Mediterranean littoral as a result of over-development of beach resorts; in parts of the Hawaiian islands; on the Gold Coast in Australia; and in parts of Nepal and Indonesia. There is no shortage of examples.

It now appears certain that environmental constraints and attempts to achieve sustainable growth will feature much more strongly in marketing decisions generally in the 1990s than hitherto. International travel and tourism organizations, such as the WTO, World Travel & Tourism Council (WTTC), World Travel and Tourism Environment Research Centre (WTTERC), Pacific Asia Travel Association (PATA), International Federation of Tour Operators (IFTO), Tourism Concern and many others, have taken a series of initiatives since 1990 to alert the industry to the dangers inherent in poor environmental practices. Increasingly, they are proposing new ways to develop tourism and to operate sustainable businesses. Governments, too, are active, and to choose just a few leading examples, Canada, Australia, New Zealand, USA, the Netherlands and the UK have all taken recent planning and development measures to prevent the negative impacts of tourism activity where it is possible, and to limit and ameliorate them where it is not.

Leading international companies are responding to these pressures, and some are now self-regulating their operations, as recorded in the annual reports of the WTTERC in 1992 and 1993. In 1993 some eleven of the major international hotel groups in the world published and began to implement their first manual of environmental good practice, developed as the 'International Hotels Environment Initiative' under the Prince of Wales Business Leaders Forum. At the time of writing, the first WTO statistical guidelines for measuring the impact of tourism on environments, intended to facilitate decisions leading to more sustainable tourism, were expected in 1993.

Although most of the environmental groups concerned with international tourism see small businesses as more environmentally friendly than large ones, it is the larger businesses which have the management structure and expertise to deal with environmental issues effectively. It is the larger businesses that have to act with a view to their long-term future. They can exert considerable influence over their suppliers, e.g. if tour operators implement a policy of dealing only with suppliers meeting agreed environmental criteria. They can research and respond to changing customer attitudes and influence behaviour by marketing methods. They are also the easiest for governments to regulate, and the most likely to be exposed and pilloried in the media if their actions are revealed to cause or exacerbate environmental damage. By contrast, most small firms, and the governments of many small developing countries facing impossible economic demands from their local populations, are unable to resist the prospect of short-term revenue gains and the attractions of a large source of scarce foreign currency.

Ecotourism

At the time of writing many countries around the world appear to have accepted the specious claims of a new buzz-word, *ecotourism*. Impossible to define succinctly, ecotourism is used loosely to mean any aspirational form of tourism which simultaneously conveys value to natural resources, resident communities in visited destinations, and the visitors themselves – without any of the negative and damaging implications inevitably associated with poorly managed so-called mass tourism.

In the early 1990s ecotourism is in danger of becoming the new holy grail of the travel and tourism industry. As defined by its mainly academic proponents it accounts for no more than about 5 per cent of world travel and tourism and in many areas it may produce more damage to the environment than the development of managed resorts. Ecotourism is at best a particular form of product; it is not a new paradigm for sustainable tourism and its pursuit may prove a distraction from the more important core issues of building sustainable principles and practices into the mainstream operations and marketing of the world's largest industry.

The world's largest industry is not the world's largest polluter. But the global scale of leisure time tourism activity and its particular focus on attractive environments means that future marketing will be far more concerned with these issues than hitherto.

4 More sophisticated and more repeat consumers

Chapters 4 and 5 provide the evidence on which one can predict with some confidence that customers for travel and most forms of tourism products will become more sophisticated, and more demanding over the next decade, as well as more environmentally aware. Toffler's view is that 'as we leave the industrial era behind, we are becoming a more diverse society. The old smokestack economy serviced a mass society...[The new economy] services a de-massified society. Everything from lifestyles and products to technologies and the media is growing more heterogeneous' (Toffler: 1990, p. 167).

Sophistication reflects the expectations of older, more affluent, better educated, more experienced and more confident customers. The majority of them, having grown up after the Second World War (1939-45), will have markedly different expectations for tourism products than the less demanding markets of the 1960s and 1970s. The traditional standardized package tours delivering beach holidays in rows of nearly identical hotels in dozens of nearly identical resorts are already losing popularity. They are unlikely to disappear but will certainly lose their market share.

Using a leading character to describe Honolulu in a novel published in 1991, one of the leading British authors writes: "The history of Hawaii is the history of loss." "Paradise lost?" I said. "Paradise stolen. Paradise raped. Paradise infected. Paradise owned, developed, packaged, Paradise sold" (Lodge: 1991, p. 143). This judgement may well be very unfair to the islands of Hawaii. It is of interest in that it represents a growing attitude of rejection of currently popular tourist destinations among many media commentators and prospective customers, which is already strongly held and is likely to increase. It has potentially important implications for attitudes to environments and customer reactions.

From a different perspective, in an influential study of the changing behaviour of holiday-makers, Jost Krippendorf identifies the empty pointlessness and lack of real satisfaction in much of the holiday travel experience of people in industrialized countries. 'Seized by a feverish desire to move', tourism, he argues, is all too often a form of escapism, which in the end exacerbates rather than ameliorates the dissatisfactions of much of modern living. Moreover it all too often abuses and alienates the host community, whose lives are invaded by pleasure-seekers. He argues that leisure and travel should not be trivialized, but contribute to the 'happiness of the individual and the well-being of our society' ... 'What we have failed to do is develop forms of travel that are psychologically, socially, economically and ecologically compatible' (Krippendorf:1987).

From a marketing standpoint, the response for the next decade appears to lie in more systematic segmentation and upgrading of products to meet the emerging needs of Toffler's heterogeneous future society – another way of describing market niches. The increasing segmentation of tour operators' brochures is a sure sign that this is happening already, and it looks certain to increase. Paradoxically, the search for niche products, which are environmentally satisfying, as well as meeting Krippendorf's criteria, is more likely to focus on environmentally fragile areas, than on purpose-built resorts such as Honolulu and the Costa Brava, which are best able to cope with visitor pressure. Grappling with this paradox is the subject of a book in itself and cannot be pursued here. But marketing managers will ignore the issues at their peril.

An interesting aspect of sophistication based on experience and knowledge is the growing importance to travel and tourism businesses of repeat customers. Regular repeat customers are often senior individuals in their working lives and are likely to be among the most demanding of users; they are sought after by most organizations and most are likely to know their own value. This has several dimensions. The first concerns the number of customers who use the same company on several occasions in a year. Travellers for business purposes are the obvious examples for airlines and hotels, and the same individuals might be persuaded to use the same organization for other products, e.g. weekend breaks in hotels. A second dimension is that repeat customers may be other organizations, not individuals. Repeat business from local schools or coach operators to museums are examples of repeat custom generated by group buyers.

Repeat customers, as noted later, always represent a marketing 'bargain'. They are also likely to know others who could become repeat customers in due course – another marketing bargain. A third aspect of repeat custom can be seen where a large organization, with a range of products, might aim to service the same client for more than one need over a year. American Express and Thomas Cook, for example, by providing a range of travel-related services, aim to sell several of their products to the same customer over a year. It is economically very attractive to do so. Satisfying repeat customers, and finding ways to bind them to the organization and reward their loyalty by added-value products has, not surprisingly, become an issue of major concern to marketing managers in the 1980s. It seems certain to grow further in the next decade and extend much deeper into the leisure market. Large organizations, offering a wide range of products in many destinations, are obviously better placed to satisfy repeat customers, another incentive to growth.

A final reflection on the implications of more sophisticated consumers raises the issues of domestic versus international tourism and packaged versus independent travel. In the 1970s and 1980s there was no real contest in northern European markets. Travel abroad, delivered by tour operators, held a glamour and status allied to warmth and sunshine and low prices that was irresistible to many. Markets previously content with domestic products shifted to overseas destinations. In the early 1990s there are signs of change in mature holiday markets.

To this author, a combination of more experienced and ageing markets in northern Europe for those who have several times 'been there and done that', and not enjoyed the stress of flying from congested airports to congested destinations, makes domestic travel look more attractive than at any time since the 1960s. Domestic operators, partly in response to catering also for growing numbers of overseas visitors, have invested heavily and greatly improved the quality of their products and their marketing skills. Many smaller, uncompetitive operators have gone out of business. It has to be speculation, but the omens for significantly increasing the volume of domestic travel in developed countries at the expense of overseas destinations seems a strong possibility for the 1990s. The traditional market for 2 weeks by the sea is not likely to return to northern Europe, but there are now many newer products, especially of the short-stay, impulse-purchase variety. The prospects for developing attractive marketing packages to offset the cost of fully independent travel and paying rack rates appear good.

5 Product differentiation, quality issues and refurbishment

If growing competition for more mature and discriminating markets is a major trend for the next decade, the pursuit of improved product quality and of 'excellence' will be the essential management response. Increasingly a joint responsibility between marketing and operations managers, excellence is essentially an idea and a feeling or perception of satisfaction by customers. There is nothing new about that. Most top-grade hotels and first-class cabins of airlines, for example, have been aiming at excellence for decades. Before the airlines, passenger ships were equally well aware of competing for market share on the basis of product quality. Increasingly, however, and this is relatively new, excellence is also being defined, targeted, and measured as a set of attributes and qualities to be designed into every product and its delivery. High quality in product performance, as perceived by customers, is a vital preoccupation for managers; achieving it and measuring it systematically is the basis for effective marketing competition. It is especially important as the means of keeping existing repeat customers and persuading first-time buyers to come again.

The more that markets are segmented, the more attention has to be given to designing and monitoring the performance of the particular set of attributes and qualities that comprise and signify excellence for each sub-group. In many cases the delivery of excellence may depend on seemingly marginal differences, but their importance to the sub-groups in question is what matters. Provided excellence is measured by segments, managers will be able to determine which modifications it is cost-effective to deliver. Potentially, this should lead in the 1990s to a more productive partnership between marketing and operations in all sectors of travel and tourism.

Excellence, often related to concepts of Total Quality Management (TQM), has become something of a buzz word in the early 1990s. It is often stressed, by Barker for example, as 'the base of the 21st century ... It will give a competitive edge only until the end of the decade. After that, it becomes the necessary price of entry' (Barker: 1992, p. 12). In this context Barker is referring to the delivery of quality across the whole price range of products offered by an organization to its chosen market segments.

Equally interesting is the link between concepts of product quality and the balance between new developments and the refurbishment of old products. Critics of the tourism industry frequently point to the visible problems created by over-development of visitor destinations. They assume that there is inevitability in a cycle whereby holiday destinations are discovered, developed until they destroy their original attractiveness, and then become swamped by so-called 'mass tourism' and no longer provide the satisfactions the original customers seek. Around the world there is much evidence that, superficially, appears to bear out this seemingly inevitable cycle of 'boom' followed by decline and deterioration. At least until the late 1980s that appeared to be the inevitable fate of many British and other northern European seaside resorts as they declined from their prosperity of the 1960s.

In a young growth industry, especially in the leisure sector, the ability to switch to new destinations offering much the same products in 'unspoiled' areas has been frequently exploited by tour operators with no commitment to specific destinations. But there is nothing in the 'life cycle' arguments that inhibits the refurbishment and redevelopment of products. In the 1990s proven techniques make it possible to change the character of existing destinations and the products they provide, and therefore change the customers that will buy them. Planned refurbishment can break the cycle of decline and provide new life to old visitor destinations and time-expired products, exactly as happens in other product fields.

In the next decade and beyond environmental reasons alone seem likely to make new destinations both harder to find and more expensive to develop. It can be expected that planning procedures for new resorts will be more rigorous and complex than hitherto. It follows that future development activity is likely to focus more on the planned refurbishment of existing visitor destinations to arrest decline, restore their core attractions and manage tourism more effectively. In addition, the planned development of tourism activities and revenue as a contribution to urban and rural regeneration generally – new uses for buildings and areas no longer able to perform their original economic purposes – offers one of the more exciting prospects for the tourism industry over the next decade. No other industry sector of comparable scale can provide this widespread prospect of beneficial redevelopment. If Wigan, Glasgow and Manchester in the UK, or Boston and South Street Seaport (New York) in the USA can become successful visitor destinations in their own right, there is massive hope for other destinations, too.

For developers, the systematic refurbishment and redevelopment of existing destinations was usually more difficult and costly in the 1980s than building on new or 'greenfield' sites. This was especially true in rural areas if the value of the environment was not costed into projects. Redeveloping heritage structures such as former mills or warehouses, and areas such as former mineral extraction sites or fishing industry ports, could only be achieved with extensive subsidies. Again, the growing need to protect untouched areas from unnecessary development is altering the economics of redevelopment. It is never likely to be a low-cost option but the costs appear different if values are attributed to the non-economic benefits of refurbishment.

For every refurbishment as for every new development, the need for detailed planning and justification of projects is a key requirement, especially where existing communities will be affected by redevelopment plans. Development and construction are the obvious and most visible aspects of such projects. But they are ultimately totally dependent on the projections of market size, seasonality and revenue generation, which it is the business of marketing personnel to calculate. Market size means the aggregate of all the separate segments that are to be planned for. The type and purchasing characteristics, as well as the volume of such segments, are determined by the type and quality of the products provided for them. Thus the discussion of excellence, products and segments, and refurbishment, travels full circle.

6 Marketing trends for visitor destinations

If the scenario of mature, more sophisticated, and more competitive markets emerges over the next decade, as suggested in this chapter, there will be interesting implications for the marketing of destinations. In this context a visitor destination may be broadly defined as meaning a 'village, holiday centre, seaside or mountain resort, town, city or country park; within the boundaries of which particular management policies and practices are implemented to influence visitor movements and their impact on the environment' (WTTERC:1992). Under this definition the area focus for visitor destinations is generally wider than a single site, but smaller than a country or a region. In most developed countries visitor destinations include residential communities whose interests are the responsibility of elected local authorities.

It follows from the views put earlier about more sophisticated customers that there is likely to be growing interest in newer forms of active, participatory leisure travel. This will be accompanied by a relative shift away from traditional, passive, sightseeing and beach-based types of holiday, so long associated with so-called 'mass tourism'. The shift will put added pressure on visitor destinations possessing scenic and other environmental attractions, and on towns and cities offering cultural activity. Urban and rural destinations of established (or reconstructed) heritage appeal will be especially attractive.

Inevitably, this shift to outdoor interests such as walking, golfing, equestrian, water-based activities, and nature-watching, will increase the pressure on relatively fragile areas least able to cope with visitor numbers. Even with allowance for refurbishment, as noted above, there is likely to be a relative shift away from purpose-built coastal resorts, which are better able to deal with visitor numbers at relatively low cost to the environment. Although most large towns and cities can absorb additional visitor numbers without difficulty, most rural and heritage destinations cannot.

The major implication of this shift is that the visitor-management techniques currently practised at destinations are due for radical overhaul and development. Traditional planning and development controls call for master plans and planning regulations for land and buildings. Subsidies, licences, price controls and fiscal measures are used to support such plans, and will remain the cornerstones of regulatory policies. But these are essentially supply-side techniques. Indirectly they influence market

behaviour, but there will be a growing need for better marketing and information techniques – first, to target desired segments, and, second, to persuade, cajole, educate and generally to influence the behaviour of visitors (including sometimes decisions not to visit). Because in many destinations visitors will arrive by public transport and use commercial accommodation and other visitor facilities, the marketing and information influences will operate best if they are a shared responsibility via partnership schemes between the public involving commercial sectors. For reasons amply described in this book, marketing techniques will only be effective if they are organized around targeted visitor segments.

This author believes that better co-ordination is needed between the planning controls over the supply side available to local authorities, and influences over the demand side (marketing) mostly wielded by commercial interests. Co-ordination requires better targeted planning for destinations, and major improvements in market research information at destination level. Research will be needed also to monitor the performance of visitor-management techniques against objectives.

In the 1980s, led by environmental interests, it became part of received wisdom in many countries that good practice in tourism planning meant avoiding high-density tourism resorts (contemptuously dubbed ghettoes) and achieving a wider dispersal of visitors throughout communities. In fact there appears to be a much stronger case for the development of more enclosed tourism complexes or purpose-built villages in which local communities are isolated from visitors, and vice versa. Prime examples of such enclosed complexes are the Disney Corporation resorts, Center Parcs, most Club Mediterannée villages, some ski resorts, many holiday villages and timeshare resorts.

The value of enclosed resorts is that they can be totally planned and managed, not only to deliver the satisfactions that many customers seek but also to minimize damage to the surrounding environment, and in many cases to enhance it. The planned use of landscaping can promote biodiversity, the use of waste water treatments can avoid traditional pollution, energy conservation can be optimized, and, through programmes for targeted reduction and recycling of ancillary products, the consumption of resources per capita can be greatly reduced. Most such villages are designed to be traffic-free, and provide an ideal platform for the promotion of appropriate environmental messages. Because they are under single ownership and control, the management of visitors in successful enclosed resorts is based on an effective co-ordination of supply-side and demand-side controls and inluences. However 'sustainability' for tourism developments is defined in the 1990s, it is most likely to be delivered in controlled environments.

It seems probable that the modern trend to enclosed and managed environments will therefore continue in the 1990s as the best way to resolve conflicts. It is even more probable that the visitor-management methods the new centres have developed, though in optimum circumstances, will be copied and transferred for application in traditional, multi-ownership 'open' visitor destinations, in which the lives and often competing interests of visitors and residents mingle. It is an interesting speculation that the Disney Parks and Center Parcs of the 1990s are not so much new concepts but the logical successors of the original purpose-built seaside resorts developed in the USA and Europe over a century earlier. The old resorts gradually lost their original integrity of design and product quality, and therefore their appeal to visitors. Those that can be refurbished should look to their late twentieth century successors to find the visitor management methods essential to accompany redevelopment – a form of technology transfer in reverse. As this author put it in a study of seaside resorts in England, 'A first step... is to designate and create new management arrangements for precisely specified "core visitor areas" ... where visitors

are most likely to congregate and spend their time' (ETB: 1991, p. 13). Marketing is a key technique in such management arrangements.

7 Marketing and information technology

The growing role of information technology in travel and tourism will be perhaps the most obvious of all the trends influencing the next decade. It is discussed in several parts of the book. This final chapter focuses on two aspects especially relevant to future marketing.

Inventory Management – CRS

As recently as the late 1970s academics from Harvard Business School were able to persuade themselves that 'services are perishable; they cannot be inventoried' (Sasser *et al*: 1978, p. 16). They judged this a disadvantage compared with physical stock control for manufacturing industry. In fact inventory management is at the very heart of travel and tourism marketing. It is being driven (very fast) by developments in information technology. Whatever international regulatory bodies decide to do in influencing the ways in which computer reservation systems (CRS) can be operated, it is obvious that the next decade will see further development and internationalization of these systems. Led by airlines, the main CRSs discussed in chapter 18 are already almost universal in the transport and travel agency sectors and growing rapidly in the accommodation and car-rental sector. Commencing with business travel, they are now rapidly extending into leisure travel. The major systems are international and becoming global in operation now and, as in every other sphere, there will be growing competition by the main players for market share.

Wherever businesses are dependent on advance bookings for the provision of services, and provided that the scale of operations is large enough to produce a low unit cost of transaction, CRS inventory systems provide many advantages. They improve customer choice and convenience, increase operational efficiency through speed of access to products and ability to operate yield management programmes, reduce staff costs in handling bookings and improve their efficiency by providing instant access to relevant information, and generate valuable marketing data about customers and the characteristics of transactions. Through the use of interactive databases and on-line access for a range of travel suppliers, it is already common for the different elements of tourism products to be brought together and booked in seconds. Current technology offers the option to provide visual material as part of point-of-sale material. Parallel developments in consumer-credit arrangements through 'smart cards' and Electronic Funds Transfer at Point of Sale (EFTPOS) make it possible to link an instant booking with instant payment.

Most students of travel and tourism will be aware of these developments. It is worth noting though that, until as recently as 1982, Britain's second largest tour operator took half a million bookings a year by telephone. By 1987 its computers handled some 2 million bookings, dealing with 100,000 on a peak day, a figure unthinkable only 5 years earlier. Modern CRSs handle many times that volume of transactions, and in 1992 the UK-based Galileo system was holding and displaying more than 50 million scheduled air fares alone. It was capable of handling tens of thousands of transactions an hour. CRSs and their many applications when linked with PC systems are one of the better examples in practice of the information-society concepts developed by Toffler and others to define the driving force of the twenty-first century.

To summarize its importance, sophisticated inventory control systems are revolutionizing distribution systems in travel and tourism. CRSs are now much more than access systems: they are also primary channels for promotional techniques. CRSs are revolutionizing product design and formulation through the ability to put together the components of the tourism product in apparently bespoke ways to meet customers' interests and wants. By providing a constant stream of marketing data, especially for occupancy projections and consumer response to pricing policies, CRSs are also becoming primary tools for yield-management systems and creative revenue generation wherever gaps are identified. Finally, when used in parallel with customer databases and knowledge of repeat customers, CRSs are changing the market-research knowledge that marketing managers have of their market segments. In other words, CRSs are relevant to all four of the classic four Ps of marketing. They convey marketing advantages greater than anything available to manufacturing industries for consumer goods. They may also provide ways to circumvent costly traditional retailer distribution systems (see below).

Although CRSs are presently confined mainly to the transactions of large operators working internationally, there is reason to expect that there will be significant extension of access to smaller operators over the next decade. Smaller hotels, holiday parks and even farmhouses and the larger guesthouses can potentially benefit from access to CRSs. But they are too small to do so individually and must find co-operative intermediaries to organize collective access and share costs. With the current rate of technological development, this should prove possible over the next decade.

Management control

Most managers and students in travel and tourism will be at least aware of the trends in CRSs. Fewer are likely to have considered the changing role of information technology in facilitating the more efficient management of larger business organizations.

The proposition stressed here is that information technology is a structural component of management as organizations grow larger. There are many references in this book to the marketing advantages and economies of scale potentially achievable through larger organizations. Attention is drawn to the seemingly inexorable shift toward market-place dominance whereby a small number of commercial firms in many developed countries - usually less than six - control half or more of total sales revenue in each main sector of travel and tourism. This is characteristic of the main modes of public transport, parts of serviced accommodation, tour operation, travel retailing and car rental. Some of the organizations are transnational and global in the scale of their operations. More are likely to be in that category in the next decade.

Until recently there was ample evidence that diseconomies of scale, caused by management hierarchies and the difficulty of exercising efficient management control, offset the marketing and other economies of scale achievable in operating very large, multi-site businesses. Recognition of such problems, as well as a wish to inject greater competition, led to the worldwide move by governments in the 1980s to break up the operations of large, traditional, public-sector-owned monopolies. There is an obvious danger that the larger the organization, the slower the speed of decision-making and the more complex the hierarchies of management in comparison with leaner, smaller entrepreneurial rivals. When multi-site combines with multinational, the problems are potentially compounded. It is the capability to overcome decision-making inertia that gives IT its particular value from a management perspective.

It appears to be fairly common ground that the efficiency of management has less to do with the size of an organization and more to do with the composition of its decision-making structures. Staff motivation and morale are associated with setting clear targets and monitoring performance in cohesive parts of a business. This appears to be facilitated in a structure of market-orientated strategic units within a total business and the participation of staff in the decision making processes. As discussed in Chapter 10, that is also the basis of effective marketing and brand or product management. In the 1990s there is much scope for very large organizations to divide themselves functionally, with a small head office to set and co-ordinate corporate policy and strategy, and separate business units to manage specific market/product portfolios. But this process depends for its efficiency on the speed and quality of information available to make decisions at the functional level and to interact with corporate headquarters.

Database knowledge of customers' profile and behaviour, as discussed in Chapter 19, coupled with the continuous and immediate flow of information provided by modern CRSs, provide an information base relevant to the strategic and operational decisions of large organizations for which there are no parallels in the history of travel and tourism. The rate of technological change as databases interact indicates that the speed and quality of information flows will be further enhanced in the 1990s. Much of the traditional management inertia of larger organizations can be overcome.

As an example, in a European context, there is a quantum leap in the difference between what channel ferry shipping companies knew about their customers and cost/revenue flows in the early 1980s and what Eurotunnel knew when it opened for business. By that time the ferry companies had also radically overhauled their own information flows in order to compete. The battle for customers and market share will be fought out by marketing managers reliant on a speed and quality of information unthinkable a decade earlier. Such examples will be found in all parts of the world in the 1990s.

8 Distribution issues

Each of the four Ps, and especially the integration between them, will remain, as now, the cornerstones of effective marketing. Without denying that, there is a strong case for suggesting that particular attention will have to be paid in travel and tourism to distribution issues in the 1990s. While the techniques of product formulation, pricing and promotion are relatively well understood and developed, the evidence suggests that this is not the case for distribution and that the 1990s will see more major changes.

Efficient, cost-effective distribution, the means of creating access to attractive products for target customers, has been the subject of research and development in larger travel companies. But for most travel and tourism businesses it still appears to be widely misunderstood, and very often the costs are seriously underestimated. To this author, reflecting the characteristics of tourism discussed in Chapter 3, understanding the techniques and full costs of achieving distribution is more important than a knowledge of promotion or even product specification. An average, or even below average product with excellent distribution may be able to outsell an excellent, well-promoted product with poor distribution.

To some extent this reflects the fact that promotional techniques are very often organized around and within available distribution systems. It reflects also the continuing need to achieve sales around the break-even point (at the margin), where the incremental costs of production are low and contribution to gross profits is very high. As noted in Part Four of this book, the marketing efforts of all larger businesses have to be organized round the daily need to obtain marginal increments in occupancy or other measure of capacity utilization, and revenue 'yield'. Managing distribution channels often provides the most cost-effective way to achieve these marginal gains.

The principal issue in the distribution process is the real cost of achieving it, measured as a percentage of sales revenue or planned gross profit per unit sold. For large tour operators utilizing retailers for their distribution, the unit cost of distribution is much higher than the unit contribution to gross profit. In the early 1990s, for example, a tour operator planning to sell a package for £300.00 was unlikely to retain more than about £15 per average sale – if all went well and the market behaved as forecast (around 5 per cent of turnover). It would have to pay costs of up to £50 on average to achieve each sale through retail outlets (allowing for promotion to outlets, servicing them, maintaining computer-reservations systems, brochure production and distribution, as well as commission and possible over-rides). In other words, for every £1 earned by the operator, it paid some £4 to a retailer which did not share the operators' packaging costs and did not buy in bulk for sale at retailer risk.

The second issue reflects the changes in technology referred to earlier in this chapter. In this context the technology is continually developing and in particular offers the possibility to reach *some* targeted customers through non-retail channels at a fraction of the average cost of unit sales through retail distribution. There are major problems for operator/retailer partnerships if the former divert highly lucrative sales to book direct and leave the harder sales to retailers. But the margins in the early 1990s are so wide that they must be under constant review.

The third issue, related to the second, is the fact that directly booked products are not only more profitable, they also yield vital customer information to operators that is otherwise denied them. It seems absurd in the 1990s that operators using retail channels may have to buy expensive market research to obtain information that is virtually free to the retailers.

The fourth issue becomes more important as markets mature, and larger organizations only survive and grow through repeat customers. If, as in business travel, a key customer can produce ten bookings over a year, the marketing cost per purchase may be less than 10 per cent of the average cost of just one first-time booking.

For example, £1 spent on a telephone call or a stamp and a letter to a targeted previous customer could produce ten bookings over a year by a satisfied customer – say 10 × £100 = £1,000. The alternative of achieving a new customer on each of ten occasions by a distribution channel could easily be 10 × £20 = £200. The comparison to make is between £1 and £200 to achieve business worth £1,000 (although normally a regular repeat customer would be given a more attractive rate than first-time customers). The marketing imperative of arithmetic like that, in the light of the costs noted under the first issue, is surely overwhelming.

A fifth issue emerges as large organizations form partnerships, either by strategic marketing agreements or by formal integration or joint ownership. They then often have the possibility to serve the same client with more than one type of transaction in a year. Airline customers are also customers for hotels, holiday-product suppliers may also be able to service business needs for the same customer, and tour operators and scheduled airlines may be logical business partners. The international marketing of American Express (in its role as a travel principal) is perhaps the most obvious example of a multi-transaction operator, and it cannot be an accident that much of that business is achieved through direct-marketing methods. It is a classic case of a global operator using its customer database simultaneously for promotion, distribution, and market research.

In all these considerations travel organizations that provide only retail services appear to offer very high cost distribution measured in average costs per transaction. They must be vulnerable to the growing flexibility of distribution systems.

9 More responsible tourism marketing for the 1990s?

Most encouraging of all is the fact that businesses are beginning to respond to the demands of their stakeholders – investors, customers, suppliers, neighbours and their own workforce – all of whom are beginning to think more seriously about ways of ensuring that our children do not inherit a degraded and polluted world (HRH the Prince of Wales: 1990).

This statement focuses on the whole of business, not just travel and tourism and not just marketing. It expresses a now widely held view that traditional profit-maximizing behaviour is no longer a sustainable strategy, at least for larger businesses continuously exposed to media interest. It is another way of describing what Kotler defines as a 'societal marketing concept', in which 'the organization's task is to determine the needs, wants and interests of target markets and to deliver the desired satisfactions more effectively and efficiently than competitors **in a way that preserves or enhances the customers' and the society's well being'**. It stresses the need for balance between 'company profits, consumer satisfaction, and public interest' (Kotler: 1991, p. 26) (author's emphasis).

For travel and tourism, as for all forms of business, the major issues of the next decade and beyond will revolve around defining and attempting to balance the often competing needs of:

Economy, Ecology, Equity – Globally

Economy in this context means profit (or surplus on operations for non-commercial organizations). *Ecology*, discussed earlier in this chapter, means environmental constraints, broadly defined. *Equity* means a fairer distribution of the use of Earth's resources and consideration for the needs of present and future generations as well as the interests of economic expansion. Exact definitions of these terms will doubtless change as politicians and businesses react to current knowledge and expectations about the needs for and impacts of economic development; developing technology will increase the perceived options.

There is already evidence of a customer backlash against companies that are perceived to be polluters in a social as well as a more narrowly defined environmental sense. As they respond, the shift towards more responsible marketing appears likely to forge closer links in organizations between marketing and operations. In travel and tourism businesses operations departments deliver the products. Whatever the marketing promise, it is at the delivery stage that socially responsible programmes are practised or not. The development of performance monitoring to measure the quality of product delivery is a primary route to drawing marketing and operations together in a much stronger synergy of interest than hitherto.

The closer integration of marketing and operations in larger companies may weaken the traditional management dominance of accountants over the next decade. Accountants owe their positions to their knowledge and expertise in business monitoring and cost control, especially in the short run. But a financial strategy that is not market-orientated and validated by repeat custom is academic. To this author at least, the new forms of auditing and performance monitoring and control discussed in this chapter will come to rank with financial controls. The role of marketing managers in specifying, influencing and monitoring the delivery of responsible corporate programmes will increase. For travel and tourism this new influence should lead to better ways to market 'value added' or quality rather than sell on lowest price, and help justify to customers any price premiums essential to pay for investment in responsible product programmes.

In achieving and delivering the all-important balance implicit in the more responsible conduct of business, marketing is the primary means of defining and communicating it. The role of marketing is partly to help identify changing consumer attitudes, partly to define perceived environmental benefits so that they may be designed for prospective buyers of products, partly to communicate and promote competitive products that are sustainable over time, and partly to communicate environmental awareness and promote more responsible behaviour by visitors at destinations. Without efficient marketing, there is an obvious danger that 'societal marketing' could be no more than an academic concept. Balance has to be acceptable to consumers or it cannot be achieved. There is enough in all this to ensure that marketing strategies will be in a state of continuous development in the years ahead. They will remain at the leading edge of decisions which business organizations take concerning all their stakeholders. Product specification and promotion will play an especially important role. Any suggestions that marketing techniques have already reached maturity should therefore be refuted. The scope for new concepts, and especially new applications and linkages with operations, is immense.

In terms of more responsible marketing, travel and tourism has some key advantages. There is no other·global industry that so clearly has a long-run vested interest in maintaining healthy environments and in protecting them from over exploitation. Self-interest requires improved management of tourism operations now, in order to safeguard future business and achieve sustainable development and growth. There is also no other industry better placed to communicate with its customers and to influence them at times when they are most likely to be receptive to environment messages - to rouse their awareness and modify their behaviour. Since travel and tourism in developed countries now reaches over 90 per cent of the population, the opportunities to communicate are immense, although co-ordination will be needed to produce the maximum effect.

10 Marketing the margin

To bring us back to the all-important 'bottom line' and conclude with a view of management and marketing that expresses the *leitmotiv* of this book, the following quote is helpful:

> Excellence is a game of inches, or millimetres. No one act is, per se, clinching. But a thousand things ... each done a tiny bit better, do add up to memorable responsiveness and distinction ... and loyalty ... and slightly higher margins (Peters and Austin: 1986, p. 46).

Nothing has changed since the first edition to suggest that this quotation is any the less valid for the 1990s. It serves as a useful reminder that quality of service product delivery is always a combination of multiple actions taken by many staff. It means that, whatever skills marketing managers may possess, they will achieve little if the operations and other key divisions of an organization are not performing their part. Marketing is not effective unless it is integrated within the management structure of an organization from the boardroom down. Excellence is a continuing responsibility, vital to long-run business success, requiring systems and procedures to make it happen. It is implicit that excellence can be targeted, measured and improved.

By linking memorable responsiveness to profit margins, the quotation stresses that excellence is a customer-orientated approach to business, having particular regard to repeat custom. Good feelings about past service drive future purchase. In each of the trends affecting marketing over the next decade, this epilogue emphasizes the increasing relevance of **marketing the margin** in the conditions marketing managers are likely to face in the coming decade. Competitive edge lies at the margins, which are constantly changing. Seeking marginal improvement is as relevant to modern concepts of socially responsible marketing as it is to narrower ideas of profit maximization. Achieving the margins provides marketing managers with their organizational authority and influence, and should promote innovative thinking.

One may safely conclude that influencing and managing the direction and speed of customer-orientated responses, especially at the margin, will continue to be the principal preoccupation of marketing managers in the fascinating, volatile, increasingly global business of the 'world's largest industry'.

References and select bibliography

Abell, D. F. and Hammond, J. S., *Strategic Market Planning*, Prentice-Hall International, New Jersey, 1979.

Alderson, W., 'The Analytical Framework for Marketing', in Lawrence R. J. and Thomas, M. J. (Editors), *Modern Marketing Management*, Penguin, London, 1971.

Allport, G. W., in Murchison, C., (Editor), *Handbook of Social Psychology*, Clark University Press, Worcester, Mass., 1935.

American Society of Travel Agents, *The Dilemma in Developing Printed Materials for Travel Agents*, ASTA, New York, 1974.

Ansoff, H. I., *Corporate Strategy*, Penguin, London, 1968 (revised edition 1987).

Argenti, J., *Practical Corporate Planning*, George Allen and Unwin, London, 1980.

Baker, M. J., *Marketing: An Introductory Text*, 3rd edition, Macmillan, London, 1979 (4th edition 1985).

Baker, M. J., (ed.) *The Marketing Book*, 2nd edition, Butterworth-Heinemann, Oxford, 1991.

Barker, J. A., *Future Edge: Discovering the New Paradigms of Success*, William Morrow & Company, New York, 1992.

Bartels, R., *The History of Marketing Thought*, 2nd edition, Grid, Ohio, 1976.

Bateson, E. G., *Managing Services Marketing*, 2nd edition, Dryden International, New York, 1992.

Boyd, H. W. and Larreche, J. C., 'The Foundations of Marketing Strategy' in Cox, K. K. and McGinnis, V. J., (Editors) *Strategic Planning Decisions: A Reader*, Prentice-Hall, Englewood Cliffs, 1982. pp. 3-17.

Bottomley Renshaw, M., *The Travel Agent*, Business Education Publishers, Sunderland, 1992.

Brent Ritchie, J. R. and Goeldner, C. R., (Editors) *Travel, Tourism and Hospitality Research: A Handbook for Managers and Researchers*, John Wiley and Sons, New York, 1986.

British Tourist Authority, *Museums – Lessons from the USA*, BTA, London, 1983.

Broadbent, S., *Spending Advertising Money*, 3rd edition, Business Books, London, 1979.

Burkart, A. J. and Medlik, S., *Tourism: Past, Present and Future*, Heinemann, London, 1974 (2nd edition 1981).

Burkart, A. J., 'The Role of a Reservation System in the Marketing of Tourism Services', in HCIMA Review, No. 4, Spring, 1976.

Buttle, F., *Hotel and Food Service Marketing: A Managerial Approach*, Holt, Rinehart and Winston, London, 1986.

Chisnall, P. M., *Marketing: A Behavioural Analysis*, 2nd edition, McGraw-Hill, London, 1985.

Christopher, M., *Marketing Below the Line*, George Allen and Unwin, London, 1972.

Christopher, M., *The Strategy of Distribution Management*, Heinemann, London, 1985.

Cooper, C., Fletcher, J., Gilbert, D., and Wanhill, S., *Tourism Principles and Practice*, Pitman, London, 1993.

Cossons, N., 'Making Museums Market Orientated', in Scottish Museums Council, *Museums are for People*, HMSO, Edinburgh, 1985.

Cowell, D., *The Marketing of Services*, Heinemann, London, 1984 (2nd edition 1993).

Crouch, S., *Market Research for Managers*, Heinemann, 1985.

Davidson, J. H., *Offensive Marketing*, Pelican, London, 1975. (New edition 1987.)

Davies, A. H. T., 'Strategic Planning in the Thomas Cook Group', in Taylor, B., and Harrison, J. (eds), *The Manager's Casebook of Business Strategy*, Heinemann, Oxford, 1990.

Day, G. S., *Market Driven Strategy: Processes for Creating Value*, Free Press, London, 1990.

Doganis, R., *Flying Off Course*, Harper Collins Academic, 2nd edit., Routledge, London, 1991.

Donelly, J. H., 'Marketing Intermediaries in Channels of Distribution for Services', in *Journal of Marketing*, Vol. 40, January 1976.

Economist Intelligence Unit, *The Tourism Industry and the Environment* (Special Report No. 2453), EIU, London 1992.

Economist Intelligence Unit, 'The Role and Functions of an NTO Abroad', in *International Tourism Quarterly*, No 2, 1983.

Edwards, A., *International Tourism Forecasts to 2005*, (Special Report No. 2454), Economist Intelligence Unit, London, 1992.

Eiglier, P. and Langeard, E., 'A new Approach to Service Marketing', in *Marketing Consumer Services: New Insights*, Report 77-115, Marketing Science Institute, Boston, 1977.

Engel, J. F., and Mimiard, P. W., *Consumer Behaviour*, 7th edition, Dryden International, New York, 1992.

Fletcher, K., Wheeler, C., and Wright, J., 'The Role and Status of UK Database Marketing' in *Quarterly Review of Marketing*, Vol 16., No. 1., October 1990., pp 7-14, Chartered Institute of Marketing.

Forte, C., *Forte: The Autobiography of Charles Forte*, Sidgwick and Jackson, London, 1986.

Frechtling, D. C., 'Key Issues in US Tourism Futures', in *Tourism Management*, Volume 8, No. 2, June 1987.

Gater, C., 'Database Key to a Direct Hit', in *Marketing*, 2 October, (Journal of Inst. of Marketing) Maidenhead, 1986, pp. 41-42.

Gee, C. Y., Choy, D. J. L. and Makens, J. C., *The Travel Industry*, 2nd edition, New York, Van Nostrand Reinhold, 1988.

Greene, M., *Marketing Hotels and Restaurants into the 90s*, Heinemann, London, 1982 (2nd edition 1987).

Haines, D., 'Pictures in Advertising Research in the UK and USA', in *Market Research Society Newsletter*, No. 214, London, January 1984.

Hart, N. A. *The Practice of Advertising*, 3rd edition, Butterworth-Heinemann, Oxford, 1990.

Hart, N. A. and Stapleton, J., *The Marketing Dictionary*, 4th edition, Butterworth-Heinemann, Oxford, 1992.

Heape, R., 'Tour Operating Planning in Thomson Holidays UK', in *Tourism Management*, December 1983.

Heath, E. and Wall, G., *Marketing Tourism Destinations: A Strategic Planning Approach*, John Wiley & Sons, New Jersey, 1992.

Heneghan, P., *Resource Allocation in Tourism Marketing*, Tourism International Press, London, 1976.

Hirst, M., 'Newer and Better Ways', in *Managing Service Quality*, July 1991, pp. 247-51.

Holloway, J. C., *The Business of Tourism*, 2nd edition, Macdonald and Evans, Plymouth, 1985 (3rd edition, Pitman, London, 1992).

Holloway, J. C., and Plant, R. V., *Marketing for Tourism*, 2nd edit., Pitman, London, 1992.

Horwath Consulting, *Worldwide Hotel Industry*, Annual Report, Horwath Consulting, London.

Housden, J., *Franchising and Other Business Relationships in Hotel and Catering Services*, Heinemann, London, 1984.

Howard, J. A. and Sheth, J. N., 'A Theory of Buyer Behaviour' (1967), reproduced in Enis, B. M. and Cox, K. K., (Editors), *Marketing Classics*, 3rd edition, Alleyn and Bacon, Boston, 1977, pp. 161-185.

Hussey, D. E., *Introducing Corporate Planning*, 2nd edition, Pergamon Press, Oxford, 1979.

International Passenger Survey (IPS), a year-round survey of passengers arriving in and departing from the UK, conducted for the UK government.

Jefferson, A., & Lickorish, L. J., *Marketing Tourism: A Practical Guide*, 2nd edition, Longman, Harlow, 1991.

Jeffries, D. J., 'The Role of Marketing in Official Tourism Organizations', Paper to 23rd Congress of AIEST, in *Tourism et Marketing*, vol. 13, Bern, Switzerland, September 1973.

Joyce, T., *What Do We Know About How Advertising Works?*, J. Walter Thompson, London, 1967.

Kotas, R., (Editor) *Market Orientation in the Hotel and Catering Industry*, Surrey University Press, London, 1975.

Kotler, P., *Marketing Management: Analysis Planning and Control*, 5th edition, Prentice-Hall International, London, 1984 (7th edition 1991).

Kotler, P., *Marketing Management: Analysis, Planning, Implementation and Control*, 7th edition, Prentice-Hall International, London 1991.

Kotler, P. and Cox, K., (Editors) *Marketing Management and Strategy*, A Reader, Prentice-Hall Inc., New Jersey, 1980.

Krippendorf, J., *Marketing et Tourisme*, Lang and Cie, Berne, 1971.

Krippendorf, J., *The Holiday Makers*, Heinemann, London, 1987.

Lavery, P., 'The Financing and Organization of National Tourist Offices' in *Travel and Tourism Analyst*, No. 4, pp. 84-101, Economist Intelligence Unit, London, 1992.

Leppard, J. W., & McDonald, H. B., 'Marketing Planning and Corporate Culture' in *Journal of Marketing Management*, Vol. 7, No. 3, pp.213-235, July 1991.

Levitt, T., 'Marketing Myopia', in *Harvard Business Review*, Vol. 38, July/August, 1960.

Levitt, T., 'Improving Sales through Product Augmentation', in Doyle, P. *et al.*, *Analytical Marketing Management*, Harper and Row, London, 1974, p. 10.

Levitt, T., 'Marketing Intangible Products and Product Intangibles', in *Harvard Business Review*, May/June 1981, pp. 37-44.

Lewis, R. C., '*The Positioning Statement for Hotels*', Cornell Hotel and Restaurant Administration Quarterly, Vol. 22, No. 1, May 1981, pp. 51-61.

Lewis, R. C., and Chambers, R. E., *Marketing Leadership in Hospitality: Foundations and Practices*, Van Nostrand Reinhold, New York, 1989.

Lodge, D., *Paradise News*, Secker & Warburg, London, 1991.

Love, J. F., *McDonald's: Behind the Arches*, Bantam Press, New York, 1987.

Lovelock, C. H., *Services Marketing: Text, Cases and Readings*, Prentice-Hall, New Jersey, 1984.

Luck, D. J. et al., *Marketing Research*, 3rd edition, Prentice-Hall, New Jersey, 1970.

Maas, J., 'Better Brochures for the Money', in *Cornell Hotel and Restaurant Administration Quarterly*, Vol. 20, No. 4, 1980.

Mayo, E. J. and Jarvis, L. P., *The Psychology of Leisure Travel*, CBI, Boston, Mass., 1981.

McCarthy, E. J., *Basic Marketing, A Managerial Approach*, 7th edition, Irwin, Homewood, Illinois, 1981.

McDonald, M. H. B., *Marketing Plans*, 2nd edition, Butterworth-Heinemann, Oxford, 1989.

McDonald, M. H. B., and Leppard, J., *The Marketing Audit*, Butterworth-Heinemann, Oxford, 1991.

McIntosh, R. W., *Tourism; Principles, Practices, Philosophies*, 1974 (6th edition, with Goeldner, C. R., John Wiley & Sons, New Jersey, 1990).

McIver, C. and Naylor, G., *Marketing Financial Services*, The Institute of Bankers, London, 1980.

Medlik, S., *Profile of the Hotel and Catering Industry*, 2nd edition, Heinemann, London, 1978.

Medlik, S., *The Business of Hotels*, Heinemann, London, 1980 (second edition 1989).

Medlik, S., *Dictionary of Travel, Tourism and Hospitality*, Butterworth-Heinemann, Oxford, 1993.

Medlik, S. and Middleton, V. T. C., 'Product Formulation in Tourism', in *Tourism and Marketing*, Vol. 13, AIEST, Bern, 1973.

Middleton, V. T. C., 'Tourism Marketing: Product Implications', in *International Tourism Quarterly*, No. 3, 1979, EIU, London.

Middleton, V. T. C., 'The Marketing Implications of Direct Selling' in *International Tourism Quarterly*, No. 2, 1980, EIU, London.

Middleton, V. T. C., 'Product Marketing: Goods and Services Compared', in *Quarterly Review of Marketing*, Vol. 8, No. 4, July 1983a.

Middleton, V. T. C., 'Marketing in the Hospitality Industry' in Cassee, E. and Reuland, R., (Editors) *The Management of Hospitality*, Pergamon, Oxford, 1983b.

Middleton, V. T. C., 'Profitability Through Product Formulation Strategies', in *The*

Practice of Hospitality Management II, AVI Publishing, Westport, Conn., 1986.

Middleton, V. T. C., 'UK Outbound', in *Travel and Tourism Analyst*, December, 1986, pp. 17-27 EIU, London.

Middleton, V. T. C., 'Marketing the Margin' in *Quarterly Review of Marketing*, Vol. 14., No. 2., pp. 14-17, January 1989, I. M. Maidenhead.

Middleton, V. T. C., *New Visions for Independent Museums in the UK*, Association of Independent Museums (AIM), Chichester, 1990.

Middleton, V. T. C., 'Whither the Package Tour' in *Tourism Management*, Vol. 12, No. 3., pp. 185-192, September 1991, Butterworth-Heinemann, Oxford.

Middleton, V. T. C., 'The Tourism Product' in Witt, S. F., and Moutinho, L., (eds) *Tourism Marketing and Management Handbook*, 2nd edit., Prentice-Hall International, London, 1994.

Mill, R. C., & Morrison, A. M., *The Tourism System: An Introductory Text*, 2nd edit., Prentice-Hall International, Englewood Cliffs, New Jersey, 1991.

Morrison, A. M., *Hospitality and Travel Marketing*, Delmar Publishers, (Purdue University), New York, 1989.

Murphy, P. E., *Tourism: A Community Approach*, Methuen, New York, 1985.

Nykiel, R. A., *Marketing in the Hospitality Industry*, pp 305, Van Nostand Reinhold, New York, 1989.

Ogilvy, D., *Ogilvy on Advertising*, Pan Books, London, 1983.

Ohmae, K., *The Mind of the Strategist*, Penguin, London, 1983.

Peters, R. and Austin, N., *A Passion for Excellence*, Fontana, London, 1986. (Follow-up of Peters, R. and Waterman, R. H., *In Search of Excellence* 1982).

Petersen, C., 'Promotions Boom in Confusion', *in Marketing*, Journal of the Chartered Institute of Marketing, Maidenhead, September 1978, pp. 61-66.

Pickering, J. F., *Industrial Structure and Market Conduct*, Martin Robertson, London, 1974.

Piercy, N., *Marketing Organisation, An Analysis of Information Processing, Power and Politics*, George Allen and Unwin, London, 1985.

Piercy, M., *Market-led Strategic Change*, Butterworth-Heinemann, Oxford, 1992.

Porter, M. E., *Competitive Strategy: Techniques for Analysing Industries and Competitors*, Free Press, New York, 1980.

Porter, M. E., *Competitive Advantage: Creating and Sustaining Superior Performance*, Free Press, New York, 1985.

Rathmell, J. M., *Marketing in the Service Sector*, Winthrop, Cambridge, Mass., 1974.

Reed, A., *Airline: The Inside Story of British Airways*, BBC Books, London, 1990.

Ries, A. and Trout, J., *Positioning the Battle for Your Mind*, McGraw-Hill, New York, 1981.

Reilly, R. T., *Travel and Tourism Marketing Techniques*, 2nd edition, Delmar Publishing, New York, 1988.

Rodger, L. W., *Marketing in a Competitive Economy*, 2nd edition, Hutchinson, London, 1968.

Rooij de, N., 'Mature Market in Europe', in *Travel and Tourism Analyst*, May 1986 EIU, London.

Sasser, W. E., Olsen, P. R. and Wyckoff, D. D., *Management of Service Operations: Text, Cases, and Readings*, Allyn and Bacon, Boston (USA), 1978.

Schmoll, G. A., *Tourism Promotion*, Tourism International Press, London, 1977.

Scottish Museums Council, *Museums are for People*, HMSO, Edinburgh, 1985.

Seibert, J. C., *Concepts of Marketing Management*, Harper and Row, New York, 1973.

Shaw, S., *Air Transport: A Marketing Perspective*, Pitman, London, 1982.

Shaw, S., & Stone, M., *Database Marketing*, Gower, 1987.

Smith, V., *Hosts and Guests: The Anthropology of Tourism*, Univ. Pennsylvania Press, 1977.

Stanton, W. J., *Fundamentals of Marketing*, 6th edition, McGraw-Hill, London, 1981.

Swinglehurst, E., *Cook's Tours: The Study of Popular Travel*, Blandford Press, Poole, 1982.

Taylor, B., & Harrison, J., *The Manager's Casebook of Business Strategy*, Heinemann (Professional Publishing), Oxford, 1990.

Toffler, A., *Power Shift*, Bantam Books, London, 1990.

The Tourism Society, *Handbook and Members List*, London, 1979.

Travel and Tourism Research Association (TTRA), *Report of 17th Annual Conference*, University of Utah, 1986.

US Travel Data Center, *The 1986-87 Economic Review of Travel in America*, Washington, DC., 1987.

Wahab, S., Crampon, L. J. and Rothfield, L. M., *Tourism Marketing*, Tourism International Press, London, 1976.

Wheatcroft, S., 'The World Airline Industry in 2000' in *Travel & Tourism Analyst*, No. 3, Economist Intelligence Unit, London, 1992.

Wheatcroft, S. and Lipman, G., *Air Transport in a Competitive European Market*, Economist Intelligence Unit, London 1986.

Wilmhurst, J., *The Fundamentals and Practice of Marketing*, 2nd edition, Butterworth-Heinemann, Oxford, 1984 (3rd edition 1993).

Wilmhurst, J., *Below-the-line Promotion*, Butterworth-Heinemann, Oxford, 1993.

Witt, S., and Moutinho, L. (Editors), *Tourism Marketing and Management Handbook*, 2nd edition, Prentice-Hall International, Hemel Hempstead, 1994.

World Tourism Organization, *Presentation on Tourism Trends to 2000 and Beyond*, WTO, Madrid, 1992.

World Travel and Tourism Council, *Travel and Tourism: The World's Largest Industry*, WTTC, Brussels, 1992.

World Travel and Tourism Environment Research Centre, *Travel and Tourism: Environment and Development,* WTTERC, Oxford Brookes University, 1992 and 1993.

Index